Dying to Learn

A VOLUME IN THE SERIES

Cornell Studies in Security Affairs

Edited by Robert Jervis, Robert J. Art, and Stephen M. Walt

A list of titles in this series is available at cornellpress.cornell.edu.

Dying to Learn

Wartime Lessons from the Western Front

MICHAEL A. HUNZEKER

Cornell University Press

Ithaca and London

First published 2021 by Cornell University Press

Printed in the United States of America

Library of Congress Cataloging-in-Publication Data
Names: Hunzeker, Michael A., author.
Title: Dying to learn : wartime lessons from the Western Front / Michael A. Hunzeker.
Description: Ithaca [New York] : Cornell University Press, 2021. | Series: Cornell studies in security affairs | Includes bibliographical references and index.
Identifiers: LCCN 2020057756 (print) | LCCN 2020057757 (ebook) | ISBN 9781501758454 (hardcover) | ISBN 9781501758478 (pdf) | ISBN 9781501758461 (epub)
Subjects: LCSH: Germany. Heer—History—World War, 1914–1918. | Great Britain. Army—History—World War, 1914–1918. | France. Armée—History—World War, 1914–1918. | World War, 1914–1918—Campaigns—Western Front. | Military art and science—Europe—History—20th century. | Tactics—History—20th century.
Classification: LCC D530 .H87 2021 (print) | LCC D530 (ebook) | DDC 940.4/144—dc23
LC record available at https://lccn.loc.gov/2020057756
LC ebook record available at https://lccn.loc.gov/2020057757

For my wife, Major Yu-Ching Yeh, and my brother,
Major Adam Hunzeker

Contents

Acknowledgments

Dying to Learn tries to explain why some militaries are better at learning than others. I have struggled with this question for the better part of two decades, and I owe a great deal to those who have helped me along the way. I am particularly indebted to Aaron Friedberg, for his support and encouragement, and Stephen Rosen, whose pioneering theory of military innovation I am trying to build upon. Ezra Suleiman and Edward Erickson provided crucial guidance throughout the writing process. Ryan Grauer, Adam Grissom, and Ed Rhodes—along with Jordan Cohen, Matthew Fay, and Kendrick Kuo—offered invaluable feedback as part of a book workshop. I likewise received a number of helpful ideas and suggestions from participants of the 2018 National Security Scholars and Practitioners Program. I have valued Alexander Lanoszka's friendship, advice, and reassurance throughout this long and winding journey. I also want to thank Jonathan Askonas, Stephen Biddle, Barret Bradstreet, Ahsan Butt, Matt Campbell, Thomas Christensen, Mark Christopher, Liam Collins, Luke Condra, Zack Cooper, Mark Crow, Christina Davis, Rex Douglass, Colin Dueck, Thomas Ehrhard, Joanne Gowa, Kristen Harkness, Christopher Hamner, Jerad Harper, Gregory Koblentz, Raymond Kuo, Ellen Laipson, Adam Liff, Matthew Lundgren, Robert McGrath, Rohan Mukherjee, Joseph Petrucelli, Jim Pfiffner, Eric Reid, Mark Rozell, Thomas Scherer, John Schutte, A. Trevor Thrall, and Keren Yahri-Milo for their advice and assistance over the years. Roger Haydon, along with the entire staff at Cornell University Press, did an amazing job of helping me (finally) get this book across the finish line. And I want to gratefully acknowledge the Bradley Foundation, the Smith Richardson Foundation, and the Princeton School of Public and International Affairs for their financial support.

None of this would have been possible without my family's seemingly endless reservoir of patience, along with their willingness to give me a swift kick in the pants from time to time. I especially want to thank my parents for supporting my decision to join the US Marines Corps, my in-laws for tolerating their daughter's decision to marry a marine, and my wife for accepting my decision to go to graduate school (despite getting back at me by joining the US Army). My children unfortunately lacked a voice in these decisions, but their arrival convinced me it was time to wrap things up so I could spend more time with them.

Finally, whether they know it or not (most do not), countless US marines left their mark on this book. I owe a special thanks to a pair of battalion commanders who turned into mentors along the way: Colonel Robert Abbott and Dr. Brian Buckles. Fideleon Damian, Jason Filos, Seth Lynn, and Jacob Robinson likewise offered insight and the sort of painful but necessary critical feedback that only lifelong friends can proffer. I also want to thank Christophe Bach, Ryan Barton, John Binder, Gregory Bishop, George Camia, Scott Cooper, John Gwazdauskas, Jeffrey Jarosz, Sandor Marton, Coy McHorse, Arch Ratliff III, Matthew Rauth, Daniel Reeves, Victor Ruble, Brian Strack, Christopher Thomas, Angel Torres, James Tunney, Steven Underwood, Adam Vandegrift, Thomas Vanderhorst, Raul Villegas, Yinon Weiss, Craig Wiggers, Jayme Winders, Shawn Woodard, Darrin Wynn, and Guadalupe Zapata. Captain George "Alexi" Whitney, Lieutenant Alex Wetherbee, Master Gunnery Sergeant John Singleton, Sergeant Dustin Curtiss, Corporal Jesus Medellin, Lance Corporal Ronald White, and Private First Class Brian Cutter—I hope that you and your families will consider this book a humble attempt to honor your service and memory.

Abbreviations

ACT	assessment, command, and training
ARVN	Army of the Republic of Vietnam
BEF	British Expeditionary Force
CALL	Center for Army Lessons Learned
CDC	US Army Combat Developments Command
CHEM	Centre des Hautes Études Militaires
COIN	counterinsurgency
CONARC	US Army Continental Army Command
ExRfdI	Exerzier-Reglement für die Infanterie
FM	field manual
FSR	Field Service Regulations
GHQ	General Headquarters
GOCRA	General Officer Commanding, Royal Artillery
GQG	Grand Quartier Général
IGMTE	inspector general of military training and education
MACV	Military Assistance Command, Vietnam
MLR	main line of resistance
OHL	Oberste Heeresleitung
ORSA	Operations Research and Systems Analysis
PAVN	People's Army of Vietnam
RGA	Royal Garrison Artillery
RMA	revolution in military affairs
SAMS	US Army School of Advanced Military Studies
SS	Stationary Service
TRADOC	US Army Training and Doctrine Command
TTPs	tactics, techniques, and procedures

Dying to Learn

Introduction

Wartime Learning

> Let us not for a moment forget that, while study and preparation are necessary, war itself is the real school where the art of war is learned.
>
> —General John J. Pershing, address to officers of the American
> 1st Division, April 1918

The Puzzle

President George W. Bush ordered US ground forces into Iraq on March 19, 2003. Few military organizations were as prepared as the US Marine Corps for the invasion that followed. The Marine Corps had, after all, spent twenty-some years developing and refining a so-called maneuver warfare doctrine.[1] With its emphasis on speed, flexibility, and firepower, maneuver warfare was perfectly suited to a campaign of shock and awe.

Regimental Combat Team (RCT) 5's run-and-gun battle against the Al Nida Republican Guard Division in early April exemplified the Marine Corps' preferred war-fighting methods.[2] Already, the once deliberate advance on Baghdad had morphed into a headlong dash as the Marine Corps' ground combat element, the 1st Marine Division, sought to exploit its unexpected momentum.[3] A battalion of main battle tanks—protected by mobile scout and antitank vehicles—poured thousands of rounds of 120mm cannon and machine-gun fire into Iraqi positions, blazing a path for the rest of the RCT to follow. An infantry company embarked in amphibious assault vehicles followed in trace, clearing pockets of resistance and securing nearby buildings whenever the column came to a halt. Cobra gunships buzzed ahead, destroying enemy antiair and antiarmor assets before they had a chance to ambush the column. An artillery regiment raced up the road not far behind, protecting the RCT with counterbattery fire and neutralizing distant targets as needed. In a matter of days, RCT-5 annihilated the Al Nida Republican Guard—one of Saddam Hussein's most elite divisions—as the marines seized the ground the Iraqi division had tried to defend, killed its commander, destroyed its equipment, and scattered its surviving personnel.

The marines were not as well prepared for what came next. Despite a deep reservoir of institutional experience fighting guerrillas and insurgents, the Marine Corps initially struggled to adapt to the pacification challenge.[4] Yet learning did ultimately occur. Commanders pored over lessons learned by their predecessors in the Dominican Republic, Haiti, Nicaragua, Panama, the Philippines, and, of course, Vietnam. Units experimented with new techniques and shared their experiences with one another. For its part, the Marine Corps both encouraged bottom-up initiative and provided a top-down intellectual framework to tie these disparate actions together in the form of an overarching new doctrine, *Field Manual 3-24: Counterinsurgency Operations*, in 2006.

The differences between combat operations in 2003 and 2006/2007 were striking. Take, for example, the 1st Battalion, 6th Marine Regiment's deployment to Ramadi, the capital of Iraq's Anbar Province, in September 2006.[5] Small teams of marines who lived, ate, and patrolled alongside Iraqi soldiers and police officers replaced the massed columns of armor racing along the highway. Decisive thrusts and rapid maneuver gave way to a painstaking effort to collect intelligence and earn the population's trust. The use of firepower became judicious instead of liberal. And rather than prioritizing the destruction of enemy units, marines focused on training Iraqi units and supporting civilian-led reconstruction efforts. As the battalion's executive officer aptly observed, "combat" operations in Ramadi actually represented a "combination of improvised explosive devices, quick gun battles in the streets, and then handing out school supplies to the kids 20 minutes later."[6] Far from exceptional, the 1st Battalion, 6th Marine Regiment's methods became the rule for how Marine Corps (and US Army) units battled the insurgency in Iraq.

The Marine Corps' experience in Iraq reaffirms one of warfare's most immutable features: it changes.[7] Sometimes these shifts are subtle and hard to discern. Other times, the transformation is so profound that a conflict's opening engagements bear little resemblance to the battles that end it. In either case, wars are often a race to see which side will be the first to learn from its battlefield experiences so as to bring its prewar expectations and capabilities into line with wartime realities and requirements.

So, why do some militaries learn faster than others? What enabled the marines—masters of conventional maneuver warfare—to adapt to the demands of a decidedly unconventional counterinsurgency doctrine? Could the marines have learned faster than they did? And what can we do to ensure that the Marine Corps—and all of our war-fighting organizations—are ready to learn as quickly as possible the next time we send troops into harm's way?

These are the questions that animate this book. And the answers are anything but academic. Rare though they may be, wars play an outsize role in the international system.[8] States devote vast sums of human and financial capital preparing for—and waging—them. Some scholars even think that first movers and early adapters on the battlefield can lock in long-term competitive advantages. Moreover, the international system appears to be in the midst of both a return to wars between the great powers and a tectonic shift in how wars are fought. The US military must be ready to learn and quickly adapt on tomorrow's battlefields. To be sure, America's military leaders are taking this challenge seriously. More likely than not, they will come close to getting it right. There is already a broad consensus about what future wars will look like. Unfortunately, as the case studies in this book highlight, close might not be good enough, and the price for working out the details on the battlefield is measured in lives.

Learning How to Learn from History

History is an important source of lessons on wartime learning. Of course, it is one thing to say that we should learn from history. It is another thing to specify *where* we should look in history and *what* we should draw from it. History is long. It yields contradictory lessons, most of which are irrelevant to the challenges that today's military planners face.[9] It is not an easy task to discern which historical episodes bear a striking resemblance to our own and are therefore worth learning from and which are not.

This book's central premise is that the First World War is uniquely relevant to the challenges that today's leaders face as they prepare for tomorrow's wars. The book also contains important lessons about wartime learning. Of course, historical analogies are often inappropriate and misleading despite their intuitive appeal. Yuen Foong Khong is right to caution against picking them based on superficial similarities, because the wrong historical parallels could lead us to unsupported conclusions and ignore disconfirming evidence.[10] There are at least three reasons, however, why the First World War—and the years leading up to it—is relevant to the challenges military leaders face today.

The first reason involves the rate of technological change. Disruptive technologies, such as railroads, hydraulics, internal combustion engines, airplanes, and interchangeable parts, proliferated before the war. Europe's armies struggled to keep up as their leaders worried obsessively about falling behind in this never-ending innovation race. They devoted scarce resources to research, develop, and acquire the newest weapons, only to find their capabilities out of date by the time they were fully fielded. Smaller peacetime military budgets meant investing in future weapons, inevitably came at a cost to training and doctrinal development.

One hundred years later, technology is once again evolving at a breakneck pace. Innovation is a top priority for great powers and regional actors around the world. Most notably, the US military is spending tremendous sums of money to maintain a technological edge over its competitors.[11] Russia and China are developing precision-strike, antiaccess/area denial, cyber, and artificial intelligence capabilities. Defense budgets are on the rise. At the same time, spending levels remain a fraction of what states are willing to spend in wartime. As a result, the pressure to modernize once again comes at the expense of readiness, training, and doctrine.

The second reason concerns the character of technological change. The private sector developed many of the technological innovations that revolutionized combat during the First World War. As a result, it was nearly impossible for military leaders to predict how—or even if—these technologies might reshape warfare. The nature of these new technologies also created another dilemma for Europe's generals. While the technologies made it both possible and necessary to spread their armies out across the battlefield, they did not give generals a commensurate ability to maintain control over their increasingly far-flung forces. In essence, Europe's generals knew it was becoming dangerous to mass their men, but they also knew they lacked the tools to communicate with and provide logistical support for units scattered across the battlefield. Thus, all three European prewar armies—German, French, and British—debated whether it was better to absorb higher casualties or accept less control.

Today, the private sector is again responsible for the most important innovations, most of which are designed for civilian use. Yet there is no denying that additive manufacturing, social networking, artificial intelligence, robotics, artificial intelligence, and space exploration will reshape warfare. What is up for debate is how and to what degree existing military doctrine must change in response to these shifts. Moreover, like their predecessors a century ago, today's military leaders worry that it might take so long to identify and develop innovations that they will be obsolete by the time they are fielded. And the character of today's innovations means that military leaders are once again reassessing the proper balance between dispersion and control.

The third reason involves the relative absence of great-power wars in recent times. The First World War followed a prolonged period of peace in Europe. There were no major wars between Europe's leading states between 1871 and 1914. Desirable as great-power peace was, it had the unfortunate side effect of making military planning even harder by yielding relatively few obvious lessons from which planners could learn. Of course, Europe's armies were not idle during this period. They fought or observed a number of localized conflicts, including the Boer and Russo-Japanese Wars. Some scholars suggest that these conflicts presaged the shifting nature of warfare. They therefore criticize Europe's generals for failing to learn from these wars

and the American Civil War. These critiques ignore major contextual differences and that the lessons of the American Civil War and the Boer and Russo-
Japanese Wars were less self-evident than it seems in hindsight. The American
Civil War ended fifty years before the First World War began and was waged
on a different continent with dissimilar geography. Many of the weapons
that revolutionized warfare in 1914 were either nascent or nonexistent in
the 1860s. It is unclear whether the American Civil War dragged on for four
years because warfare itself changed or because the Union Army suffered
from inept military leadership early in the conflict.[12] Nor were the Boer and
Russo-Japanese Wars necessarily a better guide to the future of great-
power wars. The Boer War was asymmetric and primarily guerrilla in nature for its final two years.[13] The Russo-Japanese War was a limited conflict
in which sea power was at least as important as land power.[14] As a result,
the officer corps in all major European armies engaged in a fierce decades-
long doctrinal debate about the future of warfare—one that raged until the
fighting broke out in 1914.

A similar great-power peace exists today. The Second World War represents the last direct conflict between two or more great powers.[15] Strategists
and war planners therefore lack an example of what a major war will look
like when all sides have advanced twenty-first-century weapons. Recent
wars, violent and prolonged as they have been, are unlikely to be an accurate guide. Some, including the 1991 Persian Gulf War, the 2003 US-led invasion of Iraq, and Russia's 2008 invasion of Georgia, were interstate and
conventional but grossly lopsided. Others, such as the insurgencies in Afghanistan and Iraq as well as Russia's hybrid campaign against Ukraine,
were interstate but unconventional. Though the great powers did intervene,
the civil wars in Chechnya, Yugoslavia, and Syria remained primarily intra-
state conflicts. None featured large-scale combat between great-power military forces fighting over core interests and fully equipped with state-of-the-art
weapons.

Wartime Learning on the Western Front

The First World War also contains one of history's most important examples
of wartime learning. In particular, the Western Front pitted three of the
world's most advanced armies in a race to master a form of warfare none
had seriously anticipated. Moreover, these three combatants—Britain, France,
and Germany—had armies that were remarkably similar, so much so that
the historian Williamson Murray calls it the closest thing to a natural experiment in military history.[16] Except for the British Army, they were the same
size. They were organized along similar lines,[17] and their weapons were virtually identical.[18] Once they were locked in a stalemate, all three had a common goal (to penetrate the other side's defenses) and faced the same obstacles

(firepower, lack of mobility, and command and control) as they tried to achieve it.

As the case studies in this book highlight, all three went to war with virtually identical war-fighting doctrines. From 1914 to 1916, their war-fighting doctrines began to diverge as they searched for a solution to the deadlock. Then in the war's final years, all three *began* to converge on a new way of war—one organized around modern assault tactics, combined-arms infantry and artillery operations, and the elastic defense in depth.[19] The German Army was the first to make the transition. The British Army was not far behind, although the war ended before the transformation was complete. The French Army began but did not complete the transition.

That any army managed to revolutionize its doctrine in the middle of a war is surprising, given how we normally think about military organizations. It is even more shocking given that the standard narrative surrounding the First World War is one of "stagnation and military incompetence."[20] Most students are erroneously taught that the war was little more than routinized slaughter.[21] Historians have spent decades debunking this pernicious myth.[22] The Western Front was not deadlocked because its generals were coldhearted idiots and cowards. The front was deadlocked because all three main armies went to war armed with prewar doctrines that did not (and, as I argue, could not) foresee wartime realities. Nor did it take long for these armies to recognize their shortcomings. As Gary Sheffield aptly reminds us, the soldiers and officers "did not simply gape at the trenches with incomprehension."[23]

The reality is that few armies have changed how they fight as dramatically as did the British, French, and German armies between 1914 and 1918. Although none seriously prepared for trench warfare, it did not take long for all three to begin searching for a solution. We therefore should not confuse the lack of movement on the Western Front with an absence of learning. Far from the definition of insanity, with British, French, and German generals doing the same thing over and over while expecting different results, all three aggressively tested out new war-fighting ideas. They did not stop trying to learn until the war ended four years later.

The First World War's static battlefields ultimately gave rise to the military doctrines that dominated the Second World War's mobile battlefields. Some scholars even go so far as to suggest that the Western Front represents the birthplace of modern conventional warfare.[24] This basic story is already well developed in the existing historiography. However, an important question remains. Why did the British, French, and German armies pursue roughly the same set of solutions (assault tactics, combined arms, and elastic defense in depth) to the same tactical problem (stalemate) *but at different speeds and to varying degrees of success?*

A Theory of Wartime Learning

The German Army learned faster than its competitors. It combined arms to a greater degree, at a lower level, and at an earlier point in the war than either the French or the British.[25] German Army assault tactics, although perhaps no more advanced than those used by the British or French armies by war's end, were employed with greater uniformity and to greater effect in Erich Ludendorff's spring 1918 offensives.[26] And the German Army was the only army to truly master the elastic defense in depth. What about the German Army made it better at learning?

I offer a theory of wartime learning, which I call assessment, command, and training (ACT) theory, to answer this important question. ACT theory predicts that three organizational characteristics will play an outsize role in wartime learning:

- The degree to which a military delegates command on the battlefield,
- Whether it possesses a particular type of doctrinal assessment mechanism, and
- The degree to which it controls training in the classroom.

Independently, each attribute influences a different part of the learning process. The degree to which subordinate commanders can exercise autonomy on the front lines determines the speed with which the organization can generate new ideas. Whether or not it has an independent doctrinal assessment mechanism—which I define as a formal independent unit empowered to analyze frontline reports, test new ideas, refine best practices, and disseminate new doctrine across the organization—impacts its ability to sift through these ideas and distinguish the good ones from the bad ones. And the degree to which it centralizes control over training determines how fast it can implement a new doctrine across the entire organization. ACT theory further predicts that militaries that combine these three characteristics in a particular way will learn faster than their competition:

- Those that *moderately delegate* command on the battlefield,
- Those that possess an *independent, prestigious, and rigorous* doctrinal assessment mechanism,[27] and
- Those that maintain *centralized* control over training.

Chapter 1 develops ACT theory in greater detail, but here I offer a brief summary of the theory's basic tenants.

ACT theory begins with the observation that modern military organizations are extraordinarily large and complex. Complexity means that terms such as "hierarchical"/"flat" and "centralized"/"decentralized" inaccurately gloss over the range of activities that modern military organizations can undertake as well as the way that they can manage and coordinate these activities.[28] Specifically, modern military organizations can choose to maintain tight control over some activities while delegating significant latitude over others. This observation is especially true of an army's two most important activities: training and fighting.

COMMAND PRACTICES

ACT theory assumes a strong relationship between a military's command practices on the battlefield and how it generates new ideas.[29] Specifically, the more it delegates decision-making authority, the more likely it is that subordinate commanders will experiment. And the more those subordinates experiment, the more the organization as a whole generates new ideas.

The degree to which an army centralizes or decentralizes decision making has both short- and long-term effects. In the short term, decentralization increases the number of units willing to experiment with new approaches. As decentralization increases, so too does the variation in how units fight. This variation in turn generates new information and alternative ways of fighting. Decentralization's benefits go only so far, however.[30] In theory, an army that unleashes its commanders to fight however they want to will generate the most information. Unfortunately, this information will be of little use, because there will be too much of it as frontline units undertake countless ad hoc experiments. In any case, most experiments will fail. Thus, too much decentralization will generate too much information, overwhelming the organization's ability to meaningfully process and refine it. And too much decentralization will lead to high casualty levels, since experimenting units are more likely than not to fail. Therefore, a theoretical inflection point exists at which the costs of decentralization (in terms of information overload and battlefield losses) outweigh its benefits (in terms of generating new information). ACT theory assumes that moderate levels of decentralization maximize this utility/variation trade-off.

In the long run, moderate decentralization fosters a culture in which leaders are willing to take risks and listen to ideas from below. The intuition is that senior commanders will give junior leaders the same leeway they were once afforded. The opposite is true in military organizations that are extremely centralized or decentralized. In armies with a long-standing tradition of giving subordinates no latitude, junior leaders are less likely to experiment, and senior leaders are less tolerant of risk and new ideas from below. In armies that give subordinates extremely high levels of authority, leaders at every rung along the chain of command are unlikely to listen to one another.

TRAINING SYSTEMS

Even the best new doctrinal practices are only as good as their implementation. And there are at least two reasons a military might resist implementing otherwise effective new practices. First, change generates opposition. Military organizations are vibrant social organisms made up of subgroups and cliques, each with their own parochial interests.[31] These dynamics invariably impact organizational behavior during periods of change, because new doctrines affect the organization's internal balance of power. New winners and losers are created as some combat arms (e.g., infantry, special forces, cyber officers) benefit from the change by gaining more prestige, securing additional promotions, and improving access to resources. In a world of finite defense budgets and general/flag officer positions, the competition over such things is fierce and often zero-sum. As a result, advocates for change always face resistance, if only because someone stands to lose something in the process. The more a military centralizes control over its entry-level and unit training, the more power senior officers have to circumvent and overcome such resistance.

Second, because modern militaries are so large and complex, even the seemingly straightforward act of transmitting a new practice across the entire organization becomes problematic. Wartime conditions radically exacerbate the challenge. Centralization abets standardization, ensuring that as many people as possible are taught new practices the right way. This capability is especially important for those just joining the organization. Unlike most other organizations, militaries bring in large numbers of new personnel every year, especially in wartime. Control over entry-level training ensures that within a few years, the youngest members—who make up the largest percentage of the organization—will know nothing other than the new approach.

Standardized training also helps overcome resistance from those already in the organization. Frontline troops rarely care about doctrinal debates. They just want to survive and go home. They are, however, rightfully suspicious of new ideas should they fail on the battlefield. And when existing troops are unevenly trained in new practices, they may fail not because the new practices were unsound but instead because they were improperly trained in their application. In this way, standardization and resistance are themselves inversely related.

The preceding discussion suggests that more centralization is almost always better for training. Unlike command practices, where decentralization is beneficial in moderation, training only improves with centralization. Technology, cost, combat demands, and geography obviously place practical limits on the degree to which an army can centralize training. In theory, if an army were ever able to achieve perfect centralization (e.g., pull every soldier off the line and train them all in one classroom), then perhaps we might see a point where the returns from centralization start to diminish. Nevertheless, for practical purposes, ACT theory treats the relationship as linear.

ASSESSMENT MECHANISMS

Even if we understand the organizational characteristics that optimize experimentation and implementation, two important questions remain:

what determines whether senior leaders see a need for change, and how do leaders decide on which idea to implement?[32] After all, someone is always calling for change in any large organization. So, what decides which calls for change will be heard and which will be ignored? ACT theory argues that it comes down to whether an army has a particular type of doctrinal assessment mechanism. Wars generate mountains of information, most of which is chaotic and contradictory.[33] Military organizations that possess a dedicated analytic unit empowered to investigate frontline reports, test new ideas, refine best practices, and disseminate new doctrine across the organization are more likely to have leaders who detect the need for change and select an appropriate doctrine to meet the organization's wartime needs.

ACT theory predicts that these assessment processes work best when they meet three conditions. First, they must be *independent.* This independence must come in two forms. Officers engaged in doctrinal assessment must be free from undue political and command influence so as to engage in genuinely objective analysis. And their doctrinal assessment activities must remain separate and distinct from both the intelligence process and coordinating combat operations. Intelligence efforts are necessarily focused on the adversary. Doctrinal assessment requires a healthy dose of introspection. Combat operations require real-time decision making. Doctrinal assessment demands reflection and an ability to step back from the crisis du jour so as to holistically evaluate broad trends. Of course, doctrinal assessment cannot be completely divorced from the intelligence process or combat operations. It must still have the institutional links and authority to get the right information (about performance gaps and alternative ways to fight) into the right hands (the senior leadership) so that overarching decisions about doctrine can be made and implemented. Second, they must attract the best and brightest. In practical terms, this means officers must believe that being assigned to a doctrinal assessment billet is *prestigious* insofar as it puts them on a fast track to promotion. Third, the officers who perform doctrinal assessment must undergo *rigorous* formal training and education so as to prepare them for the difficult intellectual challenges associated with analyzing data and writing doctrine.

PUTTING IT ALL TOGETHER

In sum, ACT theory thinks of military organizations as gigantic, dynamic, and evolving search engines. During periods of peace, militaries do their best to guess what the next war will look like and then develop doctrines accordingly. As soon as the fighting begins, however, militaries must detect where their prewar doctrines fail to meet wartime realities. They then develop a range of alternatives, select the best one, implement it across the relevant parts of the organization, and reevaluate. This cycle repeats itself ad infinitum until the war ends.

Furthermore, ACT theory predicts that when a military gives its frontline leaders a *moderate* amount of discretion on the battlefield, retains tight control over what personnel learn in the classroom, and possesses an independent doctrinal assessment mechanism to help leaders wade through the mountains of incoming information, it will learn faster and more efficiently than its adversaries if they organized these activities in any other way. ACT theory therefore pushes back on the idea that armies must be highly centralized to operate effectively. It also questions the degree to which theories of change borrowed from the private sector, which emphasize decentralization, help us understand military organizations engaged in war. Finally, ACT theory questions the utility of thinking about militaries as either centralized or decentralized and implies that they can be both at the same time. The real question is what a military chooses to centralize control over and what it chooses to delegate.

Thus, ACT theory is ultimately about how organizational structure has a systematic impact on wartime learning. ACT theory *does not*, however, assume that structure is deterministic. As the case studies in this book demonstrate, other factors—most notably political and strategic demands—can trump structure's impact. From violating Belgian neutrality in 1914 to proposing a secret alliance with Mexico in 1917, Germany repeatedly committed strategic missteps that mitigated whatever advantages its army gained from doctrinal learning. The British high command knew it was not ready to attack along the Western Front in 1915, but alliance politics compelled it to do so. And the political imperative not to yield another inch of French soil prohibited the French Army from adopting elastic defenses in depth.

In the same vein, ACT theory is also probabilistic. A military can fail to learn despite exhibiting all of these characteristics, just as learning can occur in their absence. After all, it is still possible for a military practicing moderately decentralized authority to embrace a suboptimal concept. Highly centralized training structures will quickly transmit new ideas regardless of their underlying merit. And even the most rigorous assessment mechanism can overlook relevant data, fall prey to confirmation bias, and reject evidence that fails to conform to preexisting expectations.

ACT Theory and Existing Scholarship

ACT theory contributes to a vibrant and ongoing debate over the sources and causes of military change.[34] To be sure, this literature has not yet generated much in the way of consensus or conclusive findings.[35] Nevertheless, it continues to evolve in important and dynamic ways. For example, whereas the field once fixated on the most dramatic form of change—innovation—it has since broadened its aperture so as to include related phenomenon such as adaptation, emulation, and learning.[36] Similarly, early work tended to treat all military organizations as inherently conservative, risk averse, and backward looking.[37] Many scholars now reject this blanket assumption by acknowledging that military organizations vary tremendously in terms of their willingness to embrace change.[38] Such improvements allow the existing literature to address an impressive range of issues related to military change.

ACT theory contributes to this constantly evolving discussion by bringing organizational structure back to the forefront of analysis. As such, ACT serves as a useful counterpoint to the culture-centric theories that now dominate the literature. Broadly speaking, culture-based explanations fall into one of two categories: those that focus on national—or strategic—culture and those that emphasize organizational-level culture. Russell Weigley's pioneering work typifies this first approach. He argues that the United States struggled to adapt to unconventional warfare, in large part because the American Civil War changed how American elites defined war and victory so as to prefer annihilation over attrition, overwhelming force over proportionality, decisive engagement over maneuver, and the destruction of opposing military forces over other types of objectives.[39] Dima Adamsky likewise points to strategic culture as the reason Israel, the Soviet Union, and the United States responded differently to the precision-weapons revolution in military affairs.[40] Jacqueline Newmyer similarly finds that China's unique strategic culture shaped how it has responded to that same revolution.[41]

Elizabeth Kier's work typifies the organizational culture strand of analysis. She points to the French Army's culture as the reason interwar France adopted an inappropriate static defense doctrine even as Germany developed its offensive blitzkrieg doctrine.[42] Austin Long theorizes that a military organization's culture acts as a heuristic, helping leaders make sense of an otherwise chaotic threat environment.[43] Culture plays an especially vital role when the organization is taking on a new mission, helping or hindering efforts at adjustment based on the degree to which the new mission fits within the preexisting culture. Accordingly, the US Army's continental culture undercut its ability to adapt to counterinsurgency, whereas the British Army's maritime culture helped it avoid similar struggles. John Nagl likewise compares the British Army's success waging counterinsurgency during the Malayan Emergency against the US Army's failure during the Vietnam War.[44] He concludes that the British Army did a better job of adapting to counterinsurgency because it had a learning culture that encouraged frontline leaders to share new ideas and insights. Terry Terriff suggests that the US Marine Corps' culture of organizational paranoia inspired it to develop maneuver warfare doctrine in the 1980s.[45]

Finally, some scholars look at how strategic and organizational culture can interact in order to explain military change. In her study of the US Marine Corps and counterinsurgency, Jeannie Johnson compares the Corps' organizational culture with the broader American strategic culture in which it is nested, thereby highlighting the Corps' mixed record of learning from its long history with counterinsurgency.[46] Thomas Mahnken similarly documents how a mix of ethnocentrism, biases, and organizational culture caused the US military to overlook important German, British, and Japanese innovations before the Second World War.[47]

Cultural explanations have come to dominate the literature, because culture undoubtedly plays an important role in how militaries innovate, adapt, and learn. Nevertheless, theories that focus on culture face an important limitation: they have a hard time explaining cases in which a given military gets better—or worse—at changing over relatively short periods of time.[48] This gap becomes especially important when trying to understand wartime change. For example, as Chapter 3 illustrates, the British Army became better at learning over the course of the First World War. Since both British strategic culture and the British Army's organizational culture should have remained relatively fixed over the course of the war, neither can account for this shift.[49] By focusing on organizational-level structures, particularly those that leaders can control, ACT theory also fills an important gap in how we think about wartime change. By looking beyond culture—something that is not subject to control—ACT theory offers policy makers insight into factors they can influence so as to improve how their military forces learn on the battlefield.

Of course, ACT theory is not the first to suggest that organizational structures and institutional arrangements shape how military forces innovate, adapt, and learn. Looking at British, French, and German innovation during the interwar period, Barry Posen concludes that militaries are like all bureaucratic organizations in that they resist change despite obvious evidence that existing ways of doing business are obsolete.[50] In his view, change is unlikely unless senior political leaders intervene so as to force it upon an otherwise resistant military. But because politicians are usually preoccupied with other priorities, it takes a major shift in the balance of power to scare them into taking action.[51] Like Posen, Stephen Rosen also emphasizes organizational dynamics. Unlike Posen, who assumes that all organizations resist change, Rosen allows for variation. Specifically, Rosen assumes that military services are vibrant political communities composed of diverse interest groups from different communities of combat arms officers. These groups compete with one another for power, resources, and prestige.[52] Rosen also contends that political leaders lack the specialized knowledge needed to navigate these complex dynamics and so are not in a position to foist transformation on an otherwise unwilling organization. Change instead requires internal leadership by senior officers—not external intervention by civilian politicians—and becomes most likely when prochange officers effectively articulate a new theory of victory and build protected promotion pathways for younger officers who support change.

Other scholars use the relationship between organizations as well as the broader institutional milieu in which military bureaucracies operate to explain why some are better at changing than others. Matthew Evangelista argues that the US state-societal arrangement allowed it to out-innovate the Soviet Union during the Cold War.[53] The United States combined a strong society with a weak state, thereby creating an open and decentralized system that fostered innovative thinking, whereas the Soviet Union combined a strong state with a weak society, which inhibited creativity. Deborah Avant finds that institutional "rules of the game" explain why the armies of Britain and the United States approached counterinsurgency differently.[54] And in his comparative assessment of the Polaris and Trident II ballistic missile programs, Owen Coté suggests that interservice competition *fosters* innovation.[55]

Over the last ten years, a newer strand of scholarship has begun helping us understand how specific organizational structures relate to military change. Caitlin Talmdage's work on battlefield effectiveness highlights the link between organizational practices and combat performance.[56] Effectiveness, in turn, depends on how well a military learns from and adapts to changing battlefield conditions. Specifically, Talmadge finds that military forces that promote based on merit, enforce rigorous training standards, empower subordinate commanders, and encourage information flows between units will out-learn and out-perform competitors that do not. Suzanne Nielson argues that the US Army became more innovative after the Vietnam War, in large part because it created an internal command with broad authority over training and doctrine.[57] Janine Davidson similarly looks at how post-Vietnam changes to the US Army's professional military education programs, war-planning system, and lessons-learned processes helped it adapt to its stability and reconstruction mission in Iraq.[58] Ben Jensen contends that incubators and advocacy networks play an important role in fostering and transmitting new ideas across complex and resistant military bureaucracies.[59] Michael Horowitz concludes that financial and organizational costs determine whether or not a military will adopt a technological innovation developed by another state.[60] And in his study of the British Army in Afghanistan, Theo Farrell asserts that frontline combat units are most likely to adapt when they think they are losing, operate in a highly decentralized environment, and experience high turnover rates among leaders.[61]

ACT theory makes three important contributions to this organizationally focused strand of the literature on military change. First, ACT theory leverages organizational structure to help us better understand wartime change. Existing organizational studies—particularly those that explain transformational and enduring forms of change—pay more attention to how change unfolds between conflicts than how it evolves within a given war.[62] There are understandable reasons why scholars emphasize peacetime change. War is rare, and militaries spend remarkably little time actually waging war. Moreover, as Rosen aptly points out, fundamentally changing an organization usually takes a great deal of time. Yet during times of war, "innovations must be thought through and implemented within two or three years if they are to be of any use at all."[63] Nevertheless, as the historiography on the First World War convincingly demonstrates, military forces can and do change—and sometimes in profound and revolutionary ways—over the course of a single conflict. ACT theory helps us understand how and why.

Second, ACT theory helps to bridge a conceptual gap between scholars who explore military innovation and those who look at battlefield adaptation. Innovation theories tend to be top down in that they assume that wholesale transformation requires a level of support and resourcing that only high-ranking officers can provide. In contrast, adaptation theories look at change from the bottom up insofar as they recognize that frontline combat units routinely make ad hoc changes to how they fight, even without high-level sanction, direction, or support.[64] Unfortunately, both sets of explanations are incomplete. Top-down innovation theories have a hard time explaining where new ideas and alternative theories of victory come from in the first place. As the case studies in this book suggest, they often come from frontline units. Yet because bottom-up adaptation theories are content to explain ad hoc experimentation, they do not clarify how or why some impromptu changes serve as the basis for wholesale, organization-wide reform while other changes do not. By focusing on the ways in which doctrinal assessment mechanisms can capture, filter, refine, and disseminate frontline experimentation across the entire organization, ACT theory offers a useful way to connect these otherwise disparate strands of literature on military change.

Third, although other scholars highlight a role for doctrinal assessment mechanisms, ACT theory provides additional clarity and nuance in how we think about them. Existing work focuses heavily on the US Army and the role that its newly created Training and Doctrine Command (TRADOC) played in reorienting the Army after Vietnam.[65] ACT theory builds on their insights but then tests them against an important set of cases that explore how doctrinal assessment operates in wartime and in a non-US context. Moreover, existing work tends to look at doctrinal assessment dichotomously: either a military organization has the functional equivalent of a TRADOC, or it does not. In comparison, ACT theory suggests that not all doctrinal assessment mechanisms are structured or organized the same way and that subtle differences in how they function can have a major impact on the degree to which they foster wartime learning.

The Way Ahead

The rest of the book is organized as follows.

Chapter 1 describes ACT theory in detail, describing its predictions and the kinds of evidence that confirm or reject its validity. The chapter includes a detailed discussion of definitions, case selection, and scope conditions. Chapter 2 provides a basic overview of the tactical dilemma facing the British,

French, and German armies on the Western Front and identifies the optimal doctrine for ending the stalemate. Chapters 3, 4, and 5 contain the German, British, and French case studies, respectively. The final chapter discusses alternative explanations. It also introduces two shadow cases—the US Army in Vietnam (1965–1973) and Iraq (2003–2010)—so as to suggest that ACT theory can explain more than just learning on the Western Front. It concludes by identifying important policy implications for contemporary defense strategists.

Assessment, Command, and Training Theory

It is not merely the tools of warfare but the organizations that wield them that make for revolutionary change in war.
—Eliot A. Cohen, "A Revolution in Warfare," 1996

The Question

Assessment, command, and training (ACT) theory seeks to explain why some wartime militaries are better than others at learning so as to *correctly* update how they fight. It is therefore useful to start by defining two concepts that are at the center of this outcome: learning and doctrine.

LEARNING

As traditionally understood, learning involves the act of acquiring new knowledge, skills, and experience. We usually think of learning as something that individuals do. Nevertheless, scholars have long believed that organizations can also learn.[1] Of course, I must modify this definition, because I want to understand how a specific subset of organizations (militaries) learn while under extraordinary conditions (warfare). War is a complex phenomenon, and militaries invariably acquire all sorts of new knowledge, skills, and experiences from fighting them. To keep my analysis manageable, I focus specifically on one type of learning: how militaries update, revise, and otherwise change their war-fighting doctrines (which I define below). Learning is also usually treated as something worth pursuing for its own sake. Although I do not dispute this view, wartime imperatives lead me to look at learning in instrumental terms. I am particularly interested in how learning helps a military force become more effective on the battlefield.

These considerations lead me to define learning as the act of updating and refining an existing war-fighting doctrine so as to make it as effective as possible. In other words, it is the iterative process by which a military determines the best way to fight given its goals, adversaries, resources, and limitations. Previous scholars, including Richard Downie, John Nagl, and Janine Davidson, similarly highlight both doctrine and effectiveness in their definitions of military learning.[2]

It is still relatively unusual to look at military change through the lens of learning. Scholars have traditionally preferred to focus on innovation, adaptation, and emulation. Learning has an advantage over these concepts, because innovation, adaptation, and emulation overlap to such a degree that it is practically impossible—and analytically arbitrary—to distinguish between them.[3] There are, after all, few pure examples of each, particularly in a wartime context. If one looks closely enough, every innovation contains countless smaller adaptations and emulations. The opposite is also true. Emulations involve elements of innovation and adaptation, since organizations cannot copy practice, doctrine, or technology wholesale, at least not if their goal is to improve performance. Subtle differences in culture, structure, geography, and capacity mean that emulators need to modify imported doctrines to make them fit. Such modifications represent adaptations—and even innovations—in their own right.

Take, for example, the US Army's AirLand Battle, which scholars and policy makers often use as an example of doctrinal innovation. Unveiled in 1982, AirLand Battle outlined a radical new vision for defeating the Soviet Army in Europe. This vision called for American ground troops to conduct rapid combined-arms attacks against Soviet frontline units by harnessing a range of new communications and long-range precision strike technologies. Simultaneously, American airpower would conduct strikes against Soviet command-and-control assets and follow-on forces deep behind enemy lines.[4] As such, AirLand Battle represented a radical break from the far more conservative active defense doctrine that preceded it. And at least according to its most ardent proponents, AirLandBattle set the stage for institutional reforms and acquisition programs that helped the United States defeat Iraq in the 1991 Persian Gulf War.

But how innovative was AirLand Battle? Carl von Clausewitz talked about combining speed and maneuver to strike at an enemy's center of gravity. The microprocessing technologies, long-range weapons, and rapid communications technologies behind AirLand Battle had been around for decades, at least in the private sector. And American planners borrowed the entire idea of using computers and microprocessors to develop long-range deep-strike weapons from the Soviet Union, which was a generation ahead of the United States in thinking about how computers could revolutionize warfare but a generation behind in its ability to actually build them.[5]

It is ultimately hard to argue that AirLand Battle represented a pure case of innovation, adaptation, or emulation, since it clearly involved pieces of all three. This observation suggests that how one categorizes organizational change largely reflects where one chooses to look. To ignore or privilege innovation, adaptation, or emulation over the other two is to omit a critical part of the causal story.

Thinking in terms of learning helps us bypass these arbitrary distinctions. After all, most of us do not care whether a military is better at navigating wholesale transformation or empowering ad hoc modifications per se. Instead, we care about whether it can change so as to meet wartime challenges and realities—changes that will often require a mix of innovative, adaptive, and emulative behavior. A learning approach helps us pay attention to the organizational characteristics that impede and enable all three important forms of change.

DOCTRINE

If learning is the process through which a military acquires new skills, knowledge, and expertise about how to fight, then doctrine is the mechanism by which it codifies and transmits these lessons. At its most essential, doctrine refers to how a military plans to fight and win on the battlefield.[6] Doctrine plays at least five key roles. First, it provides a standard playbook that allows units to coordinate their actions on and off the battlefield. In peacetime, it serves as the basis for developing the training standards that help units prepare for combat. Once the fighting starts, doctrine helps units synchronize their operations in accordance with an overarching set of principles and objectives, even when they cannot communicate with one another directly.[7] Second, doctrine educates and socializes junior leaders. By articulating an overarching "theory of victory," it prepares new frontline officers and noncommissioned officers to make decisions under conditions of fog, friction, and uncertainty, providing them with guidelines and rules of thumb for acting in the absence of concrete direction.[8] Third, doctrine serves as a source of institutional memory, capturing experience and knowledge that might otherwise be lost.[9] This function is especially important in wartime, given the casualties and personnel turnover caused by combat. Fourth, doctrine serves as a prescriptive conceptual framework that informs long-term decisions about weapons procurement; recruitment, training, and education; and organizational structure.[10] Finally, doctrine helps the entire organization think about the future. The act of bringing officers and experts together to debate about what future battlefields will look like and the best way to prevail on them represents an invaluable opportunity.[11] In many respects, the process of developing a new doctrine is probably more important than the document that ultimately emerges.

Unfortunately, it is usually easier to describe what doctrine does than what it is or looks like. Scholars and policy makers alike have a bad habit of using doctrine as a catchall term to describe everything from national strategy (e.g., the Truman Doctrine) to nascent operational concepts (e.g., multidomain operations).[12] As I use the term, doctrine has several defining characteristics.

It is officially endorsed by top-level leadership and widely promulgated within an organization. It is usually written down, albeit in sometimes frustratingly vague language.[13] Yet imprecision does not imply irrelevance. The nebulous and abstract way in which many modern doctrines are written serves an important purpose. As military historian M. A. Ramsay reminds us, military "planners and writers can deal only in probability and estimates."[14] They must therefore write in general terms that offer "guidance for the force to use in its war preparation without being so specific that it binds too tightly the hands of the future commanders who will have to use it."[15] Doctrine is also multifaceted, not monolithic, insofar as militaries often have multiple overlapping doctrines. Scholars tend to talk about doctrine in singular terms, as if a given military can only have one doctrine at a time. However, contemporary armed forces must perform a wide range of missions, and they often develop separate doctrines for each one. Take the US Army, for example. It had 344 service-level doctrinal manuals as of early 2020, each of which applies to a distinct technical, tactical, operational, or strategic task.[16] *Field Manual 3-0: Operations*, outlines the US Army's preferred approach to deter and defeat peer and near-peer adversaries on conventional battlefields. Meanwhile, *Field Manual 3-24: Counterinsurgency*, describes its doctrine for combating insurgents, guerrillas, and other violent subversive movements.

The Assumptions

ACT theory rests upon two assumptions. The first is that there are better—and worse—ways to fight at any given point during a conflict. What this superior way looks like will depend on a wide and complex range of factors, including—but not limited to—one's adversary/ies; allies; political aims; the state of military technology; national sources of military power (e.g., industrial and technological bases, economic and financial resources, social resilience, etc.); the quality and quantity of one's military forces; and the geographic features that define the land, air, and water on which they are fighting. As these factors shift, so too does the best way to fight. The second assumption is that, all things equal, military organizations want to win and prefer to do so at the lowest possible cost in lives and matériel. In other words, militaries care about being effective and efficient. And they generally believe that the best way to be efficient is to be effective.

Taken together, these assumptions imply that that a superior war-fighting doctrine exists, even if it only becomes evident in hindsight. They also imply that fighting in the best way possible gives a military the best chance to achieve its goals at the lowest possible cost. In this way, a superior doctrine is like a Platonic ideal. It exists independent of whether or not any of the combatants manage to approximate it. However, the closer a military comes to fighting the "best" way possible, the more *likely* it is to achieve its goals at the lowest possible cost.

It is also important to clarify what these two assumptions *do not* imply. First, they do not mean the side that fights the best will always win. Many factors combine to determine victory and defeat in war.[17] Battlefield effectiveness and efficiency are of course important factors in shaping the final result, but even the most effective and efficient armies, navies, and air forces cannot overcome inept or poor political, economic, and social decisions. Wars are also stochastic. They remain a game of chance.[18] The better a military's warfighting practices, the better its chances are. Yet at the end of the day, even the best war-fighting practices in the world will not prevent lieutenants from getting lost, sentries from getting drunk, or the enemy from getting lucky.

Second, these assumptions do not mean that the superior way to fight is necessarily the same for every military. What works for one ally or adversary may not work for another. However, the more characteristics combatants share in terms of size, resources, objectives, culture, and weapons, the more likely it is that they will also share the same superior way of fighting. The opposite is true in highly asymmetric conflicts.

Third, these assumptions have nothing to say about when—or how often—the superior way of fighting changes over the course of a war. It could evolve multiple times in a short period of time or remain consistent for the entire conflict.[19] The factors and forces that determine the superior way to fight are virtually endless and may become obvious only in hindsight.

Finally, these assumptions do not imply that a change in one of the myriad factors that determine what the superior way to fight looks like (e.g., a shift in political aims or the introduction of a new technology) will yield a proportionate shift in the superior war-fighting doctrine. For example, a seemingly revolutionary new weapon might have a negligible effect on the best way to fight. Such seems to have been the case with tanks, at least during the First World War, and with atomic weapons, at least vis-à-vis twentieth-century ground combat.[20] The reverse can also be true. A small change in technology could trigger a major change in the best way to fight. The breech-loading rifle is one such example.[21] This observation has important ramifications for prediction. Being able to detect a looming shift in technology or objectives does not translate into being able to predict the best way to fight before the fighting breaks out. There is an important difference between realizing that the best way to fight is about to change and knowing both the degree and the direction in which it has changed. As the case studies in this book demonstrate, when it comes to war fighting, being off by even a little bit can prove costly.

ARE THESE SOUND ASSUMPTIONS?

These might seem like strong assumptions. However, most scholarly critiques of military effectiveness rest on even stronger ones. To criticize military performance and decision making (e.g., the French Army in the Second World War, the United States in Vietnam, or the Soviet Army in Afghanistan) relies on the assumption that there was a better way to fight *and* that political and military leaders at the time *should have known* about it. ACT theory simply assumes that a superior way to fight exists. The theory makes no claims about how quickly leaders should realize they are fighting suboptimally or how easy or difficult it is to identify the better alternatives.

Some readers might also question whether military leaders really care about being effective or efficient. Militaries are, after all, large public bureaucracies. And bureaucracies are often criticized for being inefficient and ineffective.[22] To be sure, peacetime military organizations pursue myriad goals, many of which are unrelated to efficiency or effectiveness.[23] The incentives to fight effectively and efficiently are magnified, however, once the fighting starts. Institutional self-interest suggests that militaries want to use their resources as effectively and efficiently as possible if only to dissuade politicians from interfering. Battlefield effectiveness and efficiency also helps husband resources for use in countering unforeseen contingencies. Individual self-interest likewise pushes wartime militaries to be as effective and efficient as possible. Generals and admirals know that success yields prestige and promotion. Failure often leads to the opposite. Frontline troops have even stronger incentives, since they are the ones who pay the price for inefficiency and a lack of effectiveness.

The Explanation

My explanation for why some militaries are better at wartime learning than others starts with conceptualizing wartime learning as a three-step process.[24] This simplification undoubtedly distorts reality. Militaries—and the hundreds of thousands of personnel who comprise them—are infinitely complex. At the same time, it is fair to say that all organizations must accomplish a minimum number of critical tasks if learning is to occur. In broad terms, scholars tend to agree that three are particularly important.[25] First, the organization must begin to experiment so as to develop alternatives to existing practices and praxis. I call this step *exploration*. Second, the organization must both decide which of the many possible options it wants to implement and engage in a rigorous process of testing and evaluation to refine the new practices so they are ready for widespread implementation—a process I call *selection*. Finally, because we do not care about organizational learning for its own sake, the organization must transmit these new practices so as to change how units fight on the battlefield. I call this final step *action*.

Each stage in this process presents a unique set of challenges, constraints, and opportunities. Organizational characteristics that make it easier to navigate one stage can prove counterproductive in another. To understand why, it is worth looking at each stage in isolation.

EXPLORATION: IDENTIFYING THE NEED FOR CHANGE AND GENERATING ALTERNATIVES

Learning starts with detecting the need for change. Organizations develop and rely on standard operating procedures, routines, and best practices, because these elements maximize efficiency and effectiveness. Since the need for change is rarely self-evident, most organizations usually resist learning so long as they think the existing way of doing business still works. The challenge is even greater for wartime militaries. The fog of war complicates assessment.[26] Shifts in the character of war can render existing performance standards and measures of effectiveness obsolete. Ironically, these are the very metrics commanders need to recognize that the battlefield is changing in the first place.[27] Compounding the challenge, service cultures and traditions—essential for fostering military esprit de corps and therefore combat effectiveness—can also stymie the flow of information and distort objective analysis.[28] Militaries that have information-collection processes (i.e., feedback loops) in place before the environmental shift, are receptive to new information, and have leaders or a culture tolerant of ambiguity, dissent, and alternative viewpoints are the most likely to detect those shifts and the corresponding need to undertake change. [29]

It is one thing for an organization to realize that it needs to change. It is another thing entirely for the organization to decide how—and in what ways—it should change. There are often many plausible ways to solve any given problem. Since lessons are rarely self-evident, particularly in wartime,[30] military organizations must generate a range of alternative ways to improve battlefield performance. As discussed, scholars endlessly debate whether these ideas tend to come from outside the organization, the inside, the top down, or the bottom up in wartime militaries. Regardless, there is basic consensus that decentralized organizations and those that possess a culture tolerant of risk, debate, and discussion tend to be better at generating a wide range of alternative ideas.[31] Slack resources to support experimentation are also helpful.[32]

SELECTION: DECIDING AND REFINING

Once an organization generates a range of options, it must then pick which idea(s) it wants to implement.[33] Regardless of where the new ideas came from, the decision to select one for implementation almost certainly occurs at the top of the organization or is mandated by outside political leadership. At this point, various groups inside and outside the organization will be advocating for and against various options. The right course of action is rarely self-evident.

Consensus will not necessarily be forthcoming, since these groups clash due to both principled disagreement and self-interest. As a result, top-level commanders may need to impose consensus from above. Access to power, resources, and authority make it easier for a leader to overcome resistance.

Moreover, even the best ideas need to be refined before they can be implemented and institutionalized.[34] Organizations need to test and validate innovative new technologies and practices—as well as minor adaptations to existing ones—to make sure they will work when scaled up. Emulated practices and technologies must be reconfigured to synchronize with existing routines and cultures. Slack resources help here too, especially those that can be shifted from research and development to testing and evaluation. Experimental units and feedback loops are also critical. Both help with evaluation and refinement. Resource limits are often acute during this stage, especially if the organization must simultaneously execute old tasks even as it refines new ones. Continued resistance from interest groups is another impediment.[35] Finally, there is always a risk that testing and refinement will reveal a fatal flaw, forcing the organization to restart its search.

ACTION: TRANSMITTING NEW PRACTICES AND ROUTINES

The final step in the learning process involves communicating the desired changes across the relevant parts of the organization.[36] Procedurally, this means revising training manuals, acquiring sufficient inventories of needed gear and equipment, and teaching personnel how to perform new tasks and handle new technologies. Politically, implementation often requires overcoming opponents inside and outside of the organization who continue to resist change. Any meaningful change, after all, will elicit opposition by those who resist out of principled disagreement and those who see a threat to their institutional standing and access to resources. Regardless of their motivation, those who oppose change have a range of tools at their disposal. They can shirk, refuse, or quit, although these last two options are available only to top-ranking officers in wartime. The larger and more complex and geographically dispersed the organization is, the easier it becomes for opponents of change to resist or undermine new practices. As a form of public bureaucracy, military organizations face another challenge: opponents can appeal to political leaders outside the organization to block or impede implementation. Success in this final stage increases as senior leaders who support change gain control over routines, resources, promotion systems, and external actors.

WARTIME IMPEDIMENTS: UNCERTAINTY AND DANGER

Wartime militaries must navigate two additional challenges that further complicate learning. The first is uncertainty. Organizational change always involves some degree of ambiguity, but war is unparalleled in its confusing and uncertain nature.[37] Whether and how battlefield conditions have changed is rarely obvious. As a result, debates can rage as to whether the organization is failing because its new practices are fundamentally unsound or because frontline units are implementing them incorrectly. Rational, well-intentioned leaders can reach different conclusions even after looking at the same results. Similarly, even when frontline and experimental units generate new practices and procedures, combat conditions can make it hard to distinguish those that work from those that do not. Good ideas can fail because they are inadequately resourced or poorly executed by commanders who do not fully understand them. Alternatively, bad ideas can succeed because of luck or because they are tried out on particularly inept adversary units. War is also rare, which means that the opportunity to put doctrinal concepts to the test are few and far between for most militaries.

Danger also permeates wartime learning.[38] Combat means that learning must occur under the harshest, most frightening conditions imaginable. Time lines are compressed.[39] Death and destruction—not bankruptcy or missed profit targets—are the penalty for getting it wrong. The stakes are therefore exponentially higher for wartime militaries than they are for any other kind of organization. These risks impact how the entire force performs, even if death and injury are ostensibly something experienced by individuals, not the organization writ large. As Stephen Rosen aptly reminds us, "the morale and composition of the leadership" are affected by the knowledge that the servicemen and women under their command are being wounded or killed.[40] For this reason, those who say the military can learn how to learn from innovative private-sector companies such as Google and Tesla would do well to remember that no one asks these organizations to develop new cars or apps while their best and brightest are being slaughtered.

NAVIGATING THE CENTRALIZATION/ DECENTRALIZATION PARADOX

Each step in the learning process places a unique—and sometimes *contradictory*—set of demands on wartime military organizations. Exploration requires open-mindedness, creativity, and receptivity to new ideas. Selection demands rigorous analytic capabilities. And action necessitates firm leadership, consolidated recourses, and the will to overcome resistance from within. Essentially, the characteristics that foster learning in one phase can hinder it in another. These tensions and trade-offs are especially pronounced when it comes to how much authority the organization centralizes or decentralizes control over a given activity to subordinates.[41]

Harvey Sapolsky was among the first scholars to explicitly identify this trade-off.[42] In his 1967 study of innovation among large department stores, he noticed that these chains were organized such that individual stores and managers exercised tremendous latitude over purchasing and sales. Such a structure allowed them to excel at creative thinking and problem solving but also made it hard to implement new practices across the entire chain, because the decentralization that fostered creativity also made it easy for individual stores to resist unwanted change.

Sapolsky suggests that all organizations face a similar dilemma.[43] Decentralization helps navigate the early stages of the innovation process while complicating the later stages. In contrast, centralization facilitates implementation but impedes the willingness to experiment. Sapolsky concludes that change is therefore rare because most organizations cannot simultaneously be centralized and decentralized.

Yet Sapolsky's important finding overlooks a key fact. Large organizations are composed of multiple subordinate units, and there is no reason, prima facie, that they must structure each unit in exactly the same way. A department store chain, for example, could empower individual outlets to make their own marketing decisions while retaining tight control over pricing, logistics, and human resourcing decisions.

Wartime militaries are particularly massive and complex. Most are made up of dozens of specialized units and departments. Each one can handle a different range of tasks, including acquisitions, administration, communications, education, finance, intelligence, legal, logistics, lobbying, maintenance, operations, recruiting, and training.[44] Different militaries can manage similar activities in different ways. For instance, one army might centralize logistics planning, while another delegates it to subordinate units. Moreover, militaries need not manage all of their activities in exactly the same way. They can centralize control over some activities at the same time that they delegate authority over others. For example, a navy might maintain top-level oversight and control over acquisitions while empowering individual ship commanders to make operational decisions. And militaries can change the degree to which they centralize or decentralize a given task over time. An air force that centralizes control over targeting at the start of a war might then delegate such tasks as the conflict drags on.

The upshot is that it is misleading to think of wartime militaries as either centralized or decentralized. Such labels gloss over crucial variations in how different militaries actually go about doing their job on the battlefield.[45] Military organizations can be centralized and decentralized *at the same time* by retaining high-level control over some activities while delegating authority over others. This insight helps us understand why some wartime militaries can adeptly navigate the learning process even as each step in that process places contradictory demands on it.

Although modern militaries manage a diverse portfolio of activities, three such tasks are particularly relevant to both battlefield effectiveness and doctrinal learning:[46]

- Command practices, or the norms, traditions, and values that influence how commanders lead subordinates on the battlefield;
- Assessment mechanisms, or the units and practices that shape how the organization assesses information about performance and effectiveness; and
- Training systems, or how the organization trains (and retrains) personnel on new practices and weapons in the classroom.

ACT theory's central prediction is based on how these three activities interact, namely that wartime militaries with moderately decentralized command practices, independent assessment mechanisms, and centralized training systems will learn faster than militaries that are organized any other way.

COMMAND PRACTICES

I define a military's command practices as the norms, values, and traditions that shape how much latitude superiors give their subordinates in combat. It might seem odd to focus on norms, values, and traditions, given that all three are inherently informal and amorphous. But a military's formal authority structures, such as those depicted on standard "table of organization" charts, rarely tell us much about how it actually practices command and control. Militaries are organized hierarchically. Superiors always have the statutory authority to tell subordinates what to do. Subordinates always have a legal obligation to obey. Thus, at least in structural and legal terms, it would seem that most militaries practice command and control in exactly the same way. Yet history tells us this is not the case, because militaries have varied tremendously in terms of how they actually practiced command and control in battle. Some militaries empowered captains to make decisions that others only trusted colonels to handle. The norms, values, and traditions that a military holds toward command and control paints a much more detailed picture than where its commanders sit on an organizational chart.[47]

Command practices can range from highly centralized to highly decentralized. Highly centralized command practices mean that senior leaders do not trust their subordinates to make their own decisions in combat. Instead, senior leaders expect their orders to be strictly executed, even when circumstances change. In such organizations, ideas only flow from the top down. Leaders neither solicit nor pay attention to input from below. The Iraqi Army on the eve of the Persian Gulf War (1991) stands out as an example of a military organization with highly centralized command practices.

Highly decentralized command practices exist at the other end of the spectrum. In these kinds of organizations, subordinate commanders enjoy nearly unlimited autonomy. No matter how junior they may be, they are free to make their own decisions on the battlefield. Information flows freely across the organization as well as up and down the chain of command. The real question is whether anyone is paying attention. Although this type of command practice exists mostly in theory, some extremely "flat" terrorist organizations, insurgent movements, and "Fourth Generation" criminal networks might approximate this "ideal" type.[48]

Most militaries fall somewhere in between these extremes. The midpoint is especially important. Although I discuss definitional and measurement issues later in this chapter, for now suffice it to say that moderately decentralized command practices empower relatively junior officers—those commanding platoons and companies—to make independent decisions on the battlefield. The US Army and Marine Corps today embrace moderately decentralized command practices.

Command practices matter because they influence the speed and efficiency with which wartime militaries navigate the exploration phase of the learning process. They do so in two ways. First, they impact the probability that the organization will detect the need for change. Existing scholarship tells us that frontline leaders are often the first to recognize performance gaps.[49] Command practices also determine whether their superiors are actually listening to them. Senior leaders are most likely to listen to their frontline subordinates in militaries with moderately decentralized command practices. Superiors in such organizations tend to be more receptive to subordinates partially out of necessity, because subordinates already have the ability to deviate from commands, and partially because they were themselves afforded trust and autonomy when they were junior officers. This suggests that leaders become more receptive the longer their organization practices moderately decentralized command and control, because over time subordinates become senior leaders.

Senior leaders have a harder time recognizing the need for change in militaries that practice either highly centralized or highly decentralized command and control. In militaries with centralized command practices, superiors place less weight on what their subordinates tell them, because they see little benefit—and much risk—in trusting their subordinates' input and judgment. This is especially true if highly centralized command practices have been in place for a long time. Militaries with highly decentralized command practices face the opposite problem, but the net effect is the same. Commanders at every level have little reason to listen to one another, since their prerogative is guaranteed.

Senior leaders in highly decentralized and centralized organizations face another problem: information overload. Leaders in militaries that practice moderately decentralized command and control do not need to micromanage their subordinates, freeing them to focus on more important issues such as whether there are problems with their organization's existing war-fighting doctrine. In contrast, senior leaders in militaries that rely on highly centralized command practices have less bandwidth to pay attention to truly important issues. Delegating little forces them to assume responsibility for much. Enforcement also becomes an issue, because frontline units must be monitored to ensure conformity. Both factors place significant demands on senior leaders, distracting them from the bigger picture. Senior leaders in organizations that practice highly decentralized command and control face a similar problem. For these leaders, coordination problems dominate their time and attention, because frontline units may not cooperate with one another on the battlefield. Controlling fiercely independent units likewise distracts them from focusing on important issues.

Command practices also shape the range of viable alternatives that a military is likely to generate once it realizes its existing doctrine is not working as well as it should. Frontline units are a natural source of experimentation. Command practices determine both the degree to which frontline units are willing and able to experiment and whether senior leaders will pay attention to the information these experiments generate. As decentralization increases, so too does the degree to which frontline units are allowed to deviate from orders and doctrine. The more units fight in different ways, the more experimental information they generate.

It might seem that more decentralization is always better. That is not the case, however, because information comes with two trade-offs.[50] First, battlefield experiments are like any other mutation in nature. Most will fail, which means there is a theoretical inflection point past which frontline experiments will cost more in lives and material than it will be worth in terms generating useful information. Second, more information is not always better. War is already complex and confusing. Fog and friction make even the simplest task hard. When too many frontline units start generating too much information, overload ensues.

The foregoing discussion leads to my first hypothesis, which, because it relates to the exploration phase of the learning process, I call the *exploration hypothesis*. It predicts that militaries with moderately decentralized command practices will generate more war-fighting alternatives related to the superior way of fighting before than those with either highly centralized or highly decentralized command practices. Highly centralized command practices stifle experimentation, whereas highly decentralized practices generate too much information to be of practical value and a too high a cost in terms of battlefield losses. If the exploration hypothesis is correct, it follows that militaries with moderately decentralized command practices should enter the exploration phase of the learning process before those with either highly centralized or highly decentralized command practices.

ASSESSMENT MECHANISMS

I define an assessment mechanism as any unit, agency, or cell that filters information and helps top-level commanders evaluate and update existing doctrine. To qualify as such, it must meet three criteria. First, it must be *independent* insofar as officers assigned to these units are protected from political and command influence and are free to engage in objective analysis. This requirement means it should also be separate and distinct from both day-to-day intelligence activities and managing the conduct of operations. Intelligence units turn raw information about enemy capabilities and intentions into usable data so commanders can decide how to fight tactically. Assessment units turn raw information about how both friendly and enemy units fight so commanders can decide how to change training and doctrine. Similarly, managing modern combat operations is sufficiently demanding and important in its own right that any entity attempting to balance both tasks will invariably prioritize the former over the later. Effective assessment of course requires feedback from both the intelligence and combat units, but it should nonetheless remain distinct from those efforts. Second, the assessment mechanism must be *prestigious*, which means it must attract the best officers in the organization. This requirement usually means officers must believe that being assigned to such a unit puts them on a fast track to promotion. Third, the officers who perform doctrinal assessment must undergo *rigorous, formal* training and education so as to prepare them for the difficult intellectual challenges associated with analyzing data and writing doctrine.[51]

When they exist, these assessment units help the organization navigate two crucial tasks associated with the selection step in the learning process. The first involves combing through mountains of experimental data to discern which of the seemingly plausible concepts are actually fundamentally sound, which were unsound but succeeded due to chance and luck, and which show promise despite initially failing in combat. Even with a significantly narrowed list of plausible alternatives, resource constraints usually mean that senior leaders must still pick one—or a small handful—for implementation. The existing scholarship on military change typically portrays this as a clear-cut decision: leaders opt to either maintain the status quo or implement a doctrinal change that we now know to have been the right one. History suggests that the decision is rarely so simple. Leaders usually face a range of reasonable—and sometimes mutually exclusive—alternatives. Their experts disagree. Meanwhile, internal interest groups (e.g., officer associations and combat arms communities) and external ones (e.g., defense manufacturers) lobby. And given the obvious demands on their time and attention, senior commanders are often so preoccupied by day-to-day issues that they may not have sufficient bandwidth to think as rigorously about the problem as they would like.

Assessment mechanisms therefore help senior commanders make these decisions faster than they otherwise could on their own. They do this by creating a system for collecting the information generated by frontline observation and experimentation. They scrutinize raw and unprocessed information and distinguish good ideas from flawed ones. And they present top-level commanders with a finite range of options to choose from—options that have already been vetted and refined to some degree.

Of course, selecting an idea does not automatically lead to implementation. New tactics, techniques, and procedures (TTPs) need to be tested to ensure scalability. The fact that a new tactic, technique, or procedure worked for an elite or handpicked experimental unit does not imply that it will also be effective when performed by large numbers of frontline units. Likewise, a new weapons system, no matter how effective, is of little use if the organization cannot buy or build enough of the weapons in time to make a difference. And, of course, the organization must develop new training manuals and standards to facilitate rapid transmission. This entire process is iterative, requiring constant feedback between testers, trainers, and decision makers.

Assessment mechanisms facilitate these efforts by identifying requirements, establishing performance standards, and evaluating progress toward those standards. They also serve as a transmission mechanism between those testing new concepts, those who will acquire the resources needed to facilitate implementation, and those who will train the rest of the organization.

This discussion leads to my next two hypotheses. Because both relate to the selection phase of the learning process, I refer to them as selection hypothesis 1 and 2. Selection hypothesis 1 predicts that top-level leaders in military organizations with assessment mechanisms are more likely to make decisions about doctrinal change that actually improve combat performance. If this hypothesis is correct, it should follow that militaries with assessment mechanisms will be more likely to pick the doctrinal concepts and practices that represent a superior way of fighting. Selection hypothesis 2 predicts that militaries with assessment mechanisms will refine new doctrinal concepts, ideas, and practices before those that do not have them. The observable implication is that militaries with assessment mechanisms will transition from exploration to selection—and move through the selection process—faster than militaries that do not.

TRAINING SYSTEMS

Action is the final step in the learning process. For wartime militaries, the biggest challenge related to acting on a new doctrinal concept revolves around training (and retraining) frontline units, many of which will still be engaged in active combat operations. I define training systems as the departments, agencies, or units that control how personnel learn the TTPs and weapons they will use in combat. Unlike command practices, which we must infer from norms, values, and traditions, we can directly observe training systems. In theory, these systems can vary along a spectrum ranging from highly centralized to highly decentralized. In highly centralized training systems, a single high-ranking general officer exercises control over all individual and unit training and has the authority to inspect schools, mandate curriculum changes, alter training budgets, and fire instructors. Moreover, all training and educational activity takes place on a single base, campus, or facility. The modern US Marine Corps comes close to this theoretical extreme insofar as a single general officer commands a training branch, entry-level training for enlisted personnel is consolidated at two boot camps, and all officer training and education takes place in Quantico, Virginia.

Highly decentralized training systems are at the other end of the spectrum. They are defined by the absence of a single high-ranking officer with the aforementioned authorities. Instead, individual unit commanders control training. Meanwhile, training and education take place across the organization's full geographic span. The regimental systems common in nineteenth- and early twentieth-century continental Europe exemplify a decentralized approach to training. European commanders had a great deal of discretion over recruiting, indoctrination, and combat training.

A military's training system determines the speed with which it can effectively transmit new practices across the entire organization. This is because militaries face two obstacles when they try to implement a major doctrinal change. The first involves resistance and pushback. Some officers within the organization will resist change because they disagree with it as a matter of principle. Others will resist because change threatens their parochial interests. Regardless of their motivation, those who oppose change have a range of options for resisting. The organization's top leaders will have their hands full running a wartime organization and may not have the bandwidth to monitor compliance within the training system. Those who oppose change can exploit this inattention by not teaching new doctrinal concepts or by teaching them half-heartedly so as to guarantee failure. Since wartime militaries are constantly training large numbers of new members, the longer new soldiers learn old methods—or new methods taught the wrong way—at the hands of those who oppose change, the longer doctrinal change will take. Insidiously, combat performance will continue to suffer. Yet leaders might mistakenly think that new methods are failing because they are unsound, when in reality they are failing because those inside the organization who oppose change are setting them up to fail. Organizational change might become easier as a war drags on, since older members will exit over time through casualties and transfers. However, this natural tendency is undercut the more older members who resist change remain in charge of training their replacements.

Centralized training is the most effective remedy. Top-level leaders are better equipped to identify and punish internal resistance when they wield tight control over training. Of course, wartime demands mean top-level leaders cannot personally oversee training. The next best option is to have a dedicated agency or command—led by a high-ranking officer who agrees with the changes and answers directly to the top-level leadership—with the power, resources, and authority to either conduct all training or monitor it and replace those leaders who do a poor job of it.

Ineffective transmission is another obstacle to decisively acting on a new doctrine. It may not be as nefarious as resistance, but it is no less tractable. Transmission problems exist because as large and complex organizations engage in active combat, wartime militaries will always struggle to accurately communicate new concepts and practices without losing something in the process. This problem is akin to the children's game of telephone, where a message delivered to the first child sitting in a line becomes increasingly garbled as it is passed down the line. Ideally, a military can try to put every last service member in a single classroom so as to teach them at the same time. Realistically, such an approach is hardly possible in peace, let alone in war. Usually, when a military needs to transmit a new set of precepts or lessons, it instead trains the trainer. This approach involves a small group of personnel learning new methods directly from the experts who designed them. These students then become instructors and teach a larger group of soldiers who, in turn, also become instructors. Although this snowball approach to training is highly efficient, it can leave much to be desired in terms of quality and uniformity.

Centralization helps reduce the transmission problem. Even when wartime conditions force a military to use such a training process, an empowered, resourced, and dedicated training command can monitor quality. It can likewise use inspections, audits, and the occasional firing to ensure uniformity. Thus, training almost always improves with centralization, which leads to a fourth hypothesis that, because it relates to the action phase of the learning process, I refer to as the action hypothesis. It predicts that the more a military centralizes control over individual and unit training, the faster it can transmit new doctrinal concepts. The observable implication is that militaries with highly centralized training systems will move through the action phase of the learning process—and will therefore demonstrate widespread mastery—before than those militaries that do not.

To recap ACT theory's hypotheses and observable implications:

Main hypothesis. Militaries that combine moderately decentralized command practices, highly centralized training structures, and a doctrinal assessment mechanism will optimize their prewar doctrines to match wartime realities more effectively and efficiently than those that combine these three characteristics in any other way.

Exploration hypothesis. Militaries with moderately decentralized command practices will generate more war-fighting alternatives related to the superior way of fighting before than those with either highly centralized or highly decentralized command practices.

Selection hypothesis 1. Top-level leaders in military organizations with assessment mechanisms are more likely to pick the doctrinal ideas that improve combat performance.

Selection hypothesis 2. Military organizations with assessment mechanisms will refine new doctrinal concepts, ideas, and practices before those that do not have them.

Action hypothesis. The more a military centralizes control over individual and unit training, the faster it can transmit new doctrinal concepts.

THE RELATIONSHIP BETWEEN COMMAND PRACTICES AND TRAINING STRUCTURES

It is fair to question whether two of my three explanatory variables are endogenous or causally related to one another. Intuitively, it makes sense to think that militaries with highly centralized training systems will also centralize control over battlefield decision making. After all, why maintain tight control in the classroom only to relinquish it on the battlefield? ACT theory is flawed if these command practices and training systems tend to move in lockstep, not least because it means we will never see a military that has combined moderately decentralized command practices with highly centralized training systems.

Thankfully, there are multiple reasons to think that these two variables vary independently, in theory and in practice. Theoretically, a military can impose and enforce a uniform set of training standards and policies even as those same standards and policies are used to teach junior leaders to exercise initiative on the battlefield. The reverse can also hold true. A military might teach young officers to obey every order without hesitation, but it can do so in a very decentralized way. For example, unit commanders might have complete responsibility for—and authority over—training their own personnel. Empirically, we see examples of both combinations throughout history. As Chapters 3 and 4 describe, the German and British armies both had a long history of granting autonomy to subordinate commanders on the battlefield prior to the First World War. Over the course of that conflict, the German Army gave junior leaders even more authority even as it increasingly centralized control over training. In contrast, the British Army temporarily *centralized* control over battlefield decision making while leaving its training systems relatively unregulated. As the war progressed, however, it moved in the opposite direction, yielding autonomy to frontline commanders and exercising more control over training.

SCOPE CONDITIONS

No theory can or should explain everything. ACT theory has three important limitations. The first and most obvious is that it only explains wartime learning. Organizations learn and change in different ways and under different conditions, a fact reflected in economics, business, management, and psychological theories of organizational change. ACT theory is specifically designed to explain how militaries learn under high-intensity wartime conditions, when stakes are higher, time lines are shorter, and uncertainty is greater than in almost any other situation imaginable.[52] There is no reason to expect it to capture why some organizations are better than others learning in peacetime or hybrid conflict scenarios.

Second, ACT theory only explains how ground combat forces learn. ACT theory focuses heavily on organizational structure, and there are important structural differences between ground forces and their air and naval counterparts. Size—as defined by the number of actors capable of independent action—is one such difference. Ships are expensive, so modern navies have only a few hundred combat units capable of independent action. Advanced aircraft are only slightly cheaper, so units capable of independent aerial combat usually number in the thousands at most. Ground forces are larger and more organizationally complex. As the US Marine Corps' strategic corporal concept implies, even a single soldier or marine can act independently and in ways that have strategic effects. Modern ground forces can have hundreds of thousands of such potentially independent actors. It is reasonable to think that size and complexity influence innovation, adaptation, and emulation in important and unique ways. This means that theories designed to explain ground innovation may not carry over well to air and naval innovation and vice versa.

Third, ACT theory is limited to *modern* ground forces. For the purposes of this study, I define the modern period as starting after 1870. There are several reasons for this cutoff. ACT theory relies on structural complexity and diversity to explain how some military organizations overcome the so-called learning paradox. However, it was not until the rise of the mass industrialized army in the late nineteenth century that ground forces became complex enough to operate in the way ACT theory predicts. Before 1870, a single general could effectively lead and maneuver an entire army in the field. After 1870, modern technology rendered this style of command impossible. Thus, there was no reason to expect much variation in command practices. Even if they did vary, it was unlikely to be of much causal significance. Similarly, the relative absence of organizational complexity prior to the 1870s reduced the need for—and the benefits of—centralized training. Indeed, few armies attempted such an approach to training before this period.

Methodological Issues

I now turn to a range of mundane but necessary methodological tasks. These include describing how I operationalize ACT theory's key variables, handle case selection, and address confounding factors and alternative explanations.

DEFINING AND MEASURING THE OUTCOME OF INTEREST:
DOCTRINAL LEARNING

Wartime learning implies that a military has updated its prewar doctrines to match wartime realities and improve battlefield performance. I use four criteria to determine whether learning has occurred. First, a military's highest-ranking leaders endorse and distribute a *formal* written document that mandates a specific set of conceptual, procedural, or tactical changes. Second, the organization acquires and provides the *relevant* frontline units with the training, resources, and equipment they need to employ the updated doctrine. Third, these relevant frontline units prove that they can correctly employ the doctrine on the battlefield.[53] I use a fourth criterion to distinguish between learning and change, since learning sets a higher bar than change. Learning means that a military identified, implemented, and mastered the right lessons and has adopted a war-fighting doctrine that is superior (given its goals, resources, adversary/ies, etc.) to the one it is replacing. Change, on the other hand, simply means doing things differently, for better or for worse.

I look for evidence of *doctrinal convergence* to distinguish learning from other forms of change. In other words, I take it as powerful evidence that a military has adopted a war-fighting doctrine that is superior to the one it replaces when *other* wartime militaries with similar goals, resources, and adversaries fight under similar conditions and/or with similar weapons as the military I am evaluating and adopt the same doctrine. This claim means that it may be difficult to know what the superior war-fighting doctrine ought to have been until well after the fact. Therefore, for evidence that learning did or did not occur, I compare the historical record about how an army actually fought against the consensus among military historians about how it should have fought.

Since I want to understand why some armies learn faster than others, I also need to operationalize each step in the learning process so I can track and compare them against one another. I use the following scheme: I code an army as navigating the exploration phase when individual frontline units engage in ad hoc experimentation *and* senior leaders endorse a sustained effort to capture, refine, and validate the results of those experiments *or* designated specific experimental units to do the same. In either case, at least one of these ideas must be a part of what we later know to have been the superior way to fight. I code an army as being in the selection phase when it picks what we later know to have been the right experimental concepts and then engages in a sustained effort to distill and refine TTPs; research, design, and procure the equipment; and develop the formal doctrine needed to employ this new concept on a widespread basis on the battlefield. I code an army as moving into the action phase when it wages a major demonstration battle in accordance with the principles behind the superior doctrine and/or promulgates official written doctrinal guidance organization-wide, injects this updated doctrine into the training pipeline so as to train new personnel, and undertakes a deliberate effort to reorganize relevant combat units, retrain existing personnel, and equip both to fight in accordance with the updated doctrine. Finally, I treat an army as having learned when it adopts what we now know to have been a superior way of fighting and transmits this updated doctrine across the relevant parts of the organization by disseminating formal guidance, reorganizing force structure, fielding sufficient numbers of required weapons, and retraining personnel such that the majority of frontline combat units can fight in accordance with this new doctrine.[54] I use the term "mastery" to indicate the point in time in which we can say a military has effectively navigated the entire learning process. I primarily base my coding decisions on consensus among expert historians, although I also refer to primary source documents, including after-action reports, firsthand accounts, and doctrinal publications.

I readily admit that establishing the exact moment in time at which an army transitions from one phase of the learning process to another is an imprecise art at best. To be appropriately modest about my coding scheme, I use these aforementioned sources to identify a basic time frame in which each transition occurred. Specifically, I divide each year of the war into four seasons and code shifts that occur from January through March as wintertime transitions, from April through June as springtime, from July through September as summertime, and from October through December as falltime. Throughout each case study, I clearly specify the events and developments (such as the publication of a new doctrinal manual or a major demonstration battle) behind each coding decision.

DEFINING AND MEASURING THE EXPLANATORY VARIABLES

Command Practices I distinguish between centralized and decentralized command practices by the level at which leaders delegate authority to subordinates to make *tactical* decisions. In particular, I look for the level at which commanders are typically willing to issue *mission-type orders*. Mission-type orders are a type of directive that specifies what a subordinate must do without telling him or her how to do it, thereby allowing the subordinate to exercise initiative, judgment, and discretion.[55] To measure a given military's command practices, I look for the lowest level at which the organization typically issues mission-type orders during wartime. Theoretically, this approach could lead to dozens of different categories. To keep the effort manageable, I put command practices into one of four discrete groups: centralized, moderately centralized, moderately decentralized, and decentralized. In centralized systems, the senior-most operational commander either trusts no one to exercise personal judgment or issues mission-type orders only to the commanders at the division level and above. In moderately centralized systems, only career officers with decades of experience (which I define as battalion commanders and above) are trusted to carry out mission-type orders. In moderately decentralized systems, all officers—and even career noncommissioned officers—are empowered to carry out mission-type orders. Finally, in decentralized systems, personnel of every rank and experience level are allowed to execute mission-type orders.

As a practical matter, armies rarely put on paper the degree to which they plan on letting subordinates exercise autonomy and initiative. Even when they do, there is often a gulf between policy and practice. As Chapter 4 illustrates, at one point during the First World War, official British doctrine called on junior officers to demonstrate initiative, "but woe to the man who displays it."[56] I therefore must infer an organization's command practices based on the norms, traditions, and expectations actually described in primary and secondary resource documents.

Assessment Mechanisms Most modern military organizations have units that collect after-action reports and disseminate lessons learned. Yet I do not take the presence of such units alone as an indication that the organization has an assessment mechanism as defined by ACT theory. To qualify as such, these organizations must do more than serve as a conduit for disseminating paperwork. True assessment mechanisms filter, evaluate, and refine information as it moves up the chain of command, such that only a small number of ideas make it into top-level commanders' hands. They also translate raw ideas into formal doctrine, which then serves as the basis for developing new training standards and curriculum.

To code a military as having an assessment mechanism, I must find evidence of a dedicated analytic unit that does three things. First, it must possess the independence to make recommendations that go against traditional thinking and parochial interests. It must also be formal and permanent insofar as it establishes stable, predictable, well-understood, and accessible conduits between frontline units and the highest levels of command. Second, this dedicated analytic unit must have sufficient institutional prestige to attract the most intelligent officers in the organization and the educational programs and policies to teach them how to conduct rigorous analysis. Third, the military's personnel must undergo rigorous training to prepare them to produce high-quality analysis. I code assessment mechanisms dichotomously. In cases where all three conditions are present, I code a military as having an independent assessment mechanism. If one or more conditions are not met, I code the organization as not having an assessment mechanism. I draw information from primary and secondary sources.

Training Systems Although training systems can theoretically vary along a spectrum from highly centralized to highly decentralized, in practice I will look at a single factor to categorize a military's training system: the degree

to which a single high-ranking command or officer controls training and education. In contrast to command practices, which I infer from norms, traditions, and expectations, I use objective measures to categorize training
systems. This approach leads to a dichotomous coding scheme. A centralized training system is one in which a single, high-ranking command (or
general officer) has the authority to inspect training schools, dictate curricula, alter funding, and fire instructors. Decentralized training systems are
defined by the fact that no single officer has the power to control curricula,
instructors, or budgets, and training activities take place across the organization's full geographic span. The same caveats and trade-offs that exist
with command practices also pertain to training systems. There are lesser
and greater degrees of centralization even among armies with centralized
training structures. ACT theory predicts that centralization's positive effects
will increase as centralization increases. I rely on evidence from the historical
record, training reports, and secondary historical literature to categorize
each organization's training structure.

CASE SELECTION, CONFOUNDING FACTORS, AND ALTERNATIVE EXPLANATIONS

There are challenges when selecting historical cases with which to test ACT
theory. Wartime outcomes are complex and often overdetermined. Overdetermination is particularly problematic when analyzing tactical outcomes,
because it becomes hard to isolate the most important causal factors.[57]

I do two things to avoid oversimplifying complex outcomes. First, I acknowledge from the outset that ACT theory's variables are not always learning's most important determinants. Strategic imperatives, resource constraints,
and a wide range of other factors can stymie change. I think it is sufficient
to prove that ACT theory captures something *predictable and consistent* about
why some militaries are better at wartime learning than others, even in
cases where command practices, assessment mechanisms, and training systems are not the dominant factors.

Second, I test ACT theory against a historical case that allows me to capture as much variation as possible while accounting for as many confounding factors as possible. As I argued in the previous chapter, the First World
War's Western Front lets me rigorously assess ACT theory's internal validity. The three primary combatants engaged in that theater—Britain, France,
and Germany—had armies that were remarkably similar. The Western Front
therefore serves as a natural experiment, which contains three army cases
that share a single operational context.[58] I am therefore using John Stuart
Mill's method of difference to test ACT theory.[59] I select army cases that
shared many of the same background characteristics but varied in terms of
the variables of interest. The British, French, and German armies learned at
different speeds. They also evolved over time in terms of their respective

command practices, assessment mechanisms, and training systems. Chapters 3, 4 and 5 demonstrate that armies learned more effectively as they shifted toward moderately decentralized command practices, developed coherent and independent assessment mechanisms, and exerted centralized control over training. The Germans were the first to reach this ideal setup and were also the first to adopt (most of) the elements of a superior combined-arms doctrine. The British Army was close behind, although because it struggled to centralize training until the summer of 1918, its units never demonstrated as much uniformity in how they fought.[60] The French Army was the slowest of the three to learn. That all three armies also varied in the key independent variables from 1895 to 1918 allows for in-depth process tracing.[61] In sum, looking at the British, French, and German armies as they struggled to break the deadlock allows me to leverage both cross-case and within-case variation to test ACT theory's casual mechanisms.

Controls The shared context of the Western Front also allows me to control for many of the important alternative explanations for organizational change, including:

Objectives States and their military organizations might choose to adopt suboptimal war-fighting doctrines. Even in wartime, states can have multiple political and military objectives, and these goals can be in tension with one another. For example, in the midst of fighting large-scale counterinsurgencies in Iraq and Afghanistan, the United States still sought to deter major peer competitors.[62]

In a world of limited resources, states must prioritize certain objectives over others. Senior political and military leaders sometimes subvert learning if it comes at a price in terms of their ability to pursue goals that are more important to them. For example, Adolf Hitler's willingness to divert resources from his military forces to pursue his racial policies stands out as a stark example of this logic at play. There are also cases in which political leaders do not care about combat effectiveness. History is littered with military organizations designed to do something other than fight. Autocratic leaders might not care about the lives of their citizens and soldiers, or they might care more about other objectives, such as ensuring regime stability, enhancing social equality, maintaining social inequality, supporting domestic weapons production, rallying domestic support, undermining political adversaries, signaling resolve, or reassuring allies.[63]

Even if suboptimality has a strategic logic, we should expect such situations to be the exception, not the rule. Losing wars is costly, even for the most powerful despots. Deliberately forcing a military to fight inefficiently is a risk-laden gamble. In any case, the First World War helps us deal with this factor. Despite their reputation for callous disregard, the reality is that military and political leaders on all sides were obsessed with maximizing efficiency—or, to use their terminology, minimizing wastage. Indeed, prevailing on the Western Front was a top priority for all three militaries and their political leaders throughout the war. Although both the Entente and the Central Powers sometimes prioritized other theaters, they were never willing to risk defeat along the Western Front.

All three armies also shared similar political, strategic, and tactical goals. Politically, Britain and France wanted to end the stalemate to push Germany out of France and Belgium. As the war escalated, both wanted to neuter Germany's future ability to wage war. Germany's political objectives were a bit more puzzling. From 1914 onward, it is hard to see how their tactics and operations fed into a coherent strategic-political framework. Indeed, it is curious to imagine what exactly the Germans planned to do had they reached Paris in 1914 or in 1918 for that matter.[64] Strategically, generals on both sides wanted to penetrate the other side's defensive network so as to restore maneuver on the battlefield. Tactically, all three armies recognized that political and strategic success depended on finding a solution to stalemate at the tactical level.[65]

Organizational Size and Resources Scholars have long hypothesized that an organization's size and resources might impact its ability to change.[66] Unfortunately, it is not clear *how* size and resources impact learning. Large diverse organizations have an advantage over their smaller competitors in that they often have extra personnel to work on research and development. At the same time, larger organizations can be unwieldy or can have more so-called veto players capable of blocking change. Small organizations tend to be more agile, but they may not be big enough to adequately manage operations and research and development at the same time. The same debates can be had over slack resources. Leaders can use excess resources to invest in innovation and learning, and they are better positioned to absorb the inevitable failures. Yet excessive resources can also lead to malaise and complacency. After all, efficiency and effectiveness are less of a worry when leaders can simply throw resources at the problem. Thus, it is equally plausible that hunger—not bloat—fosters learning.

Thankfully, the First World War lets me sidestep these debates. Uniformity along many of the parameters usually associated with organizational change allows us to dismiss these factors as learning's causes. The British, French, and German armies were all enormous once the war was under way. The French Army had almost five million soldiers at any given point in time. The German Army had nearly six million. Although Britain only had ninety thousand men in Europe at the start of the war, by 1918 it too had millions of men under arms. These armies were also organized in remarkably similar ways. They likewise enjoyed many of the same resources and endured many of the same scarcities. All three suffered from matériel shortages early in the war. All three faced manpower deficiencies as the war dragged on.

Nevertheless, the First World War was a total war insofar as Britain, France, and Germany mobilized the entirety of their citizenry, colonies, and economies to support the war effort. Even if the Western Front was not always the focus of effort, it remained a top priority for all three sides from the war's beginning until its end.

Nature of the Problem   Some learning problems are harder to solve than others. However, all three armies faced the exact same problem in the exact same place: stalemate on the Western Front. As a result, they also fought under the same conditions, which helps control for factors such as weather, terrain, and even uncertainty.[67]

Duration   Learning becomes more likely over time, all things equal. The longer a military fights, the more information it generates and the more time leaders have to select, refine, and implement changes.[68] It is misleading to compare an organization that fails to learn during a thirty-day lightning war to one that successfully learns over the course of a ten-year war of attrition. The First World War easily controls for time and duration, since the war on the Western Front lasted almost exactly the same amount of time for all three armies.

OTHER CONFOUNDING FACTORS AND ALTERNATIVE EXPLANATIONS

Using the First World War as a test of ACT theory helps control for a range of factors. However, this approach has limits. It does not allow me to control for other confounding factors and influences that might plausibly impact wartime learning, including shifts in the intrawar balance of power, culture, or regime type. I therefore rely on process tracing to deal with these potential alternative explanations.

Culture   Cultural differences can make some states and military organizations more innovative, adaptive, and flexible than others. At first glance, distinguishing a military's command practices from its overarching culture might seem difficult. Conceptually, command practices refer only to the organizational norms, traditions, and expectations that govern how much decision-making autonomy superiors grant to their subordinates. All other norms, practices, traditions, and expectations belong under the broader umbrella of organizational, strategic, and national culture.

The best way to distinguish between command practices and culture in practice is to look for two types of evidence: (1) Did a military's command practices change to become moderately decentralized over the course of the war, and (2) which occurred first, the change in command practices or doctrinal learning? When a military moderately decentralizes its command practices *and then* adopts a superior war-fighting doctrine, we have evidence that command practices—not culture—facilitated learning. Culture is, after all, sticky: it should change slowly if at all over the course of a single conflict. Conversely, if learning occurs in the absence of a shift toward moderately decentralized command practices or if learning does not occur despite the presence of moderately decentralized command practices, there is strong evidence that culture—not command practices—is driving events.

Shifts in the Balance of Power A changing balance of power can make war more likely.[69] Such shifts can also shape how and why militaries change.[70] Rising states often seek new military capabilities to realize their ambitions. Status quo powers might also seek to update their military doctrines to meet these new challengers, and this can influence wartime learning. As one side starts to win, the other side might face pressure to change. Situations in which highly salient battlefield defeats or significant changes in one side's access to resources, allies, and other determinants of military power *precede* doctrinal change indicate that the balance of power—not ACT theory's variables—is driving learning. Evidence that key civilian and/or military leaders initiate a search for new options and alternatives because they perceive defeat as likely also casts doubt on ACT's core hypotheses.[71]

Civilian Intervention Political leaders can force change on their militaries. Abraham Lincoln, Georges Clemenceau, Winston Churchill, Harry Truman, Robert McNamara, and Donald Rumsfeld were all political leaders credited with—or criticized for—imposing change from the outside in.[72] Two types of evidence should be present to make a compelling case that civilian intervention, not ACT theory's variables, drove learning. First, we should see evidence that civilian leaders were aware of and took an active interest in changing *doctrine*. Simply showing that civilian leaders perceived a performance gap or were otherwise unhappy with how the war was progressing is not enough. Civilians generally pay more attention to and have more leverage over nondoctrinal sources of poor performance. Second, we should also see clear evidence of the mechanism through which civilian leaders imposed their will. Principal-agent theory tells us that guidance from the top does not automatically translate into action at the bottom. Wartime militaries are large, complex, and isolated from both society and other government agencies. Political leaders cannot take a fire-and-forget approach to doctrinal learning. They must possess a lever or transmission mechanism to ensure that their mandates are acted upon. If political leaders are responsible for wartime learning, we should see clear evidence that they used internal mavericks, fired insubordinate high-ranking officers, threatened to cut budgets, or relied upon some other enforcement mechanism.

Shadow Cases Although detailed analysis and process tracing can help confirm that ACT theory does indeed explain why the German Army learned faster than its British and French adversaries, it does not help establish the degree to which ACT theory explains wartime learning beyond the Western Front of the First World War. Thus, to at least begin to get at my theory's external validity, I introduce two short shadow cases in the final chapter: the US Army in Vietnam (1965–1973) and the US Army in Iraq (2003–2010).

METHODOLOGICAL MODESTY

It is ultimately impossible to develop an exhaustive list of plausible alternative explanations and confounding variables. This section of the chapter simply attempts to capture some of the most important alternative ways of explaining learning. Again, my goal is not to prove that ACT theory captures the only—or even the most important—explanation. The literature on military innovation and change has long suffered from this kind of regressive competition.

I am satisfied if I can show that a military's command practices, assessment mechanisms, and training systems exert a consistent and predictable impact on how wartime militaries learn *even* if other variables prove to be more important in any one case. As a result, we should still observe two things in militaries that have moderately decentralized command practices, assessment mechanisms, and highly centralized training systems *but nevertheless fail to learn*. First, we should see the three explanatory variables behave in the ways that ACT theory predicts. The organization should generate a reasonable number of new ideas, and high-ranking leaders should be receptive to them; its assessment mechanisms should collect, analyze, test, and refine ideas and pass them along to top-level leaders for endorsement; and the training system should transmit endorsed practices across the entire organization. If these variables do not behave as predicted, then this is strong evidence against ACT theory.

Second, we should see another factor intervene in the process to disrupt learning. Examples include political leaders vetoing a doctrinal concept, wars that end abruptly before the process can play out, and situations in which high-ranking officers reject what we now know to have been the superior doctrine. If military organizations that possess moderately decentralized command practices, assessment mechanisms, and highly centralized training systems fail to learn in the absence of a clear intervening factor, then this is also strong evidence that ACT theory is wrong.

Learning on the Western Front

The potential for defensive superiority had not been overlooked by European military thinkers before the First World War. But it is one thing to diagnose that a problem exists, and another to prescribe the proper response.

—M. A. Ramsay, *Command and Cohesion* (2002)

Military historians have convincingly shown that the British, French, and German armies tried to learn. The puzzle is that they did so at different speeds and to varying degrees of success. Again, the British, French, and German armies faced the same problem: stalemate. They started the war with roughly similar doctrines, weapons, and resources. And at various points throughout the war they experimented with roughly the same set of tactical solutions—assault tactics, combined arms, and elastic defense in depth. But the German Army mastered these methods before its opponents. As shown in figures 1a-c, 2a-c, and 3a-c, it was the first army to master the elastic defense in depth, which it used to defeat the French Army at Chemin des Dames in early 1917 and to reverse the British Army's gains at Cambrai later that same year. The German Army also combined arms to a greater degree, at a lower level, and at an earlier point in the war than either the French or the British. And the German Army's assault tactics, although perhaps no more advanced than those ultimately used by the British or French, were employed with greater uniformity and to greater effect in Ludendorff's spring 1918 offensives.

Chapters 3, 4, and 5 argue that assessment, command, and training (ACT) theory captures a systematic reason for the variation between how well and how fast the British, French, and German armies learned. To make sense of this explanation, however, it is important to first establish why the Western Front was deadlocked; what I mean by the terms "assault tactics," "combined arms," and "elastic defense in depth"; and why these methods represented a better way to fight under the conditions of trench warfare.

Figure 1a. Learning assault tactics, German Army.

SUMMER '14	FALL '14	WINTER '15	SPRING '15	SUMMER '15	FALL '15	WINTER '16	SPRING '16	SUMMER '16	FALL '16	WINTER '17	SPRING '17	SUMMER '17	FALL '17	WINTER '18	SPRING '18	SUMMER '18	FALL '18
		Exploration			Selection									Action		Mastery	

Figure 1b. Learning assault tactics, British Army.

SUMMER '14	FALL '14	WINTER '15	SPRING '15	SUMMER '15	FALL '15	WINTER '16	SPRING '16	SUMMER '16	FALL '16	WINTER '17	SPRING '17	SUMMER '17	FALL '17	WINTER '18	SPRING '18	SUMMER '18	FALL '18
	Exploration							Exploration			Selection			Action			

Figure 1c. Learning assault tactics, French Army.

SUMMER '14	FALL '14	WINTER '15	SPRING '15	SUMMER '15	FALL '15	WINTER '16	SPRING '16	SUMMER '16	FALL '16	WINTER '17	SPRING '17	SUMMER '17	FALL '17	WINTER '18	SPRING '18	SUMMER '18	FALL '18
Exploration											Selection			Action			

Figure 2a. Learning combined arms, German Army.

SUMMER '14	FALL '14	WINTER '15	SPRING '15	SUMMER '15	FALL '15	WINTER '16	SPRING '16	SUMMER '16	FALL '16	WINTER '17	SPRING '17	SUMMER '17	FALL '17	WINTER '18	SPRING '18	SUMMER '18	FALL '18
			Exploration				Selection							Action		Mastery	

Figure 2b. Learning combined arms, British Army.

SUMMER '14	FALL '14	WINTER '15	SPRING '15	SUMMER '15	FALL '15	WINTER '16	SPRING '16	SUMMER '16	FALL '16	WINTER '17	SPRING '17	SUMMER '17	FALL '17	WINTER '18	SPRING '18	SUMMER '18	FALL '18
			Exploration								Selection			Action		Mastery	

Figure 2c. Learning combined arms, French Army.

SUMMER '14	FALL '14	WINTER '15	SPRING '15	SUMMER '15	FALL '15	WINTER '16	SPRING '16	SUMMER '16	FALL '16	WINTER '17	SPRING '17	SUMMER '17	FALL '17	WINTER '18	SPRING '18	SUMMER '18	FALL '18
Exploration											Selection			Action			Mastery

Figure 3a. Learning elastic defense in depth, German Army.

SUMMER '14	FALL '14	WINTER '15	SPRING '15	SUMMER '15	FALL '15	WINTER '16	SPRING '16	SUMMER '16	FALL '16	WINTER '17	SPRING '17	SUMMER '17	FALL '17	WINTER '18	SPRING '18	SUMMER '18	FALL '18
			Exploration							Selection/Action			Mastery				

Figure 3b. Learning elastic defense in depth, British Army.

SUMMER '14	FALL '14	WINTER '15	SPRING '15	SUMMER '15	FALL '15	WINTER '16	SPRING '16	SUMMER '16	FALL '16	WINTER '17	SPRING '17	SUMMER '17	FALL '17	WINTER '18	SPRING '18	SUMMER '18	FALL '18
	Exploration													Selection/Action			

Figure 3c. Learning elastic defense in depth, French Army.

SUMMER '14	FALL '14	WINTER '15	SPRING '15	SUMMER '15	FALL '15	WINTER '16	SPRING '16	SUMMER '16	FALL '16	WINTER '17	SPRING '17	SUMMER '17	FALL '17	WINTER '18	SPRING '18	SUMMER '18	FALL '18
	Exploration																

The Origins of Deadlock

When Europe went to war in August 1914, statesmen and families alike hoped that their soldiers would be home by Christmas. Although their optimism seems naive today, it was not entirely unfounded. Standard wisdom at the time held that modern states had grown too fragile and interdependent to survive prolonged conflict. Such assumptions help make sense of why both sides sought a quick victory in 1914. Nor were French and German leaders oblivious to the risks. Germany recognized that sending troops through neutral Belgium might provoke Britain. And France knew it was leaving Paris dangerously exposed when it sent forces headlong into German territory. Both sides accepted these risks because they assumed that the costs of fighting a lengthy war would be much higher.

Ironically, speed helped create the problem it was supposed to avoid. For Germany, operational speed came at a steep political and strategic price. The violation of Belgian neutrality gave Britain the casus belli to send its rapid-reaction force, the British Expeditionary Force, to France. For its part, the French Army's rapid plunge into Germany—followed by an equally quick defeat—enabled it to fall back on Paris in time to block the German right hook.[1] Already hampered by logistical challenges, the German advance collapsed in the face of a combined French and British counterattack outside Paris near the Marne River.[2]

British and French forces tried to exploit the Miracle on the Marne by launching a counteroffensive, but the attack failed to dislodge German units dug in near the Aisne River. With little room for maneuver to the south, all three armies shifted their focus north. A war that began with a race to Paris now turned into a Race to the Sea.[3] The two sides clashed as they moved toward the Belgian coast. After Belgian and French troops—supported by the British Royal Navy—blocked a final flanking movement by the German Army near the Yser River in mid-October, they ran out of room. From that point on, trenches stretched from the Swiss border to the Belgian coast. With no room to maneuver, the only sure way to win in the west was to punch straight through the other side's lines.

As most history books make clear, the proliferation of new rapid-fire weapons before the war—including breech-loading rifles, machine guns, and quick-fire artillery—were one reason maneuver gave way to trench warfare. These weapons made it easier to defend than to attack.[4] Defenders could pour fire into an attacker's ranks while using trenches, shell holes, and pillboxes for protection. Advancing troops, on the other hand, had to weather an unprecedented storm of steel to press the attack.

Firepower therefore helps explain stalemate on the Western Front. But it was not the entire story. If it were, then trenches should have dominated the battlefields of every theater in the First World War. They did not, which means that at least two other key factors—the troop-to-space ratio and the imbalance between strategic and tactical mobility—combined with firepower to create deadlock. It is worth taking a moment to explain.

FIREPOWER

A series of nineteenth-century technological innovations led to the firepower revolution.[5] Rifling made individual weapons lethal at ever-longer ranges. Breech-loading mechanisms allowed soldiers to fire while lying down. Smokeless powder made it easier to fire without being spotted. Hydraulics enabled quick-firing artillery, allowing cannons to fire without pausing to readjust. The machine gun meant that a single gunner (although it usually required a small crew) could now fire hundreds of bullets a minute. Finally, the rise of mass production as well as the introduction of interchangeable parts made it financially and technologically possible to equip armies with these powerful new weapons.

Cumulatively, these advances transformed the battlefield by exponentially increasing the firepower that armies could generate. Infantry and artillery units could pump out so many bullets and create so much shrapnel that movement across open terrain became suicidal. Stephen Biddle estimates that before the firepower revolution, one thousand soldiers walking one hundred yards under fire would be exposed to two thousand bullets and shell fragments. The firepower revolution meant that those soldiers now needed to brave two hundred thousand bullets and shell fragments trying to cross the exact same ground.[6]

TROOP-TO-SPACE RATIO

Firepower revolutionized warfare, but it was the fact that the First World War involved so many soldiers—all armed with modern weapons and pitted against one another in a narrow corner of Europe—that made stalemate possible.[7] By at least one postwar estimate, the British, French, and German armies had so many soldiers in France and Belgium that they could have crammed ten men per yard along the entire front.[8] Smaller armies—or more maneuver space—might have prevented the war in the west from bogging down into a static slugfest. To illustrate this point, compare the force-to-space ratios on the Western Front to those on the Eastern Front, which remained relatively fluid throughout the war. On the Eastern Front, a division of nearly eleven thousand soldiers could cover 30 kilometers.[9] If that division were sent to the Western Front, as many German divisions were, it would usually be assigned a 2.5-kilometer portion of the front.[10]

Long-term shifts in how European armies generated manpower played an outsize role in creating this unfavorable troop-to-space ratio. It likely began with revolutionary France's levy en masse. Before the French Revolution, European armies were composed of long-serving professional troops, mercenaries, or both. Such troops were expensive to recruit, train, and retain, rendering large armies cost prohibitive. Crude logistical and supply systems also limited them from growing too large. Nor could generals trust their soldiers to forage. The risk was simply too great that they might desert while looking for food, taking their expensive training and equipment with them.

The levy en masse allowed states to mobilize citizens by appealing to nationalism. Although short-term "volunteers" were less capable than professional soldiers, quantity had a quality all its own.[11] As Napoleon discovered, conscripts tended to fight more aggressively when inspired by nationalism, and commanders could trust such troops to forage, which allowed for larger forces in the field.[12]

By 1914, the great powers could mobilize nearly 10 percent of their total respective populations.[13] Europe's armies therefore exploded in size.[14] France started the war with 4.9 million soldiers (700,000 active and 4.2 million reservists). Germany had 5.8 million soldiers (840,000 active and 5 million reservists). Britain—the lone exception—had approximately 733,000 soldiers (247,000 active duty and 486,000 reservists). By the end of the war, however, it too would have almost 5 million men under arms. Armies of this size could occupy and control enormous swaths of terrain, especially once they were equipped with modern rifles, machine guns, and artillery. For a variety of political, strategic, and operational reasons, at the start of the war France and Germany nevertheless deployed the bulk of their forces in an area already short on maneuver space.

STRATEGIC VERSUS TACTICAL MOBILITY

An underappreciated imbalance between strategic and tactical mobility compounded the problem. Early twentieth-century transportation technology made it easy to get soldiers to the front. Ships, trains, and lorries could transport hundreds of thousands of troops from their homes to the battlefield in a matter of weeks.[15] But once soldiers made it to the front, the ground was so war torn that they had to move their gear around on horses, pack mules, or, more often, their own two feet.[16]

This imbalance benefited defenders more than attackers. Defenders could build railways up to the front, which helped them shuttle reserve forces around the battlefield to rapidly reinforce weak spots and contain penetrations. The same was not true for attackers. It took time to build railways, so during an attack resupply and reinforcement units had to walk and carry everything on their backs. This limitation made it exceedingly difficult to exploit penetrations faster than defenders could plug them. Defenders also had the advantage of falling back on their supplies and reserves, whereas attackers had to move farther away from theirs.

The fact that attacking units had to carry almost everything they needed meant that weight also became a major factor. Machine guns, for example, were quite heavy at the start of the war. The Vickers and MG08 machine guns weighed sixty pounds, *excluding* the tripod and ammunition needed to fire them. The Maxim machine gun was only ten pounds lighter. Artillery was far heavier, and soldiers needed horses to move everything except the lightest of field cannons. The relative absence of lightweight firepower at the start of the war further strengthened defenses. After all, weight was less of an issue for defenders because they had time to prepare machine-gun positions and did not have to worry as much about mobility.

Finally, the state of early twentieth-century communications technology reinforced the tactical mobility challenge facing attackers. In an age before reliable, robust, and portable radio systems, commanders had no way to communicate in real time while on the move.[17] The only way to adjust a plan once it was in motion was to use a vulnerable system of runners, signals, telephones, and even carrier pigeons. Unfortunately, the chaos of battle meant lost runners, cut telephone lines, and dead birds.[18] These limitations made it hard to respond and adapt to unanticipated setbacks and unexpected successes. Communications presented less of a challenge for defenders. Unlike attacking units, which advanced into the unknown, defenders knew exactly where they were going to fight. They could rehearse their plans on the ground over which they would fight. They could reinforce their communication systems by burying telephone cables. And they could pretarget the battlefield to reduce the need for real-time coordination with artillery.

The Tactical Dilemma

In essence, the Western Front bogged down into a stalemate because there were too many soldiers fighting in too small a space with too many bullets and not enough trucks or radios. Trench warfare evolved as a logical response to this situation. Early trenches were hastily constructed and ad hoc. Soldiers and units instinctively dug in when defending or after a failed attack. Such trenches appeared on the battlefield as early as the Battle of the Marne. These first trenches were not designed as part of a coherent and permanent defensive network.[19] Most were less than a foot deep and barely capable of protecting a single soldier.[20] By mid-September 1914, however, units began to connect individual fighting holes.[21] This process continued until an interconnected line of trenches ran the entire length of the Western Front.

THE DILEMMA FACING ATTACKERS

That neither side managed to break out of its opponent's trench network until 1918 leads many to conclude that the dominant tactical problem was one of surviving the storm of steel. Just as firepower was not solely responsible for creating the stalemate, however, it was also not the only problem that had to be overcome to restore maneuver to the battlefield. In fact, penetrating (or breaking into) enemy lines was far less of a problem than popular history suggests.[22] It was costly to attack across no-man's-land, but all three armies were more than willing to pay the price.[23] Both sides seized opposing trenches with regularity. Attackers gained ground in even the most disastrous and ill-fated offensives.[24] The real challenge was transforming a break-in into a breakthrough. Breaking through meant finding a way to "exploit a penetration more rapidly than the defender could redeploy to prevent or seal it off."[25] Therefore, it was not enough to just generate more offensive firepower. Armies also had to devise new ways to organize their combat power, develop better methods and mechanisms for battlefield coordination, and strike a tough balance between two difficult sets of trade-offs.

Firepower We know that firepower was only part of the solution; deadlock endured despite the fact that all three armies quickly found ways to give their offenses more firepower. At first, they did so by improving infantry-artillery coordination. Ironically, this step mostly involved relearning lessons they already knew. As we will see, prewar doctrine in all three armies warned against launching an infantry assault without adequate artillery preparation and support. Unfortunately, in the heat of battle, inexperienced commanders routinely ignored the admonition early in the war by pushing their infantry into the assault before supporting artillery could properly soften the objective.

Both sides quickly learned to use artillery to compensate for their infantry's relative lack of mobile firepower. By the end of 1914, lengthy preassault bombardments usually preceded most offensives. Commanders hoped that such barrages might so thoroughly smash an opposing trench system that infantry assault units could sweep across no-man's-land unopposed. Unfortunately, defenses adapted to the threat, which I discuss later in this chapter. Preassault bombardments evolved as well, becoming ever longer and more powerful. By the middle of the war, artillery bombardments were major multiday operations in their own right. Commanders spent days pounding defenses with thousands of guns and millions of shells. The preassault bombardment that preceded the Somme offensive in late June 1916 is emblematic of this approach. British gunners fired more shells in the week before the assault than they did in the entire first year of the war.

All three armies also equipped their assault forces with (relatively) lightweight weapons that they could carry themselves to generate more firepower. By 1916, infantry on both sides had access to a wide array of such weapons, including light machine guns, mortars, rifle grenades, and hand grenades.

Organization Commanders also began to reorganize their infantry units so they could make the most of this newfound combat power. This was especially important when assault units inevitably found themselves fighting without artillery support. Reorganization meant rethinking long-standing habits and doctrines. Ever since firearms supplanted bladed weapons, European infantry units had been exclusively made up of riflemen. Later as they acquired newer forms of firepower, such as the machine gun, Europe's armies tended to organize and consolidate them into specialized units. Meanwhile, artillery typically remained under the control of division and corps commanders.

As a result, smaller infantry units—including the companies and battalions that did the bulk of the frontline fighting—had to coordinate with other units or ask higher-level commanders for the extra firepower they needed to press the assault. This approach rarely worked, given how hard it was to communicate on the modern battlefield (which I also discuss below). All three armies needed a better way to give frontline commanders immediate access to and control over more firepower than their riflemen could generate on their own.

Assault units also needed new tactics and formations. Early in the war, they advanced across no-man's-land in long columns or large unwieldy waves. Such formations meant braving the storm of steel while walking in a line with just two or three meters between each soldier. Linear formations were hard to control and too inflexible to adapt to unforeseen circumstances. They also made it hard for attacking infantry to get the most out of their new weapons. And of course, linear formations meant that soldiers were dangerously exposed to the full force of the defender's firepower.

Coordination Beyond these daunting firepower and organizational challenges, commanders also had to resolve a number of coordination problems. Three such issues proved especially vexing.

The first involved infantry-artillery coordination. Infantrymen were vulnerable as they lumbered across no-man's-land, so both sides used artillery to keep defenders pinned down until the last possible moment. Ideally, artillery would shift away just as the first assault waves poured into the defender's trench lines. Timing was everything. When artillery shifted too quickly, defenders had time to climb out of their shelters and mow down the attacking infantry. When artillery shifted too slowly, assault units ran into their own shells. Radios would eventually help solve this problem, but the state of communications technology during the First World War made real time coordination next to impossible. It often took hours for a front line unit to send a message back to headquarters, or vice versa.[26] Such delays made it impossible to change an artillery support plan after the infantry went over the top.

The second coordination challenge revolved around achieving surprise. Commanders needed to use preassault artillery bombardments to soften defensive positions before deploying their infantry. Defenses evolved in response to this threat. As defensive networks grew in depth, strength, and complexity, attacking commanders had no choice but to increase the power and length of their preassault artillery bombardments. Unfortunately, the longer the preassault bombardment, the harder it became to catch a defender off-guard. After all, it took weeks to stockpile the hundreds of thousands—if not millions—of shells needed to fire a multiday bombardment, and it was impossible to hide preparations of this magnitude from spies, patrols, and reconnaissance aircraft.[27] Moreover, even as they wreaked havoc on front-line defensive positions, these massive artillery bombardments were also a clear indication that an attack was imminent. Defenders used these warnings to shift extra units into place.

Logistics represented a third coordination challenge. Assault units almost always needed water, ammunition, and reinforcements by the time they reached their assigned objectives. Moreover, since attacking invariably meant moving away from friendly supply lines, the more successful the attack, the harder it was to resupply and reinforce. The massive preassault artillery bombardments made matters worse by rending the terrain impassible for resupply troops. On the other side of the equation, logistics usually became easier for defenders as a battle progressed. Defenders often built their supply lines all the way up to the front. And they had a critical advantage over attackers: retreat put defenders *closer* to their reserve units, rail networks, and supply depots.

Trade-offs Beyond firepower, organization, and coordination challenges, commanders also faced two unenviable trade-offs. The first revolved around depth. Commanders had to decide whether to assign deep or shallow (limited) objectives to their assault forces. Assigning a deep objective made a rapid breakthrough more likely, since assault units could lodge themselves far behind enemy lines so as to destroy command posts, supply depots, and artillery positions that defenders relied on. Defenders also had less time to react to a deep penetration. Yet defensive positions had grown so large and complex that deep objectives were almost always too far away for an attacker's artillery to support. As a result, the deeper the penetration, the longer assault units had to fight without the benefit of artillery support and the easier it became for defenders to maneuver counterattack units against them with impunity.

Shallow objectives, on the other hand, kept assault units within range of supporting artillery. By stringing a series of so-called bite-and-hold attacks together in quick succession, commanders hoped to methodically chew through a defense by quickly grabbing a nearby objective, pausing long enough to move artillery forward, and then taking a slightly deeper piece of ground.. Unfortunately, shallow attacks tended to sap momentum and bog down. Each set-piece attack took time—time that defenders could use to deploy reserve units and organize counterattacks.

The second trade-off involved breadth. Commanders had to decide whether to attack on a narrow or a broad front. Attacking on a narrow front made it easier to concentrate combat power. But a narrow front also made it easier for a defender to concentrate its reserve forces. There was also a risk that a successful narrow attack might create a pocket (or salient) that defenders could surround and pour fire into from all sides. Conversely, attacking along a broad front kept defenders from concentrating their reserve units. But a broad-front attack made it harder for attacking infantry to mass decisive combat power. Commanders also had a harder time coordinating operations across a wide front.

THE DILEMMA FACING DEFENDERS

That attackers could not break through Western Front defenses does not mean that defending was easy. Defending units absorbed appalling casualties and often lost as many men in a battle as the attacker.[28] Defenses therefore had to constantly adapt. In many respects, they changed at least as much as offenses if not more so, since neither side gave sufficient thought to defensive operations before the war.[29] As a result, the complex defensive networks in place by war's end bore almost no resemblance to the crude trench lines that started to appear in its first months.

Firepower In particular, defenders had to evolve in order to keep pace with the constant increase in offensive firepower. To give some sense of how much firepower attackers could generate by the middle of the war, in June 1917 a group of German soldiers counted twenty-five hundred shells exploding around their pillbox in one four-hour period.[30]

Defenses initially responded by digging deeper trenches and building underground bunkers. Attackers responded with gas, mines, and more powerful artillery. Defenders quickly realized there was a limit to how deep they could dig, because at a certain point the shelters became so deep that assault troops could take a trench before defenders could scramble up to meet them.[31] Obstacles bought defenders additional time by slowing the assault waves down, but they were vulnerable to sappers and artillery, particularly after the introduction of point-detonation artillery shells. Defenders therefore also started digging reverse-slope trenches whenever possible. Putting a trench on the backside of a hill made it harder for artillery observers to ensure that their shells were actually hitting the trench.

Equally important, defenders started adding additional lines of trenches beyond the effective range of the other side's artillery. These so-called defenses in depth were an important adaptation. They meant that defenders had a safe place to prestage supplies and reserve troops during an attack. At the same time, even this approach had limits. Having too many lines of trenches—or positioning them too far apart—meant that reserve forces were too far away to rapidly respond to a break-in. This problem was especially acute when attackers shifted to the aforementioned bite-and-hold operations. Such attacks were characterized by their shallow objectives, which ensured that the advancing force neither progressed beyond its artillery's maximum range nor occupied dangerously overextended positions. The goal was to grab a series of shallow objectives so as to slowly devour a defensive position piece by piece while ensuring that each individual attack was over before the defense could commit reserves or organize a counterattack. Defenders initially had a hard time dealing with bite-and-hold attacks, which turned depth into a liability.

Defenses in depth faced another problem. Depth, by itself, did not mitigate offensive firepower so long as defending commanders insisted on keeping most of their men in the front trenches. Indeed, by rigidly holding on to every inch of ground and fighting to keep the front line, defenders left themselves dangerously exposed to the most powerful weapon in the attacker's arsenal: the preassault bombardment. Therefore, defenses needed to become more flexible. Ideally, defenders could conserve manpower by putting as few soldiers in frontline trenches—and therefore within enemy artillery range—as possible. But this was a risky approach because an attacker could more easily mount a quick bite-and-hold attack. Commanders also worried that if they let their soldiers abandon frontline positions during a bombardment, they might never stand and fight. If this happened, a penetration anywhere might turn into rout everywhere. Thus, commanders needed to design a defense that could bend without breaking. This challenge meant figuring out how to both organize rapid effective counterattacks and ensure that flexibility would not sap a defense of its fighting spirit. Finally, flexibility came at a political price. After all, senior commanders and political leaders disliked voluntarily giving up ground that had been so costly to take in the first place.

Converging on a Better Doctrine

By war's end, the British and German armies—and to a lesser degree the French Army—converged on a core set of solutions to these problems and challenges. This new way of fighting revolved around three core elements: assault tactics, combined arms, and elastic defense in depth. Taken together, they represented a more effective way to attack and defend given the core challenges that all three armies faced on the Western Front.

ASSAULT TACTICS

The storm of steel imposed fearsome casualties on units as they tried to advance across no-man's-land. The best way to conserve manpower was to disperse and maneuver in small groups, because a formation larger than eight to twelve soldiers attracted unwanted attention from enemy gunners. Yet dividing a large assault force into thousands of small teams created its own command-and-control problems. A commander could not simply unleash hordes of small units and hope something useful would come of their uncoordinated actions. The only way to make this approach work was to organize, train, and equip small-unit leaders to fight independently. This requirement meant giving small units weapons to generate their own firepower. It also meant teaching small-unit leaders how to identify gaps and strongpoints so they could exploit the former and avoid the latter.

Accomplishing these tasks meant organizing assault tactics around five interrelated concepts: dispersed formations, independent action, fire and movement, organic firepower, and deep objectives on a narrow front.

Dispersed Formations One of the most effective ways to mitigate the storm of steel was to shift from rigid lines to irregular, flexible, and dispersed formations. Appropriately nicknamed "blob" formations by British soldiers, these loose formations helped small units take advantage of the terrain for cover and concealment and kept soldiers far enough apart from one another that a single bullet (or shell fragment) would not injure or kill too many at once.

Independent Action Dispersion increased survivability but complicated command and control. Before the war, companies (made up of two hundred fifty or so soldiers) were the smallest unit allowed to operate independently in all three armies. But a single officer could not control hundreds of men spread out in an irregular formation. Thus, all three armies began training junior officers to lead smaller units. These units grew successively smaller—and the leaders in command of them successively less experienced—as the war progressed. At first, the British, French, and German armies experimented with platoons, consisting of forty or so men under a young officer. When these formations proved almost as unwieldy as companies, all three armies shifted to half-platoons of twenty or so soldiers led by a senior enlisted noncommissioned officer. By war's end, it was common to let an enlisted soldier lead a squad of eight to twelve infantrymen. These small units were further empowered to make independent decisions so they could respond to unforeseen setbacks, exploit unexpected opportunities, and take advantage of terrain that could protect them from the storm of steel.

Fire and Movement Long before the First World War, it had become suicidal to advance across open terrain without first suppressing enemy gunners.[32] Before the war, all three armies taught attackers to use fire and movement to suppress the enemy. Fire and movement meant that part of an attacking unit stopped to shoot while the rest of the unit continued to advance under the cover of their fire. It was akin to playing a game of leapfrog, albeit with guns. Oddly, in the war's first months, inexperienced commanders in all three armies tended to ignore their respective prewar doctrines, repeatedly sending their infantry forward in a single massive thrust. France's senior general at the time, General Joseph Joffre, as well as contemporary historians blamed the failure to practice fire and movement on a lack of realism in prewar training, which itself resulted from a lack of training space, austere training budgets, and the desire to impress inspectors during large-scale maneuvers.[33] The combination of inexperience, excitement, and chaos likely played a role in causing commanders on both sides to ignore their pre-war doctrine too. In any case, infantry units did not have the kinds of light-weight mobile firepower needed to effectively suppress entrenched defenders early on in the war. Therefore, all three armies gave up on asking their infantry units to generate their own suppression by 1915. Instead of firing *and* moving, they shifted to firing and *then* moving. In other words, commanders on both sides began to depend on artillery to suppress enemy defenders. Infantry would advance behind massive preassault bombardments and creeping barrages. Although this approach was better than advancing without any suppression, it still left attackers exposed once they moved beyond their artillery's range or fell behind the preplanned timetable.

All three armies eventually recognized that infantry units still needed to be able to suppress the enemy on their own. Part of the solution involved modifying prewar doctrine so as to reemphasize fire and movement, albeit at much lower levels of command. All three armies also paid more attention to training their infantry how to do proper fire and movement. Although leapfrogging might sound simple, doing so while under fire proved hard. There was a very real risk that some soldiers might get down on the ground only to refuse to get back up again, especially considering the firestorm awaiting these young conscripts. Moreover, controlling thousands of individual units as they moved across the battlefield—in conjunction with an overarching artillery plan—required an unprecedented degree of preparation, training, and coordination.

Organic Firepower The other part of the fire-and-movement solution involved giving small, independent, and self-contained infantry units enough firepower to go up against heavily armed and fortified defenders. Riflemen armed with bolt-action rifles simply could not press an assault on their own. It did not take long for all three armies to begin supplying their attackers with a menagerie of weapons, including light machine guns, grenades, rifle grenades, mortars, and field guns. Even then, for much of the war all three armies tended to put these weapons in the hands of specialists. This practice precluded the familiarity and camaraderie that serves as the basis for unit morale and combat effectiveness. Moreover, even when specialists were attached, higher-ranking commanders tended to retain control over their use, making them unavailable for frontline service in most cases.

Eventually, all three armies integrated the full range of weapons within the platoons and squads by issuing them to regular infantrymen instead of specialist units. Armed with their own light machine guns, rifle grenades, and hand grenades, small units finally had the kind of firepower needed to press forward without artillery support.

Deep Objectives on a Narrow Front Assault tactics required attackers to aim for objectives deep within the defensive network. The goal was to strike as deep as possible to disrupt the defender's command, support, and artillery assets. To do this, attackers needed to concentrate combat power on a relatively narrow front—preferably where the defense was weakest. To offset the aforementioned drawbacks associated with deep attacks and narrow fronts, assault units needed to bypass strongpoints, leaving them for follow-on forces to mop up. Because it was impossible to know exactly when and where assault forces might encounter unexpected success or resistance, planning had to be flexible, and frontline commanders had to have the autonomy to make on-the-spot decisions. These requirements reinforced the need for organic firepower and independent action. Deep penetrations made it likely that assault units would have to fight without artillery support, and frontline commanders had to be comfortable deviating from the battle plan.

In many respects, these assault tactics had a lot in common with prewar doctrine, which called on attackers to avoid assaults into the teeth of enemy defenses (hence the preference for flanking attacks) and to seek deep objectives that might disrupt the adversary's so-called center of gravity. Of course, the devil remained in the details. Prewar doctrines shared similar principles but remained vague as to the specific tactics, techniques, and procedures needed to act on them. And prewar infantry units did not have the requisite training, autonomy, or firepower.

COMBINED ARMS

Better infantry tactics represented an important piece of the doctrinal puzzle. But all three armies also needed to improve infantry-artillery coordination. After all, although only infantry could take and hold ground, artillery still did most of the killing. Artillery units also needed new techniques to support the new assault tactics. Given the limits imposed by geography and the absence of self-propelled artillery and reliable real-time communications, artillery-infantry coordination evolved to encompass four interrelated practices: the hurricane barrage, predicted fire, flexible command and control, and all-arms integration.

Hurricane Barrage No matter how advanced infantry equipment and tactics became, it was still suicidal to attack a prepared defensive position without adequate artillery preparation. Given the degree to which defenses had advanced, artillery support had to include both a bombardment *before* the infantry went over the top and suppressive fire to pin defenders down *during* the assault. The dilemma, of course, was that stronger defenses required longer bombardments. But longer bombardments robbed an offensive of the element of surprise.

The solution was to shift from destruction to neutralization. For most of the war, commanders on both sides tried to use their artillery bombardments to pound opposing defenses into oblivion. But destruction was an illusory goal.[34] Defenders always managed to dig deeper holes, build stronger pill-boxes, or husband reserves just outside of artillery range. Neutralizing a defense set a lower—more realistic—bar. Destruction demanded a physical outcome, namely ensuring that a high percentage of the other side's machine guns, strongpoints, trenches, and artillery were physically incapable of fighting. Neutralization implied a psychological outcome: disorienting defenders so they were unwilling to put up a fight, even if the amount of physical destruction was minimal.

Neutralization required combining speed, accuracy, and intensity, none of which were sufficient on their own. The costly attacks in late 1914 showed why fast but weak bombardments did not work. And the epic battles of Verdun, the Somme, and Passchendaele demonstrated that defenders could adjust to even the most powerful bombardment over time, especially when they knew one was coming. Powerful *surprise* bombardments, however, could shock defenders just long enough for assaulting infantry units to take advantage of their confusion. These quick but brutal artillery attacks came to be known as hurricane barrages, which momentarily disrupted defenses by catching frontline units off guard and knocking out key command posts and communication nodes. Since the defenses themselves were left largely intact, the infantry had to attack before defenders could to reestablish communications and start moving reserves into place.

Predicted Fire Both sides knew early in the war that surprise bombardments were better than long drawn-out ones. In fact, British units experimented with prototype hurricane barrages as early as 1915.[35] But technological limitations prevented hurricane barrages from becoming a practical tool. Hurricane barrages worked only when gunners could hit their targets without warning. Yet for most of the war, the only way gunners could hope to hit anything with accuracy was to fire a number of so-called registration shells before initiating the actual bombardment.[36] It could take days just to register all of the guns before a major bombardment, making surprise impossible. And gunners could not skip this step for most of the war. Without registration rounds, they could not be sure they would actually hit their targets.

It was not until the armies figured out a way to use a combination of accurate maps, precise meteorological reports, and scientific gun tables that gunners could accurately fire their guns without registering them first. Called predicted fire, this approach represented a major technical innovation that took years of experimentation and refinement. In many ways, it was the most important technical achievement in a conflict known for its scientific accomplishments.[37] All three armies had to learn predicted firing from scratch, since none had seriously studied indirect fire techniques before the war, having largely assumed that field artillery would always be able to position itself close to advancing infantry.

Flexible Command and Control Whereas assault tactics meant decentralizing autonomy and decision-making authority far beyond anything prewar doctrines had imagined, effective combined arms required flexibly switching between centralized and decentralized control over artillery assets. For much of the war, divisions, corps, and army groups in all three armies possessed their own organic artillery. Division commanders in particular ferociously guarded control over their artillery. Allowing every division to control its own artillery plan made sense during the assault, when gunners focused on suppressing defenders as the infantry made its way across no-man's-land. After all, units had different objectives, crossed different terrain, and faced different defensive networks. It was therefore impractical to have a single creeping barrage act as suppression for multiple assault divisions.

Bombardments, however, worked best when coordinated and unified across the entire zone of attack. This was especially true for hurricane barrages, where surprise was of the essence. It was impossible to coordinate multiple hurricane barrages, meaning a decentralized barrage was unlikely to surprise defenders. The solution required flexible command-and-control techniques that allowed the highest-ranking commander to control all artillery during the preassault barrage and then return control to subordinate units during the infantry assault.

All-Arms Integration The final component to effective combined arms mirrored the need for organic firepower at the small-unit level. Larger units— brigades, divisions, and corps—similarly needed to integrate all available weapons, including tanks, aircraft, and heavy and field artillery. All-arms integration required dedicated training and intense coordination so that infantry, artillery, armor, and air staffs knew how to work well together. It also entailed extensive task organization, such as putting field guns or tanks under the command of an infantry unit or allowing reconnaissance or close air support aircraft to communicate directly with frontline commanders.

ELASTIC DEFENSE IN DEPTH

Defenses evolved on the Western Front alongside the attacks that sought to penetrate them. The defenses reached their optimal form when the German Army introduced the elastic defense in depth in late 1916. Elastic defenses in depth shared three basic elements: depth, elasticity, and the counterattack.[38]

Depth Trench networks that began as hastily dug holes slowly transformed into complex defensive systems spanning miles from front to rear. At Passchendaele in July 1917, the British attacked a German defensive network that was ten thousand meters in depth at some points. Depth offered two advantages. First, it prevented an attacker from exploiting momentum. Even when assaulting infantry managed to take the first trench in a position, they had to pause, regroup, and launch another attack against the next position. Each successive attack sapped time, ammunition, and energy while creating more casualties. Depth also bought time for defenders to shift reserve forces into place. The second advantage was that the deeper the defensive system, the harder it was for the attacker's artillery to range the entire network. Depth therefore made it hard for an attacking commander to provide continuous artillery support for his assault units. The more successful the attack, the more vulnerable it became. Depth also helped conserve defensive manpower, particularly when defending commanders were willing to keep the bulk of their infantry outside of enemy artillery range.

Elasticity Elasticity meant both maintaining a relatively small garrison in the forward-most trenches and giving frontline commanders the authority to fall back to a main line of resistance if faced with overwhelming force. This approach saved lives by exposing fewer defending infantrymen to snipers, patrols, and harassing artillery fire on a day-to-day basis. It also gave commanders the flexibility to decide whether they should fight hard for the front line if threatened by a small force or pull back in the face of a major assault. Of course, pulling back was not the same thing as retreating. In an elastic defense in depth, frontline units would fight long enough to slow down the initial waves of an attack before falling back on prepared positions.

Depth was intuitive. Elasticity was not. As late as 1918, some officers still insisted on keeping most of their men in the front trenches, even in contravention of official doctrine and direct orders. There were several reasons senior officers had a hard time accepting elasticity. First, they were worried about the political ramifications of not fighting to hold on to every inch of ground. This concern was especially acute for French generals but was also an issue even for German commanders. Second, many officers worried that if they made it too easy for attackers to gain a foothold, it would become much harder to then repel the invader with a counterattack. Third, senior leaders worried that frontline commanders might abuse elasticity by pulling out at the first sign of danger or by letting an orderly withdrawal turn into an unorganized rout.

Counterattack Giving commanders the latitude to fall back constituted only part of elasticity. The other element, equally critical, was ensuring that units aggressively counterattacked as soon as possible so as to retake lost ground. Elastic defenses in depth were therefore actually quite offensive in nature. Instead of pointlessly squandering lives, frontline defenders were free to pull back in the face of an overwhelming attack. But as soon as the attackers halted to regroup, reorient, and rearm—particularly when they had moved beyond the range of their supporting artillery—the same units that had fallen back would immediately retake their position with a counterattack. To facilitate counterattacks, defenders built concrete pillboxes and strongpoints between lines of trenches. They would of course camouflage these outposts or position them beyond artillery range. These positions would serve as rally points and a base of fire for counterattack units. Aggressive training was also crucial. Counterattacking had to be instinctive. Units of every size, even down to the squad level, were expected to organize a counterattack as soon as possible. Small-unit commanders therefore needed training in offensive assault tactics. In fact, the German Army used counterattacks as a testing ground for developing and refining their offensive assault tactics.

Assault Tactics, Combined Arms, and Elastic Defense in Depth: A Better Way to Fight on the Western Front?

There are two compelling reasons to think that assault tactics, combined arms, and elastic defenses in depth were a more effective and efficient way to fight on the Western Front than the war-fighting methods that preceded them. First, as the case studies in this book illustrate, all three armies either converged on assault tactics, combined arms, and elastic defense in depth or were trying to do so as the war ended. Although the German Army was the first to (almost fully) adopt these techniques, the British Army was never far behind. And in the case of combined arms in general—and all arms integration in particular—the British Army was probably ahead. Even the French Army made significant strides toward implementing many of these concepts and were actually the first to sketch out assault tactics and defense-in-depth concepts on paper.

Second, there is a powerful argument to be made that one hundred years later, assault tactics, combined arms, and elastic defenses in depth *remain* the best way to fight on conventional battlefields. At a minimum, these techniques unambiguously shaped how the world's best armies waged war for much of the twentieth century. Stephen Biddle takes the argument a step further. In his seminal work on the sources of military power, he suggests that

> By 1918, a process of convergent evolution under harsh wartime selection pressures had produced a stable and essentially transnational body of ideas on the methods needed to operate effectively in the face of radically lethal modern weapons. . . . Taken together, they broke the trench stalemate in 1918 and defined the standard for successful military operations throughout the post-1918 era.[39]

Although not all historians and military analysts agree with Biddle, it is at least clear that assault tactics, combined arms, and elastic defenses in depth as they were developed in the First World War went on to form the core of the German Army's blitzkrieg doctrine in the Second World War as well as the maneuver warfare doctrine that guided the US Army to victory in the Persian Gulf and the initial phases of Operation Iraqi Freedom.[40] It is therefore very unlikely that there was a more effective and efficient way to have attacked and defended on the Western Front.

Road Map

The next three chapters offer a detailed look at the development and evolution of German, British, and French doctrine from 1895 to 1918, respectively. The case studies are arranged chronologically to reflect the order in which each army mastered assault tactics, combined arms, and elastic defenses in depth. The chapters are also organized chronologically by year (prewar, 1914, 1915, etc.). This approach allows me to explicitly compare the causal relationships between my dependent variables (assault, combined arms, and elastic defenses in depth) and ACT theory's preferred explanatory variables (command practices, assessment mechanisms, and training structures). I discuss key political and strategic developments insofar as they might plausibly influence tactical doctrine. To support my analysis, I draw on the secondary literature as well as primary source documents such as action reports, intelligence documents, and training manuals.

The German Army on the Western Front

The German Army learned faster than its adversaries. It was the only army on the Western Front to master a holistic doctrine consisting of elastic defenses in depth, combined arms, and assault tactics. And it did so earlier and on a more widespread basis than the British and French armies. To be sure, the British Army was rarely far behind. Although it lagged behind the Germans in adopting elastic defenses in depth, the British Army kept pace in terms of combined arms and was ahead of the German Army in developing and integrating armor. The British Army also used assault tactics by the end of the war, but implementation remained more uneven than it was on the German side.

For its part, the French Army was often more creative than its German opponent. Early in the war, French officers raced ahead in terms of thinking about assault tactics, combined arms, and elastic defense in depth. Unfortunately for the French, German soldiers were effective copycats. Since combat respects neither originality nor copyrights, good ideas proved necessary but not sufficient. As I discuss in chapter 5, the French Army struggled to both translate its cutting-edge ideas into practical doctrine and transmit them across the entire organization.

The German Army's experience on the Western Front highlights several important themes in this book. First, it illustrates the way organizational structure influences learning. The German Army was better at learning because it was systematically better at coming up with (or emulating) new ideas, refining them to meet its needs and limitations, and implementing them across the relevant parts of the organization. In other words, the German Army was structured to learn. Its often-cited command practices were part of the story, but as assessment, command, and training (ACT) theory predicts, its assessment mechanisms and highly centralized training systems were also important.

Second, the German Army's experience also reminds us *not* to overstate the degree to which individual leaders shape organizational learning. History tends to give too much credit to a small cadre of brilliant officers for

the German Army's tactical acumen, but its learning process turned on organizational efficiency, not individual brilliance. As one British officer succinctly
put it in a prewar meeting of the Imperial General Staff:

> We say, after our way, that our rivals are a nation of well-trained mediocrity.
> Could there be a more formidable thing? We say that Germany has, indeed,
> vast numbers of males, but no *men*. The land of Luther, Frederick, Stern, and
> Brunswick has never in modern time lacked personalities equal to her crisis.
> But genius is not necessary. . . . It is the system that matters. It is the mass of
> well-trained mediocrity that turns the scale. It is the best machine that wins.[1]

Individual leaders, including Erich Ludendorff, Georg Bruchmüller, Fritz
von Lossberg, and Hans von Seeckt, undoubtedly influenced learning. After
all, no matter how much structure constrains and incentivizes, people still
(at least for now) make decisions. Nevertheless, none of them had the wherewithal to conceive, develop, implement, and enforce a novel set of doctrinal
practices across a multimillion-soldier army engaged in a global war.[2] In any
case, individual genius is too stochastic to explain why the German Army
consistently outlearned its competitors.

The third theme is that learning offers a more useful way to think about
wartime change than innovation, adaptation, or emulation. The historical
record clearly shows that the German Army was not more creative or original than its competitors. It was, however, better at turning good concepts
into practical doctrine. Nor did the German Army care where good ideas
came from. It was an army of intellectual scavengers. Some concepts, such
as hurricane barrages and flexible command and control over artillery, may
have originated within the German officer corps. Other key ideas came from
below. And, of course, the German Army seems to have borrowed crucial
ideas from the French. French units were the first to add depth to their defensive networks. A young French captain, André Laffargue, wrote a monograph
on assault tactics in 1915, but his superiors seem to have largely ignored his
suggestions. The German Army, however, had no such reservations.[3] It is also
worth noting that no matter how central plagiarism was to German wartime
learning, the German Army usually did not adopt outside concepts wholesale.
Rather, it refined and adapted "stolen" practices so as to meet its unique capabilities, demands, and limitations. This was something the British Army
did not do when it copied German elastic defenses in early 1918—a failure
that nearly cost them the war.

The fourth—and perhaps most important—theme is that the German
Army lost despite being better at learning. This observation serves as a poignant reminder that tactical performance is only one variable in the military
effectiveness equation. The fact that the German Army outfought its competition on the battlefield ultimately proved less important than the German
state's pathological inability to formulate a coherent political-military strategy.[4]

As Jonathan Boff argues, "the tendency of the German military to seek military solutions to political problems and to attempt to offset operational weakness with tactical brilliance is a recurring theme in its history from Schlieffen to Stalingrad."[5] In the context of the First World War, Germany proved better at making enemies than defeating them. Violating Belgian neutrality pushed Britain into the war. The Zimmerman telegram and the unrestricted U-boat campaign pushed the United States into the war. Neither outcome was inevitable, but collectively they made the war unwinnable.

The Evolution of German Politics, Strategy, and Operations

A deep-seated fear of encirclement drove German prewar strategy.[6] Such fears may not have been baseless. *Potential* enemies did surround the young German state. At the same time, Germany's policies and strategies became a self-fulfilling prophecy, transforming theoretical adversaries into real ones.[7] Germany's Triple Alliance with Austria-Hungary and Italy, for example, pushed France and Russia into a counterbalancing coalition.[8] German belligerence likewise pushed Britain, France, and Russia—former adversaries— closer together.

Whatever its causes and reasons, encirclement meant that the Germany Army had to prepare for a two-front war. Although historians now debate the degree to which a coherent Schlieffen Plan ever existed, let alone pushed German leaders over the brink in 1914, it does seem clear that German politicians and generals believed that the best way to avoid such an outcome was to defeat France and Russia in sequence.[9] Thus, the German Army planned and trained to knock France out before its ally Russia could mobilize. By quickly securing its western flank, Germany could then concentrate against the larger Russian threat.

In accordance with these plans, the first German units violated Belgian neutrality on August 4, 1914. German strategy depended on tactical and operational speed. The Belgians, however, had a say in the matter. Their forces and fortresses held out longer than German planners had anticipated. The delay gave Britain time to deploy its British Expeditionary Force, whose intervention set the German Army's precise timetable back even further. Collectively, these setbacks gave British and French forces time to mount a decisive defense of Paris along the Marne River in early September.

The Race to the Sea ensued, after which the German Army shifted to a defensive posture along the Western Front. The speed with which the Russian Army mobilized forced the German army's high command, Oberste Heeresleitung (OHL), to send as many units eastward as possible. The German Army remained on the strategic defensive in the west for most of the next four years. Aside from offensives in Ypres in 1915, which were mostly about rationalizing the army's defensive lines, and Verdun in 1916, the German

Army focused on fending off British and French attacks with as few men as possible. This posture reflected both manpower constraints and the decision to prioritize the war against Russia. The Eastern Front therefore consumed most of the army's attention and resources. In August 1915, for example, only six divisions were available in reserve for the entire Western Front.[10]

Even the Verdun offensive seems to have been designed to drag the French Army into a backbreaking battle of attrition instead of seeking a decisive breakthrough in its own right.[11] Whatever Erich von Falkenhayn's true intentions, manpower constraints and demands from other fronts meant that German forces in the west spent the rest of the year absorbing the Entente's increasingly powerful blows. A combined British-French force landed the strongest blow along the Somme River starting on July 1, 1916. The grueling five-month-long battle pushed the German Army to its breaking point. Despite spending most of the battle on the defensive, it lost more men in the first two months at the Somme than it did in the first six months attacking at Verdun.[12]

Multifront warfare proved costly, and German leaders grew desperate. A manpower crisis loomed by late 1916 as the army started to run out of suitable conscripts, having already called up its draft classes of 1916, 1917, and 1918.[13] Domestic support also started to waver as battlefield setbacks suggested a decisive victory was impossible. As Ludendorff reported in the waning months of 1916, the "outlook for the coming year was exceedingly grave. It was certain that in 1917 the Entente would again make a supreme effort, not only to make good its losses, which it was certainly in a position to do, but to add to its strength everywhere and swell its superiority in numbers."[14] Germany responded by floating a "peace balloon" in December 1916, which the Entente rejected out of hand. Desperation fueled an increasingly disconnected political-military strategy as the German high command laid the groundwork for an unrestricted U-boat campaign and a secret military alliance with Mexico.

Both plans backfired. As a result, by the late spring of 1917, the German Army found itself spread thin across the Western, Eastern, Romanian, and Italian theaters and awaiting American entry into the war. Yet the German high command somehow came to believe either that the tables were actually starting to turn in its favor or that it faced an implacable adversary with whom negotiation was impossible.[15] Either way, from the OHL's perspective, a fleeting window of opportunity existed. Russia was on the verge of collapse, the French Army was in mutiny, and Britain was facing a manpower crisis of its own. And even though the United States had finally entered the war, it would take time for US forces to arrive in strength. The OHL therefore sought to bring the war to a successful conclusion by planning for a major offensive in the West.[16]

Germany attacked on March 21, 1918. Its early successes paved the way for its eventual defeat. By early June, German forces inflicted nearly half a million casualties on the British and French armies but at a cost of nearly the same number of German soldiers.[17] The combination of logistical failures, ambiguous strategic objectives, and the arrival of American forces proved insurmountable, and the German Army abandoned its push. The British, French, and American coalition then counterattacked. Under constant pressure, German units lacked the time, resources, and manpower they needed to reconstitute an elastic defense in depth. The same German Army that started 1918 with 190 combat-ready divisions was reduced to 98 by August 1, 47 by September 1, 14 by October 15, and 4 by November 11.[18]

The Evolution of German Tactical Doctrine

OFFENSIVE DOCTRINE

Prewar Germany's self-perceived strategic predicament—and the war plans devised to ameliorate it—shaped the army's prewar doctrine. The political and strategic imperative for speed caused planners to overemphasize the offense and neglect the defense. Again, the decision to emphasize offensive operations does not mean the German Army ignored the firepower revolution. Rather, it means German officers saw higher casualty levels as a necessary price to pay to enable offensive operations under modern conditions. From the German General Staff's perspective, "the destruction of a regiment[] or even the destruction of a division was seen . . . as inconsequential when compared to considerations that affected the campaign as a whole."[19]

Despite this strategic imperative to press the attack, German tactical doctrine nevertheless fluctuated a great deal before the First World War. These shifts reflected a vigorous internal debate within the German officer corps over the best way to assault an enemy equipped with modern firepower. Two schools of thought emerged. One school held that modern rapid-fire weapons made the battlefield too lethal to attack in large formations of tightly packed riflemen. These firepower advocates wanted to break assault forces into smaller teams, which would use flexible tactics, dispersed formations, and independent movement to minimize exposure to enemy firepower.[20] Those officers on the other side of the debate conceded that firepower now dominated modern battlefields. Yet they worried that the cure proposed by firepower advocates might prove worse than the disease. These shock-power advocates believed that commanders would struggle to coordinate hundreds of small units maneuvering independently toward the objective. They also thought individual soldiers might feel isolated if spread out across the battlefield, causing them to hesitate and falter. Their point was not entirely illogical, especially because conscripts made up the bulk of the German Army. Shock-power advocates therefore saw large tightly packed formations as a necessary evil to give soldiers the courage they needed to brave the storm of steel.

This debate raged from the end of the Franco-Prussian War (1870–1871) until the beginning of the First World War and in the process shaped doctrine. The German Army adopted three different sets of doctrines during this period: the 1888 Exerzier-Reglement für die Infanterie (1888 ExRfdI), the 1906 Exerzier-Reglement für die Infanterie (1906 ExRfdI), and the 1908 Felddienst Ordnung (1908 FSR).[21] Each reflected a unique compromise between the firepower and shock-power camps.

The 1888 ExRfdI captured the lessons that the German Army drew from the Franco-Prussian War. This doctrine was noteworthy insofar as it implied that firepower mattered more than the force derived from an infantry charge.[22] The 1888 ExfdI also identified a new type of assault formation—the (swarm of riflemen)—and a novel set of procedures for its employment. Specifically, the doctrine called on commanders to halt just outside of the enemy's maximum range, shifting their lead units into *schutzenswarm* while waiting for German artillery to soften the objective. After German artillery effectively suppressed enemy defenders, the *schutzenswarm* would then close with the objective as quickly as possible. Once within rifle fire range, it would initiate a firefight with surviving defenders, allowing follow-on assault units to mount a decisive infantry charge.

Its novel aspects notwithstanding, the 1888 ExRfdI did not represent a complete break from previous doctrine. The doctrine still called for units advancing behind the *schutzenswarm* to maneuver in tightly packed formations and emphasize speed over cover and concealment. Despite acknowledging firepower's paramount importance, the 1888 ExRfdI also still called for a final infantry charge. And even though the doctrine warned commanders that they had to win the firefight *before* charging an objective, the admonition was so subtle that it was lost on many German officers.[23]

The Boer War and the Russo-Japanese War reignited the debate, and the German Army dispatched liaison officers to observe both conflicts. Although military historians have argued that both conflicts clearly presaged firepower's dominance, at the time they seemed to have created more questions than answers among German officers.[24] It is therefore unsurprising that the German Army's next doctrinal manual, the 1906 ExRfdI, reflected such uncertainty. It was, in many respects, an unhappy if not incoherent compromise between the firepower and shock-power positions. On one hand, the doctrine appeared to side with shock-power advocates, suggesting that modern firepower was not as destructive as previous doctrine had suggested.[25] On the other hand, the 1906 regulations continued to advise against launching an infantry assault without adequate artillery support or charging an objective without first winning the decisive firefight.

This uncomfortable compromise was apparent in how the 1906 ExEfdI amended its predecessor's instructions for mounting an infantry attack. Echoing these earlier regulations, the 1906 manual again told commanders to hold their units just beyond the effective range of a defender's rifles so that German artillery could pound the objective. However, in order to maximize speed, shock and control, the 1906 ExEfdI called for the infantry to race into action using tight formations, not loose swarms, particularly if the artillery preparation adequately did its job.[26]

German officers did not have a chance to master this new manual before another one arrived two years later. The 1908 FSR—the final set of prewar regulations—indicated a shift back toward the firepower school of thought. This doctrine divided an infantry attack into three phases: forming up (*Aufmarsch*), deployment (*Entfaltung*), and an extension (*Entwickelung*).[27] During the forming-up phase, the 1908 FSR instructed commanders to shift their units from tight linear formations into a dispersed line at least 2,500 yards from the objective to afford protection from enemy artillery. The deployment phase occurred roughly 1,500 yards from the objective and involved a second formation shift, as assaulting infantry moved into three successive skirmisher lines, with several yards separating each soldier and about 300 yards (in depth) between each line.[28]

Finally, during the extension phase, the front line of skirmishers spread out even farther, with individual soldiers standing up to 4 yards apart. Following an artillery barrage, the 1908 FSR told commanders to initiate a firefight while simultaneously pushing their troops toward the objective. At approximately 160 yards from the objective, the firing line was to mount its final assault, with parts of the line advancing in 50- to 100-yard bounds as other parts of the line poured suppressive fire into the enemy position. The 1908 FSR still called for a decisive bayonet charge, although it echoed the 1888 ExEfdI by reminding commanders that they had to use artillery and their infantry firing line to keep the enemy pinned down.[29]

1914 As the preceding discussion suggests, German Army's prewar tactics were a far cry from blindly charging into machine-gun fire. Nevertheless, many inexperienced commanders ignored official doctrine by assaulting British and French positions without adequate artillery support or in dense formations.[30] Yet even had commanders adhered perfectly to prewar doctrine, they likely still would have struggled to penetrate the defensive systems that began to appear by late in the year.

Frontline units therefore began to experiment with new tactics almost immediately.[31] Within months, a new approach began to emerge. Commanders would initiate an attack by sending patrols as close as possible to enemy trenches.[32] The rest of the unit would then start to advance, moving in successive waves of skirmisher lines roughly two hundred yards apart. As soon as the lead wave also came under fire, its soldiers formed a firing line to suppress enemy defenders. Subsequent waves reinforced this firing line until it reached a density of about one soldier every two paces. At this point, individual squads started making their way forward. Each squad would dig in again when it could no longer advance. If a commander managed to build up enough combat power near the defensive position, he would launch a final charge. Although this kind of approach was far less costly than earlier war tactics, it also proved too laborious and time-consuming to facilitate a break-through. Moreover, because these experimental approaches did not entail any of the key elements of true assault tactics, I do not consider the German Army to have entered the exploration phase of the learning process in 1914.

1915 Despite remaining on the defensive for most of 1915, German units continued to experiment with different assault tactics. Battles in and around Soissons, Neuve Chapelle, and Aubers Ridge, small though they may have been in comparison to the epic clashes of 1916, nevertheless served as a tac-tical laboratory. In many respects, 1915 witnessed a high degree of doctrinal creativity and flexibility. Many regiments and divisions tried to use small heavily armed shock-troop teams instead of large waves.[33] Following the Battle of Soissons in January, for example, Colonel Seeckt, a General Staff officer serving as the chief of staff for the III Corps, argued that assault units needed more firepower, especially when moving beyond the German artil-lery's maximum range or deviating from the preestablished support plan.[34]

The OHL acted on these experiments by creating a test storm troop unit in March 1915. This event serves as unambiguous evidence that the German Army had clearly entered the exploration phase of the learning process by the spring of 1915. The OHL tasked a relatively junior engineering officer, Major Kalsow, with figuring out how to use small, independent, and heavily armed units to penetrate enemy defenses.[35] Kalsow and his detachment of nearly seven hundred men spent April and May 1915 working on new tac-tics. To test its progress, the OHL used the unit to support a small-scale at-tack in June 1915.

The initial test was an abject failure. Kalsow lost 184 men and six field guns in two weeks. The OHL therefore had to decide whether to abandon the ex-periment because the underlying concepts were flawed or whether failure resulted from poor leadership and soldiers who failed to correctly execute the new concepts. In hindsight, poor execution seems to have been the main cause of failure. The infantry unit to which Kalsow's detachment reported ignored his advice and piecemealed his assault troops into the fight. More-over, the unit's 3.7cm field guns were too small to destroy strongpoints but too big to conceal. Therefore, they attracted enemy fire before they could do any real damage.[36]

The OHL nevertheless relieved Kalsow. His replacement, Captain Willy Rohr, took command on September 8, 1915. Rohr made several adjustments.[37] He reorganized his assault force into small eight-man squads and instructed them to maneuver independently instead of in waves. He did away with cumbersome body armor and traded the unit's 3.7cm guns for lighter guns captured from the Russian Army.[38] Rohr also equipped his men with a mix of trench mortars, rifle grenades, and captured Lewis light machine guns, which meant each eight-man squad could now fight as a self-contained all-arms team in miniature.

By October, the unit settled on a new scheme for attacking.[39] Individual squads made their own way across no-man's-land using whatever formation they deemed useful to take advantage of terrain. Since each squad had a different objective, they also maneuvered without trying to maintain contact with one another. Finally, these squads *bypassed* strongpoints instead of attacking them head-on, leaving them for mop-up units following closely behind.

The OHL decided to test these new tactics by sending Rohr's into action on the Eastern Front in October 1915. The OHL was satisfied with the results and instructed Rohr and his men to create a school to teach its methods to other units. The 8th Bavarian Reserve Division was the first unit to rotate through Rohr's course in December 1915.[40] Although not yet official doctrine, Rohr's pioneering concepts served as the basis around which the army eventually organized its new assault tactics. Evidence that the German Army was systematically developing and refining these tactics, techniques, and procedures (TTPs) indicates that the German Army had progressed to the selection phase of the learning process by the fall of 1915.

1916 Nevertheless, these changes were not yet evident in official doctrine or practice. The German Army's TTPs at the beginning of the year were not totally unlike the ones it had been using since the end of 1914. The army's initial assault at Verdun is illustrative. Although some divisions used storm troop detachments to infiltrate French lines, most attacked in waves, with soldiers usually standing a few meters from one another.[41] To be sure, some things had changed. German soldiers now followed creeping barrages instead of crossing open terrain without artillery support. The forward-most assault units now carried machine guns, and commanders were incorporating pioneers—combat engineers carrying demolitions—into the assault.

Yet important doctrinal changes were coming. In late May, the OHL published a tactical manual written by Captain Rohr titled *Instructions for the Employment of an Assault Battalion.*[42] The manual suggested attaching an eight-soldier assault squad to each battalion. These squads led attacks by scouting ahead to look for gaps and weak spots. Platoon-size units from the battalion would follow these assault squads, using irregular formations to take advantage of the terrain. Moreover, the manual called for integrating heavy weapons into every echelon of the assault force, including machine guns for flank protection, field guns to reduce fortifications and strongpoints, and mortars and grenades to kill defenders in their trenches.

General Ludendorff, who along with General Paul von Hindenburg took command of the army in August 1916, became an advocate for assault tactics.[43] The OHL officially endorsed assault tactics as part of its December 1916 *Training Manual for Foot Troops in the War*. This document represented the first wholesale update to German infantry tactics since the beginning of the war. Of course, it was one thing for the army to publish a new doctrine but quite another for German troops to demonstrate that they had mastered this new way of fighting. Thus, although the new manual was a necessary step toward assault tactics, it was far from sufficient. It would take more than a year for Ludendorff and the OHL to ensure that large numbers of German soldiers were ready to execute these new assault tactics on the battlefield.

1917 The German Army remained in the selection phase of the learning process throughout most of the year as it continued to refine its new assault tactics. As much as he advocated them, Ludendorff nonetheless wanted to make sure that these new tactical principles were fundamentally sound and that they would work on a large scale. The army therefore integrated assault tactics into their offensive plans for Riga on the Eastern Front in September and in Caporetto, Italy, in October.[44] The German Army also incorporated assault tactics into its counterattack operations, which took on a decidedly offensive orientation.[45] As I discuss below, the army's new elastic defenses in depth required precisely the same kind of aggressive, independent, and mobile small-unit actions as assault tactics.

In fact, it was the German Army's *defensive* victory at Cambrai that helped convince Ludendorff his army was ready to launch a massive offensive built around assault tactics in early 1918.[46] Cambrai initially looked like a major British victory. British units made enormous initial gains after making use of both a surprise hurricane barrage and effective infantry-tank tactics. In fact, it took German commanders ten days to counterattack. But the counterattack, once finally organized, was a masterpiece.[47] It too began with a hurricane barrage. Specially trained storm troop units then advanced behind a creeping barrage and quickly penetrated the forward-most British lines. Infantry squads followed behind, moving across no-man's-land in flexible formations, bypassing British strongpoints, and using field guns to knock out those positions they could not avoid. The German counterattack regained almost all of the ground the Germans initially lost and even managed to create a minor political crisis within the British high command.[48]

1918 The OHL definitively moved into the action phase of the learning process when it published an official assault doctrine on January 1, 1918. Titled *The Attack in Position Warfare*, this manual served as the conceptual basis for how Ludendorff wanted the army to fight. The assault doctrine called on attacking units to rely on speed and surprise to disrupt enemy units before they could bring their artillery and reserve forces to bear. In addition, the doctrine gave these units the autonomy and firepower to exploit weak points and transformed them into miniature all-arms teams.[49]

Ludendorff sought to reorganize as much of the army as possible around this new doctrine before launching his spring offensive.[50] To this end, the

OHL issued a copy of *The Attack in Position Warfare* as well as an updated *Training Manual of the Foot Troops* to every battalion staff in the army. Both documents "legitimized and systematized what had been going on at the front for nearly two years."[51] Time and resource constraints, however, presented an obstacle. Ludendorff wanted to launch his offensive in a matter of months and so did not have time to train the entire army on the Western Front. Troop quality was also a problem. The army was starting to run out of soldiers and had therefore resorted to drafting men previously deemed unfit for service. Many of these new soldiers were physically incapable of fighting like storm troopers.

Ludendorff's solution was to implement a tiered system. The OHL consolidated younger, healthier soldiers into first-line assault divisions and put everyone else in second-line trench divisions. The OHL then instituted a rotational training program. Between December 1917 and March 1918, the OHL withdrew 56 divisions—roughly equivalent of the entire British Expeditionary Force—from the front lines and sent them to one of the aforementioned monthlong assault training centers behind the Western Front.[52]

The German Army's performance during Operation Michael (March 21–April 5, 1918) and the remainder of its spring offensives offers compelling evidence that it mastered assault tactics. Frontline German units used these TTPs to penetrate 60 kilometers behind enemy lines in a little over two weeks.[53] Proficiency remained uneven, of course.[54] Many units continued to rely on old techniques even until the end of the war, not least because of Ludendorff's aforementioned decision to train only part of his army. Nevertheless, from a comparative perspective, the German infantry fought with greater doctrinal uniformity than its British and French adversaries.

COMBINED ARMS DOCTRINE

Prewar The prewar German Army did not pay sufficient attention to infantry-artillery coordination. Although German infantry officers knew artillery needed to soften defenses and destroy enemy guns,[55] they assumed their artillerymen would always be close enough to the action to see where their shells were landing, even if it meant advancing alongside the infantry in an attack.[56] Moreover, indirect-fire techniques remained cumbersome, particularly given the state of prewar communications technology. Since German commanders believed that speed was of the essence, they did not put much time and energy into developing the complex procedures needed to conduct long-range fire.[57] That said, because Germany's war plans required the destruction of Belgian forts, the prewar German Army at least had more heavy artillery than the British and French armies.[58] Since heavy artillery was capable of long-range precision fire, German gunners did probably start the war with a modest advantage over their British and French counterparts in terms of the basic conceptual building blocks needed to use indirect fire.

1914 Whatever advantages the German Army enjoyed in heavy artillery and long-range gunnery experience proved fleeting. Because they were tasked with reducing enemy fortifications, only Foot (heavy) Artillery units seem to have used indirect-fire techniques to destroy opposing forts. Meanwhile, because the prewar German Army had largely ignored infantry-artillery coordination and because Field Artillery units rarely trained alongside their infantry counterparts, many German infantry units raced into action without waiting for adequate artillery support.[59] Worse yet, German artillery sometimes hit German infantry.[60] And even when infantry commanders did wait for artillery support, Field Artillery units often suffered heavy casualties as German gunners fired from exposed positions.[61]

1915 The German Army began studying infantry-artillery coordination in earnest in 1915. First, German units on the Eastern Front started experimenting with so-called creeping (or rolling) barrages, which involved firing a line of shells just ahead of advancing infantry so as to keep defenders pinned down until the last possible moment.[62] The rest of the army was quick to adopt the practice. Second, over the summer, artillery units worked on incorporating flexibility into defensive fire plans. For example, when German commanders thought an enemy bombardment signaled an imminent infantry attack, German gunners would start targeting assembly areas where the attacking units would mass before going over the top. As soon as the pre-assault bombardment lifted, some German guns shifted fire to create a protective wall of shells directly in front of German trenches, while other guns shelled no-man's-land to wear down the assault force and interdict reinforcements.[63] Finally, on June 30 German gunners used a proto-hurricane barrage for the first time in support of a small-scale attack in the Argonne.[64] Although the attack failed, German commanders began to recognize the merits of trading destructive power for tactical surprise. These indicators suggest that the German Army entered the exploration phase of the learning process by the summer of 1915 at the latest.

1916 The German Army developed and began refining some of its most important infantry-artillery coordination concepts in 1916. These included the predicted-fire techniques needed to fire hurricane barrages as well as flexible command-and-control techniques. Many of these ideas came from German units fighting on the Eastern Front. One officer, Colonel Bruchmüller, was especially influential. Medically retired before the war, Bruchmüller was recalled to active duty and sent to the Eastern Front. While preparing a divisional artillery plan during the Lake Naroch offensive (March 18–April 14), he approached the Tenth Army's chief of staff, Colonel Hell, and suggested that the Tenth Army adopt a unified artillery plan for the initial bombardment before returning control to the divisions to support their respective individual assaults.[65]

Bruchmüller's artillery plan at Lake Naroch represented a key piece of the combined-arms puzzle.[66] His main innovation involved combining predicted fire with flexible command and control.[67] As described in a manual he wrote after the battle, the Bruchmüller process involved four steps. First, units conducted reconnaissance to produce a detailed list of enemy command posts, reserve depots, and communications nodes. Second, German gunners used predicted-fire techniques to fire a hurricane barrage against these key centers of gravity. Third, German guns shifted so as to concentrate their fire on enemy artillery. Finally, German artillery fired a creeping barrage to provide cover for the infantry assault.

The senior artillery commander within the area of operations controlled all German artillery during these first three steps. Centralized command and control made sense, because hurricane barrages and counterbattery fire tended to benefit from detailed and consolidated planning. Only corps and armies had the reconnaissance capabilities and assets to locate key command posts, reserve depots, and communication exchanges deep behind enemy lines. Moreover, since these kinds of targets were often scattered across the enemy's defensive sector, it was easier for a one senior commander to control fire against them to ensure they were neutralized before the infantry assault.[68] Flexible command and control came to play in the final phase. Division commanders regained control of their artillery so they could fire a creeping barrage in support of their division's infantry assault. Decentralized command and control made sense during the assault, since division commanders were in a better position to understand the terrain and enemy defenses within their sector. They were also closer to the fight and therefore were better able to adjust their fire support plan in light of their unit's progress. That the Bruchmüller process became standard practice across the Eastern Front soon after Lake Naroch offers compelling evidence that the German Army was engaged in a sustained effort to distill and refine Bruchmüller's methods and had therefore moved into the selection phase of the learning process by the spring of 1916.

1917 Bruchmüller's methods spread across the army over the course of 1917. They featured prominently in German battle plans at Riga, Caporetto, and Cambrai. The artillery plan for the counterattack at Cambrai shows the degree to which German infantry-artillery coordination had evolved since Lake Naroch.[69] In the week leading up to the counterattack, German gunners secretly emplaced thirteen divisions' worth of supporting artillery. Without firing a single registration round, German gunners unleashed a sixty-minute barrage, neutralizing British defenders. By this point in the war German artillery batteries were fully integrated with the infantry units they supported, as each assault element had its own field artillery battery in direct support. Because this was an exceedingly dangerous assignment for artillery gunners—they were in range of both enemy artillery and small-arms fire—infantry units also attached a platoon of engineers and a light machine gun to each artillery battery for mobility and protection.

Widespread dissemination across multiple fronts required a concerted effort to disseminate Bruchmüller's ideas and train frontline artillery units on their employment. I therefore conclude that the Cambrai counteroffensive offers compelling evidence that the German Army was well into the action phase of learning combined arms in the fall of 1917.

1918 The infantry-artillery coordination techniques developed, refined, and implemented over the preceding three years played a central role in the German Army's spring offensives. To be sure, the artillery plan for Operation Michael did not take full advantage of predicted-fire techniques. Nevertheless, German gunners made extensive use of predicted fire—in conjunction with the other aspects of the Bruchmüller process—when supporting the remaining spring offensives.[70] This widespread implementation indicates that the German Army successfully mastered combining infantry and artillery operations by the spring of 1918.

DEFENSIVE DOCTRINE

Prewar Germany's aforementioned political and strategic imperatives led the prewar German Army to prioritize offensive operations, tactics, and weapons.[71] Its doctrine therefore had little to say about defensive warfare.[72] Prewar manuals did suggest that fieldworks, including trenches and fortifications, might prove useful for protecting against enemy fire. Most officers nonetheless saw firepower as the key to holding a position. Firepower in turn depended on troop density, which meant putting as many men as possible in the defensive firing line. The 1906 ExEfdI also suggested using outposts to slow and break up an enemy assault. Yet here too, prewar commanders prioritized keeping the bulk of the defensive force in a single defensive line.

1914 German defensive practices were unsurprisingly ad hoc in 1914. The fluid nature of the fighting and the degree to which the army had overlooked defensive operations before the war meant that units received little guidance on how to hold ground. In fact, the OHL did not publish its first note on defensive tactics until early 1915. Therefore, early German defensive positions usually consisted of hastily built linear trenches, which were vulnerable to shell bursts and enfilading fire.[73] These positions lacked depth, which meant that German infantry also had nothing to fall back on when British or French infantry penetrated part of the line.[74] And because units continued to dig their trenches on the forward slopes of hills, they were easy targets for opposing artillery.

1915 The German Army responded to the lessons of 1914 with a number of minor doctrinal updates.[75] The first two modifications, dated January 7 and

January 25, firmly committed German defenses to the principle of *halten, was zu halten ist* (hold whatever can be held). This dictum obligated units to rigidly cling to every inch of ground and remained a guiding principle for units until late 1916.[76] Commanders obliged, putting as many troops as they could in the foreword-most trenches—now called the main line of resistance (MLR)—and prohibiting them from falling back until the entire position was about to be overrun.[77]

The OHL also acknowledged that positions needed a second line of trenches behind the MLR. These trenches represented an insurance policy of sorts, which could slow assault units down enough to bottle them up with reserve forces. German defenses therefore started to add depth over the course of 1915.[78] Along much of the Western Front, German units started adding strongpoints designed to cover the ground behind the MLR with machine-gun fire. And some commanders learned to billet their reserve units closer to the front, usually in unprotected houses or barns another few kilometers behind these strongpoints.

Not every unit incorporated sufficient depth into its defensive network. As a result, German positions remained dangerously shallow across much of the Western Front. Two factors seem to have contributed to uneven implementation. Some commanders felt that the army's long-standing practice of letting leaders adjust doctrine to meet local conditions meant they could ignore the guidance. Other commanders thought a second line of trenches generated a sort of moral hazard by making it more likely units might abandon the MLR when they had a second position to fall back on.

The fact that German defenses withstood a series of major offensives in the spring probably owed much to luck and poor intra-allied coordination.[79] For example, when British forces penetrated German lines at Neuve Chapelle in March, the nearest German reserves were at least twenty-four hours away. Yet instead of capitalizing on their unanticipated success, British assault units spent hours waiting for orders.[80]

These near misses, combined with the growing power of British and French artillery bombardments, convinced the OHL to take a more authoritative stance. The OHL directed units to build a three-trench secondary position outside of enemy artillery range.[81] The goal was to rob an attack of momentum by forcing British and French commanders to pause long enough to shift their artillery forward before exploiting any break-ins.[82] As a result, by early summer German defenses on the Western Front often extended at least 2.5 kilometers in depth from front to rear.[83] The emphasis on holding the MLR at all costs remained.

The OHL used a summer lull in the fighting to make additional refinements, many of which were based on lessons learned in May 1915. The OHL now called for a *three*-layered defensive network.[84] Instead of serving as the MLR, the first layer now consisted of small trenches dug on a forward slope to provide early warning and to slow an initial assault. The second layer held the bulk of the defensive force and became the new MLR. It consisted of two continuous trenches built on the *reverse* slope, usually at least two hundred meters behind the crest of a hill. The third layer, now called the "second zone," consisted of smaller trenches and strongpoints built at least a kilometer behind the MLR. Reserves were billeted two to four kilometers behind this second zone.

The OHL's summer updates to its doctrine also addressed counterattack operations. Prewar doctrine called on each unit to vigorously counterattack as soon as it lost control of part of its defensive line. New OHL guidance called for each unit to wait for an attacker to begin consolidating its new position before counterattacking. The OHL reasoned that this approach might both help German commanders catch an assault unit in the midst of an awkward transition and avoid wasting men by throwing them into the middle of the fight while the attacker's artillery was still effective.

These official doctrinal changes were important, but they do not entirely capture the entire learning story in 1915. The German Army also spent the year debating and experimenting with new techniques. Many such experiments were ad hoc and bottom up. Although these frontline adaptations were not yet enshrined in official doctrine in 1915, some served as the basis for important changes to come. The most important experiments involved Colonel Lossberg's work on defending in depth. During its Champagne offensive in September 1915, the French Army managed to break in along an eight-mile-wide front. Tasked with taking over as the chief of staff for the beleaguered Third Army, Lossberg, a General Staff officer, reorganized the Third Army's defensive positions so they were now arrayed 8 kilometers in depth.[85] In addition to the existing forward trench and MLR, he added a new defensive zone spanning from the MLR to a third trench line 2.5 kilometers back. Within this zone he positioned additional observers, artillery, and machine guns. He called this line the first rearward position and used it to house reserve units. Lossberg also instructed his units to build a second rearward position 2.5 kilometers back to house even larger reserve forces.

Lossberg's ad hoc adaptation represented the army's first comprehensive defense in depth. It was not yet elastic because Third Army defenders still tried to hold their ground at all costs. But Lossberg clearly showed that when a defense was deep enough, attackers could neither sweep through the entire position in a single thrust—at least not with the organic firepower available in 1915—nor chew through it because of the time it took to reposition artillery for each successive push.

In sum, the OHL's decision to release a series of continual updates to its defensive practices in the winter, spring, and early summer indicates that it entered the exploration phase of the learning process by the summer of 1915 at the latest.

1916 Many German positions still remained relatively shallow at the start of the year. Indeed, the typical German defense in early 1916 consisted of three sets of trench lines.[86] The first set was arrayed with two hundred meters between each trench. Two massive obstacle belts up to thirty yards in depth protected the forward-most trench, and concrete strongpoints were built approximately one thousand meters behind it. The second set of trenches, located approximately three thousand yards behind the forward-most trench in the first trench system, served as the MLR. A series of covered communications trenches now connected these second-line trenches to the first line. The third line of trenches held local reserve units. The entire defensive network therefore extended some five thousand yards in depth from front to rear. Despite these changes, most commanders continued to rigidly cling to their positions while keeping most of their soldiers in the first line of trenches.[87] Such practices were ill-advised in 1915. They proved catastrophic in 1916. By this point in the war, the British and French armies had the shells and artillery to annihilate anything within range. Entire German units simply disappeared during preassault bombardments.[88]

In fact, it seems to have taken the appalling casualties suffered during the opening phases of the Somme offensive to finally push the army to consider incorporating elasticity into its defenses. Once again, the first experiments were ad hoc responses to local conditions.[89] During preassault bombardments, frontline German units realized they were better off hiding in no-man's-land than remaining in their trenches. They used lulls in the bombardment to slip out of their trenches and into nearby shell holes. British attackers found the resulting nonlinear defenses hard to fight through, as German troops used their irregular positions to fire on assault waves from all sides.

From this experience, German commanders started toying with the idea of holding ground amid the "tangle of shell holes, mined dug-outs, quarry excavations and cellars that [now] formed the German front zone" and organizing their own rapid counterattacks with whatever forces they could quickly get their hands on.[90] Casualties and shell-hole defenses meant most German units along the Somme were spread too thin to repel an assault force. Nor could local commanders wait the eight or more hours it took for a typical counterattack order to make its way from headquarters to the front line, especially if the goal was to hit an assault force while it was still trying to consolidate. In response, some units also empowered frontline commanders to launch counterattacks without waiting for an order.[91] Lossberg, for example, divided his army's zone into subsectors, put a single officer in charge of each sector, and allowed the officers to both counterattack on their own and request reinforcements directly from division headquarters. He even gave his sector commanders control over any units that entered their sectors, even in cases where a senior officer arrived with reinforcements.[92]

Far from initially endorsing these elastic methods, the OHL continued to prohibit units from preemptively giving up ground throughout the Somme campaign.[93] It was not until Ludendorff arrived on the Western Front in late August that the German Army began to seriously consider elasticity. The issue was a key agenda item during Ludendorff's first commanders' conference, held at Cambrai in early September. Ludendorff left the meeting convinced that German units "fought too doggedly" for ground, resulting in needless casualties to hold useless ground.[94]

Ludendorff set out to revise the army's defensive doctrine. In his words:

> In sharp contrast to the form of defense hitherto employed, which had concentrated in regular and easily recognizable lines, a broad defense was now organized in deep formations, mobile and handled in loose groups. At the end of the fighting the position should, of course, still be held by us, but the infantryman need no longer say to himself, "Here I must stand or fall," but had, on the contrary, the right, within a limited range, to give way in any direction before strong enemy fire. Any part of the line that was lost was to be recovered by counter-attack. The group (of a non-commissioned officer and eight men), the importance of which had been strongly emphasized by many intelligent commanders before the war, now became officially the unit of the infantry in fighting disposition.[95]

The fact that Ludendorff and the OHL moved decisively to develop, distill, and disseminate the core tenants behind the elastic defense in depth following the commanders' conference at Cambrai in September provides compelling evidence that the German Army entered the selection phase of the learning process in the fall of 1916.

1917 The German Army wasted little time transitioning from selection to action. With input from Lossberg, Bauer, and others, the OHL issued a new defensive manual to the army on December 1, 1916.[96] Titled the *Principles of Command in the Defensive Battle in Position Warfare*, it espoused four key principles: defenders needed to remain mobile and active, firepower was more important than manpower, terrain held no intrinsic value of its own, and depth was essential.[97] The OHL published a second manual, *Principles of Field Fortification*, which provided detailed instructions for building defensive positions, a month later. Collectively, these documents indicate that the German Army entered the action phase of the learning process by the early winter of 1917.

The German Army spent the rest of the winter and early spring reorganizing its defensive positions, an effort that included its infamous withdrawal to the so-called Siegfried Position.[98] By April, German defenses along much of the Western Front were prepared to support elastic defense-in-depth operations. Divided into three zones, German positions often extended nearly 10 kilometers in depth.[99] Small groups of sentries held the forward-most sector, which was called the outpost zone and extended between 600 meters and 1 kilometer in depth. The second zone, or battle zone, started with a series of trenches located at the rear of the outpost zone. It ranged from 1.5 to 3 kilometers in depth and was littered with strongpoints, machine-gun nests, and obstacles. Unlike the outpost zone, second-zone units held out against minor attacks, raids, and incursions. When confronted with a massive assault, however, second-zone commanders could yield elastically so as to trade space for time. Official doctrine admonished them to "not be tied rigidly to one point when they can no longer find cover" and to, "within certain limits, change their position in order to escape from a very intense bombardment."[100] Another set of trenches holding a much larger force of troops was located at the rear of the battle zone. Finally, the rearward zone extended an additional 3 kilometers behind the second zone. This position held storm troop battalions and reserve units so they could launch rapid counterattacks.

Counterattacks held the scheme together. German units needed a way to retake lost ground for elastic defenses to work so as to prevent British and French forces from using bite-and-hold attacks to slowly chew through even the deepest and most flexible defenses. Therefore, the new doctrine infused German defenses with a remarkably offensive flavor by requiring units to retake ground before assault forces could consolidate.[101] The doctrine also distinguished between immediate counterattacks (*Gegenstoss*)—those carried out within twenty-four hours by nearby units—and deliberate counterattacks (*Gegenangriff*), which were well-prepared minioffensives launched by assault divisions when immediate counterattacks were not feasible.[102] To facilitate rapid planning, German doctrine allowed on-scene commanders—all the way down to the squad level—to initiate counterattacks without asking higher headquarters for permission.

These defenses quickly proved their value. They withstood a major British attack near Arras in early April.[103] More important, they blunted the French Army's Nivelle offensive (April 16–May 7), nearly knocking France out of the war in the process.[104] In fact, aside from local penetrations, German defenses on the Western Front continued to hold until the Hundred Days offensive (August 8–November 11, 1918), which brought about an end to the war. For these reasons, I consider the German Army to have mastered elastic defense in depth by the spring of 1917.

The Evolution of German Command Practices, Assessment Mechanisms, and Training Systems

The German Army, as I have argued, learned faster than its adversaries. German combat units adopted elastic defenses in depth by the spring of 1917 and practiced combined-arms and assault tactics on a widespread basis by the spring of 1918. Of course, it is entirely possible that the German Army was better at learning for reasons that had nothing to do with its organizational structure and practices. To show that ACT theory offers a valid and important explanation for this outcome, I now discuss how the army's command practices, assessment mechanisms, and training systems evolved from the late nineteenth century until the end of the war. My purpose is to demonstrate that the German Army was better at learning *because* of its moderately decentralized command practices, assessment mechanisms, and centralized training system.

COMMAND PRACTICES

Prewar The prewar German Army practiced moderately *centralized* command and control.[105] This claim might seem odd, given the popular conception of the German Army as "a rigidly hierarchical organization, with the relationship of inferiors to superiors being one of strictest obedience."[106] To be sure, German society had a reputation for being rigid and hierarchical. And the German Army, like all military organizations, was hierarchical. Yet it seems clear the German Army's command practices did not mirror that of the nation it protected, at least at the top of the organization.

In particular, senior German commanders had a long tradition of empowering subordinate leaders to exercise initiative (*Weisungsfuerhrung*).[107] Some historians trace this practice back to at least the 1860s, although others suggest it took root during the Napoleonic era.[108] Whatever its origins, the German army ultimately enshrined decentralized command and control in the concept of *Auftragstaktik*, or mission-oriented command.[109] Introduced in the 1888 ExRfdI, the practice was further detailed in the 1908 FSR, which devoted an entire chapter to the topic of how a commander should communicate orders.[110] According to this manual,

> An *order* should contain, and *only* contain, everything which the recipient requires to know to enable him to carry out independently the task assigned to him. . . . In issuing orders, detailed instructions should be especially avoided in cases where circumstances may have changed before the order can be carried out. This point is especially important in field operations . . . when orders may have to be issued extending over a period of several days. In such a case a commander's general intention should be emphasized. . . . The general views of the commander for the conduct of the intended operations should be given, but the method of execution must be left open.[111]

As unique as the practice of *Auftragstaktik* was, it is important not to overstate the degree to which the prewar German Army delegated authority. *Auftragstaktik* came with a built-in restraint against excessive decentralization. Although subordinates could diverge from established practice, they were only allowed to do so when the situation required. Officers were also professionally obligated to master regulations and doctrine before deviating from them.[112] Nor did delegation mean total freedom. *Auftragstaktik* came with the implied expectation that subordinates would operate within their commander's general framework.

In any case, the prewar German Army may have been decentralized by the standards of the time, but it remained relatively centralized in modern terms. The army did not allow junior officers, let alone noncommissioned officers, to make independent decisions. In fact, even Helmuth von Moltke (the senior) tended to empower only his senior-most commanders and preferred to issue rigid, detailed orders to even corps and division-level commanders.[113] To be sure, the German Army continued to delegate authority and autonomy to successively lower levels of command throughout the latter half of the nineteenth century. Thus, by the beginning of the war even battalion commanders were trusted to make independent decisions, making the German Army's command practices moderately centralized by the start of the war.[114]

1914 The German Army's command practices during the first months of the war defy precise categorization. At the operational level, Helmuth von Moltke (the junior) sometimes delegated autonomy to subordinate commanders. It was an approach that was not without risk. Indeed, his decision to issue *Vollmacht*—an emergency delegation of authority—played a role in his army's defeat at the Marne when one of his staff officers used it "to make the most important operational decision of the German Army in World War I: the decision to retreat from the Marne."[115] Moltke also attempted to manage the war's conduct despite often remaining far away from the front lines. In contrast, his successor—Falkenhayn, who replaced Moltke in September— was an inveterate micromanager.[116]

At the tactical level, however, the army continued to practice *Auftragstaktik*. Even when the OHL intervened in operational matters, subordinate commanders retained authority over tactical decisions.[117] Although we should be careful not to draw too many inferences from the war's chaotic first few months, it further appears that moderate levels of centralization, which meant high-ranking officers exercised autonomy that junior officers and noncommissioned officers did not, led to moderate levels of experimentation. Infantry units began working on new formations and methods almost immediately. For example, some units experimented with night attacks as early as the fall, while others tried mounting company-level assaults in December.[118]

1915 There is little evidence to suggest that the army's command practices evolved a great deal in 1915. As the Third Army's experiments with defense in depth suggest, units continued to work on new techniques and technologies. This autonomy still pertained mostly to tactical decisions, since the OHL continued to dominate—if not micromanage—operational and strategic planning.[119] At the same time, delegation over tactical matters still remained by and large in the hands of division and corps commanders, not small-unit leaders. Thus, the German Army ended the year with the same moderately centralized command practices that had defined its battlefield operations for most of the war.

1916 The army's command practices began to change in 1916 as units increasingly delegated tactical decision-making authority.[120] This shift did not mean relatively low-ranking officers now enjoyed a blank check to fight how they wished. Commanders delegated authority only under specific conditions, and they did so with the clear expectation that their subordinates would exercise their initiative and judgment in accordance with the commander's overarching plan and intent.[121]

At least three factors enabled this shift. First, the army's nascent tactical concepts required senior commanders to delegate more authority and subordinates to exercise greater initiative. Assault tactics and rapid counterattacks worked only when small-unit leaders had the training and authority to make quick on-the-spot decisions.[122]

Second, Ludendorff, after replacing Falkenhayn, pushed his generals to do more to delegate tactical autonomy to subordinates. In Ludendorff's words:

> In the long period of trench warfare, the subordination of minor leaders increased to a regrettable extent. This was a most unfortunate development, due in part to the ample supply of telephones, but also to some extent to the inexperience of subordinate leaders. Every leader needed scope for his activities. Again and again, I insisted, both with the various staffs and at General Headquarters, that there should be no limitation to these leaders' authority.[123]

Third, the army's long-standing practice of *Auftragstaktik* served as a sort of conceptual precedent that made delegation more palatable and reduced institutional resistance. To be sure, many senior officers were skeptical about devolving even more tactical control to junior leaders.[124] Nevertheless, the German Army's longstanding practice of delegated command may explain why it found it relatively easy to delegate control. For all of these reasons, I argue that the German Army employed moderately decentralized command practices by the end of 1916.

1917–1918 This practice continued to take hold throughout the rest of the war. At the lowest levels, both elasticity and counterattacks required small-unit leadership and initiative to work. Elastic defenses also required higher levels of operational flexibility. To reduce response times when organizing a counterattack, the German Army allowed frontline battalion commanders to bypass their regimental and brigade staffs entirely and coordinate directly with division headquarters. And after months of debate and confusion, the army finally gave frontline commanders total control over reinforcements entering their sector, even when a senior officer was in command of those reinforcements.

Prewar The prewar German Army arguably had one of the most sophisticated doctrinal assessment mechanism in Europe if not the world. This staff system traced its roots back to the Napoleonic wars and was composed of three main elements: the chief of the General Staff, the Great General Staff (Großer Generalstab), and the General Staff serving with the troops (Truppen Generalstab).[125] The chief of the General Staff supervised the Great General Staff and served as the kaiser's top military adviser. In peacetime, the General Staff chief did not exercise operational command over army divisions and corps, which remained under the control of the army's twenty-four regional commanders.[126] In times of war, however, the chief of the General Staff became the commander in chief of the entire army.

If the chief of the General Staff was the army's head, the Great General Staff served as its brain.[127] Centrally located in Berlin, the Great General Staff represented the best of an already elite cadre of officers. General Staff officers serving with troops were, as the term implies, staff officers attached to operational units. Each division had either a General Staff major or a lieutenant colonel who served as the division chief of staff as well as one or two additional General Staff officers as assistants.[128] Each corps had one General Staff colonel serving the corps chief of staff and up to seven other General Staff officers. Every field army had one general officer from the General Staff, who served as the army chief of staff, as well as five or more additional General Staff officers. These liaison staff officers served as the Great General Staff's eyes and ears, providing a critical conduit for transmitting information between Berlin and the front lines. General Staff officers also rotated between serving on the staff and serving in command billets.[129] This practice helped to prevent the General Staff from becoming too disconnected from operational units and vice versa.

The General Staff was perhaps best known for its operational planning. However, it also played a major role in doctrinal development.[130] Since at least Helmuth von Moltke's (the senior) term as chief of the General Staff, one of its key responsibilities was to analyze and publish historical accounts of recent conflicts. General Staff officers serving with troops acted as a systematic conduit between frontline units and the highest levels of command. Equally important, General Staff officers also "formed an informal network within the German Army, often communicating with each other outside the formal chain of command. Staff officers wrote and spoke to each other frequently and shared experiences."[131]

General Staff officers were also equipped to do more than exchange ideas. They had the training to perform rigorous analysis. Much of this capacity owed to the General Staff's ability to attract the army's best and brightest. Indeed, it was the most selective, prestigious, and meritocratic institution in the prewar army.[132] Each year, over one thousand officers applied for the 160 slots in the German War Academy (Kriegsakademie). Successful applicants usually discovered that graduating was harder than getting in. The academy's hypercompetitive three-year curriculum was arguably more demanding than most professional military education programs today, not least of which was because students had to successfully pass comprehensive exams at the end of each academic year to remain in the program.

Finally, the General Staff had the autonomy and independence to make unpopular recommendations, because staff officers enjoyed protected career pathways. Not only were they seven times more likely to be promoted to general officer, but they also received accelerated promotions, advancing an average of four years before their peers to the rank of major.[133] Such trends suggest that General Staff officers were relatively well insulated from parochial interests and payback from senior officers who might disagree with their work. Taken together, the fact that the prewar General Staff was formal, prestigious, and independent suggests that the German Army started the war with a fully functioning assessment mechanism.

1914 The General Staff spent most of 1914 adjusting to its wartime role. As chief of the Prussian General Staff, Moltke (the junior) took command over the entire German Army. General Staff officers assigned to combat units and the OHL acted as a conduit between the Great General Staff, which remained in Berlin, and the front. And the Great General Staff almost immediately began collecting and analyzing after-action reports to update doctrine and training. Even in 1914, the staff was often able to alert the entire German Army to changes in enemy tactics within two weeks.[134]

At the same time, several factors limited the General Staff's ability to immediately prioritize doctrinal analysis. The task of mobilizing millions of soldiers and then transporting them from one theater of operations to the other proved all-consuming. The prewar General Staff was also undermanned. It started the war with a mere 625 officers, many of whom were assigned to frontline units.[135]

1915 Fully adapted to the wartime environment, the General Staff began functioning as a genuine doctrinal assessment mechanism in 1915. General Staff officers rotated between the Great General Staff, the OHL, and the front lines. They often played a prominent role advocating or personally developing new doctrinal concepts. Colonel Lossberg worked on adding depth to defenses. Another General Staff officer, Lieutenant Colonel Max Bauer, was instrumental in helping to develop assault tactics and defensive doctrine.[136]

General Staff officers with the Great General Staff and the OHL actively solicited ideas from frontline units and pursued those that appeared to have value.[137] They were also willing to copy the British and the French. For example, the staff obtained a copy of a captured French memo in April 1915 that suggested adding elasticity to defensive positions, principles that the OHL would eventually incorporate into its defensive schemes.[138] They also eventually obtained a copy of Captain André Laffargue's pamphlet on assault tactics.[139]

Finally, General Staff officers fiercely debated the mandate to hold the front line at all costs, which is indicative of the degree to which the institution tolerated dissenting points of view.[140] Most senior officers still believed in rigidly defending the MLR. Despite his pioneering work on defending in depth, even Lossberg held this view. A vocal group of relatively junior staff officers, however, including Major Bauer, began to argue for adding more flexibility, holding frontline trenches with small garrisons, and affording the on-scene commander the latitude to fall back as needed.

1916 The OHL and the General Staff solidified the German Army's after-action processes over the course of 1916. These efforts served as the basis for analyzing lessons learned and distributing what they saw as the best practices.[141] In particular, the OHL and the General Staff finally required frontline divisions and corps to submit lessons-learned reports (*Erfahrungsberichte*) to the OHL after major engagements.[142] Such practices were particularly important given the frontline adaptations and learning that occurred during the Somme offensive. As Robert Foley highlights, General Staff officers "were responsible for writing the lessons-learned reports and creating new doctrine within the German Army."[143] Indeed, many of the concepts on which assault tactics, combined arms, and elastic defenses in depth were based can trace their origins or development to 1916. To be sure, some of these ideas were transmitted directly between frontline units. Yet even this horizontal transmission inevitably entailed General Staff officers serving with troops communicating directly with one another. More crucially, it is hard to imagine how the necessary process of capturing, refining, and disseminating new ideas as formal doctrine could have occurred without the General Staff functioning as both a conduit and analytic mechanism. Nor was formal top-level endorsement a mere rubber stamp. Individual units— even corps and armies—lacked the resources to rebuild enormous swaths of the German Army's defensive network on the Western Front (e.g., the Siegfried Position) or to fundamentally revamp training programs for conscripts, combat units, staffs, and general officers to ensure uniformity to the degree that the German Army did in 1917 and 1918. Fundamental transformation of this magnitude required buy-in from the highest levels of command, which the General Staff made possible.

1917 Ludendorff, the OHL and the General Staff continued to assess and refine elastic defense in depth, combined arms, and assault tactics in 1917 in response to the ever-evolving British and French tactics[144] and spent much of the latter half of 1917 finalizing and writing a new assault doctrine. It is important to point out that the OHL did not rule by fiat when it came to doctrine. However much it might have micromanaged operational decisions, the OHL encouraged discussion, debate, and even dissent over doctrine. For example, two key aspects of the elastic defense in depth generated resistance. As discussed, many frontline commanders disliked voluntarily giving up ground. Others opposed letting a junior on-scene commander lead counterattacks, especially when this meant taking over reinforcement units led by a senior officer.[145] Although Ludendorff advocated both practices, he not only tolerated disagreement—he actively supported it. For example, Lossberg was a critic of incorporating elasticity into German defenses.[146] Although he would eventually warm to the idea, he wrote a memo outlining reasons why units should not voluntarily yield ground. After reading Lossberg's memo, Ludendorff published and promulgated it to every division in the army.[147] He even incorporated some of Lossberg's views into updated versions of the army's defensive doctrine. Ludendorff recognized that the defensive fight would have to be waged both for and within the front lines, thereby accepting Lossberg's preferred method of putting more troops in the outpost zone and ensuring that that they did not pull out at the first signs of a pending attack.[148]

TRAINING SYSTEMS

Prewar The prewar German Army took a relatively centralized approach to training. Two-year conscripts made up the bulk of the active-duty army, which had approximately 840,000 soldiers in 1914. The army inducted its entire cohort of new conscripts every October, which meant it had to provide introductory training for nearly half of its active force every single year.[149] Each of the peacetime army's twenty-four administrative districts contained one corps. New conscripts reported for duty to their local administrative districts, which in turn assigned them to a regiment near where they lived. Regiments then divided their conscripts among their subordinate battalions, which turned around and assigned them to their companies for training.

This approach perhaps seems like an example of extreme decentralization. After all, each of the army's administrative districts contained one corps, each corps had two divisions, each division had two brigades, each brigade had two regiments, each regiment had three battalions, and each battalion had four companies. The implication is that over two thousand different units handled training for hundreds of thousands of new soldiers every single year. However, the army used a number of tools to impose order and consistency on the process. First, the entire army followed a standardized training calendar.[150] From October to January, units focused on physical fitness, close-order drills, and individual combat skills. From the end of January until

March, they shifted to small-unit training. In March, units put new recruits into sections and platoons with seasoned (second-year) conscripts and conducted company-level maneuvers. Battalion-level exercises consumed April. Finally, the entire army spent May to August preparing for large-unit (regimental and above) exercises, which were usually held from August to September. The army used September to usher second-year conscripts out of the army and prepared to repeat the entire process again in October.

The German Army also had an inspector general of military training and education (IGMTE). The IGMTE had the authority to inspect regimental depots and access the highest echelons of command.[151] Although the billet's power ebbed and flowed over time, it nonetheless helped offset the otherwise centrifugal forces of decentralized training. Created in 1855, the IGMTE sat on the Defense Commission alongside the chief of the General Staff, the commanding general of the Guard Corps, and the commanding generals of the Army Corps, which made him a powerful figure in the army.[152] The IGMTE managed an extensive network of inspectors, who in turn supervised the army's rigorous inspection system. The Superior Military Committee of Studies, for example, was composed of thirteen senior generals and controlled the training and education for every military school except for the War Academy. Other inspection agencies included the Superior Military Examination Committee, the Corps of Cadets, the Combined Artillery and Engineer Schools, and the Inspector of the Infantry Schools.[153] The kaiser thought inspections sufficiently important that he issued inspection guidance in his royal order of March 31, 1889.[154] Inspections were a regular part of the training cycle, and every infantry battalion in the army was inspected at least thirteen times a year. IGMTE inspectors also had the authority to discipline errant units and instructors.[155]

The German Army maintained an even tighter grip over officer training. Not only were officer candidate schools subject to the same rigorous inspection system as conscript training, but the IGMTE also maintained control over every aspect of officer screening, selection, and training.[156] Furthermore, unlike conscript training, most initial officer training was done at a relatively small number of geographically consolidated schools. Young men who wanted to become officers usually had to enroll in a cadet school, which fell under the IGMTE's purview. After graduating from cadet school, all aspiring officers then had to attend a war school (not to be confused with the War Academy). These schools, which taught weapons, ordnance, tactics, fortification, topography, survey, drawing, regulations, correspondence, riding, fencing, gym, and swimming, also fell under the IGMTE. To ensure quality control, the army created a specific department under the IGMTE in 1875 called the Inspektion der Kriegsschulen with the sole purpose of monitoring instruction at officer candidate schools.[157]

Compared to officer training, noncommissioned officer training remained less centralized, but it was still supervised and inspected. Prospective noncommissioned officers attended training at specifically designated noncommissioned officer schools operated by each division. Such schools were subject to IGMTE inspection, as were noncommissioned officers' sustainment training courses held in each unit.

1914 Training took a back seat to operations in 1914. The demands of rapid mobilization and the chaos of the first months of fighting meant the army had neither the time nor the resources to worry about training new soldiers. In fact, the army's aggressive pace of operations did not allow time for reservists, retirees, and recruits to receive sufficient training despite the fact that such troops played a leading role in offensive actions throughout the war's opening phase.[158]

1915 Despite its massive expansion, the German Army's prewar training structure remained intact throughout 1915. At the beginning of the war, mobilized regiments left a small cadre behind to train new conscripts, who were then formed into replacement drafts for the unit.[159] The army did, however, implement two minor changes. After commanders complained that regimental depot training was not preparing recruits for life in the trenches, the OHL created a series of additional training depots immediately behind the front lines to give replacements additional combat training.[160] The OHL also organized specialty and refresher courses for seasoned troops and units already at the front. Rohr's *sturmabteilung* became the cadre for one such school.[161]

1916 The army began to exert more control over training in 1916.[162] In April, it expanded Rohr's *sturmabteilung* so as to increase its ability to train other units.[163] In May, Falkenhayn further directed that every field army on the Western Front send a cadre to Rohr's assault battalion for initial training. These cadres would then return to their respective field army to serve as an internal assault training battalion.[164]

Training became even more standardized and centralized under Ludendorff.[165] The army established new schools, including those for company and platoon commanders, noncommissioned officers, and specialists.[166] The OHL also issued training manuals that the entire army was obliged to use.[167] Furthermore, Ludendorff recognized that senior officers were among the most likely and powerful sources of resistance to resist his new doctrine. To deal with this challenge, he authorized the creation of two training schools for general officers and their staffs at Solesmes and Sedan. The school for division commanders at Solesmes even had an infantry division at its disposal to facilitate realistic and rigorous training.[168] On January 1, 1917, he gave General Otto von Moser command over both of these schools.[169] Thus, it seems clear that the German Army developed a centralized training system by the end of 1916. This system combined a high-ranking general officer with power over inspections and administration with as much geographic consolidation as would have been possible given that the army was waging a multifront war.

1917 Training remained centralized in 1917. Ludendorff continued to send commanders and staffs to schools in light of a number who either did not understand or chose not to implement elastic defenses in depth.[170] The OHL promulgated new instructions and training manuals,[171] while also updating the curriculum at Sedan and Valenciennes so as to prepare frontline units to use assault tactics. In December, Ludendorff began pulling units off the line to train on the army's new assault tactics.[172] Training for commanders and staff at the aforementioned officer schools was likewise revamped to ensure they were prepared for the upcoming spring offensives.[173]

1918 In the final analysis, the German Army could not have retrained one-third of its Western Front divisions in a matter of a few months had it not already possessed a highly centralized training system. By 1918 the army already had years of experience running large training centers, which provided both the infrastructure and the standard operating procedures in place to enable a rapid doctrinal shift. What the schools taught was less important than that they existed in the first place and were subject to tight control in the second place. Finally, these schools played a critical role in overcoming institutional inertia and resistance. Although frontline soldiers made up the bulk of the trainees, Ludendorff knew that the real obstacle to change came from career officers and senior leadership and insisted that senior leaders attend training just like their men.[174]

The German Army's experience on the Western Front offers compelling evidence in support of ACT theory. The theory's explanatory variables operated as predicted. The German Army started the war with moderately centralized command practices, an effective assessment mechanism, and a moderately centralized training system. The army moved toward a war-fighting doctrine based on what we now know to have been a better set of war-fighting tactics, particularly after it loosened control over its command practices (at least at the tactical level) while increasing control over training. Moreover, the key explanatory variables were in place *before* the German Army mastered these superior war-fighting practices. Although the German Army did start exploring assault tactics, combined arms, and elastic defenses in depth before it fully embraced moderately decentralized command practices, recall that the exploration hypothesis does not predict that *only* militaries that practice moderately decentralized command and control will experiment or are capable of entering the exploration phase of the learning process. Rather, exploration hypothesis simply expects that a military with moderately decentralized command practices will begin exploring *before* one practicing moderately centralized (or highly centralized or highly decentralized) command and control. And as the next two chapters will show, the British and French armies both practiced moderately decentralized command and control at the start of the war, and both entered the exploration phase of the learning process before the German Army.

The evidence presented in this chapter also suggests that learning was not simply correlated with the German Army's command practices, assessment mechanism, and training system. Rather, these factors helped it learn faster than its adversaries. Frontline units experimented because the army's command practices allowed them to do so, especially after 1916. The army's culture also ensured that senior generals listened to suggestions from below. And many of these ideas helped transform the army's war-fighting doctrine. The General Staff collected, analyzed, and selected from among the best concepts and decided which ones to invest in for further testing and refinement. This was especially evident in the case of the army's work on assault tactics but also played out with combined arms and the elastic defense in depth. And the army was able to rapidly transmit its new tactical doctrines, no matter how radical, through an efficient top-down approach to training.

The British Army on the Western Front

Of all the armies that struggled to break the deadlocked Western Front, history has been especially unkind to the British Expeditionary Force (BEF).[1] A myth of British military incompetence took root in the mid-twentieth century in books, film, television, and literature.[2] This image of "lions led by donkeys" persists,[3] even in the face of a forty-year-old historiography debunking it.[4] To be sure, the BEF fell behind the French and German armies in terms of doctrinal development early on in the war. There were a number of reasons for this lag. Some had to do with the BEF's organizational attributes and practices. Others, such as exponential growth between 1914 and 1916, owed to long-standing political and grand strategic choices that were beyond the BEF's power to control. Regardless, by war's end the BEF had moved beyond its ally and closed the doctrinal gap with its enemy. Thus, the real story of the BEF is one of an organization that evolved into a learning organization and was able to undertake profound change as a result.

The BEF's experience with doctrinal learning aligns with assessment, command, and training (ACT) theory's predictions. Although confounding factors complicate the causal story to a greater degree, it nevertheless seems clear that the prewar British Army practiced moderately centralized command and control. However, unlike the German Army, the BEF increased control over tactics and operations from early 1915 until at least mid-1916. The BEF also lacked a doctrinal assessment mechanism for the first half of the war and maintained a loose grip over training. Then, starting with the Somme offensive, senior commanders began to delegate authority again. General Headquarters (GHQ) established a formal assessment mechanism, called the Training Branch, in February 1917. The BEF began converging on the right tactical concepts shortly thereafter. The war ended before the process of fully mastering assault tactics and elastic defenses in depth was complete. British combined arms, however, were at least as advanced as those used by the German Army by war's end.

The fact that the BEF's command practices, assessment mechanism, and training systems changed over the course of the war offers compelling evidence that a causal link existed between the army's organizational structure and practices and its ability to learn. The army's transition to centralized command and control inadvertently reduced frontline experimentation, which made it harder for new ideas generated on the front lines to reach the army's high command. As the BEF transitioned back toward moderately decentralized command and control, the opposite occurred. Training Branch enabled the BEF to systematically capture, test, analyze, and disseminate new ideas. And although the army did not truly centralize training until the very end of the war, this is the point at which we see its frontline units progress most rapidly toward what we now know to have been the superior way to fight on the Western Front.

The Evolution of British Politics, Strategy, and Operations

Long-standing British grand strategy meant the prewar army had to juggle three competing—if not irreconcilable—missions.[5] The British Army had to garrison Britain's far-flung colonial empire, which meant scattering troops across the globe. The army had to be ready to wage a large-scale high-intensity war on the continent, which meant rapidly consolidating and projecting power across the English Channel. And the army had to defend the home islands against invasion, which ironically meant protecting a nation that feared its own army almost as much as it did an invading one.[6]

The army prioritized its colonial mission for a number of reasons. Empire fueled the economy, which kept Britain atop the international system. Colonial crises seemed far more likely than a continental war, let alone an invasion.[7] Finally, many senior officials assumed that the Royal Navy would serve as Britain's main effort in a general European war.[8] A widespread consensus also held that the best way to fulfill the colonial mission was to build the army around a small force of long-serving volunteers. Britain rejected mass conscription for a number of practical and philosophical reasons. They saw it as incompatible with colonial duty, since it took years to rotate units to far-flung garrisons and back again. Many also saw mass conscription as fundamentally opposed to liberty.

By emphasizing its colonial mission, the army had less time and fewer resources to prepare for high-intensity conventional warfare. The Second Boer War made this trade-off glaringly apparent.[9] The government implemented a range of far-reaching changes in the wake of the army's disastrous performance in that conflict. These so-called Haldane reforms included abolishing the post of commander in chief, creating a general staff, reorganizing the reserve force, and, perhaps most important, organizing a standing expeditionary force, the BEF.[10]

These reforms notwithstanding, the British Army was still not ready for war in August 1914. Hew Strachan suggests that Britain tried to wage war on a continental scale without bothering to first raise a continental army.[11] Ready or not, the BEF spent early August mobilizing and deploying to France. Originally, the government planned to send the entire BEF—six infantry divisions and one cavalry division—to France, where it would protect the French Army's left flank. However, at the last moment Field Marshal Lord Horatio Herbert Kitchener, the newly appointed secretary of state for war, decided to retain two infantry divisions for home defense.[12] Therefore, by August 20, four of the BEF's six divisions plus the aforementioned cavalry division were ready for action on the French Army's left flank.[13]

They did not have to wait long. The German First Army smashed into the recently arrived BEF near Mons on August 23. British soldiers mounted a stout defense but were ultimately forced to withdraw. They conducted a fighting withdraw through early September, buying time for France to pull its army back.[14] Following the Miracle on the Marne and the Race to the Sea, the BEF blocked a final German attempt to break through at Ypres in late October and early November. The BEF spent the rest of the year holding about twenty miles of front.

An unambiguous imperative drove British strategy, operations, and tactics from this point on. The BEF had to expel the German Army from Belgium and France. Because it could not defeat the German juggernaut by itself, the BEF had to fight as part of a larger coalition. Coordinating its operations with the French Army allowed Britain to generate far more military power that it could on its own. But as France's junior partner, the BEF was not free to decide when or where to fight.[15]

Britain's initial plan was therefore to husband its manpower while building a mass volunteer army as quickly as it could, with an eye toward seeking decisive victory in 1917.[16] Yet this strategy left many questions unanswered. How should Britain assist its allies in the meantime? Was the Western Front the decisive theater? No one could answer these questions in 1914, leaving the BEF to react to events as best as it could. It did what it could to reinforce frontline combat units. Soldiers entrenched wherever they happened to stop. And British commanders, under pressure to do something to help their ally, launched small-scale attacks on German lines.

The British Army's strategic conundrum grew worse in 1915. The army was still too small to wage a multitheater war of attrition. The crash expansion also placed a tremendous burden on government and military leaders. It is also an important confounding factor that must have had an impact on the BEF's ability to learn early in the conflict. The army absorbed 2.46 million volunteers in the war's first fifteen months, ten times the number in its prewar regular component,[17] and struggled to absorb this influx.[18] Industry and manufacturing also took time to adapt to surging demand. Units therefore dealt with crushing ammunition shortages through 1916.[19]

Complicating matters further, not everyone agreed that the Western Front represented the main theater of action. The war had already morphed from a continental conflict into a global one, with British troops engaged around the world. As a result, even as the army was frantically building up its combat power in France, Sir Winston Churchill, David Lloyd George, and other powerful political leaders pushed for a so-called Eastern strategy.[20] In contrast to army leaders, who thought the only way to defeat Germany was to defeat its army in France, Churchill and others wanted to target its weakest ally, the Ottoman Empire.[21]

Again, the BEF could not sit idle, biding its time until it had enough combat power to mount a decisive push.[22] France needed immediate help. The commander in chief of the French Army at the time, Marshal Joseph Joffre, described the situation in stark terms. "The best and largest portion of the German Army was on our soil, with its line of battle jutting out a mere five days' march from the heart of France."[23] Operationally, this reality forced the BEF to thread a needle between alliance imperatives and material limitations. The BEF responded by mounting a series of relatively small-scale attacks at Neuve Chapelle, Aubers Ridge, Festubert, and Loos. These were usually timed to coincide with larger French offensives. As I discuss at length below, these attacks became ever more artillery-centric as increasingly complex and powerful bombardments preceded infantry assaults, especially after the Battle of Neuve Chapelle in March 1915.[24] Still, it is important to remember that these offensives were neither designed nor intended to achieve a decisive breakthrough. Douglas Haig, who assumed command of the BEF in December 1915, long believed that a continental war would be one of attrition. Since he now commanded an army that could not yet mount a decisive operation, he sought to wear down the German Army until a chance to break through presented itself.[25]

The BEF finally reached full strength in 1916. Haig wanted to hit the German Army in Flanders, but alliance considerations compelled him to support a French-led offensive along the Somme River instead.[26] Joffre believed that a combined attack in that sector might draw German units in, enabling Russia and the BEF to launch follow-on offensives on the Eastern Front and in Flanders, respectively.[27] Germany unfortunately preempted the plan by launching an offensive of its own at Verdun in late February. Thus, the Somme offensive, which started as a French-led campaign to draw German forces away from the British Army, turned into a British-led attack designed to relieve pressure on the French Army. The campaign devolved into a five-month-long quagmire.[28] It was one of several crises that caused Prime Minister Herbert Asquith's government to collapse in December. The man succeeding him, Lloyd George, was one of Haig's chief critics and therefore played a more active role in both managing the war and attempting to marginalize Haig.[29]

Operationally, by 1916 the BEF embraced "the artillery conquers, the infantry occupies" concepts it had started to explore in 1915.[30] Scale and power notwithstanding, these bombardments suffered from the shortcomings discussed in Chapter 2. Modest gains were still possible so long as commanders kept their objectives limited.[31] But the results were disastrous when units received more ambitious assignments that took them beyond the range of British guns.[32]

By early 1917, the Entente was in disarray.[33] Verdun and the Somme were costly, hurting stalemates. Germany managed to erase Russia's gains during the Brusilov offensive, knocking Romania out of the war in the process. The United States remained firmly planted on the sidelines. And having just won reelection on an isolationist platform, President Woodrow Wilson was now pressuring the Entente to seek peace. Nor did either the British or French armies possess a proven tactical solution to deadlock, although the French Army's new chief of staff, Robert Nivelle, claimed to have one. And yet, having just rejected twin peace offers from Russia and the United States, the British high command was confident it could win the war in 1917.

The overarching allied strategy called for coordinated offensives by the British, French, Italian, and Russian armies to overwhelm the German Army and its reserves. The BEF's role was to attack at Arras in early April, drawing in German units and creating an opening the French army could then exploit with an even larger attack along the Aisne River. The British attacks succeeded, but German defenses eviscerated the French Army's thrust. The consequences were catastrophic for French morale and compelled Haig to mount a diversionary attack at Messines and another major offensive—the Third Battle of Ypres—in Flanders.[34] This period also signified an important moment for the alliance, as the BEF transitioned from junior to leading partner on the Western Front.

Operationally, the BEF took the lessons of the previous year to heart. As a result, 1917 represented the high-water mark for set-piece bite-and-hold attacks for limited objectives. These operations showed that the BEF could now seize almost any position through a combination of methodical planning, overwhelming artillery firepower, and shallow infantry objectives.[35] Unfortunately, they also revealed a crucial shortcoming: "the BEF still had major problems in capitalising on initial success, in moving from static and semi-mobile warfare into battles of manoeuvre."[36] It would take a holistic doctrine incorporating modern combined-arms techniques and infantry assault tactics to achieve that goal.

By year's end, the BEF launched a series of attacks that suggested it was working toward just such a solution. The Battle of Menin Road in late September featured both a hurricane bombardment and flexible infantry tactics.[37] The attack near Cambrai in November turned out to be one of the BEF's most innovative operations—and biggest tactical successes. Combining a hurricane barrage with effective tank-infantry operations, British troops penetrated almost six miles into German defenses. But the BEF was not able to capitalize on its success. Domestically, casualties suffered during the Third Battle of Ypres robbed Haig of the political support he would need to mount another offensive. Mutinies and manpower struggles prevented France from resuming large-scale offensives to the south. And Britain was finally start-ing to suffer from a manpower crisis of its own. For the first time since 1914, the BEF had no choice but to revert to the strategic defensive.[38]

The year 1918 dawned with no one in the British high command seriously thinking that victory was possible until 1919 at the earliest. Britain's man-power situation worsened.[39] The French were still not ready to resume of-fensive operations. Russia and Italy were out of the war, and the United States, for all practical intents and purposes, was not yet in. Haig knew that the German Army planned to exploit this window of opportunity and there-fore expected to spend the entire year defending along the Western Front.

Lloyd George was also ready to fire Haig but did not because he felt that "no one could be found who was significantly better than Haig" and, in any case, knew that Haig still enjoyed widespread support within the army.[40] Lloyd George therefore did the next best thing: he dismissed Haig's most powerful advocates within the military, including Field Marshal Sir William Robertson, chief of the Imperial General Staff, and Sir Launcelot Edward Kig-gell, the BEF's chief of staff and Haig's principal adviser. Lloyd George also agreed to subordinate the BEF to a French general, Marshal Ferdinand Foch.[41] Nevertheless, neither Lloyd George nor Foch tried to tell the BEF how to fight. Lloyd George may have been convinced of Haig's incompetence, but the prime minister remained oblivious to the technical and tactical challenges facing troops on the Western Front.

Operationally, the British Army spent the first half of the year on the de-fensive, absorbing the German attacks. The army shifted to the offensive in July, launching a series of rapid strikes and maintaining pressure against German lines for the rest of the war. First came the spring offensives, span-ning from March to July, followed by a French counterattack on the Marne River. The war ended with the British Army's final Hundred Days offensive, which spanned from August until November.

The Evolution of British Tactical Doctrine

OFFENSIVE DOCTRINE

Prewar The same basic debate over firepower versus shock power that roiled the prewar German officer corps also played out in the British Army. But the one that unfolded in the British Army was informed by firsthand experience. Indeed, the Second Boer War (1899–1902) triggered intense de-liberation within the British officer corps, not least because it took the army three years, nearly half a million soldiers, and the might of an entire empire to subdue a ragtag army of Dutch farmers.[42]

A slew of official inquiries and reforms followed. Debate over doctrine likewise intensified. Most officers agreed that breech-loading rifles, machine guns, and rapid-fire artillery unleashed an unprecedented level of firepower on the modern battlefield.[43] They did not, however, agree on a definitive set of tactics that would enable infantry to defeat a well-prepared defense.[44] British firepower advocates wanted units to spread out and carry their own lightweight rapid-fire weapons.[45] They also called for swarm formations and tactics so that small teams could make their own way toward the objective. They accepted that dispersion might slow an attack down. But they thought the loss of speed was an acceptable prince to pay, since flexible formations would let units reduce casualties by taking advantage of terrain. Shock-power advocates, on the other hand, admitted that dense linear formations increased losses.[46] Yet they thought that higher casualties were worth the price, because density also helped maintain speed, which reduced exposure to enemy fire, and created the psychological pressure needed to keep men moving across an increasingly lethal battlefield.

The British Army also published its first true doctrinal manuals during this period, including a series of new field service regulations (FSR) and infantry training (IT) guides.[47] "A landmark in British military thinking, the FSR manuals were intended to provide officers with precise instructions designed to meet every wartime contingency that could be imagined."[48] Between the Boer War and the First World War, the army published four IT (1902, 1905, 1911, and 1914) and two FSR (in 1909 and 1912) manuals. When considered in conjunction with a number of other subordinate training guides, these manuals captured and shaped official British tactical thinking before the war.[49]

The contents of the 1902 IT suggest that firepower advocates had gained the upper hand, since it departed from a number of the army's long-standing tactical practices.[50] It told commanders that "the main object of the attack is to attain superiority of fire," although it continued to insist that linear formations were best for massing fire.[51] The manual suggested that commanders divide their attack force into three echelons: scouts, a firing line, and reserves. The idea was for scouts to advance roughly half a mile ahead of the main force to locate the enemy position and take it under fire.[52] The firing line would then move up. Its goal was to achieve fire superiority over the defense by putting as many men in the firing line as possible—at least one soldier per yard.[53] Although the idea that units needed to mass men in order to mass firepower was decidedly a shock-power idea, the 1902 IT nevertheless recognized that "on open ground and at effective ranges, long lines of men rising simultaneously, and making even short rushes forward, will generally suffer heavy losses."[54] The manual instead instructed soldiers to advance in groups, which would take turns shooting and moving. The obligatory bayonet charge occurred only after the firing line decisively overwhelmed the enemy position with fire.

The 1902 IT manual represented the high-water mark for firepower advocates, especially in comparison what subsequent manuals called for.[55] Moreover, the 1902 IT manual implied that infantry units needed more than just rifles to generate firepower on the battlefield.[56] And the manual suggested that commanders demonstrate caution when moving across open terrain, something future manuals discarded.[57] At the same time, the 1902 IT did not espouse assault tactics. Despite meaningfully breaking tactical tradition, it still had a great deal in common with the doctrines that preceded and followed. Tactical formations remained linear, and the assault still ended with a final sweeping bayonet charge.

In any case, the British Army's shift toward firepower tactics proved short-lived. The army published its two-part FSR in 1909 (and updated the manual in 1912) along with supporting IT manuals in 1911 and 1914. These documents reveal an army reverting back to shock-power tactics. Although we now know that shock-power tactics were the wrong answer to the firepower problem, the British Army compounded its mistake by reverting in an incomplete way. Like the German Army's doctrine from which the British Army liberally borrowed, the 1909 and 1912 FSR struck something of an untenable middle ground between shock-power and firepower tactics. The army's final set of prewar doctrinal concepts continued to emphasize that rapid-fire weapons dominated modern battlefields, discouraged commanders from moving across open terrain without suppressing enemy gunners, and left the basic scheme of maneuver essentially intact.[58] The 1912 FSR also reminded commanders that "the climax of the infantry attack is the assault, which is made possible by superiority of fire," implying that far from a wild dash into the teeth of an enemy defense, assaults needed effective suppression to succeed.[59]

At the same time, the 1912 FSR called for firing lines to achieve a density of *three to five* soldiers per yard.[60] Moreover, during the 1909 General Staff Conference, several shock-power advocates complained that infantry units were ignoring the requirement to increase the density of their firing lines before the assault. Colonel Haldane phrased the critique as such:

> If a battalion builds up a very thick firing line, so fixed is the idea—an idea for which the South African war is to blame—in the heads of umpires [exercise observers] that it is laying itself open to suffer heavy casualties, that in nine cases out of ten it would be put out of action [by the umpires observing the exercise]. Our infantry officers in many battalions still regard a thick firing line as an absurdity and think that troops can only advance when spread out over a very wide front, instead of realizing that it is by obtaining superiority of fire and not by avoiding loss that infantry alone can win battles.[61]

The 1912 FSR contained other inconsistencies.[62] Despite focusing on the importance of achieving fire superiority before mounting the final assault, the manual did not consider using machine guns or other rapid-fire weapons to augment the infantry assault force. The manual also maintained that firepower alone could not win a battle and that the bayonet remained king even in an age of rapid long-range firepower. Nor did the 1912 FSR suggest a practical way for a commander to decide when he had—or, more importantly, when he had not—achieved fire superiority. Perhaps most problematic, rhetoric sometimes substituted for substance. For example, the 1912 FSR warned against mounting a bayonet attack in the absence of fire support but used language that seemed to endorse rash action, pushing commanders to act "decisively," avoid "half-hearted measures," and "press forward at all costs."

In the end, we should not be surprised that many frontline commanders ignored the letter of the law while adhering to its spirit in August 1914. Military historian Paddy Griffith succinctly describes the doctrinal confusion on the eve of the First World War:

> The whole officer corps therefore remained uncertain about just what assault tactics it was supposed to follow. . . . It all made for a central ambiguity, which has been rightly blamed for many of the disasters of the war. Although it was far from the case that everyone embraced a reckless cult of the offensive, it remained true that too little prohibition was imposed upon those who might be leaning in that direction.[63]

1914 Like its ally and its adversary, the BEF did not have time to fundamentally alter tactics in the war's first chaotic months. Gary Sheffield even goes so far as to suggest that the BEF's prewar tactics were fundamentally sound and that many of the early setbacks resulted from commanders misapplying them.[64] Units nevertheless identified a range of problems with prewar regulations and showed a willingness to experiment with alternatives. For example, they discovered that dispersion was more important than prewar doctrine allowed. Because German artillery outranged the BEF's guns, units learned to spread out after coming under fire. The General Staff also circulated an early set of tactical notes that advised against using column formations when under attack, suggesting that units instead adopt "loose, elastic formations adapted to the ground with men at 8 to 10 paces," although this did not become standard practice until the end of the war.[65] Infantry units realized they needed more firepower. At the start of the war, British infantry battalions had only two machine guns each.[66] Companies and platoons had none.[67] However, commanders were willing to explore alternative ways to use what few machine guns they had, even if this sometimes meant suboptimal employment. For example, it was not uncommon for units to use machine guns as a form of light artillery, firing from behind cover so as to rain bullets down on top of defenders.[68] The foregoing suggests that the BEF entered the exploration phase of the learning process by the fall of 1914.

1915 Frontline units continued working on innovative infantry techniques through the first part of 1915. January to May represented a high point for small-unit experimentation, as units searched for ways to integrate firepower and maneuver.[69] British divisions in particular seemed willing to test new tactics. Most such work focused on giving infantry units more firepower and allowing them to advance under the effects of their own suppression.[70] At Neuve Chapelle in March, British commanders used the cover of darkness to sneak field artillery into the front-most trenches and send small groups of soldiers forward to begin infiltrating German lines.[71] The attack failed but not because the tactics were fundamentally unsound. Rather, the assault units did not know what to do after successfully breaking into the German line.[72] By the time the assault units renewed their attack seven hours later, German commanders had established a hasty reserve line blocking the breach.

British tactics at Aubers Ridge in early May proved even more progressive. Having learned that field guns were too vulnerable when positioned in the front trenches, Haig's First Army instead put light cannons, heavy machine guns, and engineers in the assault waves.[73] But these tactics did not prevent disaster. The BEF lost ten thousand men in the first ten minutes of the battle.[74] The failure had more to do with poor infantry-artillery coordination and inappropriate formations than experimental firepower practices.[75] The preassault barrage lifted before the first infantrymen climbed out of their trenches, and the infantry crossed no-man's-land in long waves with men standing three paces apart.

Thus, by late spring some British units were using techniques that were arguably more advanced than anything the German Army was working on at the same time.[76] But this period of intense experimentation did not last. The BEF began to embrace a new approach to offensive operations—one emphasizing methodical artillery bombardments to pulverize defenses before the infantry went into action—over the course of the spring. Commanders therefore decided that infantry tactics needed to adapt to the artillery plan. They became increasingly rigid, linear, and stereotyped in the process. At Festubert in mid-May, British infantry went over the top in dense waves and equipped with only rifles and bayonets following a multiday bombardment. Commanders packed even more men in the assault waves when the BEF attacked again at Loos in September. Worse yet, German defenders had superior observation and reverse slope positions.[77] As a result, the BEF lost over forty thousand men, imposing ten thousand casualties on the German Army in return.[78]

For these reasons, I code the BEF as moving back *out* of the exploration phase of the learning process in the spring of 1915. We can certainly understand why infantry units traded flexible experimental tactics for linear rigid ones. Rigid timetable tactics were an easier way to ensure that the infantry scheme of maneuver supported the all-important artillery plan. It was easier to coordinate linear formations with artillery fire. They were also easier to control, protected an assault force's flanks, and, given the number of new troops, easier to teach. Nevertheless, these techniques represented a step away from what we now know to have been the superior way to fight. Flexible formations and small-unit maneuver may have been harder to teach, but they were far from incompatible with artillery-centric operations. Moreover, by increasing dispersion and allowing small-unit commanders to take advantage of microterrain and local conditions, assault tactics saved lives. These were painful lessons the BEF would soon begin to (re)learn.

1916 British infantry doctrine in 1916 defies straightforward categorization. The BEF's manuals continued to insist that fire and maneuver should be kept distinct and that infantry tactics should correspond to artillery plans. Nowhere was this more evident than it was on July 1 at the Somme River when German troops cut down fifty-eight thousand British as they lumbered across no-man's-land following a seven-day bombardment. Assault troops advanced into German defenses packed into multiple dense waves without making any attempt to conduct small-unit maneuver.[79]

Nor did official doctrine change in the wake of July 1. For example, a lessons-learned report disseminated by the Fifth Army in October reiterated that "the decisive factor in every attack is the bayonet" and reminded assault troops that "there must be; (a) No lying down, (b) No firing on the part of assaulting troops, (c) The men . . . will move over the open and keep out of the communication trenches."[80] A GHQ-issued pamphlet, *SS 135: Instructions for the Training of Divisions for Offensive Action*, similarly discouraged attempts at making "complicated maneuvers" or using flexible formations.[81] Despite absorbing appalling casualties when troops tried to advance in rigid and dense formations, British commanders still worried that dispersed and flexible movement slowed down the attack and jeopardized the artillery plan. And although the BEF did supplement the assault force's organic firepower by issuing more Lewis machine guns, official regulations nonetheless suggested giving Lewis gunners only half their allotted ammunition for fear that the gunners might lose or damage their magazines.[82]

Unofficially, some frontline units began to once again deviate from officially sanctioned practice. The most promising experiments involved organizing infantry platoons and allowing them to maneuver independently. Before the war, platoons had existed as a primarily administrative unit, although by 1916 it was common practice to use specialist platoons in combat.[83] Now the army began to experiment with employing platoons as self-contained fighting forces, dividing each platoon into two sections of riflemen, one section of bombers, and one section of light machine gunners.[84] Regardless of how they might be employed, the basic idea behind giving platoons tactical autonomy represented an important step toward modern assault tactics. Again, these efforts remained experimental and bottom up in 1916. Even by the end of the year, most battalions on the Western Front had not yet organized a single platoon, and regulations also continued to endorse linear formations.[85] Nevertheless, the fact that such experiments were once again occurring across multiple divisions and corps—and with explicit support from senior commanders—indicates that the BEF reentered the exploration phase of the learning process by the summer of 1916.

1917 The BEF made remarkable progress toward assault tactics in 1917 but started the year still in the exploration phase of the learning process as divisions, corps, and armies continued to pursue a wide range of bottom-up experiments.[86] But the BEF quickly shifted to the selection phase. This transition owes much to an important change within the GHQ, which I discuss below. Almost immediately thereafter, the GHQ began to officially endorse previously experimental concepts. The GHQ established a definitive structure for all infantry platoons in February.[87]

In the same month, the GHQ also released two of the most important tactical-level updates of the war, *SS 143: Instructions for the Training of Platoons in Offensive Action* and *SS 144: The Normal Formation for the Attack*.[88] These manuals made it clear that platoons were now the primary unit of action in the assault and that they needed to generate their own firepower and cover their own movement.[89] Platoons required a full range of lightweight weapons to fight as a self-contained force. At least in early 1917, the idea was for each section within the platoon to specialize in one weapon system (e.g., a rifle section, a Lewis gun section, a bomber section, and a rifle grenade section).[90]

The Training Branch continued to aggressively develop and disseminate new concepts throughout the year.[91] The aforementioned Battle of Menin Road (September) and Battle of Cambrai (November) demonstrated how far British infantry tactics had come.[92] At the same time, gaps remained in doctrine and practice alike. For example, the GHQ continued to endorse moving across no-man's-land in linear formations, with companies advancing in waves by platoon, with two platoons forward (abreast in two lines) and two platoons back (also abreast in two lines).[93] Instead of allowing for independent maneuver, doctrine also insisted that platoons maintain positive contact with the units on their flanks.[94] And because they were organized into four specialized sections, platoons were not yet as flexible as they would soon become.

Collectively, the manuals released by the Training Branch suggest that a major turning point in British infantry doctrine occurred in 1917. Although the GHQ did not yet espouse a truly comprehensive assault doctrine, the Training Branch's work did demonstrate that a systematic attempt to update how frontline infantry units fought was under way. I therefore use the publication of these first and most important two manuals—*SS 143* and *SS 144*—in conjunction with Training Branch's creation and subsequent work to indicate that the BEF entered the selection phase of the learning process in the winter of 1917.

1918 The BEF continued to develop and refine its assault tactics over the course of 1918. By war's end, its assault tactics were as sophisticated and advanced as anything found in the German Army, at least on paper. Three interrelated changes were especially important. First, the BEF freed its infantry of the need to adhere to rigid timetable tactics by giving them the mandate and the weapons to generate their own firepower. An updated and renamed version of *SS 135: The Division in Attack* released in November made these points explicitly. *SS 135* reminded commanders that "the infantry must always be prepared to fight its way forward by means of its own weapons."[95] The manual acknowledged that although artillery and tank fire support were essential auxiliaries, the entire tactical system was predicated on the infantry's ability to provide fire so as to support its own maneuver.[96] Moreover, organic firepower enabled the infantry to attack without waiting for a massive artillery bombardment that made it impossible to catch German defenders off guard.[97] Perhaps most important, *SS 135* asserted that "the infantry must never for a moment be permitted to consider that it merely exists to follow up an artillery barrage or to accompany a 'tank attack.'"[98]

Second, the BEF empowered infantry units to operate as independent small units, using flexible formations. The GHQ released an updated version of *SS 143*—now redesignated as *The Training and Employment of Platoons*—in February. Sections now replaced platoons as the smallest-size unit capable of independent action.[99] In July, the BEF shifted from specialized to balanced sections, which meant that every section contained a mix of riflemen, grenadiers, and Lewis gunners.[100] This move also meant that noncommissioned officers now had battlefield decision-making authority.

Third, the BEF pushed commanders to pursue deeper objectives when the opportunity presented itself. Instead of the methodical bite-and-hold attacks designed to grab shallow objectives—a defining feature of British offensive operations in 1917[101]—doctrine now avoided placing explicit limits on how deep commanders should set their objectives.[102] *SS 135: The Division in Attack* went further, advising that "if the degree of resistance encountered is less than was anticipated, or if for any other reason the attacking troops after reaching their objectives are still capable of further action, commanders should push forward in order to exploit their successes to the utmost limit."[103] General Sir Ivor Maxse's guidance to junior leaders was even more straightforward. "When in doubt, go ahead. When uncertain, do that which will kill the most Germans."[104] To be sure, the BEF's doctrine pushed for relentless—not reckless—operations. Far from endorsing headlong plunges into the teeth of the German elastic defenses in depth, the manual called for detailed planning and reconnaissance, effective all-arms coordination, and paying close attention to local conditions and the degree to which troops were physically capable of pushing forward.

The fact that the GHQ released a near-continuous series of doctrinal updates throughout 1917 and 1918 speaks to the BEF's ability to capture, assess, and disseminate lessons learned. Unfortunately, this also makes it hard to definitively establish a precise moment at which we can confidently code the BEF as transitioning from selection to action or from action to mastery. Gary Sheffield suggests that *SS 143: Instructions for the Training of Platoons for Offensive Action* and *SS 144: The Normal Formation for the Attack,* first published in February 1917, "covered essentially the same ground as *Der Angriff in Stellungskrieg* (The Attack in Position Warfare) issued by the German Army eleven months later."[105] The implication is that the BEF possibly transitioned from exploration to selection and on to action almost instantly. However, the fact that several key elements of assault tactics were missing from these manuals suggests that the BEF remained in the selection phase of the learning process through most of 1917. The Battle of Menin Road and the Battle of Cambrai, in September and November 1917, respectively, also stand out as potential transition points. However, absent evidence that the GHQ deliberately sought to replicate the tactics employed in these innovative operations across the entire BEF, it is hard to justify using these demonstration battles as a turning point either. Therefore, I ultimately code the BEF as transitioning from selection to action in the winter of 1918. I select this point because it is when the GHQ released a second and final version of *SS 143: The Training and Employment of Platoons, 1918.* A month later it distributed an updated version of *SS 135: Instructions for the Training of Divisions for Offensive Action.* It seems likely that all of the most essential elements of an effective tactical assault doctrine were in place from this moment on. Although this designation is perhaps disputable, it seems more defensible than the alternatives.

Regardless of when the BEF transitioned from selection to action, the historical record suggests that the BEF did not master assault tactics before the war's end. British infantry units varied significantly in terms of their ability to execute assault tactics throughout 1918.[106] Jonathan Boff painstakingly reconstructs how elements of Julian Byng's Third Army were remarkably proficient at using assault tactics during the Hundred Days offensive.[107] Yet a larger proportion of the BEF continued to use tactics that would not have been out of place on the Somme. For example, in August, the 32nd Division lost seventeen hundred men in a frontal assault against a prepared German defensive position. In September another division, the 62nd, was chastised by its corps commander for taking a town by frontal attack despite explicit orders to envelop and assault it from behind.[108]

It is difficult to establish how many units adhered to the army's new doctrine. The historical record lacks data on how many units effectively used modern assault tactics at any level.[109] However, it seems clear that the British high command did not control implementation and training to nearly the same degree as the German Army. To be sure, not every German soldier was trained in storm troop tactics. Less than half of the German Army's divisions on the Western Front received such training. The difference is that Erich Ludendorff deliberately selected some units for training based on his perceived operational constraints and requirements. The GHQ appears to have left this decision to chance.

COMBINED-ARMS DOCTRINE

Prewar No army paid enough attention to interarms coordination before the war.[110] The British Army was no exception. To be sure, British officers recognized that artillery and infantry units would need to do a better job of cooperating than they did in the Boer War.[111] The army tested new technologies, debated the best way to synchronize infantry and artillery operations, and produced a provisional infantry-artillery training manual in 1902.[112] The army's prewar regulations even outlined a clear set of *principles* to guide artillery and infantry commanders, including the importance of preceding infantry assaults with artillery bombardments, ensuring that artillery units moved forward with the infantry,[113] and maintaining positive communications during the attack.[114]

Crucial gaps nevertheless remained.[115] Many came back to haunt the BEF in 1914. Despite reevaluating infantry and artillery tactics after the Boer War, the two arms did so in isolation.[116] Moreover, the prevailing view that the next war would be highly mobile caused the artillery to see direct fire support as its primary role.[117] This assumption created a range of path-dependent problems that the British Army would spend years overcoming. It had too many field guns (fifty-four 18-pounders per infantry division) and too few howitzers (eighteen 4.5-inch howitzers and four 60-pounders per infantry division). The army lacked a dedicated artillery adviser to coordinate planning and fires above the division level and overemphasized direct fire missions while undervaluing long-distance, counterbattery, and precision fires.[118] In addition, the British Army did not have enough communications equipment to facilitate infantry-artillery communications.

1914 Combat revealed these deficiencies. Although the basic concepts outlined in the army's prewar regulations were perhaps sound, commanders needed concrete tactics, techniques, and procedures (TTPs) more than abstract principles. In Bidwell and Graham pithy phrasing, these "texts were admirable for supporting a prejudice but useless to young officers as guides or even philosophers."[119] For example, prewar regulations did not specify how infantry units were supposed maintain contact with their artillery given both technological limitations and ever-growing distances from which artillery needed to fire. Nor did they resolve key command-and-control problems, such as the best way to rapidly transfer control over artillery to lower levels of command as a battle unfolded.[120]

The prewar emphasis on lightweight and mobile artillery also hindered the BEF once the Western Front devolved into stalemate.[121] Field guns fired shells that were too light to penetrate fieldworks and followed flat a trajectory, which caused them to sail over entrenchments.[122] In September, the BEF asked the army to send Royal Garrison Artillery units, which had heavy siege guns, to France.[123] Gunners also found that they could no longer support their infantry with direct fire, since in practice it meant being exposed and well within range of the enemy.[124] Material shortages meant that units did not have enough shells to maintain doctrinally prescribed rates of fire, let alone what combat actually required. Finally, prewar principles notwithstanding, infantry units did not sufficiently coordinate with their supporting artillery before racing into action.

1915 There was little the BEF could do about its material shortages in 1915.[125] That did not, however, stop artillery units from aggressively exploring new methods and ways to correct problems with their pre- and early-war doctrine. Gunners learned to conceal their positions by firing from behind intervening terrain. They incorporated detailed intelligence collected by air reconnaissance units into their artillery plans, put radios for air observers in every squadron, tried out new ways of organizing phone networks, and experimented with using shrapnel shells to cut the wire in front of German trenches.[126]

One of the most noteworthy experiments involved using a protohurricane bombardment before the Battle of Neuve Chapelle.[127] To catch German units off guard, British gunners spent three weeks emplacing 354 guns under cover of darkness.[128] The thirty-five-minute bombardment indeed stunned German defenders.[129] But problems with accuracy, technical limitations (especially the lack of predicted fire techniques), and a high number of dud shells rendered the barrage less effective than it otherwise might have been.[130] British commanders concluded that the short bombardment was insufficient. Neuve Chapelle, along with the Battle of Aubers Ridge in early May, therefore marked an inflection point in British progress toward combined-arms tactics. Afterward, the BEF moved away from rapid intense barrages to neutralize German positions in favor of "the existing French practice of long methodical bombardments" to destroy them.[131] British gunners spent nearly three days pounding German positions before the Battle of Festubert in mid-May.[132] A four-day bombardment preceded the infantry assault during the Battle of Loos.[133]

Methodical battle was likely a necessary interim step in the learning process. Sequencing—instead of integrating—fire and maneuver nevertheless took the BEF away from a better approach to combining arms. At the same time, British commanders were right: their infantrymen needed more firepower than they could generate on their own. Moreover, in 1915 they did not yet have ready access to several key techniques (e.g., predicted fire) and technologies (e.g., light machine guns and the tank) that made modern combined arms possible. And by combining methodical battle with attacks for limited objectives, commanders could at least keep their infantry within the effective range of their guns, thereby creating an opportunity to chew through the German Army's increasingly complex defenses.

Although sequencing fire and maneuver had an unnecessarily deleterious effect on infantry learning,[134] the same was not true within the BEF's artillery arm. Artillery units continued exploring a variety of concepts and methods, approaches that ultimately helped the BEF master combined arms. For example, units tested new command-and-control arrangements, developed lifting-barrage techniques (an important precursor to the creeping barrage), and continued to improve infantry-artillery coordination.[135] Based on this evidence, I use the protohurricane barrage, which preceded the infantry assault at Neuve Chapelle in March 1915, to indicate that the BEF entered the exploration phase of the learning process in the spring of that year.[136]

1916 The sequential approach to synchronizing fire and maneuver took root in 1915 but came to define the BEF's artillery and infantry operations in 1916. The phrase "the artillery conquers, the infantry occupies" may be French in origin, but it aptly captures how the BEF operated during the Somme offensive.[137] The battle began with a bombardment that dwarfed its predecessors. British guns spent seven days hammering German trenches with 1.6 million shells before the infantry went over the top on July 1.[138] Rigid artillery timetables drove combat operations.[139] Infantry-artillery coordination remained poor.[140] As late as October, senior commands were still circulating lessons learned proclaiming, "the assault no longer depends upon rifle fire supported by artillery fire, but upon the artillery solely with very slight support from selected snipers and company sharp-shooters."[141]

Despite this overarching commitment to methodical infantry-artillery operations, learning still occurred. The prolonged nature of the fighting during the Somme offensive gave commanders a chance to identify problems with existing methods. A range of adaptations and innovations followed.[142] Two proved especially critical. The first was the rolling—or creeping—barrage. An improvement on existing artillery support methods in its own right, the creeping barrage also "marked the beginning of the return to emphasizing covering fire, designed to neutralise enemy fire until the infantry could close with him, rather than artillery preparation intended to destroy the enemy."[143] An enhanced version on the lifting barrage introduced the year before, the creeper involved firing a line of shells parallel to and approximately one hundred yards in front of the infantry's line of advance. British gunners would then shift their fire forward in increments so as to keep German soldiers pinned down until the first waves of British infantrymen could begin clearing their trenches.[144] Although the creeping barrage on July 1 raced ahead of the infantry,[145] British gunners eventually learned to advance their line of fire at a rate of seventy-five yards a minute over good terrain and fifteen yards a minute over rough ground.

The tank represented the second innovation, which had been under development by both the army and the navy since 1914.[146] Haig had hoped to use them en masse on July 1. However, a range of technical obstacles meant they did not see action until the Battle of Flers-Courcelette in September. It was an inauspicious debut. Of the fifty tanks that participated in the attack, eighteen broke down before the action started. Fourteen more were knocked out in the initial fighting.[147] Tank commanders were disoriented, because they moved into position under cover of darkness to maintain the element of surprise. The units to which tanks were attached were also assigned the most difficult objectives. Meanwhile, because the tanks were distributed across the entire front, their shock power was diluted. Initial setbacks notwithstanding, tanks still represented a key piece to the army's combined arms puzzle. Although rarely decisive on their own, they combined armor, mobility, and firepower, which proved invaluable when the infantry they supported advanced beyond the range of British artillery.[148] These benefits were unfortunately out of reach in 1916: tanks were still too unreliable, the army had yet to fully work out its armor-infantry tactics, and infantrymen needed more experience training and fighting alongside tanks.

Ultimately, I code the BEF as spending 1916 in the exploration phase of the learning process. The tank and the creeping barrage undoubtedly indicate that the BEF had made meaningful progress toward a superior combined-arms doctrine. The fact that the BEF—and indeed, the entire army—was engaged in an effort to acquire, develop, and refine the technologies and the techniques behind combined arms further suggests that the BEF was on the cusp of moving from exploration into selection. But a key piece of a genuine combined-arms doctrine was still missing. As *SS 135: Instructions for the Training of Divisions for Offensive Action,* published in December, made explicit, preliminary bombardments were still supposed to demolish German defensive positions instead of neutralizing German defenders.[149]

1917 If anything, bombardments grew longer and more powerful. The Battle of Messines began with more than 750 heavy guns firing 3.5 million shells between May 26 and June 6.[150] Three thousand guns spent weeks pounding German positions before the Third Battle of Ypres.[151]

But changes were coming. Much of the impetus came from the highest echelons of command. Some senior leaders wanted to restore operational surprise by trying to forego lengthy preliminary bombardments. Edmund Allenby, for example, initially wanted to precede the Third Army's attack at Arras with a forty-eight-hour bombardment.[152] The GHQ also published a key new manual, *SS 139/4: Artillery in Offensive Operations,* which despite still espousing the destruction of enemy defenses as a primary goal nevertheless also emphasized counterbattery operations, long-range strikes against German reserve and command-and-control networks, and better integration with infantry operations.[153]

The BEF also found a better way to control artillery operations. Before 1917, the senior artillery officer in each corps advised the infantry commander but "exercised no influence whatever over the heavy Royal Garrison Artillery (RGA) which might be supporting the corps' operations."[154] This arrangement made it hard to design and implement a coherent bombardment plan for the entire area of operation.[155] In December 1916, the GHQ redesignated artillery advisers as general officer commanding, Royal Artillery. With the new title came the authority to issue orders to all heavy artillery attached to the corps.[156] "These centralising arrangements laid the foundations for considerable technical advances in all fields of gunnery during 1917 and even, paradoxically, provided the background for a rational increase in flexibility and decentralization during the fast moving battles of 1918" by creating larger artillery staffs and standardizing call-for-fire procedures.[157]

Senior commanders may have set the conditions that allowed the BEF to move toward a superior combined arms doctrine in 1917. Yet it took a concerted effort by a constellation of frontline and staff officers to refine the techniques and technologies behind predicted fire. Much of this work, which included aerial observation, photography and spotting, better mapmaking, the development of gun tables, and improved meteorology, resulted from bottom-up learning.[158] In the case of sound ranging—the technique by which gunners could ascertain the exact location of an enemy battery—bottom up was quite literal. In mid-1915, the GHQ assigned a young BEF artillery officer, Sir Lawrence Bragg (who would soon receive the Nobel Prize in Physics for his prewar work on X-rays) to work on the problem.[159] One day, in the midst of his struggle to figure out how to detect the low-frequency sound waves that guns emitted when they fired, Bragg was sitting on a latrine. He noticed that his "bottom was elevated perceptibly off the seat, even though he often heard nothing at all."[160] This experience convinced him that he needed to build a better microphone, since existing ones could not capture low-frequency sound waves. One of his corporals, W. S. Tucker, solved the problem. A physics student before the war, Tucker built a device to measure air currents by placing a hot wire near an opening such that the blast of air from a gun report would cool it. Bragg's team then paired this device with yet another officer's suggestion to position microphones at equal distances along a straight line.[161] These various efforts finally paid off in 1917. At least some corps started employing predicted fire by mid-1917, and the concept reached the GHQ by year's end.[162]

Another key strand of combined-arms work in 1917 involved the tank. The army finally began producing tanks that were more capable and more reliable than earlier models.[163] Doctrinally, the GHQ encouraged commanders to integrate tanks into their artillery and infantry plans so as to use their armor and mobile firepower to breach obstacles, suppress strongpoints, and protect against shrapnel and small-arms fire. In turn, infantry could offset tanks' shortcomings. Tanks made large targets and drew heavy fire. Their visibility was poor, they were vulnerable to land mines, and they were easy to destroy if isolated. Later as German artillery gunners developed sophisticated methods for knocking out tanks, the British Army even incorporated artillery into the effort by firing smoke to hide the tanks and counterbattery missions to knock out German antitank guns. Senior commanders did not ignore the GHQ's doctrinal guidance. They recognized that tanks could fill the firepower gap when artillery was not available, when their infantry moved beyond artillery's range, or when their need for surprise precluded a long preparatory barrage. As a training update circulated by the Third Army pointed out in late 1917, "Where surprise is essential, occasion may arise when it is advisable to launch an attack at such short notice that it is not possible to prepare it methodically by artillery; in this case it may be found feasible to use Tanks instead."[164]

I use the publication of *SS 139/4: Artillery in Offensive Operations* in February as evidence that the BEF moved into the selection phase of the learning process by the winter of 1917. Although the BEF still officially embraced the use of artillery firepower to destroy—not neutralize—German defenses, this document nevertheless signified a meaningful shift toward a "genuine combined arms doctrine," particularly in its emphasis on counterbattery fire and targeting German centers of gravity.[165] In any case, the BEF was engaged in an active effort to develop and refine the other key elements of a modern combined-arms doctrine, including predicted fire, flexible command and control, and all-arms integration, by this point.

These various strands came together at Cambrai in late November.[166] The Third Army organized its attack to maximize surprise. Artillery and assault units arrived in the sector at night and maintained strict light discipline as they moved into place. Each assault division had a tank battalion operating in close support. After a hurricane barrage, advance tanks breached the obstacle belt and attacked German strongpoints. Next came main body tanks behind a creeping barrage. The first infantry units followed in platoon columns about a hundred yards behind. The tanks leapfrogged ahead to suppress German infantry for the assaulting infantry. The attack was a stunning success, at least until German units counterattacked. The foregoing leads me to conclude that the BEF entered the action phase of the learning process in the fall of 1917.

1918 The British Army possessed a workable combined-arms doctrine throughout the final year of the war, although it did not have an opportunity to apply it on a large scale until July. The army continued to refine and integrate its infantry-artillery operations even as it fielded larger numbers of higher-quality tanks.[167] I therefore use the Battle of Amiens at the outset of the Hundred Days offensive to mark the point at which the BEF demonstrated mastery of combined-arms operations. After Amiens it became clear that "the bad old days of 1915 and 1916, of infantry and artillery fighting what amounted to separate battles, were long past."[168] Artillery, infantry, and armor coordination improved even as commanders adapted to the increasingly mobile battlefield.[169] The BEF's combat operations also became more balanced. Instead of relying on its artillery to crush German defenses, the BEF now used it to "get its infantry into battle at an advantage."[170] Hurricane barrages routinely provided this edge. Yet despite being "enamored of the surprise attack,"[171] British commanders did not make the mistake of applying these new methods formulaically or treating them as a one-size-fits-all solution. For example, the Fourth Army reverted to a methodical two-day artillery bombardment before attacking the Hindenburg Line, because commanders knew that they had lost the element of surprise and that German defenses in that sector were especially stout.[172] Application of these methods across the BEF also seems to have been far more consistent than was the case with assault tactics. In fact, unit for unit, the British Army was arguably more advanced in how it used combined arms than the German Army had been during its offensives the previous spring.[173]

DEFENSIVE DOCTRINE

Prewar Although the prewar British Army focused on offensive warfare, it nonetheless arguably spent more time thinking about defensive warfare than the French and German armies. The British Army's firsthand experiences during the Second Boer War undoubtedly helped British officers appreciate the effects of modern firepower. At least some veterans of that war suggested adapting defenses by making them less linear, reducing troop density, improving camouflage and concealment efforts, and incorporating fieldworks and fortifications.[174] One prewar manual even suggested that defenders might have an edge on future battlefields.[175]

Prewar regulations of course emphasized principles over details.[176] They instructed commanders to divide their units into two parts, keeping half the force in the primary position—consisting of a noncontinuous firing line with one soldier every yard—and the rest in reserve. Regulations also encouraged entrenching if time permitted[177] and the use of outpost positions to provide early warning. Once under attack, commanders were to mount a four-phase defense. First, the outposts signaled that an attack was imminent before returning to the main firing line. Second, the firing line engaged the enemy. The commander kept his reserve force concealed until the he could ascertain the enemy's main effort. Third, the firing line would achieve fire superiority over the enemy force, thereby allowing the commander to maneuver his reserves into place for a decisive counterattack. Finally, the commander would launch a counterattack, defeat the enemy force, and transition to offensive operations.

The army's prewar defensive doctrine had some things in common with later elastic defenses in depth. Yet key differences remained. In a true elastic defense-in-depth defense, a commander buys time by voluntarily giving up ground. The outposts exist to slow an attack by providing advance warning. And the commander usually plans to mount a counterattack within the defensive position. In contrast, British prewar doctrine insisted on holding ground at all costs, using outposts only for early-warning purposes, and counterattacking before the enemy could penetrate the defensive position.

1914 The BEF's initial defenses blended established practice and ad hoc adaptation. Commanders quickly realized entrenching was necessary to hold onto a position.[178] Units therefore started digging in as soon as they halted. Soldiers learned to make their hasty trenches more survivable by incorporating overhead cover, traverses, and communication trenches, which helped them minimize exposure to enemy fire. Units also experimented with reverse-slope positions,[179] although their use was neither officially endorsed nor universally practiced. Despite these important changes, the army's overarching defensive principles remained unchanged. Commanders held onto ground at all costs, and units did not build secondary defensive lines to house reserve troops or to fall back on in the event of a major breach.[180]

1915–1916 The BEF fell behind its German adversary over the next two years. Learning and adaptation still occurred, of course. Units added obstacles, used camouflage, and made greater use of reverse-slope positions.[181] Most units also added second and third lines behind their primary trenches. And the GHQ distributed after-action and lessons-learned reports to help units improve their defensive positions. I conclude that the BEF entered the exploration phase of the learning process in the winter of 1915, as this was the point at which the GHQ published two doctrinal updates that captured many of these bottom-up lessons.[182]

The BEF's defenses nevertheless remained both shallower and less complex than those on the other side of no-man's-land. In fact, because British units dug their second and third trenches less than two hundred yards apart, the army's trench network often remained less than six hundred yards deep in some sectors.[183] The BEF did not move toward elasticity over the next two years. Instead of moving toward a more elastic disposition, units held their ground.[184] Nor did doctrine let commanders trade space for time. And most commanders held their reserves so far behind their front lines that it was impossible to organize a quick counterattack. This practice conserved manpower by keeping reserve units beyond the maximum reach of German guns. And it was not necessarily fatal in 1915 and 1916, since the German Army spent most of its time in both years on the defense. The habit proved hard to break, however, when the tables turned and the British found themselves on the defensive in 1918.

The fact that the BEF spent most of 1915 and 1916 on the offense helps explain why it did not keep pace with the German Army in terms of defensive depth and complexity. At the same time, it is important to remember that the BEF's offensive posture neither precluded the need to conduct defensive operations nor inhibited its ability to develop a better defensive doctrine. The German Army may have spent the period on the strategic defense—at least on the Western Front—but was hardly idle. The army launched major offensives at Ypres in 1915 and Verdun in 1916. And German units used small-scale attacks, raids, and feints to maintain constant pressure on British and

French forces. At the very least, the BEF could have conserved manpower by adding depth and elasticity.

1917 The BEF incorporated more depth in 1917 by reorganizing its defenses into a front line, a support line, a reserve line, and a buffer zone.[185] The front line included a fire trench and a supervision trench. Despite recognizing the tactical reasons for reverse-slope trenches, the GHQ nonetheless encouraged units to dig fire trenches on forward slopes, because "the occupation of the high ground gives a feeling of superiority which reacts favorably on the moral of troops."[186] To offset the drawbacks associated with putting trenches where artillery observers could easily spot them, commanders started to keep as few men as possible in the fire trench. Thus, the majority of the frontline garrison now remained in a supervision trench twenty-five to fifty meters behind the fire trench. Both trenches remained continuous.

The support line contained two more trenches. The first of these support-line trenches was one hundred yards behind the supervision trench and was designed to hold units to quickly reinforce the supervision trench or to mount a rapid counterattack. The first support-line trench also sheltered the frontline garrison during heavy bombardments. The support position had its own obstacle belt and so could even act as a new main line of resistance. The reserve line, which held local reserve units, was three hundred yards behind the support line. While the frontline and support-line positions consisted of continuous trenches surrounded by obstacles, the reserve line was mostly composed of bunkers and dugouts. A buffer zone extended for three to five miles behind the reserve line to slow a German penetration and had additional bunkers to act as a base of fire around which commanders could organize counterattacks.

Thus, it seems clear that the BEF adopted a defense-in-depth posture by late 1917. However, I still code the BEF as remaining in the exploration phase of the learning process because it was still missing the most important element of an elastic defense in depth: elasticity. The GHQ continued to insist that commanders cling to their positions.[187] The lack of elasticity compounded another flaw in how the army practiced defense in depth: most of the depth in British defenses lay in the buffer zone, which was *behind* the frontline garrison. The absence of an outpost zone *in front* of their positions meant that most British soldiers remained within range of German guns. And because British commanders continued to put their fire trenches on forward slopes and insisted on digging continuous trench lines instead of relying on shell hole defenses, German artillery observers found them easy targets.

1918 Strategic realities in late 1917 and early 1918 finally forced the British Army to shift into a defensive posture. Haig knew that Ludendorff was going to attack and so thought that it was "a matter of vital urgency" for the army to update its defensive practices, "since it was clear that the existing system of rigid linear defense was inadequate to cope with the major German attacks that could be expected."[188] Given the time and manpower constraints it faced, the British Army took the sensible step of copying the German Army.[189]

Three senior British officers mined German documents for ideas but unfortunately did not fully grasp the concepts they were trying to copy.[190] This so-called Jeudwine Committee made a key mistake by copying a single translated manual instead of considering the German Army's doctrine in its holistic entirety. Worse yet, the committee inadvertently copied an engineering manual instead of the operational one for commanders. As a result, the committee fixated on the technical details and aspects of a German defense instead of its underlying logic. Although Haig rejected the Jeudwine Committee's conclusions, the GHQ ultimately turned around and authorized a new defensive doctrine that made many of the same mistakes.

The GHQ issued its updated guidance for defensive operations in mid-December 1917.[191] The guidance reorganized British defenses into an outpost zone, a battle zone, and a rearward zone. The outpost zone provided both early warning and a way to buffer British defenders from German artillery and the initial infantry assault. It was to be held with as few soldiers as possible. The battle zone, which started four kilometers behind the forward edge of the outpost zone, held most of the defending garrison, while the reserve zone behind it contained local reserve forces.

Although British defenses began to resemble German ones, the similarities were often superficial. The new doctrine still told units to rigidly cling to their positions, even in the outpost zone. According to guidance issued by one British corps, "the guiding principle of the defense of the Army Battle Zone is that the forward system must be held at all costs. Troops will on no account retire from the position they are in but will defend it to the last, even if their flanks are turned."[192] Also, even as it pushed commanders to counterattack aggressively, the GHQ continued to insist on deliberate and meticulous planning.[193] Such planning took time and prevented the counterattack force from hitting German assault units while they were still vulnerable. This defect almost proved fatal during the spring offensives.

British units also did not have much time to reorganize and retrain. The GHQ published the new doctrine in mid-December 1917. Ludendorff attacked at the end of March. British defenses fared poorly. Some German assault divisions made it forty miles behind British lines in nine days.[194] Again, British defenses failed in large part because British doctrine neither grasped nor conveyed the fundamental principles behind the elastic defense in depth it sought to emulate.[195] Too many British soldiers remained in the outpost zone, which was hastily built in any case. British units clung to their positions and were slow to counterattack. And across most of the British sector, the rearward zone existed only on maps and in the minds of commanders.

Other factors undoubtedly played a role too. The British Army's official history of the war offers three additional reasons that its defenses failed. First, time, resource, and manpower constraints prevented the army from properly building an elastic defense in depth across its entire defensive front. Second, the army's southernmost army, the British Fifth Army, bore the brunt of the German assault despite having assumed responsibility for an additional twenty-five miles of front from the French Army in January. Third, the army faced unusually challenging weather conditions on March 21. Fog in particular obscured the battlefield and gave German assault divisions a major advantage.

These are important mitigating factors to be sure. At the same time, they cannot completely explain why British defenses performed as poorly as they did. After all, Haig was clearly expecting the Germans to mount a major offensive. In fact, he accurately predicted the window in which it would fall.[196] Despite facing acute manpower shortages in early 1918, the British army nevertheless possessed a better force-to-space ratio than the German Army enjoyed at any point in 1917.[197] Fog impacted German command and control at least as much as it did British operations. Thus, in the final analysis, it is hard to fully account for the army's performance without considering the conceptual flaws inherent in its new defensive doctrine.

The BEF learned from its experiences during the spring. In May, the GHQ released an updated defensive manual, *SS 210: The Division in Defence*. The manual acknowledged the need for elasticity, admonishing commanders not to hold ground "merely for the sake of its retention. The advantages to be gained by proper use of ground in defense must be tested by the prospects of economizing numbers, reducing casualties, increasing the power of the defender[,] . . . [and] rendering as costly as possible an attack by the enemy."[198] *SS 210* also said that commanders had the authority to pull back as the situation required.[199] The GHQ also suggested that defenses be built with sufficient depth so that German assault units could not take the rearmost defenses under fire without stopping to shift artillery forward.[200] The GHQ also said that firepower and counterattacks, not soldiers, trenches, and obstacles, anchored the entire scheme, although it continued to insist on meticulous planning.

With *SS 210*, the BEF finally had a defensive doctrine that at least on paper was as sophisticated and advanced as the German Army's. I therefore code the BEF as moving simultaneously into both selection and action—a feat made possible by directly emulating another army's proven war-fighting practices—in the spring of 1918. This outcome, of course, begs the question: was the British Army ready and able to actually implement its newest defensive doctrine? Logic suggests that it probably was but we will never know for sure. After all, the Ludendorff offensive collapsed by late spring, and the British Army shifted to offensive operations in July. Therefore, the British Army was never again in a position where it needed to defend against a major German attack and so never had the opportunity to demonstrate true mastery of elastic defense-in-depth concepts.

The Evolution of British Command Practices, Assessment Mechanisms, and Training Systems

The BEF unquestionably transformed itself into a genuine learning organization by war's end. Yet from a comparative perspective, aside from developing a combined-arms doctrine that was arguably superior to the German Army's, the BEF lagged behind its chief adversary in terms of implementing assault tactics and adopting elastic defense in depth. Even more puzzling, the BEF was better at exploring new ideas and technologies than it was at implementing them in a sustained and systematic fashion. The BEF started experimenting with new ways to attack as early as the fall of 1914. In fact, except for the case of combined arms, the BEF entered the exploration phase of the learning process *before* the German Army. Yet the BEF struggled to move beyond exploration so as to progress into selection, action, and mastery. ACT theory helps us make sense of this learning story. As I argue below, the BEF became better at learning *after* a range of factors caused it to adopt moderately decentralized command practices, organize a genuine doctrinal assessment mechanism, and centralize control over training.

COMMAND PRACTICES

Prewar The prewar British Army practiced moderately centralized command and control. Senior leaders and commanders enjoyed considerable autonomy but expected strict obedience from those below them. Unlike the conscripts who made up the bulk of the French and German armies, British soldiers were all long-serving volunteers and were widely considered among the best trained and most disciplined in the world.[201] Nevertheless, instead of empowering them to make independent decisions, the prewar army practiced paternalism.[202] As described by Gary Sheffield, "paternalism in this era meant a rather coherent social theory of authoritarian, hierarchical values. . . . Officers tended to regard their men as children: they needed to be closely supervised because if left to their own devices they would get into trouble."[203]

Junior officers enjoyed more authority than their soldiers, at least in principle. In practice, however, their senior leaders expected them to be deferential and obedient. Some historians go so far as to suggest that a cult of rank existed within the British officer corps. Prewar officers therefore believed that "an officer of a particular rank was ipso facto more able and more knowledgeable than any officer of a more junior rank," which meant that "suggestions or criticisms made by subordinates were seen as a challenge to the authority of the commander."[204] Officer training reflected this way of thinking.[205]

Senior leaders, in contrast to their subordinates, possessed extraordinary autonomy and authority. In particular, officers commanding battalions and larger formations exercised considerable latitude in how they interpreted and executed their missions. Aimée Fox suggests that devolving authority and deferring to the "man on the spot" helped commanders develop solutions "peculiar to their own formations" while encouraging debate and diversity of practice (even if some of the resulting applications of doctrine were "manifestly wrong").[206]

Such command practices represented a logical response to the demands of garrisoning a global network of outposts. Battalions deployed for years at a time to the British Empire's far-flung colonial garrisons, reinforcing already fiercely independent unit identities. And given the state of communications technology at the time, battalion commanders enjoyed unfettered autonomy while deployed. The army's regimental structure amplified decentralization. Regiments played an important role in every prewar European army, but British regiments were more independent and idiosyncratic than their counterparts on the continent.[207] Each one was unique in its identity, traditions, and culture. Soldiers and officers often felt more loyalty toward their regiment than they did toward the army or even the nation.[208] In some ways, the prewar army was an amalgamation of semiautonomous fiefdoms.[209]

The Boer War caused the army to reconsider some of these practices. Many senior officers called for delegating more responsibility to junior leaders.[210] These ideas began to make their way into official doctrine. For example, the 1902 *Infantry Training (Provisional)* manual claimed that "since the conditions of modern warfare render decentralization of command in action an absolute necessity, no good results are to be expected unless the subordinate leaders have been trained to use their wits."[211] In the preface to another manual, the army's commander in chief similarly argued that

> Success in war cannot be expected unless all ranks have been trained in peace to use their wits. Generals and commanding officers are, therefore, not only to encourage their subordinates in doing so . . . but they will also check all practices which interfere with the free exercise of the judgment, and will break down, by every means in their power, the paralyzing habit on an unreasoning and mechanical adherence to the letter of orders and to routine.[212]

The prewar officer corps, however, did not necessarily embrace this new approach. Deference, paternalism, and the cult of rank remained deeply embedded. And hierarchy, as Martin Samuels points out, tended to be self-perpetuating. "The more adherence to strict regulations was insisted upon, the more individual initiative was repressed. The more individual initiative was repressed, the greater the need for strict regulations."[213] Reformers therefore found it "difficult in the extreme to create a system of devolved command on to a rigidly hierarchical army whose other ranks were regarded and treated as little more than cogs in a machine . . . or as children who had to be spoon fed by their officers."[214] Moreover, the fact that the prewar army had long deferred to its commanders' judgment ironically gave those same senior leaders the latitude to resist delegating some of their authority to their subordinate officers.[215]

1914 The "Old Contemptibles" fought well. Vastly outnumbered, they made the German First Army pay a heavy price at Mons and Le Cateau.[216] The long-serving professionals who formed the core of the BEF are certainly an important reason it acquitted itself well in these early battles. Yet professionalism alone cannot account for the BEF's tactical acumen in 1914. The BEF's moderately centralized command practices also deserve credit. Senior commanders exercised considerable autonomy. Some of this latitude was probably the inadvertent result of a leadership vacuum, since the GHQ struggled to establish control during the war's fluid opening weeks. Indeed, the BEF's two corps essentially waged separate campaigns until the Battle of the Marne.[217] At the same time, moderately centralized command and control was clearly in line with the army's prewar practices. Senior officers routinely seized the initiative—even to the point of sometimes taking it upon themselves to countermand orders. Horace Smith-Dorrien went against the GHQ's wishes when he decided to wage a delaying action at Le Cateau on August 26.[218] The day before Haig, commanding the I Corps, defied an order to help Smith-Dorrien's II Corps.[219] Although it is hard to definitively categorize the BEF's command practices after maneuver gave way to static warfare in the fall, there is evidence that moderate command practices persisted through the latter part of the year. For example, a brigadier general, Charles FitzClarence, staved off disaster by seizing the initiative and ordering units—including those which were not under his command—to counterattack during the Battle of Ypres.[220]

1915 The BEF's long-standing tradition of practicing moderately centralized command and control slowly gave way to centralization over the course of 1915. By year's end, meticulous top-down planning was the norm.[221] Initiative turned into inaction as even higher-ranking officers began "waiting for orders from higher command."[222] Such practices steadily permeated decision making at every level, leading M. A. Ramsay to conclude that the "net result was a command structure lacking in flexibility from the army to the platoon level."[223] One staff officer claimed that British generals were "far more 'terrified of their own rules and regulations' than they were 'of the Germans; or of losing the war; or of getting uselessly killed many thousand men.'"[224] Officers became increasingly hesitant to question orders, debate doctrine, or suggest new ways of fighting.[225] One company commander put the matter succinctly in late 1915 when he said that "initiative was 'asked for, but woe to the man who displays it.'"[226]

A range of factors was likely behind this dramatic shift. The methodical artillery-centric battle concepts that the army began to embrace in mid-1915 certainly required a higher degree of centralized control. Centralization likewise represented a logical response to the army's rapid expansion.[227] Senior officers were skeptical about how untested citizen-soldiers might perform in combat.[228] As one general put it, "'We must remember that owing to the large expansion of our Army and the heavy casualties in experienced officers, officers and troops generally do not now possess that military knowledge arising from a long and high state of training which enables them to act instinctively and promptly on sound lines in unexpected situation.'"[229] Complicating matters, the prewar army did not have enough reserve officers. Since someone had to train and lead these untested men, the army had to recall retired officers and commission civilians and enlisted soldiers. And although we might imagine that a massive influx of civilians might have diluted the army's rigid hierarchy to some degree, the opposite seems to have happened, as the British New Armies mimicked the prewar army's discipline and culture, not the other way around.[230]

1916 The year of epic battles on the Western Front represented another turning point in the BEF's command practices. Haig, who replaced French at the end of 1915, consolidated the GHQ's control over the BEF and its operations. Haig's efforts may have reflected a broader organizational shift toward highly centralized command and control already in motion. Or they may have pushed the BEF to embrace a more extreme form of top-down decision making than it otherwise would have in his absence. Either way, military historians have used scathing terms to describe how the BEF practiced command and control for much of 1916. Martin van Creveld calls it "as extreme a form as can be found."[231] Williamson Murray suggests that the army's hierarchical culture was responsible for the catastrophe on July 1.[232] Martin Samuels contends that "the British soldiers' inability to carry out anything but the simplest of maneuvers may have owed more to their commanders having little faith in their capabilities than to any actual deficiency in potential skill."[233] Sanders Marble points out that by 1916 divisions "were becoming cogs in the machine."[234]

This swing toward extreme centralization was relatively short-lived. The British Army's long-standing tradition of trusting the man on the spot (at least when he was a sufficiently senior officer) to deviate from established practice soon began to reassert itself. Almost immediately after the debacle on July 1, some high-ranking commanders took it upon themselves to try out new ideas. For example, on July 2, the 19th Division launched an attack in which two infantry battalions—having left all heavy gear behind—raced across no-man's-land to catch the German defenders off guard.[235] Weeks later, elements from the 23 Royal Fusiliers used prototype infiltration tactics to take a German strongpoint.[236] To be sure, these experiments were not bottom up in the strictest sense of the term. Only division and corps commanders appear to have deviated from established practice, although it is possible that the ideas came from subordinates.[237] It is difficult to isolate the precise moment that the BEF transitioned from moderately centralized command practices to highly centralized command practices and back again. Therefore, I take the admittedly simplistic approach of coding the BEF as having practiced highly centralized command and control from mid-1915 to mid-1916 and shifting back to moderately centralized command and control for the remainder of 1916.

1917 The trend toward decentralization continued over the course of the next year. Initially, army and corps commanders began to relinquish control over minutiae. Battalion, brigade, and division commanders once again enjoyed the level of latitude and discretion that had been commonplace before the war. Yet instead of simply returning to the prewar status quo, by year's end the BEF arguably practiced moderately decentralized command and control as company-grade and noncommissioned officers began to exercise initiative and independent judgment on the battlefield.

Several factors account for this shift. First, Haig's grip on the army began to loosen. His loss of influence represented freedom for his senior army, corps, and division commanders. Of course, Haig's relative decline explains only why senior British commanders wielded more power. It does not explain why they then used this new latitude to empower their battalion, company, and platoon commanders. Thus, we must consider a second factor: tactical necessity. They also realized that many of the tactical ideas they wanted to explore needed junior leaders empowered to make independent decisions. Self-contained platoons, for example, could not function without platoon commanders authorized to make on-the-spot decisions.

The army also took active steps to cultivate initiative among junior leaders. The GHQ issued a book of tactical games for young officers and noncommissioned officers in May 1917. The introduction of the handbook said that its goal was "to increase the initiative of junior officers and NCOS . . . to teach them: to grasp sudden situations. To act quickly. To give verbal orders clearly and concisely. To write messages and reports. No opportunity should be lost in impressing on them the value of prompt decision and bold action."[238] Again, the nature of command practices is such that it is sometimes difficult to pinpoint discrete inflection points. Therefore, recognizing that this shift could have occurred earlier or later, I once again rely on a simplifying coding decision and identify the BEF as transitioning to moderately decentralized command and control in July 1917.

1918 Regardless of the exact moment at which the shift occurred, British units continued to practice moderately decentralized command and control throughout the war's final year. By this point, junior officers and noncommissioned officers routinely exercised the authority to make independent tactical decisions. The army officially endorsed such practices. *SS 135: The Division in Attack* made the GHQ's position on command and control explicit:

> The successful conduct of a battle depends upon the rapidity with which local successes are gained and exploited. As the advance proceeds and the enemy's organized defences are overcome, the actual direction, and to a large extent the control, of the operations must necessarily devolve upon the commanders on the spot. It is absolutely essential, therefore, that commanders of all grades should be able quickly to grasp the salient features of a tactical situation and to act with boldness and decision.[239]

ASSESSMENT MECHANISMS

Prewar The prewar British Army did not have an effective doctrinal assessment mechanism. The Imperial General Staff, organized in the wake of the Boer War, did not attract top talent. Its staff was not trained to perform rigorous analysis. And it lacked autonomy, power, and prestige.

In theory, the army's post–Boer War reforms should have created an institutional home and a focal point to foster critical thinking about warfare. At least on paper, the British Army had a reasonable system for generating, processing, and acting upon new doctrinal concepts by 1906. Sitting atop the director of military training and the director of operations (the offices of which both resided in the War Office), the chief of the General Staff should have been able to coordinate—and protect—an ongoing conversation about how the army should prepare for the next war.[240]

Unfortunately, the system rarely reached its potential. Many of its shortcomings reflected the British General Staff's relative youth, since Britain was the last European power to centralize staff planning.[241] The army had long resisted centralized planning because of is tradition of regimentalism and the demands of garrisoning a global empire. Moreover, British politicians did not relish the idea of copying the continental general staff model. Many worried that centralized staff planning led to militarization, which threatened liberty and made war more likely.[242] It took the army's disastrous performance during the Boer War to overcome such opposition. Thus, while the German Army had over a century before the outbreak of the First World War to refine how its general staff operated, the British Army had less than a decade.[243]

Like any new institution, it took the Imperial General Staff time to develop a corporate identity and refine its practices. One of its biggest flaws was that no single staff section was responsible for doctrinal analysis.[244] Its chief of staff even recognized this problem, proclaiming that "until some systematic method of interpreting and amending our war regulations is adopted, it is impossible for the general staff to gain the confidence of the army."[245] Unfortunately, the staff did not manage to fill this critical gap before war broke out in 1914.

Even if it had, the Imperial General Staff also lacked authority and prestige.[246] The staff was only one part of a much larger institutional decision-making apparatus that controlled long-term planning. Far from directing the process, the General Staff officers had to compete with other bureaus, including those under the quartermaster general and the adjutant general.[247] In fact, the General Staff was at best a "first among equals." If anything, the adjutant general's staff was actually more prestigious, given that it was composed of senior officers and had a longer institutional history.[248]

The Imperial General Staff also lacked access to the army's highest-ranking officers. Although the chief of the General Staff was supposed to replace the commander in chief when the latter position was dissolved in 1906, the chief of the General Staff did not inherit many of the commander in chief's powers. The chief remained an adviser to the secretary of state for war.[249] Nor did General Staff officers attached to field units have the right to communicate directly with their commanding general.[250] This was in stark contrast to the German General Staff, whose chiefs of staff possessed de facto veto power over their commanders' decisions.

The staff college system did not sufficiently prepare British General Staff officers to perform their work. The British Army's Staff College remained a pale imitation of the German War Academy. The British Army Staff College's curriculum was only two years long and had only nine permanent instructors. And the curriculum was not challenging, given that only two students failed in one three-year period. Even so, barely forty officers a year graduated from the Staff College, a number that was far too small to meet even the prewar British Army's admittedly modest needs.[251]

One reason so few British officers sought to attend the army's Staff College was that most officers did not hold it (or the General Staff) in high regard. The officer corps had long history of viewing staff assignments with skepticism.[252] Even the prewar officer corps retained its amateur, anti-intellectual bent.[253] Officers did not see professional military education as a necessary requirement for promotion or command. It speaks volumes that in 1913 only 65 of the 252 regular cavalry, artillery, and infantry regiments had a commanding officer or executive officer who had graduated from the Staff College.[254] This perception likely had much to do with promotion in the prewar British Army often being based more on patronage and personal connections than on qualifications or merit.[255] As a result, the prewar General Staff struggled to attract talent. There were almost always fewer applicants than available seats at the Staff College. Moreover, regiments actively discouraged officers from leaving for a multiyear posting at school and on staff.[256]

There is also no evidence that the British Army decided to institutionalize doctrinal assessment outside of its General Staff. The army's regimental system, combined with colonial deployments rarely requiring anything larger than a battalion, meant that all high-level staffs (brigade, division, and corps) were assembled on an ad hoc basis. Although division staffs sometimes existed in peacetime, they usually included only the commanding general, an assistant commander, and two field-grade officers. With the exception of Aldershot, there were no standing corps commands. Nor did the army have a permanent organization or institution for experimenting with new tactical ideas. Its School of Musketry at Hythe tested new technologies but was not formally empowered to develop new war-fighting concepts.[257] This limitation did not stop all its officers from endorsing new ideas. The school was, after all, a home for firepower advocates. However, it still lacked the capacity and the authority to translate its ideas into official doctrine.

1914 The British Army was as quick as any other to realize that prewar tactics were not going to break the stalemate.[258] Unfortunately, its General Staff was not in a position to coherently generate or identify viable alternatives. Not yet a decade old, the rapidly escalating conflict overwhelmed the Imperial General Staff. Sized to support six forward-deployed divisions,[259] it started the war with roughly 450 trained staff officers.[260] The General Staff lacked the bandwidth to engage in rigorous doctrinal analysis, in large part because of the inevitable demands of managing the army's breakneck mobilization, deployment, and subsequent expansion. Nor could the hastily assembled army or corps staffs fill this role.[261] As a result, army and corps staffs found it almost impossible "to overcome the unprogressive idiosyncrasies and to create common doctrines."[262] The result, as M. A. Ramsay describes, was that "early tactical reforms would offer an uncoordinated chorus of innovation rather than an orchestrated refrain."[263]

To be sure, the British Army did what it could to facilitate doctrinal learning in 1914. The army was receptive to ideas and suggestions flowing upward from frontline combat units[264] and actively disseminated these insights. In October, the War Office's Central Distribution Section began producing a series of updates with the moniker *Notes from the Front*.[265] Yet, reflecting the army's long-standing practice of deferring to the judgment of the commander on the scene, senior staff officers "resisted the temptation either to centralize power either in its hands or in the hands of others, or to serve as or to create a clearing house for information, doctrine or analysis."[266] Unfortunately, these pamphlets did little more than distribute lessons learned, passing them along without deep reflection or analysis. It is not clear how these best practices were chosen. Nor is there evidence that staff officers made an effort to systematically experiment with and refine the most promising ideas.

1915 Doctrinal assessment did not improve appreciably over the course of the next year. Shortages in manpower and matériel continued to consume the General Staff's time and energy. The GHQ continued to distribute lessons learned, producing some ninety pamphlets in 1915,[267] but failed to institute a systematic "method for analysing lessons learned or for a meaningful discussion of tactics."[268] It did not help matters that the GHQ stopped sending staff officers to visit the front for fear that too many of them might become casualties.[269]

Two other factors compounded the problem. The first is related to the BEF's command practices as they evolved over the course of the year. Doctrinal analysis is only as good as the information on which it is based, and by late 1915 centralization caused many frontline officers to feel compelled to whitewash their reports to avoid "unpalatable truths."[270] Second, the army's transmission practices left much to be desired. Rotation practices meant that army and corps commanders did not "own" their subordinate units. For example, the IV Corps had twelve different divisions rotate through it in 1916; the XVII Corps owned thirty different divisions in 1917. This practice was not unique to the BEF. However, the BEF had not yet standardized staff procedures across divisions, corps, or armies, which hampered the flow of information between units and up and down the chain of command.[271]

1916 Little changed in how the BEF produced doctrine in 1916. Again, this is not to say that the BEF ignored doctrinal learning. The GHQ continued producing *SS* pamphlets, releasing at least fourteen new or updated *SS* manuals between March and December alone.[272] Yet it is important to remember that the *SS* monographs were intended as a way to keep units up to date on ever-evolving tactics, not as definitive doctrinal statements.[273] It is also not clear the degree to which they were read or applied.[274] Again, "this idiosyncratic implementation of the lessons learned was one of the consequences of the lack of a staff section responsible for manuals and notes."[275]

Haig, who by this point in the war possessed near-complete authority over the BEF and a preference for exercising centralizing control, certainly could have created such a mechanism in 1916. The fact that he did not made it difficult for the BEF to systematically capture, analyze, refine, and distribute the countless lessons then being generated across the entire force.[276] Frontline units did what they could to fill the void. For example, the Fourth Army implemented a new system for collecting and circulating tactical notes for junior officers.[277] Moreover, as Aimée Fox and Robert Foley convincingly demonstrate, the BEF leveraged informal, horizontal, and external learning to adapt to warfare on the Western Front.[278] Yet the absence of a formal, prestigious, and independent assessment mechanism at the top of the organization, acting as a linchpin to harmonize these otherwise disparate efforts, prevented the BEF from learning as quickly or as coherently as it otherwise could have.

1917 A formal doctrinal assessment mechanism finally took form in 1917. In February, the GHQ established a new directorate—the Training Branch— to coordinate doctrinal analysis. The Training Branch had an important impact on how the BEF captured frontline lessons learned; assessed new tactics, techniques, and procedure; and produced doctrinal updates for widespread distribution.[279] In addition, the Training Branch acted as a focal point for collecting the hitherto ad hoc experiments that various frontline units were undertaking with increasing frequency at this point in the war. Moreover, since the Training Branch's remit included producing the *SS* pamphlet series, it improved the rigor of the thinking and analysis that went into these documents. Prior to the Training Branch's establishment, "the production of doctrine seems to have been just another task for the busy operations staff at GHQ. It would appear that they assigned a writer or simply convened committees on an ad hoc basis whenever a doctrinal need was identified."[280] After 1917, the process by which these manuals were written became much improved. The Training Branch routinely convened working groups of staff officers and commanders to assess and recommend doctrinal updates.[281] For all these reasons, I code the BEF as having a doctrinal assessment mechanism by early 1917.

1918 The Training Branch hit full stride in the war's final year.[282] The branch published a series of new and updated *SS* pamphlets, including *SS 135: The Training and Employment of Divisions, 1918* (January), *SS 143: The Training and Employment of Platoon 1918* (February), *SS 203: Instructions for Anti-Tank Defence* (February), *SS 204: Infantry and Tank Co-Operation and Training* (March), *SS 210: The Division in Defence* (May), and *SS 135: The Division in Attack* (November).[283] These manuals identified and redressed some of the most glaring flaws in the BEF's tactics and operations. For example, within a few weeks of the start of Ludendorff's spring offensive, the Training Branch released *SS 210*, which made important adjustments to the BEF's defensive doctrine. Nor was this simply an issue of quantity over quality. Substantively, the manuals were of much higher quality, reflecting sound analysis while balancing general principles against the need for concrete examples. As this chapter has endeavored to demonstrate, by this point in the war the BEF's doctrine had converged on the tactical concepts that, with the benefit of hindsight, we now know represented a superior way to fight on the Western Front.

TRAINING SYSTEMS

Prewar The army's colonial mandate unsurprisingly caused it to adopt a decentralized approach to training.[284] Some soldiers spent years on routine garrison duty, while others battled active insurrections and insurgencies. The tactics that worked for one regiment were unlikely to work for another.[285] Regiments therefore handled their own recruit training. Unique training schemes proliferated. The result was that units varied dramatically in how they interpreted and executed doctrine. For example, during one major exercise, two divisions established defensive positions on the exact same piece of ground. One division occupied thirteen miles of frontage, while the other occupied only three.[286]

Commanders resisted attempts to standardize training.[287] But not every-one agreed with this laissez-faire approach. Critics wanted to inject a de-gree of order and uniformity into the system as early as the 1830s, but their efforts were in vain.[288] By the turn of the century, firepower advocates were among the loudest advocates for training reform, since they realized that central schools and standardized training would make it easier to dissemi-nate their new methods. At least some of these reform-minded officers wanted the newly formed general staff to play a more active role in train-ing.[289] And the army did make some progress toward centralization immedi-ately before the war. As part of its broader General Staff reforms, the army established the Directorate of Military Training section within the Imperial General Staff. Ostensibly empowered to impose order, the directorate lacked the authority to inspect units or fire commanders. Some British staff officers therefore agitated for more change, suggesting that the army create a perma-nent army recruit depot and issue a manual of applied tactics.[290] The Impe-rial General Staff ultimately quashed these suggestions. Ironically, senior officers worried that standardized training might undercut their authority while encouraging units to adopt stereotyped tactics.

1914–1915 The army was too busy dealing with the exigencies of mobiliz-ing its colonial force for a global war to worry about training. For the most part, the volunteers who flocked to the army after August did not even see action until 1915. In fact, the eleven divisions that the army sent to reinforce the BEF in France 1914 were built around existing Territorial Army units augmented by reservists.

By 1915, however, the British Army had no choice but to find a way to train the hundreds of thousands of civilians answering the call to arms. The army responded by standardizing training, although completing the pro-cess took three years. The army's first attempts to concentrate authority over how new recruits trained were modest. Volunteers still reported to their local regimental depot for their uniforms and gear. These depots han-dled basic training with the goal of mentally and physically toughening up the men so they were ready for life on the front.[291] The regimental depots then shipped recruits to their respective battalions, which handled the bulk of their combat training just as had been the case before the war.[292]

The most meaningful changes involved junior and noncommissioned of-ficer training. The GHQ was worried that many new officers lacked experi-ence and therefore created new schools for junior officers and noncommissioned officers in each field army. The first such school seems to have been orga-nized in the Third Army.[293] Over time, commanders came to realize that it was easier to train other specialists at central schools rather than in the unit itself.

Again, these were modest initial steps toward centralization. Most new soldiers continued to receive their training from the units in which they served. Most commanders saw no need to relinquish their grip over individual and unit training. Even within the various field army schools, training remained uncoordinated, and the length, content, and quality of training varied accordingly.[294] Neither the army nor the GHQ thought to appoint a senior officer over the entire process.

1916 The army took more incremental steps toward centralized training in 1916. The introduction of conscription caused it to further standardize the training pipeline.[295] New recruits continued to report to regimental depots for initial training. After roughly two weeks, the depots then transferred them to training reserve battalions, of which there were 112. These specialized training units provided another six to eight weeks of individual and small-unit combat training before forming recruits into replacement drafts for service in France.

This approach to training was certainly more systematic than pre- and early-war training. However, the process still left much to be desired. Officers returning from India, retirement, or convalescent leave often led training. The army made no attempt to train the trainer, and because these officers were often out of touch with new doctrine and best practices, recruits often received outdated training. As a result, frontline units still ended up handling the bulk of a soldier's combat training.[296]

1917 Following its creation in February, the Training Branch ostensibly oversaw training within the BEF, although it still lacked the authority to enforce compliance.[297] Nevertheless, 1917 saw the BEF and the GHQ push the army toward centralized training. In June, the BEF outlined a single coherent framework for organizing all training in France.[298] It called for a streamlined three-tiered system of schools: the GHQ-controlled schools, field army–controlled schools, and corps-controlled schools. The GHQ schools handled all staff officer, engineer, junior officer, and noncommissioned officer training. The army schools provided training for new company commanders and their enlisted advisers, artillery commanders, and signals and gas instructors. The corps schools managed platoon commander and platoon sergeant training as well as specialist courses for bombers, mortar men, and machine gunners.

The Training Branch also acted as a "connecting file" between the GHQ and frontline units. The branch attached staff officers whose primary responsibility was to manage training and maintain direct lines of communication between the Training Branch and every field army and corps headquarters.[299] Beyond their duties as training liaisons, these officers also organized demonstrations, scheduled expert lectures, and led periods of instruction. Unfortunately, this responsibility came without power, as these officers still lacked the authority to fire wayward instructors.[300]

The army took another step toward centralized training in December when it released additional regulations to synchronize depot training in Britain and field training in France.[301] These changes were particularly important because they helped the regimental depots stay abreast of new frontline TTPs. Cumulatively, these important changes suggest that the British army possessed a moderately centralized training system by the end of 1917.

1918 The BEF was a true learning organization by end of the war. Unfortunately it remained better at learning than teaching. M. A. Ramsay frames the dilemma well, arguing that "the failure to institutionalize training with a central authority responsible for both tactics and training and for awareness of the conditions at the front was, ironically, a failure to concentrate authority in the one area that could have alleviated the consequences of excessive centralization elsewhere."[302] The norm that only commanders could train their men slowed the last step in the competitive learning process, because many commanders chose not to train their soldiers how to employ the army's new assault and defensive doctrines. Several senior officers recognized the link between inconsistent training and battlefield performance and called on the GHQ to do a better job of monitoring and enforcing training.[303] The problem was not fully resolved until July 1918, when the GHQ appointed Ivor Maxse as the inspector general for training. Maxse's appointment marked the army's transition to a centralized training structure. He was "empowered to visit any formation, unit or training establishment at 24 hours notice."[304] More importantly, he had the authority to fire any instructor—including school commanders—even over the objections of division, corps, and army commanders.[305] Throughout his brief tenure, he fought to eliminate all army and corps schools in France and replace them with GHQ schools. The changes were too little too late.

We cannot say with absolute certainty that the army's centralized approach to training would have helped the BEF do a better job of employing its new assault and defensive tactics had the war lasted into 1919. But the fact that training for artillerymen and tankers was more tightly controlled than it was for infantrymen and that combined arms was the one doctrine that the army managed to consistently implement on a large scale is also highly suggestive.

The British experience both lends support for ACT theory and suggests its conceptual boundaries. A consistent relationship existed between the army's command practices and its ability to generate new ideas or remain receptive to outside ones. The BEF practiced moderately centralized command and control from the start of the war through early 1915. As ACT theory predicts, this was a period in which larger formations experimented with novel solutions to the deadlock. But because the BEF did not have an independent assessment mechanism, bottom-up experimentation did not translate into organization-wide learning.

The shift toward centralized command practices in mid-1915 had a deleterious impact on experimentation. Units stopped exploring assault tactics altogether and struggled to make additional progress toward elastic defense-in-depth puzzles. To be sure, this was also the period when the BEF began exploring combined arms in earnest. That said, the GHQ's intense focus on artillery-centric methodical combat operations almost certainly acted as a confounding factor by causing the army to significantly increase the time, energy, and resources directed toward developing new artillery and tank capabilities.

The Somme offensive renewed the push toward decentralization, as senior commanders began to reassert their prerogative and experiment with new methods. As the BEF's command practices changed over the course of the next year—first from highly centralized to moderately centralized and then to moderately decentralized—it experienced a resurgence in frontline experimentation and exploration.

Then in early 1917, the GHQ organized an independent assessment mechanism in the form of the Training Branch, which helped capture and process new ideas and lessons learned. It is telling that the army moved from exploration to selection vis-à-vis assault tactics, combined arms, and elastic defenses in depth *after* creation of the Training Branch. The Training Branch also helped the BEF produce a more effective doctrine, as evidenced by its ability in all three cases to move from selection to action in a year or less.

By war's end, the Training Branch had developed an assault doctrine that was at least as sophisticated as the German Army's and a combined-arms doctrine that was perhaps more so. But the Training Branch lacked a centralized training structure to rapidly and uniformly transmit these crucial ideas across the organization. The GHQ redressed this deficiency by mid-1918. The war ended before these reforms had time to bear fruit in terms of assault tactics, as frontline implementation and employment remained uneven throughout the rest of the war. The BEF did, however, master combined arms. The discrepancy between these two outcomes probably has much to do with both the technical nature of combined-arms techniques—which will lend itself to rapid dissemination via centralized transmission—and a relatively larger number of infantry units that required training on assault tactics. Chapter 5 suggests that a similar phenomenon played out in the French Army.

None of this is to say that the British won only because the Germans failed or that the British Army emerged victorious in spite of itself. The point is simply that in 1918, the best army in Europe did not fully employ the superior war-fighting doctrine that it had already developed. The British did not lose as a result. As Chapter 1 suggests and the German case affirms, tactical learning does not lead to victory. However, it is almost certain that the BEF paid a higher price than it necessarily had to.

CHAPTER 5

The French Army on the Western Front

France fell behind its ally and its adversary in the race to learn on the Western Front. By war's end, the use of assault tactics among frontline infantry units remained uneven. Although the French Army mastered combined arms, it moved more slowly through the learning process than both the British and German armies. French gunners were firing prolonged artillery bombardments well into 1918. In terms of defensive doctrine, the French Army did eventually incorporate depth into its defensive positions but never embraced elasticity.

This outcome challenges the notion that decentralized organizations learn faster, because the French Army was arguably the most decentralized and adaptive army on the Western Front. French infantry units experimented sooner and more aggressively than their British and German counterparts. French officers were likewise among the first to work on nascent assault tactics and elastic defenses. Furthermore, the prewar French Army was more democratic and meritocratic than the British and German armies.

The case of the French Army on the Western Front therefore serves as a poignant reminder that the ability to adapt to frontline conditions is only part of the learning story. After all, the French Army practiced moderately decentralized command and control for most of the war. French officers felt empowered to debate doctrine. And the army's high command—the Grand Quartier Général (GQG)—was receptive to the resulting proliferation of bottom-up lessons learned. Unfortunately, the army also lacked a coherent doctrinal assessment mechanism to rigorously distinguish between the right lessons and the wrong ones from the cacophony of ideas being generated from below. Nor did those in charge of writing doctrine have the institutional authority to impose their ideas onto combat units, which often viewed new doctrinal mandates as suggestions. It was not until Marshal Philippe Pétain created a specialized unit within the GQG's Third Bureau[1] with a specific mandate to develop and disseminate doctrine that the army was able to identify a better way to fight. Its name notwithstanding, this Training Section had relatively little control over how frontline units trained. With the exception of specialized schools for artillery and tanks, training remained decentralized throughout the war. As a result, even when the army had identified a superior war-fighting doctrine, it struggled to ensure widespread compliance among the frontline units that actually did the fighting.

Methodologically, this case is also an important source of both within and between case variation against which I can test assessment, command, and training (ACT) theory. Within case variation comes from the aforementioned story of how the French Army assessment mechanism evolved over the course of the war. Before the Training Section, the GQG struggled to isolate, identify, and promote the sort of assault, combined-arms, and defensive tactics that we now know represented a better way to have fought on the Western Front. The GQG was also slower to converge on these tactics than the German—and to a lesser degree the British—high commands. However, the Training Section's creation helped the army move beyond exploration and into selecting and acting upon a more effective way to fight. In terms of between case variation, the French Army's command practices, assessment mechanism, and training structure differed from those found in the British and German armies at the start of the war. French learning likewise varied from the British and German experience in ways that ACT theory predicts. The French Army's moderately decentralized command practices enabled frontline units to actively explore alternatives to their prewar tactical doctrine almost as soon as the fighting started. Senior offices were receptive to the lessons generated. But the combination of an incomplete assessment mechanism and decentralized training caused it to fall behind its ally and adversary in capitalizing on frontline learning so as to move from exploration into selection, action, and mastery.

There are nevertheless two factors to take into account when testing ACT theory against the French Army. First, political and strategic imperatives limited the army's doctrinal options. Both have the potential to stymie learning.[2] Politically, French civilian leaders inserted themselves into military decision making to a greater degree than was the case in Britain and Germany. Prewar politicians maintained tight control over the French Army. Although political oversight remained weak for much of the war, Prime Minister Georges "the Tiger" Clemenceau immersed himself in military matters after rising to power in late 1917.[3] Moreover, voluntarily giving up ground to the hated German invader was politically impossible, making it difficult for the French Army to embrace elastic defenses. Strategically, the French Army was under immense pressure to remain on the offensive. And the disastrous Nivelle offensive in the spring of 1917 forced it to conserve manpower and rebuild morale. These factors invariably shaped how the French Army learned.

The second reason for circumspection is that the French Army occupies a blind spot in the English-language military historiography on tactical change during the First World War.[4] The renaissance of how we understand the doctrinal revolution that occurred on the Western Front has yet to fully capture the French Army's experience.[5] Literary and anthropological work continues to dominate how we think about the French Army. This lacuna is somewhat understandable given that there is a gap in the historiography when it comes to how the French Army actually fought the war. The official French history is overwhelming,[6] and relatively few primary source documents have been translated into English. Still, it is imperative that scholars interested in military change do a better job of scrutinizing the historical record, because the French Army was far more innovative than history has thus far given it credit for.

The Evolution of French Politics, Strategy, and Operations

A range of daunting political challenges beset the prewar French Army. A deep civil-military divide was chief among them. An ideological chasm separated the Left from the Right as politicians on both sides used the army as a weapon in their struggle for power.[7] The debate often centered on manpower policy and conscription. Liberal politicians wanted a nation in arms made up of short-serving conscripts to act as a bulwark against militarism. They also wanted conscripts to serve for two years, which they saw as sufficient to teach recruits how to fight but not so long to enable the army inculcate them with militaristic values. Conservatives thought mass national armies were outdated and favored a small army composed of long-serving professionals. Although conservatives knew the army could not completely abandon conscription, they thought conscripts should at least serve for longer periods of time. The two sides fought hard over what might otherwise seem like a relatively minor difference in manpower models, because each side worried that the other might use the army against it. The Left worried that conservatives might use the army to suppress liberty. Meanwhile, conservatives feared that the Left wanted to transform the army into an "instrument of revolution."[8] Conservatives held the upper hand from 1870 to 1905, a period in which conscripts served in the army for three to five years. From 1905 to 1913, left-wing politicians reduced this obligation to two years, although it was increased back to three years immediately before the war.[9]

This power struggle had a toxic effect on the army. Two especially deleterious effects stand out. First, patronage, ideology, and religion played an outsize role in selecting and promoting senior officers.[10] Politicized promotion schemes systematically eroded the army's ability to learn and analyze by both empowering underqualified leaders and creating incentives to toe the line. Second, since conservative and liberal politicians alike feared what might happen if the other side gained control over the army, both sides tried to splinter their ability to plan and coordinate.

French politicians did at least share a common threat perception. Both sides of the divide saw Germany as the primary rival and most likely wartime adversary. Conservatives and liberals also agreed on the need for allies.

France therefore began forging an alliance with Russia in 1891 and squeezed a military commitment out of Britain in 1906.[11] The French government hoped the prospect of a two-front war might deter German aggression or, if deterrence failed, force Germany to divide its army. Of course, this strategy meant *both* France and Russia had to attack at the first sign of hostility. Otherwise, Germany might find a way to fight and defeat the two in sequence.

This overarching grand strategy is one reason the army prioritized offensive operations before the war.[12] Between 1871 and 1914, the French Army developed a series of sequentially numbered operational plans in the event of another war with Germany.[13] Based on the traumatic experiences of the 1870–1871 Franco-Prussian War, early versions of the plan were built around the assumption that Germany would mobilize faster than France, so the French Army anticipated using an extensive fortress network to buy time for the army to marshal its forces.[14] Three developments caused subsequent plans to take on a more aggressive and offensive tone. First, the aforementioned alliance with Russia created incentives for both sides to attack as soon as possible so as to prevent the German Army from concentrating against either. Second, the development of high-explosive shells in the mid-1880s rendered fortresses obsolete. Third, the Franco-Prussian War convinced the French government to upgrade its rail network such that by the turn of the century it was possible for France to mobilize as fast as Germany. Plan XV (1903) therefore replaced a passive defensive scheme with a flexible active one.[15] Plan XVI (1909) called for an immediate push into Germany.[16] It was General Joffre's often-maligned Plan XVII, however, that guided the army's push into Germany during the opening stages of the war.[17]

As much time as the French Army spent planning for the opening stages of a war with Germany, neither it nor the nation were adequately prepared for a prolonged total war in 1914. The army faced almost immediate shortages in shells, labor, and military manpower.[18] Casualties were also much higher than expected. French generals knew the war would be bloody, but the war's initial campaigns exceeded their grimmest expectations. In August and September alone, 329,000 French soldiers died.[19] Partisan infighting at least temporarily ended with the outbreak of war.[20] So too did any attempt to maintain political control over the French Army and its most powerful officer, Joffre.[21] Although Joffre nearly lost the war before it had even begun, his status as the perceived architect of the Miracle on the Marne made him politically unassailable for a time. The government did not reassert full control over the GQG until Clemenceau became prime minister in November 1917. As a result, from August 1914 until late 1917, political factors exerted relatively little influence over the army's tactics or doctrine.

Strategically, in accordance with Plan XVII, Joffre sent the bulk of his army into Germany to recapture France's "lost" provinces and deliver a knockout blow to Germany before its army could reach Paris. Ironically, the army's headlong plunge failed so quickly that it gave Joffre time to pull his forces back to Paris.[22] Had the attack been more successful, it is entirely possible that the bulk of the French Army would have been too far away to block Helmuth von Moltke's right hook before it landed on the capital.

Once the Western Front solidified in mid-October 1914, the French Army's overarching strategic goal became as clear as it was intractable: it had to eject the German Army from French soil. The French high command of course preferred to wait on Britain to arrive in full force before attempting a decisive breakthrough.[23] But Russia needed France to keep pressure on the German Army so it could not concentrate its forces in the east.[24] For all of these reasons, the French Army had no choice but to remain on an almost constant offensive footing after late 1914.

From this point on, Joffre was committed to the idea of achieving a decisive breakthrough, even though he acknowledged that his army needed tactics and more artillery to end the stalemate, neither of which it had at in the war's first year.[25] He still launched a series of relatively small offensives in early 1915, including in the Vosges (January) and in Champagne (February to March). These were followed by larger attacks in the spring and fall in Artois and Champagne. The army spent the rest of the year nibbling away at German defenses. Alliance politics ostensibly justified the constant attacks, because they kept Germany from concentrating against an increasingly beleaguered Russian ally.[26]

Joffre intended to deliver a decisive blow in 1916 via a series of coordinated offensives with France's allies on the Western, Eastern, and Italian fronts.[27] Germany of course preempted the plan with its assault on Verdun. The fighting in Verdun persisted until mid-December. The Somme offensive did at least take pressure off the French Army. But France's other allies were unsuccessful in their attacks. The German Army defeated both the Italian assault across the Isonzo River and the Russian offensive near Lake Naroch. Manpower concerns also became acute. The French Army lost hundreds of thousands of soldiers at Verdun and the Somme. By July, the French units on the Western Front were ninety-two thousand men understrength, despite the army having received its contingent of conscripts for the year.[28] French finances were even worse. The government spent approximately seven times what it generated in revenue in 1916 alone.[29] Because France relied on loans to cover 85 percent of its wartime expenses, its debt to grew to 124 percent of gross domestic product.[30] The government was forced to implement the country's first income tax.[31] These failures and setbacks had enormous political consequences. Prime Minister Aristide Briand sacked Joffre in December, and Briand's government would itself collapse three months later.

Despite these enormous setbacks, 1917 still dawned with the government and the French high command confident that victory was just around the corner. Such unwarranted optimism was largely predicated on the hope that the army's new commander in chief, General Robert Nivelle, had found a way to break the deadlock.[32] In fact, the government promoted Nivelle over more experienced generals because he claimed his that so-called *bataille de rupture* could finally win the war. To be sure, Nivelle's new method produced success in a series of counterattacks at Verdun near the end of 1916. And his concept, as I discuss below, did incorporate several key pieces of the assault tactics and combined-arms puzzle.

Yet the government's faith proved unfounded, and the spring offensive was a disaster. The army lost 134,000 men in the first nine days of April alone.[33] Widespread mutinies followed as nearly 40,000 soldiers refused to fight.[34] Nivelle lost his job, and two governments fell in short succession, which paved the way for Clemenceau to become prime minister. Pétain, the new commander in chief, made it clear that he was not going to win the war in 1917. Instead, he put the army on a defensive footing and focused on ending the mutinies, which he did with an exceedingly soft touch. Pétain did authorize a series of small-scale offensives late in the year, although these were primarily designed to get his units back into fighting shape. He otherwise insisted that the French Army wait for the United States to arrive in force and for French industry to produce more tanks, neither of which he thought would happen until 1919 at the earliest.[35]

But Clemenceau was not about to let his army remain in a defensive crouch. Even if he shared Pétain's view that France could not win in 1918, the Tiger wanted to keep pressure on Germany so as to set the conditions for success in 1919. Of course, Clemenceau could not relieve the immensely popular Petain and instead jockeyed with his American and British counterparts to promote a more aggressive general, Ferdinand Foch, as the supreme commander of the Allied armies. Unlike Pétain, Foch wanted the French Army to attack. Unlike Nivelle, Foch sought to conserve manpower by mounting continuous attacks for limited objectives along the entire front instead of a decisive battle at a single point. Although Foch knew that no single attack could achieve a decisive result, he believed that this approach, which he termed *bataille generale,* would allow the French Army to wear its adversary down and set the conditions for victory in 1919.

The Evolution of French Tactical Doctrine

ASSAULT DOCTRINE

Prewar French officers wrestled with the same doctrinal questions as their British and German peers. But the debate over shock power versus firepower unfolded against a different backdrop in the French Army: namely, what French officers saw as their army's humiliating defeat in the 1870–1871 Franco-Prussian war. The loss took on a life of its own, turning into "a key feature in the collective imagination of the officer corps. . . . So great was the trauma that all tactical and strategic thought was linked, directly or indirectly, . . . to this disaster."[36] At least at first, defeat inspired an open-minded reassessment and a willingness to embrace change. The government rationalized the Ministry of War, organized a General Staff, and authorized the creation of a staff college. And the army revisited and revised its operational and tactical doctrine with astonishing frequency.[37]

Two sets of prewar doctrinal guidelines had a particularly important impact on French operations in 1914 and 1915 and are therefore worth exploring in detail. The first set of regulations revolved around the army's 1895 operational doctrine, the *Service of Armies on Campaign*.[38] These regulations espoused a set of concepts designed to enable offensive operations in the face of modern firepower, reminding commanders that they needed an overwhelming firepower advantage before moving against an objective; the regulations also called for flexible formations and emphasized the need for surprise.

The 1895 regulations—in conjunction with their associated *Infantry Training Regulations*—also prescribed a multiphase infantry assault.[39] The attack was to begin when the commander identified the enemy's position and divided his force into preparatory, shock, and reserve elements. Scouts would stealthily guide units into position, with the units themselves remaining in dense formations so as to facilitate quick movement. Next, a preparatory force would shift into a skirmisher line between four hundred and seven hundred meters from the objective. Since this transition was perilous and time-consuming, especially for large units or if attempted under fire, regulations held that a commander should not attempt to deploy his force until it was close enough to its objective to return fire and suppress enemy gunners. The commander then needed to decide when and where to deploy his shock echelon. He could use it to flank the enemy, or he could send it through the firing line into a direct assault on the objective. In either case, troops would advance in bounds, with skirmishers advancing in front of the line as needed. The attack would culminate with the inevitable bayonet charge. The 1895 regulations were also clear on the need to wait until the objective was effectively suppressed before mounting the final charge. Élan was not a substitute for firepower.[40] The regulations also advised commanders to focus their final assault on weak points in the defensive line, shifting reserve forces as required to achieve numerical superiority at a decisive point and to penetrate as far into the enemy position as possible.

The 1895 regulations represented a high-water mark for firepower advocates and espoused some of the basic principles behind assault tactics. Yet the ink was hardly dry on the last of the supporting infantry training manuals when the Boer War led many officers to wonder if they were already obsolete and to fiercely debate what the recently concluded war should mean for the army's offensive doctrine.[41] Firepower advocates wanted to decentralize command and control during the assault—the 1895 regulations gave the senior-most commander on scene the authority to decide when and where to mount the decisive push—while shock-power advocates thought those conflicts validated the existing emphasis on centralized decision making.[42] Firepower advocates prevailed on this issue insofar as the 1904 *Infantry Training Regulations* made the infantry *section* (the equivalent of a British platoon) the primary tactical unit in the assault and empowered *section* commanders to use flexible formations and maneuver independent of one another.[43] Nevertheless, sections were still supposed to move as a single unit under the control of one officer with no more than one pace between soldiers.[44]

The Russo-Japanese War reignited the debate.[45] Some firepower advocates once again saw a need for decentralized command and control. But the army rejected their argument. The firepower and shock-power camps also argued over what lessons to learn about mounting an assault against a well-defended position. Firepower advocates pointed out that mass attacks shattered against entrenched defenders, but shock-power advocates argued that a number of Japanese assaults prevailed because of energetic leadership and decisive action.[46]

The debate culminated with the publication of three new doctrinal manuals on the eve of the First World War: *The Conduct of Large Units* (October 1913), *The Decree on the Service of Armies in the Field* (December 1913), and the *Regulations for Infantry Maneuver* (April 1914).[47] Collectively, these regulations suggest that shock-power advocates had gained the upper hand. After the war, they came to be seen as synonymous with the doctrine of *offensive à outrance* (offensive at all costs), which, to quote General Joffre,

> Affirmed as sort of dogma, that success in war could come only to him who sought to bring the opponent to battle and was capable of delivering the offensive with all his power; the idea of security rested upon the requirement that commanders maintain their freedom of action in the face of an enemy's efforts to impose his will.[48]

On a rhetorical level, the 1913 regulations were nothing if not provocative. On its first page alone, *The Conduct of Large Units* proclaimed that "the purpose of military operations is the annihilation of the organized forces of the enemy;" argued that "a decision should be sought within the shortest possible time so as to promptly end the fighting," and insisted that "the offensive alone leads to positive results by seizing the initiative in operations [when] we take control of circumstances instead of submitting to them."[49] It is therefore not surprising that the prewar French Army earned a reputation for "attacking the enemy everywhere, anytime, with all available forces, even without regard for traditional security precautions of the effects of enemy firepower."[50]

At the same time, we should not confuse rhetoric with substance. A closer inspection suggests these manuals were not as single-minded as their postwar reputation might imply. First, they neither ignored firepower nor substituted élan for good tactical sense. The preface to the *Regulations for Infantry Maneuver* implored officers to remember that

> The experience of the most recent [wars] were given abundant proof that the continued increase in the rate of fire and of the flatness of the trajectory of the infantry projectile, and the continued increase of the rate of fire and the power of artillery fire expose troops to *destructive effects which are becoming more and more redoubtable*, which requires them to use very supple formations which may be rigorously adapted to the terrain. Experience equally proves *the greatest importance of fire* for the support of movement, which alone is decisive and irresistible, and which alone is capable of producing victory.[51]

This last sentence is especially important, because it demonstrates that French doctrine recognized the indispensable and complementary relationship between firepower and maneuver on the modern battlefield.

In many respects, the 1913–1914 regulations were not significantly dissimilar to those found in the German and British armies. All three armies worried that soldiers might not press an attack against modern firepower, although French doctrine certainly used more aggressive language to make the same point. Rhetorical excess notwithstanding, the 1913–1914 regulations did not tell French commanders to attack with reckless abandon. The regulations instead reminded them to plan methodically, conduct meticulous reconnaissance, coordinate closely with supporting artillery, and rely on judgment and experience instead of blindly deferring to regulations—tenets with which most infantry officers already agreed.[52]

The army's 1913/1914 doctrine also acknowledged that modern firepower rendered traditional formations obsolete.[53] Similar to the regulations that preceded them, the 1913/1914 doctrine still encouraged commanders to base their formations on the terrain and the situation, including extensive use of cover and concealment as well as night attacks. Dense formations were proscribed except, of course, during the final bayonet charge.[54] And these updated regulations even suggested that the best way to prevent an enemy commander from shifting his reserves was to attack without attempting to maintain contact with friendly units on either flank while implying that modern battles could take days to play out.[55]

Ultimately, perhaps the greatest flaw in the army's prewar doctrine was that it tried to incorporate key viewpoints from both sides of the firepower debate, a balancing act that caused it to be inconsistent if not contradictory.[56] As a result, many young officers going into action for the first time in 1914 found it easier to adhere to the bombastic rhetoric rather than the moderate if not contradictory substance. And it is easy to see why inexperienced officers might find extreme rhetoric so alluring when experiencing the heat of battle for the first time. According to Michel Goya, Lieutenant Colonel Louis

Loyzeau de Grandmaison, one of the leading shock-power advocates, liked to get his officers' attention by proclaiming, "'Let's go to extremes, for it is possible even that may not be enough.'"[57]

At the same time, the army's prewar doctrine was not so far off the mark that it created an insurmountable obstacle to learning. Moreover, many influential officers disagreed with the army's new doctrine, including Pétain, General Louis de Maud'hy, and Marshal Émile Fayolle.[58] Nor, at least on paper, was French doctrine necessarily more flawed than British and German doctrine. French doctrine reflected the same attempt to reconcile shock-power and firepower approaches. If anything, by emphasizing the decisive use of reserves, breaching along a narrow front, and aggressively pursuing deep objectives, even at the expense of flank security, French doctrine contained key elements of a truly modern assault doctrine. As a result, at least in some respects the French Army may have started the war *closer* to the superior doctrine than either its ally or its adversary.

1914 The unfortunate reality is that the outsize rhetoric surrounding the army's prewar doctrine had a profound impact on inexperienced infantry commanders. Units went to extremes, seeking speed and surprise instead of waiting for their supporting artillery to do its job.[59] They suffered appalling casualties as unsuppressed German gunners poured fire into their ranks.

Although the GQG saw no reason to fundamentally revise its prewar doctrine during the first months of the war, it did start to disseminate lessons learned almost as soon as the fighting started.[60] Three such notes—two in mid-August and one in early September—reminded commanders to wait for artillery to suppress German positions before launching their assaults, to use skirmisher lines, and to do a better job of using the ground to conceal their movements.[61] Nor did combat units wait on the GQG for top-down guidance. "Regiments began spontaneously at the end of August 1914 to try and rid themselves of their most deadly flaws and to come up with new and more effective methods."[62] Some units experimented with makeshift innovations; others tried to copy German methods.[63] Frontline experimentation continued even after the front began to solidify in mid-October. Indeed, although the army's constant attempts to hammer away at German trenches throughout the late fall and early winter were costly in terms of lives lost, they also served as a source of bottom-up lessons learned to which, as we will see, the GQG was highly receptive.[64] The preceding discussion indicates that the army entered into the exploration phase of the learning process almost as soon as the war began in the summer of 1914.

1915 The French Army spent the war's first full year trying to modify its prewar doctrine. Far from breaking with offensive à outrance, the GQG's sought to achieve a breakthrough by way of mounting rapid direct attacks against German lines—operations in which élan was still thought to play a central role.[65] The first such high-level adaptations came on January 2 and 3.[66] The January 2 memorandum was only about two and a half pages long but introduced three important changes. First, it encouraged commanders to continue setting deep objectives while also warning against trying to take them in a single thrust because artillery units could not move across the shell-torn ground fast enough to support a single rapid penetration. Instead, the GQG wanted commanders to use a series of successive shallow attacks, seizing interim objectives en route to their ultimate goal. Second, the memo said that planning needed to be far more meticulous and detailed. Breaking a single deep thrust into multiple successive attacks required more reconnaissance, coordination, and liaison than commanders were used to. Nor did battlefield conditions permit modifying or adjusting a plan once an attack was under way. Third, the GQG directed division and corps commanders to coordinate their attacks in order to hit the Germans along as large a front as possible, thereby preventing German reserves from concentrating on a single breach.[67]

The army's late winter and early spring offensives followed this model. The approach unfortunately had a critical flaw.[68] Although multiple shallow attacks prevented infantry from outrunning its artillery support, halting each successive attack to allow artillerymen to move their guns forward robbed units of momentum and surprise. This also gave German commanders more time to reinforce their defenses, which meant the first stage of an attack was also usually the last. Moreover, many units still failed to coordinate sufficiently with the artillery that was supposed to support them.[69]

New doctrinal instructions followed in mid-April. The *Instruction on the Aim and Conditions of a General Offensive Action* called for units to try to take objectives far behind German lines in a single thrust on a relatively narrow front (of 1–1.5 kilometers).[70] Given the increasingly sophisticated defenses they faced, the GQG further suggested that French assault units be "imbued with the idea of piercing, of getting beyond the first trenches which may be conquered and of pushing the attack without interruption, without respite, day and night, to a final conclusion."[71] The GQG knew this approach would lead to higher casualties and also recommended continuously feeding reinforcements into the assault waves.[72]

The army put this approach to the test in its Artois offensive in early May. The results were satisfactory insofar as the army seized eighteen square kilometers from the German Army in over a month of fighting.[73] But this progress was illusory, since the updated regulations traded one set of problems for another. Successive attacks on a broad front may have given Germans time to reinforce but also forced German commanders to divide their reserves. By 1915, the increasingly long bombardments that preceded French offensives gave German commanders plenty of warning about when and where they needed to send their reserves. Moreover, attacking along a narrow zone meant German commanders could concentrate their reserves. The army nevertheless used the same approach—albeit with even more artillery support—during its fall offensives in Champagne and Artois.[74] Both failed not only because of the aforementioned flaws but also because French assault units now encountered the German Army's new defenses in depth.[75]

To be sure, the French Army's doctrine in 1915 evolved so as to encompass several key aspects of a modern assault doctrine. For example, regulations suggested that advance waves should avoid strongpoints so as to penetrate as far into German lines as possible while letting specialized follow-on units clear pockets of resistance. Jonathan Krause even suggests that recommendations such as these show that the GQG embraced a nascent form of modern assault tactics.[76] However, as Chapter 2 points out, modern assault tactics require more than just a willingness to bypass strongpoints. The GQG did not yet endorse flexible formations and independent small-unit maneuver. Indeed, French infantrymen continued to lumber across no-man's-land in line, with men standing one meter apart from one another. Infantry companies remained the smallest unit capable of maneuvering independently. Nor did small infantry units possess much in the way of organic firepower in 1915. Only battalions had access to the kind of weapons and firepower needed to fight only as an all-arms team. The process of augmenting companies, sections (platoons), and *groupes de combat* (squads) with a diverse range of high-firepower weapons would not begin in earnest until 1916.

Below the level of official doctrine, frontline units also continued to explore alternative ways to attack. One particularly important experiment occurred in May. During the Second Battle of Artois a young French captain, André Laffargue, tried out a number of new techniques, many of which resembled modern assault tactics. He summarized his ideas in a memo while recuperating from wounds suffered in the battle. Laffargue advocated using specialized assault troops, equipping them with mobile firepower, and relying on surprise artillery attacks instead of prolonged bombardments to precede an assault.[77] His ideas were of course incomplete. For example, he still thought in terms of centralized command and control on the battlefield, stating that "the will of each soldier must, to a great extent, be so moulded as to respond automatically to commands" and suggesting that small-unit leaders were still useful primarily for relaying orders from officers instead of making decisions in their own right.[78] He also thought assault troops should continue to move in wave formations instead of irregular and flexible formations.[79] And he rejected the idea of having assault waves revert to fire and movement unless they found it absolutely necessary.

Laffargue nevertheless had the right idea, and the practices he endorsed were closer to the mark than the army's official doctrine. Foch received a copy of Laffargue's memo and tried to personally deliver a copy to Joffre but was turned away by Joffre's staff for having a dirty uniform.[80] Joffre did eventually read the memo and ordered its dissemination, but the GQG neither endorsed nor sanctioned Laffargue's ideas.[81] Nor did Joffre invest in further conceptual development. Without top-level sanction, Laffargue's ideas went nowhere (at least in the French Army; a wayward copy eventually wound up in German hands). For these reasons, I code the French Army as having remained in the exploration phase of the learning process throughout 1915.

1916 The GQG responded to the disappointing fall campaigns by undertaking its first major doctrinal shift of the war. By early 1916, the GQG replaced the rapid, direct, and decisive approach, which had for so long defined the army's offensive operations, with a methodical battle concept.[82] The GQG communicated the change by releasing a series of manuals in January, including *Instruction of the Offensive Combat of Small Units* (January 8), *Instruction on the Air and Conditions of a General Offensive Action* (January 16), and *Instruction on the Offensive Combat of Large Units* (January 26).[83] Collectively, these manuals signaled that "no longer were men to be pitted against matériel."[84] Methodical doctrine instead emphasized penetrating German lines through the use of meticulous planning and overwhelming firepower to systematically isolate and seize a series of limited objectives in succession.

The shift from swift decisive attacks to *l'artillerie conquiert l'infanterie occupe* represented a dramatic and in many respects understandable response to the problems the army faced in 1915.[85] But it was also a step in the wrong direction, as it took infantry units further away from the sort of flexible tactics, techniques, and procedures (TTPs) they would need to develop and master in order to adopt a modern assault doctrine. Instead of acknowledging that infantry and artillery had to fight as a mutually interdependent whole, methodical battle instead held that artillery—and artillery alone—set the conditions for movement.[86] To this end, the GQG now endorsed a range of new tactical practices.[87] Instead of lumbering across no-man's-land in a single unwieldy wave, units now moved in three consecutive waves. The army did start to equip infantry sections with light machine guns but did not let them operate independently. In fact, more than ever before, the French Army left it to the artillery to provide most of the firepower. Joffre and the GQG believed that sufficiently powerful preassault artillery bombardments would destroy German defenses, thereby allowing the infantry to sweep across the battlefield unopposed.

The Somme offensive exposed that many methodical battles had inherent flaws.[88] Limited objective attacks did not threaten the German Army's increasingly deep defenses. Nor could French artillery displace fast enough to support a series of limited attacks in quick succession, giving German commanders plenty of time to move reserves into place. And the multiday artillery bombardments of course made surprise impossible and the ground impassible for French infantry.

To compensate for these shortcomings, the GQG responded with another round of doctrinal updates, starting with the *Interim Note Appended to the*

Instruction of 8 January 1916 on the Offensive Combat of Small Units issued in late September.[89] The changes, although modest, did represent progress back toward assault tactics. The GQG told infantry units to modify their wave formations by spreading their men out even further, with one man every four to five paces.[90] The GQG also instructed units to reorganize their waves around the section and officially endorsed the idea that sections—not companies—were now the lowest level at which arms could be combined.[91] This was initially achieved by dividing the section in half such that bombers and light machine gunners made up half of a section, while the other half was entirely composed of riflemen. During an attack, the half section of bombers and light machine gunners—augmented by engineers—was to advance in a wave formation until it came into contact with German defenses. At this point, a second wave, containing the section's riflemen, would leapfrog past the lead wave in order to take the objective. Finally, a third wave of moppers would clear pockets of resistance and consolidate around the objective. These were meaningful steps in the right direction, but they could not mask the fundamental problems with the overarching methodical battle concept. In any case, despite reorganizing the assault waves around platoon-size units, the army still did not allow them to maneuver independently. And the fact that they continued to advance in waves prevented them from taking advantage of local terrain or protecting their own flanks.

Nor did the shift to *l'artillerie conquiert l'infanterie occupe* preclude tactical experimentation among frontline units. Infantry units became increasingly diverse in the methods they employed.[92] They continued to explore flexible small-unit tactics, looser formations, and the new lightweight weapons that the army began distributing over the course of the year.[93] Larger formations also felt free to test concepts that diverged from the army's official doctrine. One such experiment proved especially influential: Nivelle's *bataille de rupture*. Nivelle, who led Second Army during the Battle of Verdun, launched counterattacks in October and December. He ignored official doctrine by setting objectives far behind German lines. However, unlike French operations in 1914 and 1915, a massive artillery bombardment preceded both attacks. Nivelle also instructed his commanders to ignore their flanks, which allowed some of them to reach their objectives before German commanders could shift reserve forces into place.

The counterattacks were a stunning success. By trading flank security for speed, Nivelle's so-called Verdun method even contained several critical pieces of a modern assault doctrine. At the same time, *bataille de rupture*'s tactical underpinnings remained incomplete. Crucially, at the small-unit level it did nothing to increase dispersion, allow for irregular formations, empower independent small-unit action, or encourage infantry units to generate their own firepower. Nivelle's infantry continued to advance in waves and depended on artillery to cover their movement.

Equally important, the unique conditions at Verdun may have played a major role in Nivelle's apparent success. As Joffre noted after the war:

> These attacks, to a great extent, had succeeded because, on the ground where they took place, the enemy's defensive organizations had virtually disappeared, as a result of the almost incessant bombardment, which had pulverized this area during nine months of struggle. . . . There was no barbed wire; . . . bomb-proofs were few . . . ; [and] the trenches [were] caved in.[94]

Joffre was certainly not unbiased. He did, after all, lose his job to Nivelle. Nevertheless, Joffre raised important questions: Did *bataille de rupture* work at Verdun because it was fundamentally sound, or did exceptional circumstances mask crucial flaws, thereby suggesting that the Verdun method might work only at Verdun? In any case, neither Nivelle nor the GQG put much thought into understanding why his methods worked so well despite their similarity to French doctrine in 1914 and 1915. Instead, Nivelle focused on tying his "alluring formula" with "what would nowadays be called a skillful 'messaging' targeted at politicians."[95] This politically advantageous but analytically suspect combination would lead the army to the brink of disaster in a matter of months in 1917.

Ultimately, I consider the army to have remained in the exploration phase of the learning process throughout 1916. Frontline units continued to experiment freely, almost to the point that their diverging methods might have undercut effectiveness. With the benefit of hindsight, we now know that the GQG endorsed several important pieces of the doctrinal puzzle. That said, the GQG made these changes so as to improve the efficacy of a war-fighting approach—methodical battle—that was in many important respects the *opposite* of the modern assault doctrine toward which it would eventually begin moving by the end of the war.

1917 The French Army suffered from doctrinal whiplash in 1917. Nivelle replaced Joffre at the end of 1916, and Nivelle's *bataille de rupture* correspondingly displaced *l'artillerie conquiert l'infanterie occupe* as official doctrine. The GQG issued the necessary doctrinal updates in December 1916 and January 1917. These modifications represented a significant departure from methodical battle yet were in many respects simply a variation on the decisive battle concepts that guided the army in 1914 and 1915.[96] The Verdun method called on units to attack in depth along a relatively narrow front so as to concentrate artillery firepower against a relatively small part of the German line. An obligatory multiday artillery bombardment preceded the infantry assault, after which infantry advanced (in waves) as rapidly as possible to capture objectives within the first line of German artillery.[97] There was no expectation that infantry would generate its own firepower. Sections did still carry light machine guns and grenades, but the GQG made no other provisions to provide infantry with additional firepower. Nor were small units expected to maneuver independently. Instead, a fast-moving rolling barrage would guide and protect the lead assault waves. *Bataille de rupture*'s emphasis on speed also meant that assault units needed to bypass pockets of resistance and ignore their flanks.

Even though most French units did not receive the new doctrine until early 1917, *bataille de rupture* nevertheless served as the basis for Nivelle's scheme of maneuver at Chemin des Dames in April. Nivelle promised that the offensive would win the war, but the offensive was such an abject failure that it almost lost it instead. French assault units could not keep up with their creeping barrage, which advanced at a blistering pace of one hundred meters every four minutes.[98] The absence of artillery support might not have mattered had the French infantry not lacked the weapons and tactics to generate suppressive fire on their own and still depended on artillery to support their movement. Beyond employing an intrinsically unsound concept, Nivelle also attacked into the teeth of Germany's new elastic defense in depth.[99] Compounding an already bad situation, he made no attempt to keep his offensive a secret beforehand. He openly discussed his plans with French newspapers, and in any case German intelligence officers obtained a copy of his operation order.[100]

Pétain replaced Nivelle in May. Despite putting the army on a defensive footing, Pétain nevertheless implemented a range of profound changes to how units attacked. A series of doctrinal updates followed in June, July, and September.[101] Collectively, these documents represented a new phase in French offensive doctrine: the combined-arms battlefield.[102] Perhaps the most important changes involved transforming infantry sections into true combined-arms units capable of generating sufficient firepower to operate and maneuver independently.[103] The half-section became a *groupe de combat*, which was organized around an all-arms team of infantrymen carrying light machine guns, bombs, and rifles. The GQG further authorized the noncommissioned officer who led each *groupe de combat* to issue tactical orders. Sections and *groupe de combat* alike could use flexible formations and break apart (or reintegrate) so as to bypass strongpoints and pockets of resistance.

To conserve manpower and rebuild morale, Pétain reverted back to attacks for limited objectives. Meticulous planning, massive artillery preparation, and modest goals defined these minor operations. Indeed, Pétain did not think the army had enough artillery to successfully mount a series of limited attacks in close succession and so made no attempt to achieve any sort of breakthrough or to let assault units move beyond their assigned objectives if the opportunity presented itself.[104]

Over time, however, a system born of necessity evolved into a full-fledged doctrine, which "sought to solve the tactical problem by taking caution and method to an extreme . . . [and] thereby turned into a system what should have remained a temporary phenomenon."[105] The GQG codified the transition when it released the *Instruction on the Offensive Action of Large Units in Battle* at the end of October.[106] The Battle of La Malmaison in October 1917 represented one of the most important such limited actions.[107] Pétain amassed three infantry corps, nearly two thousand heavy and field artillery pieces, and dozens of tanks to attack a ten-kilometer-wide section of the German line.[108] A six-day artillery bombardment preceded the infantry attack. And assault units did not try to capitalize on their successes after seizing their objectives within the first position of the German defensive network.

Based on the foregoing assessment, I code the French Army as moving into the selection phase of the learning process in the late spring. This corresponds with the GQG's release of the first of a series of updates that, taken together, capture the core elements of a modern assault doctrine. Furthermore, I consider the army to have transitioned from selection to action that fall. I base this assessment on the GQG's publication of *Note on the Reorganization of the Infantry Company* in September, which codified the aforementioned changes to the infantry section, and *Instruction on the Offensive Action of Large Units in Battle* in October as well as on the large-scale demonstration battle involving many of these techniques at La Malmaison in late October. These efforts did not, however, indicate that the army mastered assault tactics in 1917. These new tactics required extensive training, and throughout the year infantry units continued to "march only in the wake of artillery shells," depending on artillery support instead of their newfound firepower, flexible formations, and organizational structure.[109]

1918 The French Army defeated its German adversary in 1918. The French Army prevailed because it, in concert with its American and British allies, masterfully undertook "a continuous shaking of the enemy defence, 'by means of hammering that would cease whenever the artillery became unable to extend its action any further, and would then continually resume on another point of the front.'"[110] Victory did not, however, mean that French infantry had mastered modern assault tactics. Implementation remained uneven as units struggled to use the methods introduced in mid to late 1917. Methodical preparation and a heavy reliance on artillery-generated firepower proved a hard habit to kick.[111]

The GQG did what it could to provide clear doctrinal guidance. A GQG-issued note in April reminded commanders to use flexible formations, integrate fire with maneuver, delegate authority to subordinates, and dispense with detailed planning when the situation required.[112] "Yet this note appeared too late to have an immediate impact, as did the more general *Directive Number 5* issued on 12 July 1918."[113] Ultimately, French units did not employ assault tactics on a widespread basis, as was the case in the German Army.[114] This limitation may reflect the fact that the German Army had a deliberate training plan and did not attempt to retrain the entire army on the Western Front. Pétain, however, rejected this approach for fear that doing so would create elite assault units that might rob the best soldiers from regular units.[115] That said, reflecting the army's long-standing emphasis on decentralized command practices, some units nevertheless still experimented with creating *grenadiers d'elite*. In many respects, as I argue below, the army's commitment to decentralization allowed it to act as a hotbed of experimental activity but impeded its ability to ensure uniformity across the fighting force.

COMBINED ARMS DOCTRINE

Prewar The French Army's prewar rhetorical emphasis on speed, shock, and élan is certainly one reason French infantry often raced into action without waiting for their supporting artillery once the war broke out. But this was not the only source of poor infantry-artillery coordination in 1914. The way the army prepared the two arms to fight alongside one another also bears much responsibility. It was a two-part problem. Doctrinally, the army's prewar regulations were light on details on how to effectively combine the two arms, although they were no worse than their British or German equivalents in this regard. Materially, the army started the war overinvested in the wrong type of gun. The army doubled down on the Matériel de 75mm Mle 1897 (the French 75) quick-fire field gun before the war. This lightweight rapid-fire weapon was certainly well suited to the war the army wanted to fight but was wholly inadequate for the war it was actually called upon to win. The army therefore had to play a game of catch-up before it could start the race to master combined-arms warfare.

In terms of doctrine, the army's 1895 regulations called on artillery to fire a preassault bombardment and suppress defenders once the infantry assault was under way. The 1913 regulations, however, dispensed with the need for a preliminary bombardment entirely, instead suggesting that artillery need not open fire until after infantry units were already pushing toward the objective.[116] The regulations also prioritized supporting the infantry assault and destroying the enemy's defensive position over counterbattery fire.[117] Problematically, despite giving lip service to close coordination between infantry and artillery units, they did not offer concrete guidance specifying how the two arms should actually communicate under fire. The fact that on the rare occasions that artillery and infantry units did train together, they almost always operated within visual range of one another.[118] This habit seems to have caused the army to overlook the need for detailed coordination techniques.

In terms of material, the army started the war almost exclusively equipped with light field guns.[119] The German Army had two thousand modern heavy guns in August 1914. The French Army had three hundred.[120] The disparity reflected a deliberate choice predicated on a vision of future wars that prioritized speed and mobility.[121] The army therefore spent heavily procuring a large arsenal of French 75s. This field gun certainly provided light, maneuverable, accurate, and devastating firepower, at least at close ranges. But by investing in the French 75 to the exclusion of almost everything else, the army inadvertently created two problems. First, because shells fired from the French 75 had both a short range and a flat trajectory, French gunners had less experience conducting long-range and indirect fire than their British and German counterparts.[122] Second, the investment in French 75s caused French artillery planners to focus almost exclusively "on speed and direct fire at high rates from close distances."[123] In some respects, the gun's technical capabilities and limitations may have shaped its artillery doctrine instead of the other way around. Most notably, French officers believed that artillery was ineffective against entrenched positions.[124] Convinced that only infantry could defeat an entrenched enemy, the army made no attempt to acquire a gun that was more effective against fieldworks. Instead, doctrine dispensed with preparatory bombardments against prepared enemy positions entirely.[125]

1914 Infantry-artillery coordination reached its nadir during the mobile battles of August and September. Infantry commanders routinely thrust their soldiers into the assault without waiting for adequate artillery support. And the French 75 proved "an easy mark for the German howitzers when the latter were more than 8,500 meters away."[126] Frontline units were quick to recognize the problem and did what they could to respond. Bottom-up adaptations included attaching artillery liaisons to infantry units, experiments with longer-range fire and aerial observers, and early attempts to fire proto–rolling barrages.[127] For these reasons, I code the army as entering the exploration phase of the combined-arms learning process in the late summer of 1914.

Nevertheless, frontline adaptation could only do so much to solve the path-dependent problems that the army's prewar procurement strategy created. Units could not instantly rid themselves of their French 75s. It would take French industry years to produce enough long-range howitzers and high-trajectory mortars to make a decisive difference on the battlefield. The GQG did what it could in the interim by giving units permission to strip antiquated siege cannons from forts (including those at Verdun) for use in the field.[128] The army also suffered from a shell shortage.[129] No one had enough munitions at the start of the war, and France's crisis was not nearly as desperate as Britain's. At the same time, French gunners were still at a disadvantage compared to the German Army. The army had stockpiled a "mere" 5.244 million shells before the war. The German Army, in contrast, started the war with 12 million shells for its 77mm guns alone.[130]

· These impediments invariably complicated the quest for a modern combined-arms doctrine. The fact that the GQG had to worry about procuring a new artillery arsenal and produce millions of new shells invariably distracted it from analyzing artillery TTPs, particularly in the war's most chaotic opening months. At the same time, French deficiencies in doctrine and material paled in comparison to those facing the British. Yet it is important not to overstate the problem. After all, the British Army faced a bigger gap in material yet ultimately managed to master combined arms faster than its French ally.

1915 The army remained in the exploration phase of the learning process throughout 1915 as well. Combat units continued to make tactical adjustments and improvements to infantry-artillery coordination. Infantry and artillery commanders continued to do what they could to improve interarms coordination.[131] French gunners worked on improving the tactics and techniques behind rolling barrages. Nivelle, then commanding a division in Artois, incorporated one into his attack there in the late spring.[132] And various corps organized corps-level artillery commands to facilitate centralized control over preparatory bombardments and improve information sharing about long-range and indirect fire techniques.[133]

For its part, the GQG's doctrinal update in mid-April identified four primary artillery missions. The first three—to destroy German trenches and fieldworks, kill German troops, and destroy German guns[134]—show that the GQG realized that the 1913 field service regulations were wrong to eliminate preparatory bombardments. Yet by emphasizing destruction over everything else (in fact, providing fire support for the infantry assault was listed as the fourth priority)[135] suggests that the army was moving *away* from the sort of artillery techniques it would ultimately need to fight effectively on the Western Front. The change also indicated that the GQG was starting to elevate artillery from a supporting arm to the dominant one. Preparatory bombardments inevitably began to grow longer and more powerful. The army massed 350 heavy artillery pieces for its attack at Artois in May.[136] Prior to the Third Battle of Artois four months later, the French army sent 900 heavy guns to Champagne and another 250 heavy guns to Artois before using them to fire a three-day barrage.[137]

Even as the high command embraced the sort of artillery tactics that would eventually set the stage for '*l'artillerie conquiert, l'infanterie occupe,*'" it also started to work on an important piece of the combined-arms puzzle. In December, Colonel Jean Estienne wrote a memo to Joffre in which he declared that he regarded it "'as within the bounds of possibility to create motor-vehicles that enable infantry . . . and artillery pieces to be transported across every obstacle, and under fire, at a speed above 6 kilometers an hour.'"[138] With Joffre's endorsement, the GQG began working on the idea. Although the Ministry of War had already started studying "land ships" as part of a joint commission with the British Admiralty,[139] the GQG's Third Bureau—and Estienne—were soon at the center of a diffuse and informal network of politicians, officers, engineers, and industrialists working to build a viable tank force for the army.[140]

1916 The army continued to make incremental progress on its artillery doctrine in 1916, although its overarching shift toward *l'artillerie conquiert, l'infanterie occupe,* meant that significant change would have to wait. Many of these adjustments were top-down, which was a welcome change given that the army's many frontline adaptations since 1914 had proven "remarkable, but had happened in a rather anarchic manner and in the absence of any centralizing body apart from [GQG], which was stretched to the limit by the day-to-day running of the war" and therefore resulted in the proliferation of divergent techniques.[141] Among its many efforts to begin standardizing artillery doctrine, the GQG improved infantry-artillery coordination by attaching liaison and observation sections to infantry units during an attack.[142] The GQG also gave division commanders control over artillery in their sector during the assault, which made artillery more responsive.[143] This approach did not represent true flexible command and control, but it was an improvement over the army's previous approach. And the rolling barrage also became standard practice army-wide by the middle of the year.[144]

The GQG also made considerable progress establishing an organizational structure for its nascent tank force and developing tactics for their eventual employment. In August the GQG published *Note on the Tactical Use of Tanks.*[145] Whereas the British Army wanted to use tanks as an independent maneuver element, the Third Bureau envisioned using them to provide mobile firepower for the infantry.[146] French industry never managed to produce enough tanks to translate this aspiration into reality. The fact that French officers were thinking in terms of creating an all-arms combat team, however, indicates that they intuitively grasped the best way to use tanks to restore battlefield mobility. A month later the GQG made Estienne the commander of the Assault Artillery (so named because the army considered tanks a form of mobile artillery and organized it within that combat arm).[147]

These conceptual efforts are especially impressive when you consider that the army did not yet have a single tank unit. It was not until mid-fall that French industry even began producing prototypes.[148] At the very least, these efforts represented a rare case during the First World War in which an army worked on its tactical employment concepts before actually acquiring a new technology.[149] Despite the significant progress the French Army made in developing tank technology and doctrine, I nevertheless code the army as remaining in the exploration phase of the learning process, because neither the GQG nor frontline units had yet began to seriously wrestle with a critical piece of a modern combined-arms doctrine: predicted fire. Goya argues that the French Army was slow to develop this technique—or to consider replacing destruction with neutralization as the primary objective of an artillery bombardment—because its heavy guns were technically inferior to those found in the German Army.[150] This line of reasoning seems problematic, since the British Army started working on the problem in 1915. Indeed, in 1915 Sir Lawrence Bragg served as a liaison officer with the French Army so as to study its sound-ranging capabilities.[151] Moreover, as the French Army's work on tanks shows, it was clearly possible to work on concepts even before the requisite technologies were in place. And given France's alliance with Russia, it is hard to believe that the GQG was totally unaware of Georg Bruchmüller's work on protohurricane barrages at Lake Naroch in March.

1917 For all the battlefield setbacks the French Army suffered in 1917, it also started to make significant progress toward a true combined-arms doctrine. Some of the most important work again involved tanks. French tanks went into action for the first time on April 16 as part of Nivelle's offensive.[152] The initial results were disappointing. Nineteen tanks broke down before the attack even began. German gunners knocked out another fifty-seven.[153] By day's end, the army lost nearly one-third of its entire tank inventory, including over 60 percent of those sent into action.[154] Technical limitations and malfunctions notwithstanding, the setback revealed a flaw in how they were being employed.[155] The GQG wanted tanks to provide mobile support for infantry, but the two arms had not worked well together on the battlefield.

The army tried again and again, sending tanks into action 231 times over the course of the year.[156] These engagements were an invaluable source of lessons learned, and the GQG was clearly paying attention. Two weeks after their inauspicious debut, the tank force was divided among the entire assault force, with individual tank batteries assigned to support specific infantry units and tank command posts embedded within the headquarters elements of the respective infantry divisions being supported.[157] Pétain likewise believed that tanks were a promising capability, [158] and he incorporated them into his limited offensives. The Battle of La Malmaison, for example, showed the GQG that medium tanks were too big, making them both hard to maneuver and easy to destroy.[159] From that point forward, the army prioritized light tank development and procurement—a decision that would pay dividends in 1918. Under Pétain, the GQG distilled these lessons into a new set of tank regulations, *Interim Instruction on the Use of Tanks*, which it issued at the end of December.[160] Collectively, these changes show that the army was making meaningful progress toward transforming its infantry and tank units into a true all-arms combat team.[161]

The army's artillery techniques and doctrine also improved dramatically, especially after Pétain assumed command. Artillery units finally standardized their methods and structures.[162] Artillery command and control became more flexible, as corps commanders exercised centralized control over the artillery bombardment before delegating it to division commanders during the infantry assault. And during the Battle of La Malmaison in October, French artillery units finally used predicted fire techniques for the first time (although the initial bombardment still stretched on for six days). Fire support planning likewise began to reflect a shift in emphasis from destroying German positions to neutralizing them.[163] The GQG codified these practices in November when it issued *Instruction on Artillery Fire*.[164]

I therefore code the French Army as moving into the selection phase of the combined-arms learning process in the spring of 1917, when the GQG released a number of new regulations and doctrinal updates. And I consider the army to have entered the action phase of the learning process that fall, reflecting La Malmaison's significance as a demonstration battle as well the important tank and artillery doctrines the GQG released in November and December.

Mastery, however, would have to wait until the next year. Conceptually, the army had embraced a modern combined-arms doctrine by the end of 1917. In practice, however, French infantry continued to depend on their artillery to overwhelm German defenses before attempting to maneuver. Indeed, for all of their differences, Nivelle and Pétain had a remarkably similar approach to how they used artillery. An eight-day artillery bombardment preceded Nivelle's offensive, and his assault troops simply advanced immediately behind their preplanned rolling barrage. Given that he needed to husband his army's manpower while rebuilding its morale, Pétain was even more willing to rely on massed artillery firepower to smash German defenses before sending a single French soldier over the top. At La Malmaison, French artillery had a field gun every twenty-four meters, a medium gun every eighteen meters, and had two gunners for every infantryman in the assault wave.[165] In August, French gunners fired six tons of shells for every linear meter of front attacked.[166] This approach was as understandable as it was unsustainable. French guns consumed five hundred million francs' worth of shells at La Malmaison—an expenditure that represented twice the army's total spending on tanks during the entire war—just to attack a ten-kilometer front.[167]

1918 The French Army effectively mastered combined-arms operations in 1918 as frontline tank and artillery units made widespread use of the concepts and techniques introduced the preceding year. In January, the army combined artillery units not otherwise attached to divisions or corps into the General Artillery Reserve, allowing it to "produce powerful concentrations of fire."[168] At the end of May, French light tanks went into action for the first time.[169] And in July, the GQG released new regulations that, among other things, officially endorsed sudden, violent preassault strikes in lieu of multiday bombardments; identified principles for employing light tanks; and emphasized the need for close cooperation among infantry, artillery, and tank units.[170] Frontline units also continued to experiment with new techniques, such as embedding 37mm cannons into its assault waves.[171] These guns were relatively light and maneuverable and therefore provided assault troops with organic firepower to suppress and destroy defensive strongpoints. By November, most artillery, infantry, and tank units were fighting as part of an effective, "well-integrated, combined-arms system.[172] I therefore use the July doctrinal updates as evidence that the French Army mastered combined arms warfare by the summer of 1918.

DEFENSIVE DOCTRINE

Prewar Its reputation for offensive action notwithstanding, the French Army's defensive doctrine was arguably more sophisticated defensive doctrine than those of the British and German armies. French officers paid more attention to defensive warfare, and the army's prewar doctrine incorporated a range of basic defense-in-depth concepts. Three manuals outlined the army's prewar defensive doctrine: *The Decree on the Service of the Armies in the Field*, *Practical Instructions on Field Fortifications* (issued in 1906 and updated in 1911), and *Handbook for Engineer Officers*.[173]

These regulations collectively stipulated that commanders should organize their defensive positions into three successive positions: an advance position to slow attackers and buy time for reserves to move into position, a main position in which the bulk of the fighting would occur, and a secondary position to block any attackers who managed to penetrate beyond the first two lines. Regulations further subdivided the principle position into a forward line for infantrymen and a rear line for the unit's field artillery.

French prewar regulations also went into more detail about incorporating trenches and fieldworks. Instead of calling for defenders to dig a single continuous trench, French doctrine presaged mid- to late-war defenses in depth by organizing the entire position around a series of strongpoints set roughly one thousand yards apart. Commanders could then use machine guns and artillery to cover the ground between strongpoints with fire. These strongpoints also served as a rally point for organizing counterattacks. At the same time, prewar doctrine regulations left no room for elasticity. In fact, article 112 of *The Decree on the Service of the Armies in the Field* went so far as to remind commanders that "there is one principle WHICH IS ABSOLUTE: the division must hold till the end, even if it is completely sacrificed."[174]

1914 The fact that the French Army spent relatively more time thinking about defensive operations than its ally and adversary gave it a slight advantage in 1914. As soon as the front solidified in mid-October, infantry units "instinctively grasped that digging in was the only immediate and possible answer to the effectiveness of the artillery and automatic weapons. They dug rifle-pits at first, but then continuous trenches to make communications easier."[175] Frontline commanders also abandoned key pieces of the army's prewar defensive doctrine. Specifically, the fear of being outflanked caused most units to spontaneously dig a continuous trench line instead of organizing their positions around strongpoints and centers of resistance.[176] I take all of this frontline experimentation and adaptation—particularly given that it happened in the absence of top-level doctrinal guidance from the GQG—as evidence that the French Army entered the exploration phase of the learning process in the fall of 1914.

1915 French defenses continued to evolve in 1915. These changes remained largely bottom-up. By spring, most French units added additional lines of trenches until their positions extended up to a kilometer in depth.[177] In accordance with prewar doctrine, the first trench provided local security and advance warning, the second trench served as the main line of resistance and contained most of a unit's troops, and the third trench held local reserves. In some sectors, units added strongpoints between the second and third trenches, but the trenches remained single continuous lines.

The GQG finally issued an official doctrinal update on defensive tactics in July. Unfortunately, this update confused as much as it clarified, since its main recommendations were contradictory. The GQG claimed that it was too dangerous to put large numbers of troops in the front trench lines at the same time that it continued to pressure commanders not to yield an inch of ground.[178] According to Lucas, "to be very sure not to lose the part of the line confided to him, and for fear that reinforcements would not arrive in time," commanders saw to it that their first trench remained "permanently and very strongly occupied. Such great infantry density of the first line had the serious disadvantage of causing useless losses, in normal times, and the destruction or capture of the defender, in case of attack."[179]

In October, the GQG issued another directive. This one clearly called for more defensive depth.[180] French defenses continued to grow in depth during the second half of the year.[181] Along most of the Western Front, defensive systems that started out as three trenches in early 1915 morphed into three *positions*. Each position was composed of three trenches that were two hundred to five hundred yards apart; each had its own obstacle belt and was located one thousand yards or so behind the position in front of it. Communication trenches connected the entire system. As a result, French defenses now extended up to six kilometers in some places. The GQG enshrined the defense in depth as official doctrine in a December update.[182] However, the absence of any effort—bottom up or top down—to incorporate elasticity into the defensive concept means that the French Army remained in the exploration phase of the learning process throughout 1915.

1916–1917 French defensive doctrine stagnated for much of 1916 and early 1917. This is in some respects unsurprising, since both Joffre and Nivelle focused on delivering a knockout blow. At the same time, the unexpected German attack at Verdun in February forced the army to fight a desperate defensive action. Moreover, the GQG was aware of the German Army's new assault methods and its increasingly elastic defense-in-depth schemes. Although "everything seemed to indicate, therefore, that it would be easy for sound defensive methods to be defined and learned," neither the GQG nor frontline units seemed to seriously consider adding even more depth, let alone incorporating elasticity into its defensive systems.[183] For its part, official doctrine remained adamant that "ground be held to the last man, and if lost it must be immediately recovered."[184]

Pétain was obviously more interested in defensive operations than his predecessors. In July 1917, the GQG issued its first major modifications to the army's defensive doctrine in nearly eighteen months.[185] The army continued to divide its defenses into three positions, each of which consisted of an obstacle belt and three trenches.[186] However, the GQG now wanted to add sentries scattered among the shell holes in front of the first position to improve early warning. The GQG also told commanders to build their second positions beyond the range of German field guns but close enough that soldiers could still cover the first position by fire. The GQG similarly wanted to shift the third position such that it could cover the second position by fire. Finally, the GQG suggested building bunkers throughout all three positions to serve as both a rally point for organizing counterattacks and a shelter of last resort.

Additional directives followed in December 1917 and January 1918.[187] Both called on commanders to stop massing soldiers in the forward-most trenches. Pétain even met with his senior generals to explain why it was their men "could not fight to retain every foot of soil."[188] Nevertheless, implementation remained haphazard at best. Some commanders followed the GQG's mandate. Other commanders resisted. Convinced the new doctrine was too quick to give up sacred ground, they insisted on putting as many men as possible in the foremost positions. The British Army took over dilapidated trenches that were not well arrayed in depth in early 1918, which suggests the degree to which implementation remained uneven.[189] For these reasons, I still consider the French Army to have remained in the exploration phase of the learning process in 1916 and 1917.

1918 By the time the German Army launched its spring offensive, French defensive positions were relatively deep.[190] Nevertheless, they remained rigidly defended. Commanders were reminded that:

> *Troops entrusted with the defense of an area of ground never under any circumstances abandon it.* It is important not to have any doubt on this matter in the mind of troops. The existence of stronger lines of defense to the rear, the moving of the company into *advance posts* . . . or keeping *main bodies* more to the rear, *never* imply that advanced elements can take the initiative in falling back on the main body, even if they judge their position is exposed.[191]

Such rigid defenses struggled to contain the German Army's new assault techniques. Only the Fourth Army "managed to hold on to its position in the face of the onslaught," which it was largely able to do because it fully embraced defending in depth (but not elasticity).[192] The German Army ultimately exhausted itself, although this likely had at least as much to do to with Erich Ludendorff's strategic and operational missteps than the inherent effectiveness of French defensive doctrine. In any case, the French Army emerged victorious despite having remained in the exploration phase of the defensive learning process throughout the war.

The Evolution of French Command Practices, Assessment Mechanisms, and Training Systems

The British and German armies learned more quickly than the French Army. By November 1918, implementation of assault tactics among French infantry units remained uneven. The army had adopted a modern combined-arms doctrine but refused to incorporate elasticity into its defensive schemes. ACT theory helps us make sense of this outcome. The French Army practiced moderately decentralized command and control and so was always quick to begin exploring new methods and concepts. In fact, French units began experimenting with the basic techniques behind assault tactics, combined arms, and elastic defenses in depth before than their British and German counterparts. Nor did the GQG ignore the resulting bottom-up lessons. But politicization and its fractured bureaucratic structure prevented it from being as effective at transforming good ideas into best practices as it otherwise could have been. And even after Pétain reformed the GQG in mid-1917, thereby radically improving its ability to undertake rigorous doctrinal analysis, the army still struggled to retrain units in accordance with its newfound best practices. French training remained highly decentralized throughout most of the war, impeding its attempts to transmit and enforce new TTPs.

COMMAND PRACTICES

Prewar The French Army practiced moderately decentralized command and control before the war. French officers had more autonomy and authority than their British and German peers. As the British army's *1906 Handbook of the French Army* described French command and control, "initiative on the part of all unit commanders has been much encouraged and has now become a noticeable factor in all operations."[193] This was especially true for junior French officers. Recall that the 1904 *Infantry Training Regulations* enshrined infantry sections as the primary tactical unit to promote initiative and to decentralize battlefield command and control. The regulations therefore also empowered "the lieutenant, whose role until now had been 'limited to staying in rank, in his place as a file-closer, supervising the fire of his troops, closing up the ranks and files.'"[194] In fact, Pascal Lucas goes so far as to suggest that the prewar army became *excessively* decentralized. In his view, the army overemphasized initiative.[195] Whether or not this was the case, the French Army did not practice decentralized command and control in the way that I define the term, since noncommissioned officers lacked tactical decision-making authority.[196]

The French Army probably delegated more tactical responsibility than other European armies because its officer corps was more meritocratic than any other in Europe. This emphasis on meritocracy flowed from an overarching political belief that "bridging of all classes within an officer corps based on merit" was necessary to protect a well-functioning democracy.[197] To this end, the army organized schools dedicated to helping noncommissioned officers earn a commission. By 1914, nearly half of all French Army officers had previously served as enlisted soldiers.[198] In comparison, prior enlisted soldiers composed no more than 5 percent of the prewar British officer corps.[199] The prewar French Army also practiced conscription more equitably than the German Army, allowing for fewer exemptions and postponements.[200]

1914 The army's command-and-control practices quickly became bifurcated once the fighting started. The GQG increasingly dictated operational matters while leaving it up to units to determine their tactical methods. In many respects, micromanagement was a natural reaction to the army's horrific casualties. Joffre blamed his senior generals for their inept leadership and poor grasp of established doctrine.[201] He responded by sacking 162 generals and senior colonels, including 70 percent of his corps commanders.[202] Nevertheless, the GQG's appetite for prescribing operational-level plans only increased as the front began to solidify in October and November.

Meanwhile, frontline commanders continued to exercise the tactical autonomy they had long enjoyed. There is some evidence the army may have shifted from moderately decentralized to moderately centralized command practices. Casualties were particularly severe among company-grade officers, not least because prewar doctrine encouraged them to lead their soldiers from the front,[203] which proved especially lethal during the war's bloody first months. Unit commanders may have therefore shown a reluctance to give retirees, reservists, and noncommissioned officers hurriedly pressed into service as much discretion as the active-duty officers they replaced.[204] Michel Goya also suggests that the bottom-up tactical adaptations common in frontline units occurred at the regimental level, although we cannot rule out the possibility that underlying ideas came from junior officers.[205]

1915 The GQG continued to tighten its grip over operational-level decision making as the army shifted to larger and larger set-piece battles. Krause describes it as an effort to "achieve an unprecedented level of influence" over formations in the field.[206] After the war, General Fernand de Langle, who commanded the Fourth Army in 1914 and 1915, "complained bitterly about

Joffre's interfering in operational planning and decisions" by personally reviewing and approving virtually every memorandum issued by his headquarters staff, which "paralyzed the initiative of army commanders."[207] Moreover, Joffre maintained control with brutal efficiency, relieving those senior officers who disobeyed him.[208]

Frontline commanders, however, continued to enjoy discretion in the tactical methods they employed. Captain Laffargue's story illustrates this strange dichotomy. A company-grade officer, Laffargue had the latitude to develop and test novel techniques during a major battle. His experimental tactics actually involved devolving command authority further down the chain of command. Laffargue was allowed to write a monograph detailing his tactical experiments, a work the army's senior-most commanders—including Foch and Joffre—both read and disseminated. The GQG's failure to subsequently build on Laffargue's ideas highlights the problems it faced when it had to act as a doctrinal assessment mechanism early in the war. But the fact that a "lowly" frontline company commander's novel tactical concepts reached the highest echelons of the organization, which then actively disseminated them,[209] offers compelling evidence that the army practiced moderately decentralized command and control in 1915.

1916 Joffre micromanaged operational-level planning and decision making throughout the remainder of his tenure. As Pascal Lucas recalls, the GQG, "which could quickly get information on everything which was going on, tended towards excessive centralization; nothing could no longer be done excepting upon its orders; it took over all initiative and all responsibility."[210] Yet despite his obsession with operational details, Joffre never showed much of an interest in tactical methods. This was true even at the height of *l'artillerie conquiert l'infanterie occupe*, a methodical approach that encouraged stereotyped infantry and artillery tactics. Units nevertheless continued to experiment with TTPs. Nivelle worked on his *bataille de rupture* concept. Petain's developed new defensive tactics occurred while in command of French forces around Verdun. These experiments were not restricted to high-level commanders. Frontline units tried out an increasingly diverse range of formations and different ways to integrate their new weapons.[211] And the GQG actively encouraged the continued delegation of command authority by formally calling on infantry sections to operate as independent combined-arms maneuver units.[212] For these reasons, I continue to code the army as practicing moderately decentralized command and control throughout 1916.

1917–1918 If anything, the army's command practices became even more decentralized and delegated in the war's final two years. Four days after replacing Joffre, Nivelle called on the army to delegate more tactical authority.[213] To be sure, Nivelle's operational concept, not an intrinsic commitment to empowering subordinates, caused him to push for more delegation. After all, *bataille de rupture* depended on commanders making decisions without first consulting higher headquarters.

Pétain took decentralization even further. Despite limiting the army to highly choreographed battles, he believed that empowering frontline commanders to respond to local conditions reduced casualties and improved combat effectiveness. His changes to the platoon organizational structure suggest as much. It is also telling that Pétain restored confidence and subdued the mutinies in large part because he insisted on listening to his soldiers instead of cracking down on them, as some of French officers wanted.[214] Pétain even sought to codify this approach to command and control: he used his final official directive of 1917 to encourage flexibility and initiative, even down to the small-unit level.[215] By the end of 1917, the army even began to allow noncommissioned officers to make tactical decisions on the battlefield. The decision to shift from sections to *groupe de combat* as the smallest combined arms unit capable of independent maneuver meant that noncommissioned officers no longer simply carried out orders.[216]

ASSESSMENT MECHANISMS

Prewar The basic pieces of a doctrinal assessment mechanism existed within the prewar army, but political realities kept them from being assembled and used in a coherent way. The government organized a general staff in 1871. The French General Staff's Third Bureau was responsible for handling both operational planning and army-wide training.[217] In 1880, the army established a staff college, the Ecole Supérieure de Guerre, to prepare French officers for staff duty. Admission was competitive, and graduates of the two-year program rotated between staff and command tours, thereby maintaining open lines of communication between the army's brain trust and its frontline units.[218] To further develop the most talented staff officers, the army also created the Centre des Hautes Études Militaires (CHEM) in 1910. CHEM students received an additional ten months of instruction designed to pair the army's top staff officers with its brightest minds.[219] CHEM alumni "read like a who's who in the French Army general staff system."[220] Finally, the Ecole Superieure de Guerre and the CHEM actively participated in writing the army's doctrine and played a key role in developing the army's 1913 and 1914 regulations.[221]

Yet no one within the high command had the authority to direct these various pieces so as to coordinate their efforts to produce doctrine. A comparison with the German Army is instructive. The highly autonomous German General Staff exercised consolidated control over doctrine, mobilization, training, and operations.[222] The chief of the German General Staff also enjoyed direct access to the emperor. In contrast, French politicians worried that a general staff with too much independence or power might threaten the still-fragile Third Republic.[223] The government therefore deliberately sought to fracture control over planning and analysis by dividing it among count-less agencies, directorates, and bureaus. Michel Goya suggests that the French Army had a "three-headed high command."[224] Hew Strachan points out that the General Staff had to coordinate with at least thirteen other gov-ernment agencies to do its job.[225] For example, the General Staff's Third Bu-reau had to jockey with dozens of other agencies to manage training and education. These included the First through Tenth Directorates within the administrative offices of the minister of war and the *section des acuvres mili-tares diverses* within the cabinet of the minister of war. Even within the Gen-eral Staff, the Third Bureau had to wrestle with the Personal Administration section. And of course, by law the Superior War Council had to approve any changes to training and doctrine.[226]

The net result was that prewar doctrinal analysis occurred in a feudal sys-tem in which multiple actors and agencies claimed authority and jockeyed for influence.[227] For its part, the General Staff functioned more like a bureau-cratic machine than a coherent source of guidance and thought.[228] Splintering the army's ability to plan and coordinate indeed helped to maintain political control over the army, but the effects of this excessive division of labor proved deleterious for doctrinal analysis. In the absence of a "stable, centralized body" to coordinate tactical thought, the army's prewar doctrine vacillated between "a succession of different 'poles' of thought," none of which had the authority or legitimacy to impose its views on the entire army.[229]

1914 The GQG did what it could to capture and disseminate lessons-learned doctrinal assessment as soon as the fighting started, releasing notes on August 16, August 24, and September 3. These were primarily doctrinal patches that tried to remind units to follow established prewar practices, such as waiting for adequate artillery support. The reality is that it would have been impossible for the GQG to engage in deeper doctrinal analysis in 1914. The fronts were too mobile, the fighting too chaotic, and the task of mobilizing for war too demanding. Even if the war might have otherwise reduced or eliminated some of the prewar political and bureaucratic re-strains on efficiency doctrinal analysis, Joffre's staff during the first weeks of the war consisted of fifty officers working out of a high school near Notre Dame.[230] The staff simply lacked the bandwidth to assess existing practices or rigorously explore new ideas.

At the same time, there was a potential upside to the long-standing ab-sence of a centralized authority over doctrine in the prewar army: frontline units were accustomed to ignoring army doctrine and implementing their own preferred tactical methods.[231] It should not be surprising that command-ers were therefore quick to experiment and adapt as was previously dis-cussed. They also actively shared their ideas and lessons learned with one another.[232] For its part, the GQG's nascent reporting system also did what it could to capture these experiences. It had a staff officer assigned to each large unit. These liaison officers would conduct regular visits to the front line to pass along personal guidance from Joffre and collect feedback from commanders and their staffs.[233] These liaison reports served as the basis for the GQG's early notes on lessons learned.[234]

1915–1916 The next two years of fighting exposed flaws in the army's doctrinal assessment mechanism. The biggest problem was structural. The GQG's Third Bureau was ostensibly responsible for managing the army's operations, doctrine, and training.[235] Although it is unclear whether the Third Bureau had managed to impose its authority over the prewar army's byzantine approach to doctrinal development, operations indisputably consumed most of its time and attention. Moreover, some frontline commanders began to question the degree to which Third Bureau staff officers truly understood conditions on the frontline.[236] In any case, doctrine and training, which I discuss below, took a back seat. The GQG consequently acted more like a conduit for transmitting bottom-up adaptations than an independent mechanism capable of vetting those ideas and transforming them into a coherent doctrine. The way the GQG responded to Captain Laffargue's work is again instructive. Joffre and the Third Bureau did not hesitate to circulate Laffargue's ideas. Although "Laffargue's work remained one of the many ideas floating about in 1915 on the same subject,"[237] the Third Bureau did not take additional steps to create an experimental unit akin to those being organized by the Oberste Heeresleitung at almost the exact same time. Nor did the Third Bureau suggest that commanders pay any more—or less—attention to Laffargue's concepts than any of the other lessons learned being passed around from unit to unit at the same time.

1917–1918 The absence of a doctrinal assessment meant that holistic shifts in the army's doctrine had to rely on the preferences of its commander in chief. The fact that the army's doctrine swung so dramatically between Joffre, Nivelle, and Pétain suggests as much. Pétain, however, did more than just impose restraint on the army's operations. He also implemented a critical structural change to the Third Bureau. On May 23, 1917, he directed it to create the specialized Training Section.[238] The Training Section had a profound impact on how the army both produced and disseminated doctrine.[239] The Training Section's placement within the Third Bureau meant that doctrinal development would remain sensitive to operational realities. But the Training Section's existence as a dedicated subunit also prevented urgent operational demands from crowding out doctrinal work. The Training Section also had expert personnel qualified to work on doctrine. Each combat arm had a representative in the section.[240] Doctrinal updates required consultation with frontline units. The Training Section coordinated review commissions chaired by corps-level commanders when considering broader doctrinal reforms. In addition, the Training Section circulated draft regulations and solicited broad feedback on the draft before releasing official changes. And although the Training Section staff continued to rely on liaison officers to capture bottom-up lessons learned, they also served as a source for novel ideas in their own right. For example, the section led the thinking on the creation of the *groupe de combat*.[241] Thus, from the spring of 1917 on, I code the French Army as having a true doctrinal assessment mechanism. This system remained in place until the end of the war, ultimately making it possible for Pétain to develop and transmit transformational changes to the army's doctrine. Despite having embraced a better way to attack and combine arms, the GQG unfortunately lacked a training system that could ensure the uniform transmission and implementation of these new concepts.

TRAINING SYSTEMS

Prewar The prewar French Army took a highly decentralized approach to training. Responsibility for recruit training fell to its active regiments.[242] The French Army also followed a standard annual training schedule.[243] Every year in the early fall, conscripts reported to their local regiment for induction. Regiments then conducted individual training from October to December. Small-unit training ran until March, at which point the regiments transitioned to company exercises for the rest of the spring and early summer. The annual training cycle culminated with brigade, corps, and army maneuvers in the late summer.

Unlike the German Army, which strictly controlled when, what, and how German soldiers trained, the French Army only standardized its training calendar. Regiments retained significant latitude over what their soldiers learned and how they trained. In theory, the General Staff's Third Bureau oversaw this entire training process.[244] Yet just as excessive compartmentalization and duplication undermined its control over doctrine, the General Staff also prevented the Third Breau staff from regulating training as it actually occurred at the regimental level. No single office, bureau, or agency was "capable of handing down a final verdict on disputes which would be accepted throughout the army."[245] Nor did the army empower a single officer to exercise complete control over training issues, to inspect training schools and/or relieve commanders for training failures. Compounding matters, the prewar army was drowning in doctrinal updates before the war. Michel Goya estimates that units had to absorb twenty-three hundred pages of regulations by 1888 alone.[246] The army's constantly changing regulations may have reflected a certain responsiveness to the changing character of war. Nevertheless, the absence of clear top-down guidance and direction meant frontline commanders were on their own to set training priorities. The quality of the army's training varied dramatically before the war as a result.[247]

1914 As decentralized as it was, the prewar army's training cycle was orderly compared to how recruits and reservists trained immediately after the war broke out. The magnitude of the mobilization effort quickly overwhelmed the system. Adding to the challenge, the appalling casualty rates forced the army to speed up the conscription pipeline. The army inducted the conscript class of 1914 early and then turned around and called up the entire fall 1915 class in December 1914.[248] The army grew so desperate for replacements that it even recalled the conscript class of 1892, men who were at the very end of their twenty-five- to twenty-eight-year window for being called back into active service.

The already strained training pipeline collapsed under the pressure. The regimental depots could not handle the influx of new (and old) soldiers. The depots could neither absorb so many untrained recruits at once nor compress a yearlong training schedule into a matter of days or weeks. Most recruits were fortunate if they received any training at all. Many arrived on the front carrying a rifle they had never before fired. Units finally had a chance to at least improvise a better training system once the Western Front started to solidify.[249] Army corps organized training centers behind the front lines, although in 1914 these depots focused on preparing recently mobilized reserve units for action. For the most part, most new soldiers continued to receive introductory training at their regimental depots. Learning how to actually do their jobs had to wait until they went into action for the first time.

1915 The army injected more order into the process as the year unfolded, but the system remained highly decentralized. The field armies established infantry schools behind the lines and eventually added additional training programs for new officers and noncommissioned officers.[250] Responsibility for training new soldiers, however, remained firmly on the shoulders of the frontline commanders who received them. New conscripts continued to report to their regimental depots for basic training, and the quality of that training remained poor and disconnected from the realities of life on the front lines. Most conscripts spent one month training with their regiment before reporting to a divisional depot behind the front lines for specialist training (e.g., for pioneers or machine gunners) and acclimatization.

As had been the case before the war, no staff existed to exercise singular control over—or responsibility for—training curricula and standards. Nor did any one high-ranking officer have the authority to enforce training standards or punish deviance. Training also remained geographically dispersed, as each field army ran its own network of schools. This diffuse approach to training unsurprisingly caused units to become "increasingly disparate in their tactical and technical proficiencies."[251] The fact that some commanders continued to launch infantry assaults without waiting for sufficient artillery preparation, despite the GQG's repeated reminders not to do so, indicates the degree to which lessons were being transmitted but not learned.

1916 The army continued to take incremental steps toward standardizing its approach to training over the course of the year. Previously, each regiment sent a number of companies to run basic training at the regimental depot behind the front lines as well as a number of camps for field exercises.[252] After 1916, each battalion in the division instead sent one company to train new replacements coming from their basic training in France at the newly redesignated division instruction centers behind the front lines. Unfortunately, minor changes such as these proved insufficient, not least because the soldiers and officers in these training companies had themselves not yet mastered the army's new equipment, tactics, techniques, or procedures.[253] More consequential changes came in the late summer as the GQG finally began to try to impose order and rationality on the army's training practices. In August, the GQG published *Note on the Training of Large Units in the Camps*, which established a formal and standard approach to unit training.[254] The GQG also designated inspector generals for heavy artillery and tank training. These changes were important but still too modest to fundamentally change the overall approach to training. Each division instruction center still controlled its own training program. These centers were still spread across the entire Western Front. And the army still lacked schools and courses for teaching new concepts and tactics to existing staff and general officers. Corresponding to the uneven nature of their training, frontline combat units continued to vary in the tactical methods they employed.

1917–1918 Meaningful change would have to wait until the final two years of the war. Whatever their other differences, Nivelle and Pétain both sought to impose order and standardization over how the army trained. Nivelle did so in order to prepare the army for his spring offensive as quickly as possible, creating the dedicated Army Reserve Group to train units how to fight in accordance with his *bataille de rupture* concept. Several factors contributed to the resulting debacle: the concept was not yet fully refined, the army had practiced decentralized training for decades, and units had very little time to absorb these new methods. Indeed, historians suggest that uneven execution was one of the many reasons for his failed offensive.[255]

Pétain built on his predecessor's efforts. He formally enshrined the principles behind this new approach in *Directive Number 2,* which made it clear that he considered training a "core component of the French Army's efficiency."[256] He established the position of inspectorate-general of artillery with the power to coordinate the development and dissemination of new artillery techniques.[257] Pétain also continued the practice of using the Army Reserve Group to manage the army's training, an initiative that began under Nivelle. Since this unit had a commanding general and was exclusively dedicated to the training mission, we can assume that a relatively high-ranking officer finally had at least a modicum of control over how training was handled. Pétain also directed that divisions rotating out of the front lines should pass through the Army Reserve Group for instruction on all-arms combat operations and the defense in depth.[258] Finally, under Pétain, the GQG organized a series of schools and courses to teach generals and staff officers how to orchestrate the tactics their soldiers were learning to execute.[259]

I ultimately conclude that by 1918, the French Army managed to establish centralized control over tank and artillery training. The same was not true for infantry training, which remained relatively decentralized. There is little question that the GQG exercised far more control over infantry training by the end of the war than ever practiced before or that these reforms significantly enhanced its ability to "organize the standardization, dissemination, and teaching of innovations."[260] Yet these changes could not overcome the infantry's long-standing aversion to centralized control. Few officers disagreed with Pétain's emphasis on improved training, but they did chafe at his attempts to centralize control.[261] In fact, the GQG ultimately amended *Directive Number 2* so as to reaffirm "the principle that the unit commander was the permanent trainer of his troops."[262] Moreover, the Training Section, its name notwithstanding, had no authority to impose a change in training methods on the army in the field. Nor did an equivalent to Sir Arthur Solly-Flood or Sir Ivor Maxse exist in the French Army.

The lack of centralized control over infantry training made it hard for these units to quickly adopt and employ the army's new assault tactics. Goya suggests that "the translation of doctrine into practical abilities down at the unit level had been both protracted and incomplete, partly because of the filters through which the doctrine had to pass . . . but above all because of the deficiencies of the training structure."[263] Use of the army's new assault tactics remained at best uneven through the end of the war.[264]

The army did, however, establish a degree of centralized control over tank and artillery training by 1918. The GQG organized heavy artillery training centers in 1915 and required that every heavy artillery officer in the army attend a course at one of the centers.[265] In 1916, the GQG laid out a centralized system for training new tank units before the army had even received its first full complement of tanks. And in 1917, the GQG created the inspectorate-general of artillery position, empowered to standardize training across the various branches of artillery. No such equivalent existed in the infantry. The GQG's far more active role in monitoring and supervising tank and artillery training helps explain why these units were more uniform in implementing combined-arms tactics by war's end, even as many infantry units struggled to employ the army's new assault tactics.

It is not clear why the GQG dictated artillery and tank training while leaving infantry training in the hands of regimental depots and frontline commanders. One plausible explanation is that many of the army's wartime artillery innovations were highly technical in nature, causing the GQG to assume that only a small number of experts were qualified to teach them.[266] A finite pool of instructors would necessitate bringing students to a small number of training schools. In contrast, the GQG likely saw infantry training as unspecialized and nontechnical and therefore something that any qualified infantry command could reasonably manage. The fact that tank units did not exist until 1916 meant that tank commanders had no tradition of maintaining control over how they trained their men. The relatively small number of tank units likewise facilitated top-down control over training.

ACT theory helps us understand why the French Army was slower to learn than either its ally or its rival. The army's long-standing moderately decentralized command-and-control practices empowered frontline units to begin searching for new methods and techniques almost as soon as the fighting started. The French Army was therefore the first to enter the exploration phase. The GQG was receptive to these bottom-up adaptations but struggled to move beyond simply acting as a distribution center for lessons learned. It was not until Pétain created the Training Section in mid-1917 that the army possessed a truly doctrinal assessment mechanism capable of rigorously analyzing new ideas so as to produce a coherent set of tactical regulations. Unfortunately, the army's decentralized approach to infantry training prevented it from teaching the majority of its frontline units how to use its new assault tactics. Meanwhile, because the GQG maintained a tighter grip on tank and artillery training, those units were far more effective at implementing the army's new techniques for combining arms.

At the same time, there are limits to what lessons we can draw from the French Army's experience. There is still much to learn about French tactics on the Western Front. English-language scholars are just now starting to pay as much attention to the French Army as they have long lavished on the British and German armies. Overdetermination also presents a methodological challenge. Politics played a bigger role in the development of French doctrine than was the case in the British and German armies, especially before the war and after Clemenceau rose to power. In particular, political imperatives prevented the French Army from ever seriously considering elastic defense-in-depth concepts.

Conclusion

Alternative Explanations and Policy Implications

> In looking back at the war and all its lessons we must not overlook the most important lesson of all, viz., all wars produce new methods and fresh problems. The last was full of surprises—the next one is likely to be no less prolific in unexpected developments. Hence, we must study the past in the light of the probabilities of the future, which is what really matters. No matter how prophetic we may be, the next war will probably take a shape far different to our peace-time conceptions.
> —Major-General A. E. McNamara, "Kirke Report," 1932

The Balance Sheet

War is a classroom, but not every army is ready to learn. Assessment, command, and training (ACT) theory offers a *systematic* way to understand why some military organizations are better students than others and also sheds light on an important historical case: the First World War's Western Front. Chapters 3, 4, and 5 explored German, British, and French learning in that theater of action as a way to test ACT theory's proposed causal relationships. Since these case studies necessarily examine each army in isolation, I now take a step back so as to compare them against one another and ACT theory's core hypotheses.

MAIN HYPOTHESIS

ACT theory's core proposition is that militaries that practice moderately decentralized command and control, have an independent doctrinal assessment mechanism, and maintain tight control over training will learn more effectively and efficiently than adversaries who combine these three characteristics in any other way. The case studies in this book provide robust support for this prediction. The Western Front pitted the British, French, and German armies against one another in a struggle to over-come same fundamental tactical dilemma. All three started the war with remarkably similar doctrines, weapons, organizational structures, and goals. Yet by the end of the war, only the German Army developed and implemented a holistic tactical doctrine organized around assault tactics, combined arms, and elastic defenses in depth—a system that, with the benefit of hindsight, we now know represented a better way to fight under those conditions.

The German Army was also the first to combine moderately decentralized command practices, an independent assessment mechanism, and a central-ized training system. All three were in place by 1916. Moreover, they oper-ated as ACT theory predicts. To be sure, the British and French armies were not far behind. The British Expeditionary Force (BEF) practiced moderately decentralized command and control and had an independent assessment mechanism by early 1917. The BEF moved from exploration to selection and from selection to action shortly thereafter.[1] However, because the BEF did not centralize control over training until mid-1918, its units were less uni-form in how they used assault tactics and organized their elastic defenses in depth. Only with regard to combining arms did the BEF catch up to the German Army by war's end.

The French Army lagged behind its ally, as ACT theory would also expect. Although the army practiced moderately decentralized command and con-trol for much of the war, it did not have an independent assessment mecha-nism until Philippe Pétain established the Training Section in mid-1917. And the army never fully centralized control over training. Although it did man-age to master combined arms, implementation of assault tactics remained uneven. For political reasons, the French Army never seriously considered incorporating elasticity into its defensive schemes.

THE EXPLORATION HYPOTHESIS

The exploration hypothesis predicts that militaries with moderately de-centralized command practices will generate doctrinal alternatives related to the superior way of fighting before those with more or less centralized com-mand practices. The case studies also support this prediction. The French Army practiced moderately decentralized command and control at the be-ginning of the war and started exploring the basic ideas behind assault tac-tics, combined arms, and elastic defenses in depth before the German Army, which practiced moderately centralized command and control until 1916. Moreover, the British Army, which started the war with moderately central-ized command practices, actually moved out of the exploration phase of the learning process, at least with regard to assault tactics, as it began to cen-tralize its control over command and control in mid-1915.

SELECTION HYPOTHESES

The first selection hypothesis predicts that leaders in militaries with independent assessment mechanisms are more likely to pick the doctrinal ideas that improve combat performance. The second selection hypothesis expects militaries with assessment mechanisms to refine new doctrinal concepts, ideas, and practices before those that do not have them. The evidence presented in the case studies support both predictions. The German Army started the war with such an assessment mechanism and entered the selection phase of the learning process for assault tactics, combined arms, and elastic defenses in depth months—if not years—before either of its adversaries. Moreover, the German Army did so despite the fact that the British and French combat units began exploring these concepts *before* German units did. The German Army also navigated the entire selection process behind the elastic defense-in-depth doctrine before the BEF. All three armies did shift from selection to action vis-à-vis combined arms at roughly the same time. And while the German and British armies both shifted from selection to action with regard to assault tactics in the winter of 1918, the French Army actually made that transition in the fall of 1917.

If anything, however, these developments offer further support for the selection hypotheses. After all, both the BEF and the French Army introduced genuine doctrinal assessment mechanisms in 1917. Once in place, the General Headquarters' Training Branch and the Grand Quartier Général's (GQG) Training Section helped their respective high commands quickly develop and refine their assault and combined-arms doctrines. Moreover, by this point in the war, both the Training Branch and the Training Section were fully aware of the German Army's progress in both areas. As the proverbial first mover, the German Army had to do most of the pioneering conceptual work, which invariably took longer and—once employed in combat—served as a source of information from which the Training Branch and the Training Section could learn. This helps make sense of why the German Army was always quicker to enter the selection phase of the learning process yet, except with elastic defenses in depth, also took longer to complete it.

ACTION HYPOTHESIS

The action hypothesis expects militaries that centralize control over training to transmit new practices faster than those that do not. Once again, the case studies support this prediction. The German Army centralized control over training by 1916. The army was therefore able to quickly disseminate its new tactical doctrines and usually navigated the action phase of the learning process in a matter of months. Uniform implementation remained a challenge for the British and French armies throughout the war. Although the BEF centralized control over training by the summer of 1918, it was too late to make a clear-cut difference. For example, the BEF moved into the action phase of the learning process vis-à-vis assault tactics in the winter of 1918, but the war ended before it could achieve the same degree of uniform implementation as the German Army. And even with regard to combined arms, it still took the BEF nearly a year to navigate the action phase of the learning process. The French Army's decentralized training likewise made it hard for the GQG to enforce uniform implementation of new practices. The fact that the GQG maintained more control over artillery and assault artillery training than it did over infantry training is also highly suggestive, since the French Army did demonstrate mastery of combined arms by war's end.

Alternative Explanations

History lends itself to multiple perspectives and interpretations. Even if the First World War is the closest thing to a natural experiment in military history, there are still a wide range of confounding factors and alternative ways to explain events. I discuss three below.

THE GERMAN ARMY LOST: DOES IT MATTER
IF IT WAS A LEARNING ORGANIZATION?

The fact that the German Army lost despite learning seems to imply that ACT theory is right but irrelevant. After all, most scholars and policy makers are interested in innovation, adaptation, and learning because they believe that such phenomenon will improve the odds of winning. Yet Germany's experience during the First World War proves that inept political and strategic decisions can undermine the advantages that accrue from having a flexible and adaptive military. For example, Germany might have knocked France out of the war in 1914 had Britain not intervened. Britain would not have come to France's aid had Germany not violated Belgian neutrality. The German Army invaded Belgium because German political and military leaders let their operational designs trump political realities. Germany made a similar mistake in 1917. At a point in the war when it needed more allies, not enemies, Germany initiated unrestricted submarine warfare and tried to secure a secret military pact with Mexico. These ham-fisted moves pushed a previously sympathetic Woodrow Wilson administration off the fence and into the war against Germany.[2] Finally, instead of offering to negotiate with the Entente after effectively winning the war on the Eastern Front in late 1917, Germany instead gambled everything on a decisive spring offensive along the Western Front.[3]

There is simply no world in which learning can, by itself, offset political and strategic incompetence. It does not follow, however, that tactical learning is therefore irrelevant. Learning matters *despite* not guaranteeing victory.

Military organizations that learn fight more efficiently and effectively than their adversaries, *all things being equal*. All things were not equal for the German Army, but this does not mean the German Army would have been better off were it worse at learning (although the war surely would have been shorter). The same holds true for Britain and France. Although their armies prevailed despite being less adept at learning, the reality is that they might have won sooner—and at a lower cost in terms of blood and treasure—had their armies been better at learning. Thus, ACT theory remains relevant, even if it is not the most important determinant of victory and defeat.

THE BRITISH AND FRENCH ARMIES WERE WAGING A WAR OF ATTRITION

My analysis is predicated on the assumption that the British, French, and German armies *should have* converged on a superior war-fighting doctrine that combined flexible assault tactics, integrated artillery-infantry operations, and elastic defenses in depth. I take the fact that the German Army arrived at this solution before its adversaries as proof that it was better at learning.

Some scholars might argue, however, that a superior one-size-fits-all way to fight did not exist on the Western Front. According to this view, Britain and France won because their path to victory ran through a war of attrition, and such a strategy turned on munitions and manpower, not flexible assault tactics, integrated artillery-infantry operations, and elastic defenses in depth. If this explanation is correct, then it follows that the British and French armies being slow to converge on these war-fighting practices tells us little about their ability to learn. Or it might even be the case that Britain and France were better learning organizations than the German Army.

There are three problems with this view. The first is that it conflates a broad strategic approach, attrition warfare, with a specific tactical doctrine, one based on stereotyped assault formations, methodical fire support plans, and inelastic defensive schemes. In reality, attrition warfare merely implies that one side wants to win by wearing down its opponent's military capabilities and political resolve while conserving its own. It stands to reason that assault tactics, combined arms, and elastic defenses in depth were actually *more* compatible with a strategy of attrition because they offered a less costly way to impose casualties while safeguarding one's own resources. Assault tactics protected advancing troops from the storm of steel. Combined arms disrupted enemy defenders, prevented them from shifting reserves into place, and restored surprise to the battlefield. And by definition, elastic defenses in depth conserved manpower by moving troops out of enemy artillery range and imposing higher costs on attacking units by forcing them to move across greater distances. This both increased their exposure to the storm of steel and forced them to move beyond the range of their supporting artillery. Thus, even if it is true that Britain and France were content to sit back and grind the

German Army out of existence, assault tactics, combined arms, and elastic defenses in depth were almost undoubtedly the best possible way to do it.

Second, it is not clear that Britain and France actually committed themselves to a strategy of attrition. To be sure, once the war was over, British and French politicians and generals had powerful incentives to make it seem like the four-year slaughter served a necessary strategic purpose. The logic behind almost every major Entente offensive on the Western Front, however, suggests that British and French generals usually hoped to achieve a decisive breakthrough. For example, Douglas Haig originally wanted to punch through German lines along the Somme River, not wear down German forces. Similarly, at Passchendaele, his tactical and operational objectives suggest that he was torn between wearing down German reserves (setting limited objectives such as seizing the high ground outside Ypres) and breaking through (by taking Ostend, which would have required a complete penetration of German defenses).[4]

Third, as chapters 4 and 5 clearly show, the British and French armies *did* move to adopt the same basic practices as their German opponent. This convergence became especially pronounced in the war's final two years. Thus, even if British and French grand strategy did commit to a war of attrition, the British and French armies still believed that assault tactics, combined arms, and elastic defenses in depth (at least in the case of the British Army) represented a better way to prevail in a prolonged battle of matériel.

LEADERSHIP MATTERED MORE THAN STRUCTURE

Genius and individual leadership offer yet another tempting way to account for change. Leaders also seem to loom over the story of wartime learning during the First World War. The problem with explanations that revolve around individuals is that they cannot account for the full range of activities that must occur to make wartime learning possible as well as for why some organizations seem to be *systematically* better at navigating this process over time and across multiple leaders, why previously conservative and pro–status quo leaders suddenly advocate change, and why some leaders successfully impose change on a large organization that instinctively resists change while others fail.

Erich Ludendorff, for example, casts a shadow over the story of German learning. His reputation as a tactical mastermind is burnished by the army's adoption of its most revolutionary practices almost immediately after he rose to power. But although Ludendorff supported assault tactics, combined arms, and elastic defense in depth, they were not his ideas. Moreover, Erich von Falkenhayn, the oft-criticized micromanager—not Ludendorff— supported the army's initial work on storm troop tactics in 1915. Falkenhayn authorized the creation of Kalsow's experimental unit, dispatched Fritz von Lossberg to Champagne, and told frontline units to send detachments to train with Willy Rohr's battalion. Were it not for Falkenhayn's advocacy and the work of other junior and senior officers, these ideas would not have been ready for Ludendorff to implement in 1917 and 1918. Finally, because Ludendorff eventually became a de facto dictator, it is hard to imagine how he had the bandwidth to both lead a nation at war and direct the detailed development of a radical new tactical doctrine. This gives too much credit to individual genius while ignoring structure's far more consistent influence.

The theory of individual genius has an even bigger problem explaining learning in the British Army. Haig was, after all, a constant. He served as the BEF's commander in chief from late 1915 through the end of the war. Many of his core advisers also remained in place for much of the conflict. And although Haig did not show much interest in his army's tactical doctrine, the BEF nevertheless became better at learning as the war dragged on.

ACT theory does not imply that leaders and leadership are irrelevant. Instead, it tries to give us a more sophisticated way to think about the relationship between leadership and learning. ACT theory offers reasons why some leaders are more receptive to bottom-up learning than others and helps us understand why some leaders are better at distinguishing good ideas from bad ones. Most important, ACT theory sheds light on the sorts of structural changes that leaders can make if they want to make their wartime organizations better at learning.

Shadow Cases

Even if ACT theory captures an important part of the story behind what transpired on the Western Front, it does not necessarily follow that the theory also tells us about wartime learning in other contexts or time periods. Every conflict is unique, and the First World War is an extreme outlier. It is also possible that wars, along with the armies that fight them, have changed since 1918.[5] This section therefore introduces a pair of brief shadow cases—the US Army in Vietnam (1965–1973)[6] and Iraq (2003–2010)—to suggest that ACT theory can also help us understand how and why armies learn in modern conflicts.

To be clear, these shadow cases *do not* represent definitive proof. They merely suggest that there are plausible reasons to think ACT theory can account for wartime learning beyond the First World War and that further research is warranted. There are three reasons to look at these two cases. First, looking at one army in two different wars controls for strategic culture, something the British, French, and German case studies could not do.[7] Second, these cases suggest that ACT theory can also apply to conventional armies as they struggle to master an unconventional doctrine—in this case, population-centric counterinsurgency (COIN).[8] Third, focusing on how the US Army adapted to two modern conflicts sheds light on its learning mechanisms and allows us to speculate about the degree to which it is ready to learn in future wars.

The US Army did not adopt a population-centric COIN doctrine in Vietnam.[9] The army did, however, practice moderately decentralized command and control, have an independent assessment mechanism, and maintain tight control over training. The US Army in Vietnam therefore represents a deviant case.[10] As such, this case reiterates an important limitation first identified in chapter 1, namely that ACT theory expects command practices, assessment mechanisms, and training systems to exert a consistent impact on how wartime militaries learn. ACT theory does not predict that these structural factors are learning's sole determinants. In Vietnam, political and strategic imperatives intervened so as to prevent an army that was otherwise prepared to learn from effectively doing so.

The Evolution of US Politics, Strategy, and Operations America's involvement in Vietnam began with the Truman administration's decision to support its beleaguered French ally. That decision occurred against the backdrop of the Cold War. From that point forward, American policy makers saw Vietnam as one front among many in the struggle against international communism.[11] After the 1954 Geneva Conference divided Vietnam along the 17th parallel, the United States sought to ensure South Vietnam's survival as an independent state. For Dwight Eisenhower, John F. Kennedy, and Lyndon Johnson, this meant propping up a series of illegitimate regimes in Saigon through an ever-increasing commitment of money, equipment, and advisers.[12] In spite of these efforts, South Vietnam's government was on the verge of collapse by late 1964. Hanoi tried to exploit the situation and sent division-size elements of the People's Army of Vietnam (PAVN) south with orders to defeat the Army of the Republic of Vietnam (ARVN) and present the United States with a fait accompli. President Johnson responded by committing additional American ground forces and authorizing them to engage in direct combat with communist forces operating inside South Vietnam.

From 1965 until the Tet offensive in 1968, US ground combat operations unfolded in accordance with an overarching strategy of graduated escalation.[13] In theory, this approach reconciled the need to put decisive pressure on North Vietnam with Johnson's desire to keep the war limited. However, as actually practiced by units on the ground, graduated escalation mostly involved search-and-destroy operations. These were pitched conventional battles in which US Army units tried to use their firepower and mobility to find and destroy communist units.[14] This is not to say that Johnson's senior commander in the field, General William Westmoreland, or his headquarters, Military Assistance Command, Vietnam (MACV), ignored the insurgency raging across the South Vietnamese countryside. MACV knew it was being "whipsawed by a dual guerrilla-conventional threat."[15] It therefore tried to establish a division of labor of sorts with South Vietnamese security forces.[16] MACV wanted to use US troops to defeat PAVN units operating in South Vietnam while leaving the National Liberation Front for local security forces to handle.[17]

American strategy changed course after the Tet offensive, though militarily disastrous for Hanoi,[18] nevertheless turned American public opinion against the war. President Richard Nixon therefore adopted the policy of Vietnamization, which he hoped might appease antiwar sentiment while also reflecting his broader efforts to reorient American foreign policy.[19] On the ground, Vietnamization meant withdrawing US ground troops while preparing the ARVN to assume control of the war. Operationally, Vietnamization entailed replacing large-scale search-and-destroy operations with small-unit clear-and-hold patrols designed to maximize local security.[20]

The Evolution of the US Army's Counterinsurgency Doctrine The US Army did not embrace COIN before Vietnam but did not ignore it either.[21] The army developed a coherent COIN doctrine in the 1950s and 1960s.[22] This doctrine was undoubtedly imperfect and existed more on paper than in practice. Yet the doctrine was based on the US Army's extensive historical experiences waging unconventional warfare and espoused many of the basic concepts we now associate with population-centric COIN.[23]

The US Army also updated its official COIN manuals based on experiences in Vietnam.[24] The army produced the new *Field Manual 31-16: Counterguerrilla Operations*, in 1967.[25] A revised version of *Field Manual 100-5: Operations*, released in 1968, warned units not to rely on heavy firepower and demonstrated a preference for small-unit action.[26] In February, MACV also sent every unit in Vietnam a new COIN manual, the *Handbook for Military Support of Pacification*, which captured the lessons learned and best practices over the course of the war.

Thus, by early 1968 at the latest, the US Army had a doctrine that captured the basic components of a population-centric COIN doctrine. The problem was that MACV—in accordance with its overarching political and strategic mandates and limitations—decided on a military strategy anchored on conventional warfare.[27] Operations and tactics followed suit as frontline commanders emphasized air mobility, armor, and firepower, thereby applying conventional solutions to an unconventional problem.[28]

Creighton Abrams replaced Westmoreland in mid-1968 and tried to push the US Army to do a better job of balancing between conventional and pacification operations.[29] Under Abrams's leadership, the US Army experimented with or participated in a number of innovative programs, including the Civil Operations and Revolutionary Development Support, the Hamlet Evaluation System, the Chiêu Hồi defector, and the Accelerated Pacification

Campaign programs.[30] Despite placing a greater relative emphasis on COIN operations under Abrams, MACV nevertheless continued to pour far more resources into its conventional operations.[31] COIN operations rarely amounted to a proverbial drop in the bucket.[32]

Command Practices The US Army practiced moderately decentralized command and control in Vietnam. The ground war consisted of countless small-unit actions in which company-grade officers—and even noncommissioned officers—exercised significant autonomy. In many ways, the infantry company was the primary unit of action in Vietnam.[33] Even Westmoreland's large-scale search-and-destroy campaigns were decentralized operations in which battalion, company, and platoon commanders had the latitude to decide how to accomplish their assigned tasks.[34] Given Vietnam's complex terrain, senior commanders could not have controlled combat operations even had they wanted to. Although high-ranking officers did retain centralized control over air, intelligence, and fire support assets, all were available on call to junior leaders, especially as they sought to bring firepower to bear on insurgent units.[35]

US Army units also actively experimented.[36] They tested different organizational structures—work that ultimately led the US Army to add a fourth rifle company to its light infantry battalions.[37] Combat operations also involved thousands of similar bottom-up adaptations to weapons, formations, and tactics. And junior officers did not hesitate to complain about the army's strategy, operations, and tactics.[38]

Assessment Mechanism The US Army also had an independent assessment mechanism in the form of its Combat Developments Command (CDC).[39] Although the CDC has been heavily derided for its obsession with body counts the reality is that in Vietnam the command was able to leverage what Jonathan Askonas refers to as "the most elaborate assessments, indicators, and metrics system the world had ever seen in wartime."[40] By 1966 the CDC—based in Virginia—had permanent liaison offices in Vietnam. Although the army had embedded analysts within combat units before, Vietnam was the first war in which these liaison observers remained attached to their combat on a permanent basis, thereby providing "a continuous link for the flow of observer-derived information"[41] The CDC also collected and analyzed after-action reports coming from the front lines. Each quarter, division commands and above sent an "Operational Report–Lessons Learned" to the CDC via the assistant chief of staff for force development. CDC analysts parsed these reports for useful ideas and information so as to revise official doctrine as needed.[42]

CDC personnel also had the analytic wherewithal to rigorously process and evaluate the incoming data. Much of this capacity was based on the army's newfound passion for operations research and systems analysis

(ORSA). The Office of the Deputy Undersecretary of the Army for Operations Research was established in 1965 to coordinate ORSA efforts across the entire service.[43] Vietnam was therefore the first conflict in which the US Army relied heavily on advanced analytic techniques to assess and develop doctrine.[44] Within the combat theater, ORSA-trained analysts were permanently integrated at the division, force, and MACV levels.[45] Back in the United States, the CDC also made extensive use of ORSA-trained analysts to process raw data, develop new techniques, and assess lessons learned.[46] These analysts were highly educated and well prepared for the task at hand.[47] Prior to 1967, the army picked 15 officers each year to attend a graduate-level ORSA degree program at a civilian university. In March 1967, the army created a dedicated career path for ORSA specialists called the ORSA Officer Specialist Program. Ultimately the army had 413 slots for ORSA officers, most of whom rotated in and out of the specialty to maintain credibility in their traditional (e.g., infantry, armor, signals) specialties. While some senior officers disliked letting officers specialize in ORSA, an official review of the program "reported that the program was attractive to outstanding young officers and was already one of the more popular special career programs."[48] The US Army also relied on professional civilian contractors for ORSA support, since the sheer amount of data that the army's ORSA efforts produced meant there simply were not enough qualified army officers to meet the analytic demand.[49] Contractors made up nearly 80 percent of the organization's ORSA workforce by 1968.

Finally, the CDC had the latitude to make independent recommendations. The CDC produced the army's COIN manuals during the war, many of which rejected existing praxis. For example, the 1966 US Army Combat Operations and 1967 Evaluation of United States Army Mechanized and Armor Combat Operations in Vietnam studies "involved extensive in-country data collection and analysis by a mixed team of military personnel and ORSA analysts."[50] Both studies criticized existing practices. The Army Combat Operations in Vietnam study said that the CDC needed to do a better job of incorporating lessons learned from frontline units into official doctrine, encouraged infantry commanders to keep small units foot mobile instead of relying on armor and air for transportation, called for infantry battalions to add a fourth company, and recommended the use of tactical areas of operations to assist with command and control. Less than ten months after the study began, the CDC evaluated and endorsed all of its main findings, and the army's chief of staff directed their implementation.[51]

Training System The US Army relied on a centralized training system throughout the Vietnam War. From 1955 until 1973, a single high-level command—the Continental Army Command (CONARC)—controlled the service's entry-level, individual, and unit training as well as its professional military education schools.[52] The CDC also maintained a liaison detachment within each CONARC training school so as to monitor how new ideas were being taught.[53] CONARC therefore maintained control over how new soldiers learned the army's COIN practices, how career soldiers studied COIN doctrine, and how units trained for COIN operations. And CONARC ensured that personnel and units across the entire organization received COIN training. In 1965, the US Army War College introduced a five-week course on economic development for senior officers.[54] By 1969, all US Army Command and General Staff College students received 222 hours of COIN education.[55] COIN training was also incorporated into the introductory programs for all new officers and soldiers. CONARC even required units in Europe and the United States to set aside time for COIN training each year.[56]

A Failure to Learn? The US Army practiced moderately decentralized command practices, had an independent assessment mechanism, and centralized control over training. But the army failed to master COIN. I argue that the story of the US Army in Vietnam, far from counting as evidence against ACT theory, validates the theory's internal logic while highlighting one of its most important limitations: politics and strategy trump structure when it comes to learning.

Specifically, the US Army's command practices, assessment mechanism, and training systems functioned as ACT theory predicts they should. Combat units experimented. The CDC collected and analyzed their lessons learned, producing a surprisingly coherent COIN doctrine in the process. And CONARC transmitted these ideas across the organization. Therefore, the US Army had the doctrine in place to implement population-centric COIN on a widespread basis had strategic-level decision makers made the decision to do so. The army did not go this way, because senior leaders—right or wrong—saw Vietnam through a Cold War prism.[57] This put the US Army on the horns of a dilemma. The army had to pacify South Vietnam in support of an illegitimate government, defeat a highly capable conventional adversary, and accomplish both tasks without expanding the war and while still maintaining a credible deterrent posture against communist aggression in Europe, Korea, and Taiwan.[58] Faced with these multiple irreconcilable demands, the US Army's senior leaders opted to focus on conventional warfare to defeat PAVN units operating in South Vietnam and deter the Soviet Union. The army preferred to let South Vietnam take the lead in putting down the insurgency.[59] In essence, the US Army's focus on conventional warfare prevented it from adapting to the unconventional war it was losing. Still, it is not entirely obvious that prioritizing COIN operations would have yielded a different result.[60]

THE US ARMY IN IRAQ

The US Army's experience in Iraq (2003–2010)[61] offers clearer support for ACT theory. Combat units practiced moderately decentralized command and control, just as they had in Vietnam. The service overhauled its assessment mechanism after Vietnam, making it more effective while also fully integrating it into its already centralized training system. The outcome in Iraq, however, was different, at least in terms of doctrinal learning. The US Army adopted the official COIN doctrine *Field Manual 3-24: Counterinsurgency*, in 2006, and more frontline infantry units than not operated in accordance with the population-centric COIN principles espoused in that manual. Although General David Petraeus often receives credit as the mastermind behind this transformation, the reality is that learning was the result of an organization-wide effort composed of both bottom-up adaptation and top-down vision.[62]

The Evolution of US Politics, Strategy, and Operations The George W. Bush administration relied on a three-part justification for invading Iraq and removing Saddam Hussein from power.[63] First, Bush wanted to stop Hussein from using the weapons of mass destruction Iraq had allegedly stockpiled. Second, Bush wanted to prevent future attacks against the US homeland by severing Hussein's supposed links with international terrorist organizations. And third, by eliminating a despotic regime, Bush hoped to spark democratization in the region. To achieve these goals, he wanted a quick and surgical invasion. His administration believed that leaving Iraq's institutions and infrastructure intact would eliminate the need for a prolonged military presence.[64] Bush's secretary of defense, Donald Rumsfeld, was especially emphatic that the invasion force remains small and agile.

The invasion force reached Baghdad and toppled Hussein (along with most of his statues) in a matter of weeks. However, US forces ran into trouble when they transitioned to so-called fourth-phase operations. Widespread unrest and violence overwhelmed their ability to maintain order, not least because they were not trained, equipped, or sized for long-term security and stability operations.[65] In any case, administration officials initially blamed the violence on criminals and regime "never enders."[66] The rapidly devolving security situation nevertheless ultimately forced Bush to abandon his plans for a quick exit. His administration eventually organized the Coalition Provisional Authority to coordinate a reconstruction effort.[67]

Combined Joint Task Force 7, the US Army's senior command in Iraq at that point in the war, directed combat units to support the stabilization mission by conducting offensive operations "to defeat remaining noncompliant forces and neutralize destabilizing influences in the AO [area of operations]."[68] Thus, at least initially, the army once again opted to use conventional force against an unconventional foe. From 2003 to 2005, most combat operations focused on killing or capturing insurgents. Only about 6 percent of these operations were designed to protect the Iraqi people.[69] As Ahmed Hashim describes it, "the U.S. military's response to the insurgency [was] uniformly muscular, its weapon of choice the blunt military instrument. . . . [T]he Poles have taken to calling it the 'baseball bat' strategy."[70] An American colonel put it more bluntly: "If I were treated like this, I'd be a terrorist!"[71]

Whatever the rationale, this approach did not stem the violence. Attacks on coalition troops and government forces surged despite a string of battle-field successes, including Hussein's capture in December 2003, Moqtada al-Sadr's defeat in An Najaf in mid-2004, and Fallujah's virtual annihilation in November of the same year. Nor did political breakthroughs slow the insurgency's momentum. Violence increased unabated, even after the United States ceded control to an interim Iraqi government in June 2004 and Iraqi held its first elections in January 2005.

The war reached a turning point when Sunni insurgents bombed the Golden Mosque in February 2006.[72] Pushed to the brink, Shi'ite militias began exterminating their rivals. The country descended into civil war.[73] Bush responded by deploying thirty thousand additional troops around Baghdad as part of the so-called surge. Bush also made Petraeus, one of the army's leading advocates for COIN reform, responsible for implementing the military component of this new strategy. Operationally, Petraeus ordered his forces to implement the COIN doctrine he helped author a year earlier. The US Army steadily shifted from a conventional kinetic-based approach that emphasized "large, fortified bases, mounted patrols and transition to Iraqi security forces" to a true COIN program based on "smaller, dispersed bases, dismounted patrolling, and direct provision of U.S. security for threatened Iraqi civilians."[74] Many credited these efforts for pulling Iraq back from the brink.[75]

The Evolution of the US Army's Counterinsurgency Doctrine The US Army relegated COIN to the backburner after Vietnam. The army's newest capstone doctrine, *Field Manual 3-0: Operations* (2001),[76] offered a few vague prescriptions for conducting COIN operations.[77] The army also promulgated the new *Field Manual 3-07: Stability and Support Operations* a month before the invasion, although this manual similarly lacked sufficient detail.[78] Ironically, at least in terms of doctrine, the army might have been better prepared to fight insurgents in Vietnam than it was in Iraq.

The US Army's official doctrine did not catch up until the US Army and Marine Corps jointly published *Field Manual 3-24: Counterinsurgency (FM 3-24)* in 2006.[79] FM 3-24 "gave the Army and Marine Corps the intellectual and training tools to prosecute the fight in Iraq."[80] FM 3-24 also represented the first capstone-level doctrine in the organization's history to champion a comprehensive population-centric COIN doctrine. The manual reminded commanders that their main goal in a COIN campaign was to protect the people, not kill guerrillas.[81] Doing this meant dividing and distributing soldiers throughout the community instead of consolidating them in large bases.[82] Although living and operating among the local population made

American soldiers more vulnerable in the short run, it was the only way to establish popular credibility in the long run. FM 3-24 also reminded unit leaders that when their soldiers brought their firepower to bear on the enemy, they would do so precisely and only in proportion to the threat.[83] And FM 3-24 emphasized the need for both integrated civil-military action and a heavy reliance on intelligence.[84]

FM 3-24 was not a case of a high-level doctrine that had little impact on how units operated on the ground. Many units were already using COIN tactics, techniques, and procedures.[85] FM 3-24 nevertheless served as an intellectual framework to ensure such principles were applied on a widespread basis and also shaped the concept of operations for the 2007 surge. US Army units participating in the surge divided into small teams and manned outposts *inside* Baghdad and alongside Iraqi troops.[86] The units initially focused on security for Baghdad's most violent neighborhoods. As conditions improved, these units then began to expand the zone in which they operated. Foot patrols replaced armored and motorized patrols.[87] Commanders limited the use of heavy weapons, artillery, and air strikes. And the army increased its contributions to civil-military units, including Provisional Reconstruction Teams, and adviser groups attached to Iraqi security units.[88]

Command Practices US Army combat units continued to adhere to the army's long-standing practice of empowering junior and noncommissioned officers.[89] Frontline commanders did not report being micromanaged or having their ideas and experiments ignored by their chain of command.[90] In any case, the nature of Iraq's insurgency, combined with the relative paucity of combat troops, meant that senior officers had no choice but to cede initiative and authority to the lieutenants and sergeants leading the small-unit patrols and convoys that composed the overwhelming majority of combat operations in Iraq.[91] If anything, US Army combat units took their freedom to experiment to its logical extreme. Austin Long says that "the U.S. military's actual conduct of COIN in Iraq from 2003 to 2005 can charitably be described as highly variable."[92] Combat units aggressively tested out different methods and techniques.[93] Some of these ideas eventually made their way into FM 3-24.[94] Moreover, many of the officers who were instrumental in writing FM 3-24 or advising General Petraeus as he implemented it in 2007 had previous experience as commanders on the ground in Iraq.[95]

Assessment and Training Of course, all the brilliant frontline tests and trials would have made little difference without a mechanism for collecting, selecting, refining, and turning them into coherent doctrinal concepts. The US Army had such a capability, given that it built upon its Vietnam War–era doctrinal assessment mechanism in the wake of that conflict. Ironically, this system was the result of a series of reforms designed to help the army shift *away* from COIN. After Vietnam, Abrams (by then the chief of staff of the army), General William DePuy (a former division commander and MACV staff officer who fiercely opposed using the army to conduct COIN missions), and General Paul Gorman sought to improve upon the army's Vietnam-era analytic system by streamlining data collection, centralizing analysis, and improving the links between doctrine and training.[96] Their most important reform involved combining the CDC and CONARC so as to create the new Training and Doctrine Command (TRADOC) in 1973.[97]

TRADOC improved how the US Army produced doctrine and managed training in a number of ways. Given how unwieldy the Vietnam-era Operational Report–Lessons Learned system had become, TRADOC replaced it with the Center for Army Lessons Learned (CALL) in 1985.[98] To streamline the process even further, units on the ground were allowed to submit their observations, insights, and lessons reports *directly* to CALL.[99] CALL historians and analysts then vetted submissions, selecting the most promising items for distribution to subject matter experts within TRADOC.[100] CALL also collected ideas by sending trained analytic teams to embed within frontline units.[101] More than fifty such teams had deployed to Iraq and Afghanistan by 2009.[102]

TRADOC also made the doctrinal process both more rigorous and more prestigious.[103] The command established itself as "a place of intellectual ferment where young professionals sought to be assigned."[104] TRADOC organized an in-house institute to study military history for the purposes of writing doctrine, the Combat Studies Institute.[105] And the School of Advanced Military Studies (SAMS) was ultimately created under TRADOC's auspices. SAMS allowed the top graduates of the US Army Command and General Staff College to receive an intense second year of staff officer training and education. SAMS students and faculty frequently participated in the doctrine-writing process.[106]

Finally, TRADOC increased the degree to which the service could control doctrinal change, because it created a bureaucratic structure to enforce compliance.[107] Training and doctrine now existed within a single command and made a range of subsequent reforms possible. The army consolidated its schools so as to reduce the supervision challenge, established combat training centers (e.g., the National Training Center) to evaluate how well large units were prepared to execute current doctrine, organized inspection teams to ensure schools were operating in accordance with TRADOC directives,[108] and implemented the new Army Training and Evaluation Program to facilitate standards-based training.[109]

Learning Counterinsurgency Scholarship on the Iraq War suggests that as ACT theory predicts, the US Army's moderately decentralized command culture, sophisticated assessment mechanism, and tightly centralized training system played a key role in FM 3-24's development and implementation.[110] Frontline units did not hesitate to experiment. CALL captured ideas percolating up from the bottom of the organization and processed them in a cogent, rigorous way. TRADOC formed the locus for innovative thought. In fact, FM 3-24 took form after General Petraeus took command of TRADOC's major subordinate command for doctrine writing, the Combined Arms Center (which owned and was physically collocated with CALL).[111] Finally, as was the case throughout the war, TRADOC's schools continually updated their curricula to teach students at all levels new doctrine, to include FM 3-24 and the 2008 *Field Manual 3-07: Stability Operations* and *Field Manual 3-0: Operations*.[112]

Future Work

I have tried to make a compelling case that ACT theory can help us understand wartime learning. That said, no matter how convincing the evidence may (or may not) be, there is always room for future work. Three research strands seem especially promising. First, a necessary next step is to test ACT theory against non-Western cases. The First World War's Western Front is useful because it is the closest thing to a natural experiment in warfare. Nevertheless, the Western Front involved three decidedly west European armies, and there are a number of reasons to assume that early twentieth-century European ground forces differ in systematic ways from other armies at other points in time. Nor do the shadow cases on the US Army compensate for this shortcoming. After all, the American military drew cultural, organizational, and doctrinal inspiration from the British, French, and German armies. Future scholars should consider applying ACT theory to African, Asian, South American, and Middle Eastern wartime military organizations.

Second, it is worth exploring the impact that war duration has on doctrinal learning. ACT theory seems optimized to explain cases of wartime learning in longer conflicts. It took the German Army nearly three years to master assault tactics, combined arms, and elastic defenses in depth. The US Army spent seven years in Vietnam without fully adapting to COIN and at least three years in Iraq before making a decisive move toward COIN. At a minimum, it is important to test ACT theory against shorter wars so as to better establish its conceptual boundaries.

Third, although I said that ACT theory only applies to ground forces, testing it against cases of aerial, naval, and special operations warfare might be useful so as to determine whether this scope condition is necessary. Similarly, the proliferation of joint (multiservice) and combined (multinational) warfare suggests that exploring what ACT theory does—and does not— mean is important for learning in these types of contexts.

Policy Implications

To the degree that ACT theory captures something essential about wartime learning, national security policy makers should consider at least the following four reminders.

DO NOT UNDERESTIMATE THE WARTIME LEARNING CHALLENGE

The story of learning on the Western Front serves as a poignant reminder that wartime learning is the hardest form of learning. Time lines are brutally short, and political pressure is unimaginably high. Mistakes, which are an inevitable part of the learning process, are measured in terms of lives lost. Causation becomes even harder than usual to establish. Clausewitzian friction and chance can make it nearly impossible to know if a new weapon or tactic worked for the reasons alleged. And as all three case studies in this book highlight, senior commanders and staffs are likely to be so preoccupied with mobilization, coalition building, and other early war tasks that they will not have time or bandwidth to engage in meaningful doctrinal analysis until the conflict is well underway. Finally, when it comes to wartime learning, the devil is in the details. Victory on the Western Front turned not on broad operational concepts but rather on detailed tactics, techniques, and procedures that took hundreds of thousands of lives to master.

PROTECT THE TRADITION OF EMPOWERING SUBORDINATES FROM TECHNOLOGICAL INNOVATION

American military leaders should also be careful not to take the long-standing tradition of empowering subordinate leaders for granted. History suggests that such practices can falter when the shooting first starts and that centralization can become the norm with remarkable speed. Contemporary advances in artificial intelligence, quantum computing, and real-time communications could compound this risk by convincing senior leaders that they can now make the sorts of calls once delegated to the officer on the spot. After all, why let a twenty-four-year-old lieutenant or sergeant make a decision—especially one that could have operational, strategic, or political ramifications—when technology allows a general with decades of experience, surrounded by a capable staff and augmented with the latest decision-making algorithms, to do the same? The temptation to micromanage will increase, as these technologies also make it easier for political leaders at home to keep an eye on their generals and admirals. In this way, technological innovation can inadvertently undermine the command practices that the American military has spent generations instilling.

Obviously, the recommendation is not to abandon investment in these capabilities, which will undoubtedly give the US military an important edge. As technology's strongest advocates suggest, one day it may well be possible to reduce the fog of war, kill everything that can be seen, and see everything. At the same time, ACT theory reminds us that perfect knowledge comes at a price. Indeed, total battlefield awareness may impair our ability to adapt to that same battlefield, since it is possible to know something is happening without knowing what to do about it.

PROTECT THE CAPACITY FOR RIGOROUS DOCTRINAL ASSESSMENT

ACT theory suggests that assessment mechanisms are vital to wartime learning. The US military has long enjoyed a decisive advantage in this area. Nevertheless, the military should guard against two potentially deleterious trends. The first involves the tendency to substitute routinized lessons, learned procedures, and after-action reports for genuine analysis. The proclivity is understandable. Frontline leaders have many demands on their time and may come to view after-action reporting as a nuisance. Analysts want to demonstrate that they add value and so face incentives to disseminate lessons learned as fast, as far, and as wide as possible. Senior commanders often face budgetary requirements to hire analytic contractors, further exacerbating the paperwork barrage without necessarily improving its efficacy. More insidious yet, outsourcing analytic capacity could be akin to performing an intellectual lobotomy on the staff corps. The less active-duty staff officers engage in rigorous doctrinal analysis, the more these essential skill sets will atrophy.

The second trend involves the US military's tendency to marginalize analytic careers and fields. To be sure, US Army and Marine Corps officers can become analysts, but such military occupational specialties are rarely considered elite in these services. Few analysts rise to their organizations' highest echelons. Many officers consider this arrangement appropriate, since command demands warriors and the warrior ethos, not analysts and the scholarly mind-set. Such a view is historically naive. At the very least, members of the elite nineteenth- and twentieth-century German General Staff would vehemently disagree. More insidiously, a cultural antipathy to analysis suggests that the US military methodically diverts the best and brightest *away* from analytic career paths. Every army needs more commanders than analysts. Problems may arise, however, when those with the most brilliant command prospects are discouraged from pursuing analytic training.

THE PERILS OF PREDICTION

The final lesson involves a reminder about the perils of prediction. Although the US military can and should invest heavily in thinking about—

and planning for—future wars, it should also be careful not to exaggerate its ability to predict with accuracy. Predicting what future wars will look like and the kind of armies we will need to fight them is difficult under the best of circumstances. Wartime outcomes turn on a complex combination of political, social, economic, demographic, technological, strategic, operational, and tactical factors. Wars that occur in the midst of a revolutionary shift in one or more of these variables make perfect prediction impossible.

Europe faced such a situation in the decades leading up the First World War. And European generals were at least relatively certain of who they would fight and where. Rigid alliances, for all their many obvious drawbacks, simplified planning. Even so, they still failed to see what massive armies, rapid-fire weapons, and the absence of tactical logistics and communications—*and the way these factors would interact in a specific geographical space*—would mean in terms of tactical doctrine.

Today's military planners may be faced with an even more complex security environment. Technology is advancing at a breakneck pace. The most obvious changes, of course, have unfolded in computing. The computing revolution is spawning changes in everything from artificial intelligence to social networking, business, surveillance, robotics, and space exploration. Yet the Department of Defense has almost no control over how these technologies will evolve. Compounding the difficulty of keeping up, modern armies, navies, and air forces can barely deploy the latest and greatest cutting-edge weapons before their investments become seemingly obsolete.

This high rate of technological change, when combined with the absence of great-power war, mean that doctrinal development is at least as speculative as it was before the First World War. Combined-arms doctrines have matured, and precision-guided weapons have proliferated. Although both have been around for a long time, it remains unclear what a war will look like when all sides have these legacy capabilities, let alone revolutionary new ones. Today's military planners must also wrestle with a far more ambiguous range of threats and a wider range of places where they must be prepared to fight. And although the idea that mobilization meant war might seem laughable now, we should be willing to contemplate that the ability to deliver a knockout blow via the Internet or a precision strike—capabilities that may well exist in the near future—force us to make decisions in an even more compressed time line.

I do not mean to suggest that prediction is futile. Certainly, the closer we can get to the right doctrine, the better our military forces will perform in future conflicts and the fewer casualties they will suffer. Nor do I mean to suggest that the next great-power war will bog down into trench warfare on a global scale (although there are certainly reasons to speculate what precision, cyber, unmanned, and antiaccess weapons will mean for American strategic mobility). Rather, my point is to simply suggest that prediction— and doctrinal development—ought to proceed with extreme modesty under present conditions. Similarly, political leaders would be well served to pay far more attention to their military's doctrines than they likely are. That war is too important to be left to the generals overstates the case, but no one can lay claim to experience when it comes to future war. Moreover, the use of force—rarely a surgical instrument of policy under the best of circumstances—may prove especially unwieldy under present conditions. Europe's leaders would have been better off avoiding war in 1914. The last several hundred pages of analysis notwithstanding, this lesson may have been the most important one of all.

Notes

Introduction

1. United States Marine Corps, *Marine Corps Doctrinal Publication 1-0, Marine Corps Operations* (Washington, DC: Headquarters United States Marine Corps, 2001). On maneuver warfare's conceptual origins and eventual development, see William S. Lind, *Maneuver Warfare Handbook* (Boulder, CO: Westview Press, 1985); Terry Terriff, "'Innovate or Die': Organizational Culture and the Origins of Maneuver Warfare in the United States Marine Corps," *Journal of Strategic Studies* 29, no. 3 (June 2006): 475–503; Fideleon Damian, "The Road to FMFM-1: The United States Marine Corps and Maneuver Warfare Doctrine, 1979–1989" (MA thesis, Kansas State University, 2008).

2. This engagement unfolded along Route 6 between An Nu'maniyah and the outskirts of Baghdad between April 2nd and 5th. What follows is from the author's personal journal; Jim Landers, "Marines Engage Republican Guard in Fierce Day of Battle," *Stars and Stripes*, April 5, 2003; Bing West and Ray L. Smith, *The March Up: Taking Baghdad with the 1st Marine Division* (New York: Bantam Books, 2003), 153–89.

3. RCT-5 was one of three RCTs that composed Major General James N. Mattis's 1st Marine Division.

4. On the Marine Corps' history fighting small wars, see Keith B. Bickel, *Mars Learning: The Marine Corps' Development of Small Wars Doctrine, 1915–1940* (Boulder, CO: Westview Press, 2001); Allan R. Millett, *Semper Fidelis: The History of the United States Marine Corps* (New York: Macmillan, 1980). On the Marine Corps' experiences learning (and relearning) the lessons learned from its small wars, see Jeannie L. Johnson, *The Marines, Counterinsurgency, and Strategic Culture: Lessons Learned and Lost in America's Wars* (Washington, DC: Georgetown University Press, 2018); Jonathan Askonas, "A Muse of Fire: Why the U.S. Military Forgets What It Learns in War" (D.Phil. diss., Oxford University, 2019).

5. What follows is from James A. Russell, *Innovation, Transformation, and War: Counterinsurgency Operations in Anbar and Ninewa Provinces, Iraq, 2005–2007* (Palo Alto, CA: Stanford University Press, 2011), 123–32.

6. As quoted in Russell, *Innovation, Transformation, and War*, 124.

7. War would still be a rock-throwing contest if it did not.

8. Analyzing all interstate wars from 1816 to 1980, Henry Farber and Joanne Gowa argue that the probability that any two states will go to war in a given year is approximately

0.09 percent. See Henry Farber and Joanne Gowa, "Common Interests or Common Polities?," *Journal of Politics* 59, no. 2 (May 1997): 405.

9. Carl von Clausewitz, *On War*, trans. Peter Paret and Michael Howard (Princeton, NJ: Princeton University Press, 1984), 586–94.

10. Yuen Foong Khong, *Analogies at War: Korea, Munich, Dien Bien Phu and the Vietnam Decisions of 1965* (Princeton, NJ: Princeton University Press, 1992), 3–18.

11. Scott Maucione, "DoD 2020 Budget Puts Heavy Emphasis on Development of Emerging Technologies," *Federal News Network*, March 13, 2019, https://federalnewsnetwork.com /defensemain/2019/03/dod-2020-budget-puts-heavy-emphasis-on-development-of -emergingtechnologies/; Kathleen Hicks et al., *Assessing the Third Offset Strategy* (Washington, DC: Center for Strategic and International Studies, 2017).

12. James M. McPherson, *Battle Cry of Freedom: The Civil War Era* (Oxford: Oxford University Press, 2003), 454–89; and Stephen W. Sears, *Lincoln's Lieutenants: The High Command of the Army of the Potomac* (New York: Houghton Mifflin Harcourt, 2017), 177–274.

13. Nor were the lessons it held for conventional combat operations necessarily clear-cut. Paddy Griffith, *Battle Tactics of the Western Front* (New Haven, CT: Yale University Press, 2000), 51.

14. Julian Corbett, *Principles of Maritime Strategy* (London: Longmans, Green and Co., 1911; reprint, New York: Dover 2004), 74–81. Citation refers to the Dover edition. This claim is not to discount the degree to which ethnocentrism also caused European planners to overlook these conflicts, since many European believed that "the operations of Russian and Japanese forces were unlikely to hold lessons for 'civilized' militaries." Ryan Grauer, "Moderating Diffusion: Military Bureaucratic Politics and the Implementation of German Doctrine in South America, 1885–1914," *World Politics* 67, no. 2 (April 2015): 276.

15. Even if we consider the Korean War a great-power clash, it ended nearly seventy years ago.

16. Williamson Murray, *Military Adaptation in War: With Fear of Change* (New York: Cambridge University Press, 2011).

17. All three divided their combat units into infantry, artillery, and cavalry branches; subdivided their artillery into field artillery and heavy artillery; and had roughly twelve thousand soldiers per division, although British divisions were triangular (each division had three brigades, and each brigade had four battalions), while German and French divisions were square (each division had two brigades, each brigade had two regiments, and each regiment had three battalions). By August 1914, all three armies also had four infantry companies per battalion. Companies typically consisted of approximately two hundred and fifty soldiers and were considered to be the smallest unit capable of independent action by all three armies. Stephen Bull, "The Early Years of the War," in *War on the Western Front: In the Trenches of World War I*, ed. Gary Sheffield (Oxford, UK: Osprey, 2007), 173–75.

18. If there was a difference in armament, it was that the German Army started the war with more heavy artillery than the French and British due to its war plans, which called for the rapid destruction of Belgian and French forts.

19. Chapter 2 describes each of these war-fighting concepts in detail. Technically, combined arms and defense in depth have existed for centuries. With regard to combined arms, generals have always sought to offset the weaknesses of one weapon system by integrating it with the strengths of another (e.g., archers could strike distant targets but were vulnerable to close-in attack and so were integrated with swordsmen, and early riflemen were vulnerable while loading their cumbersome weapons and were integrated with pikemen). Yet the practice fell into disuse by the eighteenth century and did not reemerge in any meaningful sense at lower levels of command until the First World War. Jonathan M. House, *Combined Arms Warfare in the Twentieth Century* (Lawrence: University of Kansas Press, 2001), 3. A similar point can be made about defense in depth. See Edward N. Luttwak, *The Grand Strategy of the Roman Empire: From the First Century A.D. to the Third* (Baltimore: Johns Hopkins University Press, 1979), chap. 3.

20. Murray, *Military Adaptation in War*, 74.

21. Hew Strachan, *The First World War*, Vol. 1. *To Arms* (Oxford, UK: Oxford University Press, 2003), xv.

22. See, for example, Timothy T. Lupfer, *The Dynamics of Doctrine: The Changes in German Tactical Doctrine during the First World War* (Fort Leavenworth, KS: Combat Studies Institute, 1981);

Shelford Bidwell and Dominick Graham, *Fire-Power: British Army Weapons and Theories of War, 1904–1945* (London: George Allen & Unwin, 1982); Bruce I. Gudmundsson, *Stormtroop Tactics: Innovation in the German Army, 1914–18* (Westport, CT: Praeger, 1995); Martin Samuels, *Command or Control? Command, Training, and Tactics in the British and German Armies, 1888–1918* (London: Frank Cass Publishers, 1995); Griffith, *Battle Tactics of the Western Front*; M. A. Ramsay, *Command and Cohesion: The Citizen Soldier and Minor Tactics in the British Army, 1870–1918* (Westport, CT: Praeger, 2002); Jonathan Boff, *Winning and Losing on the Western Front: The British Third Army and the Defeat of Germany in 1918* (Cambridge: Cambridge University Press, 2014); Robert T. Foley, "A Case Study in Horizontal Military Innovation: The German Army, 1916–1918," *Journal of Strategic Studies* 35, no. 6 (2012): 799–827; Robert T. Foley, "Dumb Donkeys or Cunning Foxes? Learning in the British and German Armies during the Great War," *International Affairs* 90, no. 2 (2014): 279–98; Jonathan Boff, *Haig's Enemy: Crown Prince Rupprecht and Germany's War on the Western Front* (Oxford, UK: Oxford University Press, 2018); Aimée Fox, *Learning to Fight: Military Innovation and Change in the British Army, 1914–1918* (Cambridge: Cambridge University Press, 2018); Gary Sheffield, *Forgotten Victory: The First World War: Myths and Realities* (London: Headline Book Publishing 2001; reprint., London: Sharpe Books, 2018), Kindle. Citations refer to the Sharpe Books edition.

23. Sheffield, *Forgotten Victory*, 162.

24. Jonathan B. A. Bailey, "The First World War and the Birth of Modern Warfare," in *The Dynamics of Military Revolution, 1300–2050*, ed. MacGregor Knox and Williamson Murray, 132–53 (Cambridge: Cambridge University Press, 2009); Stephen Biddle, *Military Power: Explaining Victory and Defeat in Modern Battle* (Princeton, NJ: Princeton University Press, 2006), 28–51; Michel Goya, *Flesh and Steel during the Great War: The Transformation of the French Army and the Invention of Modern Warfare*, trans. Andrew Uffindell (Barnsley, UK: Pen and Sword, 2018), 240.

25. The British and French were far more advanced in their work on the tank. However, the tank was only one element of combined arms and, more importantly, was not a decisive element in the First World War. See Boff, *Winning and Losing on the Western Front*, 140–45.

26. For an in-depth analysis of the German Army's spring 1918 offensives, see David T. Zabecki, *The German 1918 Offensives: A Case Study in the Operational Level of War* (London: Routledge, 2006), Kindle.

27. For brevity, I use the term "independent doctrinal assessment mechanism" as shorthand for "prestigious, formal, and independent doctrinal assessment mechanism."

28. Caitlin Talmadge, *The Dictator's Army: Battlefield Effectiveness in Authoritarian Regimes* (Ithaca, NY: Cornell University Press, 2015), 13.

29. This term is a modified version of what Jörg Muth refers to as command culture. See Jörg Muth, *Command Culture: Officer Education in the U.S. Army and the German Armed Forces, 1901–1940, and the Consequences for World War II* (Denton: University of North Texas Press, 2011), 7–8.

30. Ryan Grauer, *Commanding Military Power* (Cambridge: Cambridge University Press, 2016), 39–40.

31. Stephen P. Rosen, *Winning the Next War: Innovation and the Modern Military* (Ithaca, NY: Cornell University Press, 1994), 19–20.

32. I thank Stephen Biddle for his suggestions and advice, which contributed to the following discussion.

33. Clausewitz, *On War*, 117–21; Scott S. Gartner, *Strategic Assessment in War* (New Haven, CT: Yale University Press, 1999), 26.

34. The relevant security studies literature traces back to the Cold War. For early examples, see J. F. C. Fuller, *The Conduct of War, 1789–1961: A Study of the Impact of the French, Industrial, and Russian Revolutions on War and Its Conduct* (New Brunswick, NJ: Rutgers University Press, 1961); Bernard Brodie and Fawn Brodie, *From Crossbow to H-Bomb* (Bloomington: Indiana University Press, 1973). For a detailed overview and analysis of the literature, see Adam Grissom, "The Future of Military Innovation Studies," *Journal of Strategic Studies* 29, no. 5 (October 2006): 905–34; Stuart Griffin, "Military Innovation Studies: Multidisciplinary or Lacking Discipline?" *Journal of Strategic Studies* 40, nos. 1–2 (2017): 196–224.

35. To paraphrase Stephen Rosen's apt summary of the literature in the early 1990s: for every study that discovers one factor that seems to explain change, another study identifies a case in

which change occurs despite that factor's absence. Rosen, *Winning the Next War*, 3. At least in this regard, not much seems to have changed over the past thirty years.

36. Although scholars debate the precise boundaries between these concepts, most agree that innovation involves sweeping doctrinal, organizational, or technological changes. See Williamson Murray and Allan R. Millett, eds., *Military Innovation in the Interwar Period* (Cambridge: Cambridge University Press, 2009). Adaptation refers incremental and often ad hoc adjustments by frontline units as they struggle to adjust to new tactical challenges. See Williamson Murray, *Military Adaptation in War*. Emulation involves the decision to copy proven innovations and adaptations. See João Resende-Santos, *Neorealism, States, and the Modern Mass Army* (Cambridge: Cambridge University Press, 2007); Michael C. Horowitz, *The Diffusion of Military Power: Causes and Consequences for International Politics* (Princeton, NJ: Princeton University Press, 2010). Finally, learning transcends all three forms of change, in that it relates to how organizations incorporate new knowledge, information, and experience into existing doctrine, routine, and practice. See Richard Duncan Downie, *Learning from Conflict: The U.S. Military in Vietnam, El Salvador, and the Drug War* (Westport, CT: Praeger, 1998); John A. Nagl, *Learning to Eat Soup with a Knife: Counterinsurgency Lessons from Malaya and Vietnam* (Chicago: University of Chicago Press, 2005).

37. Barry R. Posen, *The Sources of Military Doctrine: France, Britain, and Germany between the World Wars* (Ithaca, NY: Cornell University Press, 1986).

38. Dima Adamsky, *The Culture of Military Innovation: The Impact of Cultural Factors on the Revolution in Military Affairs in Russia, the US, and Israel* (Palo Alto, CA: Stanford University Press, 2010); Russell, *Innovation, Transformation, and War*; Ben Jensen, *Forging the Sword: Doctrinal Change in the U.S. Army* (Palo Alto, CA: Stanford University Press, 2016).

39. Russell F. Weigley, *The American Way of War: A History of United States Military Strategy and Policy* (New York: Macmillan, 1973).

40. Adamsky, *The Culture of Military Innovation*.

41. Jacqueline Newmyer, "The Revolution in Military Affairs with Chinese Characteristics," *Journal of Strategic Studies* 33, no. 4 (2010): 483–504.

42. Elizabeth Kier, "Culture and Military Doctrine: France between the Wars," *International Security* 19, no. 4 (1995): 65–93; Elizabeth Kier, *Imagining War: French and British Military Doctrine Between the Wars* (Princeton, NJ: Princeton University Press, 1997).

43. Austin Long, *The Soul of Armies: Counterinsurgency Doctrine and Military Culture in the U.S. and U.K.* (Ithaca, NY: Cornell University Press, 2016).

44. Nagl, *Learning to Eat Soup with a Knife*.

45. Terriff, "Innovate or Die.'"

46. Johnson, *The Marines, Counterinsurgency, and Strategic Culture*.

47. Thomas Mahnken, *Uncovering Ways of War: U.S. Intelligence and Foreign Military Innovation, 1918–1941* (Ithaca, NY: Cornell University Press, 2002).

48. Talmadge, *The Dictator's Army*, 2.

49. A constant, after all, cannot by itself explain change. And if culture is capable of changing quickly enough so as to account for British learning on the Western Front, then it is highly likely that culture is actually epiphenomenal to some other causal factor.

50. Posen, *The Sources of Military Doctrine*.

51. In her study of Soviet innovation, Kimberly Marten disputes Posen's contention that civilians are more sensitive to new threats and opportunities. She finds that Soviet civilian leaders were as susceptible to parochial and bureaucratic interests as their generals. Kimberly Zisk, *Engaging the Enemy: Organization Theory and Soviet Military Innovation, 1955–1991* (Princeton, NJ: Princeton University Press, 1993).

52. Rosen, *Winning the Next War*.

53. Matthew Evangelista, *Innovation and the Arms Race* (Ithaca, NY: Cornell University Press, 1989).

54. Deborah Avant, *Political Institutions and Military Change: Lessons from Peripheral Wars* (Ithaca, NY: Cornell University Press, 1994).

55. Owen Coté, "The Politics of Innovative Military Doctrine: The United States Navy and Fleet Ballistic Missiles" (PhD diss., MIT, 1996).

56. Talmadge, *The Dictator's Army*.

57. Suzanne Nielsen, *An Army Transformed: The U.S. Army's Post-Vietnam Recovery and the Dynamics of Change in Military Organizations* (Carlisle, PA: Strategic Studies Institute, 2010).

58. Janine Davidson, *Lifting the Fog of Peace: How Americans Learned to Fight Modern War* (Ann Arbor: University of Michigan Press, 2011).

59. Jensen, *Forging the Sword*, 17–24.

60. Horowitz, *The Diffusion of Military Power*.

61. Theo Farrell, "Improving in War: Military Adaptation and the British in Helmand Province, Afghanistan, 2006–2009," *Journal of Strategic Studies* 33, no. 4 (2010): 567–94.

62. Scholarship on bottom-up military adaptation stands out as an exception to this claim, a point that I address below.

63. Rosen, *Winning the Next War*, 22.

64. See Farrell, "Improving in War." See also Adam M. Jungdahl and Julia M. Macdonald, "Innovation Inhibitors in War," *Journal of Strategic Studies* 38, no. 4 (2015): 467–99; Raphael Marcus, "Military Innovation and Tactical Adaptation in the Israel–Hezbollah Conflict: The Institutionalization of Lesson-Learning in the IDF," *Journal of Strategic Studies* 38, no. 4 (2015): 500–28; Kristen A. Harkness and Michael Hunzeker, "Military Maladaptation: Counterinsurgency and the Politics of Failure," *Journal of Strategic Studies* 38, no. 6 (2015): 777–800; Nina A. Kollars, Richard Muller, and Andrew Santora, "Learning to Fight and Fighting to Learn: Practitioners and the Role of Unit Publications in VIII Fighter Command 1943–1944," *Journal of Strategic Studies* 39, no. 7 (2016): 1044–67; Olivier Schmitt, "French Military Adaptation in the Afghan War: Looking Inward or Outward?" *Journal of Strategic Studies* 40, no. 4 (2017): 577–99.

65. Davidson, *Lifting the Fog of Peace*; Nielsen, *An Army Transformed*; Jensen, *Forging the Sword*.

1. Assessment, Command, and Training Theory

1. James G. March and Johan P. Olsen, "The Uncertainty of the Past: Organizational Learning under Ambiguity," *European Journal of Political Research* 3, no. 2 (1975): 141–71.

2. Richard Downie, *Learning from Conflict: The U.S. Military in Vietnam, El Salvador and the Drug War* (Westport, CT: Praeger, 1998), 22; John Nagl, *Learning to Eat Soup with a Knife: Counterinsurgency Lessons from Malaya and Vietnam* (Chicago: University of Chicago Press, 2005), 6–8; Janine Davidson, *Lifting the Fog of Peace: How Americans Learned to Fight Modern War* (Ann Arbor: University of Michigan Press, 2011), 19–23.

3. This echoes a similar finding in the business and management literature on organizational innovation, which suggests that types of innovation are less distinct than originally presumed. See Fariborz Damanpour, "An Integration of Research Findings of Effects of Firm Size and Market Competition on Product and Process Innovations," *British Journal of Management* 21, no. 4 (December 1, 2010): 996–1010.

4. John L. Romjue, *From Active Defense to Airland Battle: The Development of Army Doctrine, 1973–1982* (Fort Monroe, VA: US Army Training and Doctrine Command, 1984); Walter E. Kretchik, *U.S. Army Doctrine: From the American Revolution to the War on Terror* (Lawrence: University Press of Kansas, 2011), 196–220.

5. Dima Adamsky, *The Culture of Military Innovation: The Impact of Cultural Factors on the Revolution in Military Affairs in Russia, the US, and Israel* (Stanford, CA: Stanford University Press, 2010).

6. Barry R. Posen, *The Sources of Military Doctrine: France, Britain, and Germany between the World Wars* (Ithaca, NY: Cornell University Press, 1986): 13–14; Austin Long, *The Soul of Armies: Counterinsurgency Doctrine and Military Culture in the US and UK* (Ithaca, NY: Cornell University Press, 2016), 21; Ryan Grauer, "Moderating Diffusion: Military Bureaucratic Politics and the Implementation of German Doctrine in South America, 1885–1914," *World Politics* 67, no. 2 (April 2015): 268; Benjamin Jensen, *Forging the Sword: Doctrinal Change in the U.S. Army* (Palo Alto, CA: Stanford University Press, 2016), 4.

7. Dudley W. Knox, "The Role of Doctrine in Naval Warfare," *U.S. Naval Institute Proceedings* 41, no. 2 (1915): 334; Keith B. Bickel, *Mars Learning: The Marine Corps' Development of Small Wars Doctrine, 1915–1940* (Boulder, CO: Westview, 2001), 2; Jensen, *Forging the Sword*, 3.

8. Robert A. Doughty, "The Evolution of US Army Tactical Doctrine, 1946–1976," *Leavenworth Papers* (1979): 1.

9. Nagl, *Learning to Eat Soup with a Knife*, 7; Jensen, *Forging the Sword*, 6.

10. Doughty, "The Evolution of US Army Tactical Doctrine," 1; Harold R. Winton, "Introduction: On Military Change," in *The Challenge of Change: Military Institutions and New Realities, 1918–1941*, ed. David R. Mets and Harold R. Winton (Lincoln: University of Nebraska Press, 2000), xii; Jensen, *Forging the Sword*, 6.

11. Stephen P. Rosen, *Winning the Next War: Innovation and the Modern Military* (Ithaca, NY: Cornell University Press, 1994), 57–75.

12. Long, *The Soul of Armies*, 20–21.

13. Not every armed force writes its doctrine down. The US Navy, for example, has long claimed to have a doctrine despite officially endorsing and publishing one only sporadically. James J. Tritten, *Naval Doctrine . . . From the Sea* (Norfolk, VA: Naval Doctrine Command, 1994), 2–3.

14. M. A. Ramsay, *Command and Cohesion: The Citizen Soldier and Minor Tactics in the British Army, 1870–1918* (Westport, CT: Praeger, 2002), 10.

15. Winton, "Introduction," xii.

16. As of early 2020, US Army doctrine consists of 16 army doctrinal publications, 1 army doctrinal reference publication, 64 field manuals, and 263 army techniques publications. This count does not include relevant multinational, joint, or multiservice doctrine. See Department of the Army, *Army Doctrinal Publication 1-01: Doctrine Primer* (Washington, DC: Headquarters, Department of the Army, 2014); Army Publishing Directory, https://armypubs.army.mil.

17. Stephen D. Biddle, *Military Power: Explaining Victory and Defeat in Modern Battle* (Princeton, NJ: Princeton University Press, 2006); Risa A. Brooks and Elizabeth A. Stanley, eds., *Creating Military Power: The Sources of Military Effectiveness* (Palo Alto, CA: Stanford University Press, 2007); Ryan Grauer, *Commanding Military Power* (Cambridge: Cambridge University Press, 2016).

18. Carl von Clausewitz, *On War*, trans. Peter Paret and Michael Howard (Princeton, NJ: Princeton University Press, 1984), 85.

19. Stephen Biddle offers a strong version of this point, arguing that an optimal war-fighting doctrine has existed for mid- to high-intensity conventional warfare since the end of the First World War. Michel Goya similarly suggests that the French Army continues to use infantry methods pioneered during the First World War. See Biddle, *Military Power*; Michel Goya, *Flesh and Steel during the Great War: The Transformation of the French Army and the Invention of Modern Warfare*, trans. Andrew Uffindell (Barnsley, UK: Pen and Sword, 2018), 240.

20. In the 1950s, the US Army adopted a radical new doctrine to prepare for the nuclear battlefield. Within a few years, the army returned to a much more conventional doctrine. See Andrew Bacevich, *The Pentomic Era: The US Army between Korea and Vietnam* (Washington, DC: National Defense University Press, 1986). On the tank's impact during the First World War, see Jonathan Boff, *Winning and Losing on the Western Front: The British Third Army and the Defeat of Germany in 1918* (Cambridge: Cambridge University Press 2014), 140–45.

21. Breech-loading rifles meant that soldiers no longer needed to stand while reloading their rifles, which made it easier to fire and load while lying down. This minor technological change contributed to the radical increase in rates of fire and battlefield lethality that transformed twentieth-century battlefields.

22. James Q. Wilson, *Bureaucracy: What Government Agencies Do and Why They Do It* (New York: Basic Books, 1989).

23. Moreover, regimes facing internal challengers often take steps to make their militaries *ineffective*. Caitlin Talmadge, *The Dictator's Army: Battlefield Effectiveness in Authoritarian Regimes* (Ithaca, NY: Cornell University Press, 2015), 15–23; Kristen Harkness, *When Soldiers Rebel: Ethnic Armies and Political Instability in Africa* (Cambridge: Cambridge University Press, 2018), 38–43.

24. Although I describe this process in linear terms for theoretical clarity, I acknowledge that it is cyclical and iterative in practice.

25. My model is based on Janine Davidson's "scan, interpret, act" learning cycle. Davidson, *Lifting the Fog of Peace*, 22–23. It also draws heavily on both military and nonmilitary theories of

organizational change and innovation. See Terry N. Clark, "Institutionalization of Innovations in Higher Education: Four Models," *Administrative Science Quarterly* 13, no. 1 (1968): 1–25; G. Zaltman, R. Duncan, and J. Holbek, *Innovations and Organizations* (New York: Wiley, 1973); Lloyd A. Rowe and William B. Boise, "Organizational Innovation: Current Research and Evolving Concepts," *Public Administration Review* 34, no. 3 (May 1, 1974): 284–93; March and Olsen, "The Uncertainty of the Past"; John E. Ettlie, "Adequacy of Stage Models for Decisions on Adoption of Innovation," *Psychological Reports* 46, no. 3 (1980): 991–95; James G. March, "Exploration and Exploitation in Organizational Learning," *Organization Science* 2, no. 1 (January 1, 1991): 71–87; Richard A Wolfe, "Organizational Innovation: Review, Critique and Suggested Research Directions," *Journal of Management Studies* 31, no. 3 (May 1, 1994): 405–31; Downie, *Learning from Conflict*; Nagl, *Learning to Eat Soup with a Knife*; Mary M. Crossan and Marina Apaydin, "A Multi-Dimensional Framework of Organizational Innovation: A Systematic Review of the Literature," *Journal of Management Studies* 47, no. 6 (2010): 1154–91.

26. Clausewitz, *On War*, 117–18.

27. Rosen, *Winning the Next War*, 34–35.

28. Carl Builder, *The Masks of War: American Military Styles in Strategy and Analysis; A RAND Corporation Research Study* (Baltimore: Johns Hopkins University Press, 1989); Nagl, *Learning to Eat Soup with a Knife*; Davidson, *Lifting the Fog of Peace*.

29. Rowe and Boise, "Organizational Innovation"; Fariborz Damanpour, "Organizational Innovation: A Meta-Analysis of Effects of Determinants and Moderators," *The Academy of Management Journal* 34, no. 3 (1991): 555–90; Rosen, *Winning the Next War*; Teresa M. Amabile et al., "Assessing the Work Environment for Creativity," *Academy of Management Journal* 39, no. 5 (October 1, 1996): 1154–84; Michael D. Mumford and Brian Licuanan, "Leading for Innovation: Conclusions, Issues, and Directions," *Leadership Quarterly* 15, no. 1 (February 2004): 163–71; Michael A. Hunzeker and Kristen A. Harkness, "Detecting the Need for Change: How the British Army Adapted to Warfare on the Western Front and in the Southern Cameroons," *European Journal of International Security* 6 (2021): 66–85.

30. Torunn Laugen Haaland, "The Limits to Learning in Military Operations: Bottom-up Adaptation in the Norwegian Army in Northern Afghanistan, 2007–2012," *Journal of Strategic Studies* 39, no. 7 (2016): 1004.

31. Damanpour, "Organizational Innovation"; Crossan and Apaydin, "A Multi-Dimensional Framework of Organizational Innovation."

32. Martin M. Rosner, "Economic Determinants of Organizational Innovation," *Administrative Science Quarterly* 12, no. 4 (1968): 614–24; Wesley M. Cohen and Richard C. Levin, "Empirical Studies of Innovation and Market Structure," in *Handbook of Industrial Organization*, Vol. 2, ed. Robert D. Willig and Richard Schmalensee, 1059–77 (New York: Elsevier, 1989); Damanpour, "Organizational Innovation"; Links with external organizations (as a source of new ideas) has also been proven useful. See Michael L. Tushman and Thomas J. Scanlan, "Boundary Spanning Individuals: Their Role in Information Transfer and Their Antecedents," *Academy of Management Journal* 24, no. 2 (1981): 289–305.

33. Organizations can hedge by pursuing multiple options simultaneously. But for all except the most resource endowed, at a certain point they must consolidate behind a dominant course of action. See Rowe and Boise, "Organizational Innovation"; Crossan and Apaydin, "A Multi-Dimensional Framework of Organizational Innovation."

34. Clark, "Institutionalization of Innovations in Higher Education"; Crossan and Apaydin, "A Multi-Dimensional Framework of Organizational Innovation."

35. It is important to point out that interest group opposition can come from both inside and outside the organization. The latter can be especially problematic for public bureaucracies, including militaries.

36. Clark, "Institutionalization of Innovations in Higher Education"; Rowe and Boise, "Organizational Innovation"; Rosen, *Winning the Next War*; Crossan and Apaydin, "A Multi-Dimensional Framework of Organizational Innovation."

37. Clausewitz, *On War*, 117–18; Grauer, *Commanding Military Power*, 3.

38. Clausewitz, *On War*, 113–14.

39. Rosen, *Winning the Next War*, 22.

40. Ibid.

41. I use "centralization" to mean that decision-making authority remains in the hands of a few individuals at the top of the organization and "decentralization" to mean that many individuals closer to the bottom of the organization have the power to make decisions. Grauer, *Commanding Military Power*, 28–29.

42. Harvey M. Sapolsky, "Organizational Structure and Innovation," *Journal of Business* 40, no. 4 (October 1, 1967): 497–510. Sapolsky credits James Q. Wilson for first theorizing about this trade-off. See James Q. Wilson, "Innovation in Organization: Notes Toward and Theory," in *Approaches to Organizational Design*, ed. James D. Thompson (Pittsburgh: University of Pittsburgh, 1966), 193–218.

43. Sapolsky, "Organizational Structure and Innovation," 497.

44. Talmadge, *The Dictator's Army*, 13.

45. Sapolsky makes this point, arguing that organizations can simultaneously possess centralized and decentralized elements. However, he does not offer a systematic explanation for how, where, and why such "dual core" structures increase the probability that change will occur. See Harvey M. Sapolsky, Benjamin H. Friedman, and Brendan Rittenhouse Green, "The Missing Transformation," in *US Military Innovation since the Cold War: Creation without Destruction*, ed. Harvey M. Sapolsky, Benjamin H. Friedman, and Brendan Rittenhouse Green (London: Routledge, 2009), 7.

46. Talmadge, *The Dictator's Army*, 13–27.

47. I define the term "command practices" as encompassing more than structure, but this is nevertheless a narrower construct than "organizational culture." Scholars use "organizational culture" to refer to a broad set of consistent and deeply held beliefs, ideas, preferences, and attitudes that help an organization's members define their corporate identity, role, and purpose; inform and guide their organizational decisions; and transmit this information from one generation to the next. See Ann Swidler, "Culture in Action: Symbols and Strategies," *American Sociological Review* 51, no. 2 (April 1986): 273–86; Wilson, *Bureaucracy*, 90–113. A military's command practices are among many elements that comprise its organizational culture, but the two need not change in lockstep. Thus, a military's command practices can be fluid and can change over a short period of time. A military's overarching culture is far more sticky and can take years—if not generations—to evolve.

48. See Thomas X. Hammes, "The Evolution of War: The Fourth Generation," *Marine Corps Gazette* 78, no. 9 (1994): 35–44; John Arquilla, David Ronfeldt, and Michele Zanini, "Networks, Netwar, and Information-Age Terrorism," in *Strategic Appraisal: The Changing Role of Information in Warfare*, ed. Zalmay Khalilzad, John P. White, and Andrew Marshall (Santa Monica, CA: Rand Corporation, 1999), 76–111; Chris Dishman, "The Leaderless Nexus: When Crime and Terror Converge," *Studies in Conflict & Terrorism* 28, no. 3 (2005): 237–52. For a critique, see Antulio J. Echevarria II, *Fourth-Generation War and Other Myths* (Carlisle, PA: Strategic Studies Institute, 2005).

49. Nagl, *Learning to Eat Soup with a Knife*; Theo Farrell, "Improving in War: Military Adaptation and the British in Helmand Province, Afghanistan, 2006–2009," *Journal of Strategic Studies* 33, no. 4 (2010): 567–94.

50. Grauer, *Commanding Military Power*, 39–40.

51. Again, I use the term "independent assessment mechanism" as shorthand for "an assessment mechanism that demonstrates independence, prestige, and the ability to conduct rigorous analysis."

52. Rosen, *Winning the Next War*, 22.

53. Taken together, these two requirements mean that doctrinal shifts need not change how the entire organization operates in combat. For example, a new counterterror doctrine may be relevant only to an army's special operations units.

54. I do not consider large-scale battlefield demonstrations of a new war-fighting concept (e.g., the British offensive at Cambrai or the German counteroffensive at the end of that same battle) as proof that an army has fully navigated the learning process. If such a demonstration occurs before the army officially promulgates an updated doctrine, revises training plans for new recruits, and reorganizes and reequips existing units in accordance with the new doctrine,

then I treat it as part of the selection phase. If such a demonstration happens after these prerequisites are met, I treat it as part of the action phase.

55. Although this term is relatively new, the concept is not. With the rise of mass industrial armies in the nineteenth century, individual commanders could no longer maintain personal control over their entire force. They therefore had two basic options for exercising command. They could micromanage by issuing detailed orders that precisely directed both the tasks that needed to be accomplished and how they should be accomplished, or they could identify what subordinate commanders needed to accomplish without precisely specifying how those tasks should be performed, a practice that Western militaries now refer to as mission-type command. Jörg Muth, *Command Culture: Officer Education in the U.S. Army and the German Armed Forces, 1901–1940, and the Consequences for World War II* (Denton: University of North Texas Press, 2011), 173–34.

56. Simon Robbins, *British Generalship on the Western Front 1914–18: Defeat into Victory* (London: Frank Cass, 2005), 61.

57. Scott S. Gartner, *Strategic Assessment in War* (New Haven, CT: Yale University Press, 1999), 8; Risa A. Brooks, "Making Military Might: Why Do States Fail and Succeed? A Review Essay," *International Security* 28, no. 2 (2003): 149–91.

58. This means that one case (e.g., the First World War or the German Army) does not equal one observation on the dependent and explanatory variables. At a minimum, this approach yields eighteen separate observations (each army in the prewar era, 1914, 1915, 1916, 1917, and 1918). For more on why the number of cases do not equal observation in qualitative research, see Jack S. Levy, "Case Studies: Types, Designs, and Logics of Inference," *Conflict Management and Peace Science* 25, no. 1 (2008): 3.

59. Stephen Van Evera, *Guide to Methods for Students of Political Sciences* (Ithaca, NY: Cornell University Press, 1997), 57.

60. Hew Strachan, "The First World War," *Historical Journal* 43, no. 3 (2000): 901–2.

61. Alexander L. George and Andrew Bennett, *Case Studies and Theory Development in the Social Sciences* (Cambridge, MA: MIT Press, 2005), 6–7.

62. Richard Myers, *The National Military Strategy of the United States of America: A Strategy for Today, a Vision for Tomorrow* (Washington, DC: Joint Chiefs of Staff, 2004).

63. Talmadge, *The Dictator's Army*, 15–23; Kristen Harkness, "The Ethnic Army and the State: Explaining Coup Traps and the Difficulties of Democratization in Africa," *Journal of Conflict Resolution* 60, no. 4 (2016): 587–616; Kristen A. Harkness and Michael Hunzeker, "Military Maladaptation: Counterinsurgency and the Politics of Failure," *Journal of Strategic Studies* 38, no. 6 (2015): 778–79.

64. For a critique of German strategy in 1914, see Holger H. Herwig, "The Dynamics of Necessity: German Military Policy during the First World War," in *Military Effectiveness*, Vol. 1, *The First World War*, ed. Allan R. Millet and Williamson Murray (Boston: Allen & Unwin, 1988), 86–92.

65. Williamson Murray, *Military Adaptation in War: With Fear of Change* (New York: Cambridge University Press, 2011), 76.

66. Joseph A. Schumpeter, *Capitalism, Socialism and Democracy* (New York: Harper and Brothers, 1942; reprint, New York: HarperCollins, 2008); Cohen and Levin, "Empirical Studies of Innovation and Market Structure"; Rosner, "Economic Determinants of Organizational Innovation"; Damanpour, "Organizational Innovation"; Damanpour, "An Integration of Research Findings of Effects of Firm Size and Market Competition on Product and Process Innovations."

67. Organizational scholars suggest that different causal variables can operate in different ways under different environmental conditions. See Fariborz Damanpour and Shanthi Gopalakrishnan, "Theories of Organizational Structure and Innovation Adoption: The Role of Environmental Change," *Journal of Engineering and Technology Management* 15, no. 1 (March 1998): 1–24.

68. Rosen, *Winning the Next War*, 38.

69. James D. Fearon, "Rationalist Explanations for War," *International Organization* 49 (1995): 379–414; Robert Powell, *In the Shadow of Power: States and Strategies in International Politics* (Princeton, NJ: Princeton University Press, 1999); Graham Allison, *Destined for War: Can America and China Escape the Thucydides Trap?* (New York: Houghton Mifflin Harcourt, 2017).

70. Posen, *The Sources of Military Doctrine*; João Resende-Santos, *Neorealism, States, and the Modern Mass Army* (New York: Cambridge University Press, 2007).

71. I recognize that changes in the balance of power and the perception of changes in the balance of the power are distinct phenomenon. For simplicity's sake, I treat them as one and the same.

72. Eliot A. Cohen, *Supreme Command: Soldiers, Statesmen, and Leadership in Wartime* (New York: Free Press, 2002).

2. Learning on the Western Front

1. Robert A. Doughty, "French Strategy in 1914: Joffre's Own," *Journal of Military History* 67, no. 2 (2003): 427–54.

2. The German Army inevitably moved away from its own supply lines as it closed in on Paris. Making matters worse, by the Battle of the Marne in early September, over 60 percent of the German Army's trucks were broken down. Meanwhile, German railheads were an average of eighty miles behind the front lines. Holger H. Herwig, "The Dynamics of Necessity: German Military Policy during the First World War," in *Military Effectiveness*, Vol. 1, *The First World War*, ed. Allan R. Millet and Williamson Murray (Boston: Allen & Unwin, 1988), 85.

3. Bruce Gudmundsson, *Stormtroop Tactics: Innovation in the German Army, 1914–18* (Westport, CT: Praeger, 1995), 3.

4. Robert Jervis, "Cooperation under the Security Dilemma," *World Politics* 30, no. 2 (January 1, 1978): 167–214. See also Charles L. Glaser and Chaim Kaufmann, "What Is the Offense-Defense Balance and Can We Measure It?" *International Security* 22, no. 4 (1998): 44–82; Keir A. Lieber, "Grasping the Technological Peace: The Offense-Defense Balance and International Security," *International Security* 25, no. 1 (2000): 71–104; Stephen Biddle, "Rebuilding the Foundations of Offense-Defense Theory," *Journal of Politics* 63, no. 3 (2001): 741–74.

5. Jonathan M. House, *Combined Arms Warfare in the Twentieth Century* (Lawrence: University of Kansas Press, 2001), 16–17.

6. Stephen Biddle, *Military Power: Explaining Victory and Defeat in Modern Battle* (Princeton, NJ: Princeton University Press, 2006), 29.

7. Gary Sheffield, *Forgotten Victory: The First World War: Myths and Realities* (London: Headline Book Publishing 2001; reprint, London: Sharpe Books, 2018), 152, Kindle.

8. Robert T. Foley, "Dumb Donkeys or Cunning Foxes? Learning in the British and German Armies during the Great War," *International Affairs* 90, no. 2 (2014): 283.

9. Data on the size of a German division is from General Staff, *SS 356: Handbook of the German Army in War*, November 1918, 38, Z478, Joint Services Command and Staff College Archives, Shrivenham. The estimated frontage of a German division on the Eastern Front is from Gudmundsson, *Stormtroop Tactics*, 107.

10. The estimated frontage of a German division on the Western Front is from Gudmundsson, *Stormtroop Tactics*, 107. It is telling that the German Army did not appear to have fundamentally altered its tactical assault doctrines in the Eastern theater.

11. M. A. Ramsay, *Command and Cohesion: The Citizen Soldier and Minor Tactics in the British Army, 1870–1918* (Westport, CT: Praeger, 2002), 21.

12. Ibid., 19–21.

13. These numbers are based on data assembled from War Office, *Statistics of the Military Effort of the British Empire during the Great War, 1914–1920* (London: HMSO, 1922), 29–30; Stephen Bull, "The Early Years of the War," in *War on the Western Front*, ed. Gary D. Sheffield (Oxford, UK: Osprey, 2007), 172; Ian Drury, "German Stormtrooper," *War on the Western Front*, 29; Holger Herwig, "You Are Here to Learn How to Die: German Subaltern Officer Education on the Eve of the Great War," in *Forging the Sword: Selecting, Educating, and Training Cadets and Junior Officers in the Modern World*, ed. Elliott V. Converse (Chicago: Imprint Publications, 1998), 32; Foley, "Dumb Donkeys or Cunning Foxes?," 283.

14. For a discussion of the nineteenth century trends and innovations that enabled the great powers to recruit, mobilize, and field armies of this size, see Martin van Creveld, *Command in War* (Cambridge, MA: Harvard University Press, 1985), 104–6; Martin van Creveld, *Technology*

and War: From 2000 B.C. to the Present (New York: Free Press, 1991), 161–63; Ramsay, *Command and Cohesion*, 19–22.

15. Some historians argue that mobilization plans drove strategic thinking and made conflict all but inevitable in August 1914. See Barbara W. Tuchman, *The Guns of August* (New York: Presidio Press, 2004; reprint, New York: Macmillan, 1962). For a critique of this view, see Marc Trachtenberg, "The Meaning of Mobilization in 1914," *International Security* 15, no. 3 (1990): 120–50.

16. Michel Goya, *Flesh and Steel during the Great War: The Transformation of the French Army and the Invention of Modern Warfare*, trans. Andrew Uffindell (Barnsley, UK: Pen and Sword, 2018), 240. René Louis Jules Radiguet, *The Making of a Modern Army and Its Operations in the Field: A Study Based on the Experience of Three Years on the French Front (1914–1917)*, trans. Henry P. Du Bellet (New York: Putnam, 1918), 115–16.

17. Creveld, *Command in War*, 160; Sheffield, *Forgotten Victory*, 154–56; House, *Combined Arms Warfare in the Twentieth Century*, 35–36.

18. A plaque commemorates the "Pigeon of Verdun" at Fort de Vaux in Verdun, France.

19. Bull, "The Early Years of the War," 191; Gudmundsson, *Stormtroop Tactics*, 28.

20. Bull, "The Early Years of the War," 187–88.

21. Pascal Lucas says that during the Battle of the Marne, French infantry units were surprised to find some German positions "outlined by lines of trenches and dug-in machine gun emplacements." Pascal Lucas, *The Evolution of Tactical Ideas in France and Germany during the War of 1914–1918*, trans. P.V. Kieffer (Paris: Berger-Leorault, 1925), 37, LCCN 5102270, Library of Congress, Washington, DC. (Author's note: A typographical error exists in the translated document. Page 27 is mislabeled as page 37.)

22. War Office, "Notes on Certain Lessons of the Great War" (1934), 9–10, WO 32/3116, National Archive, Kew; War Office, "Report on the Committee on the Lessons of the Great War (Kirke Report)" (1932), 11, WO 32/3116, National Archive, Kew.

23. As Douglas Haig wrote in his diary on July 2, 1916 (the day after his men went over the top for the first time during the Somme offensive, which was to be the bloodiest single day in British military history): "The A.G. [adjutant-general] reported to-day that the total casualties are estimated at over 40,000 to date [note that the battle had only been raging for twenty-four hours.] This cannot be considered severe in the views of the numbers engaged, and the length of front attacked." Douglas Haig, *The Private Papers of Douglas Haig, 1914–1919, Being Selections from the Private Diary and Correspondence of Field-Marshal the Earl Haig of Bemersyde*, ed. Robert Blake (London: Eyre & Spottiswoode, 1952), 154.

24. In analyzing trench warfare during the American Civil War, British staff officers noticed that General Winfield Scott Hancock habitually told his men to dig three lines of trenches when in defense, because "the first was almost invariably captured by surprise, and sometimes the second also." *Report of a Conference of General Staff Officers at the Staff College 18th to 21st January, 1909* (1909), 9, Joint Services Command and Staff College Archives, Shrivenham. See also Martin Samuels, *Command or Control? Command, Training and Tactics in the British and German Armies, 1888–1918* (London: Frank Cass, 1995), 86–87.

25. House, *Combined Arms Warfare in the Twentieth Century*, 39.

26. Paddy Griffith, *Battle Tactics of the Western Front* (New Haven, CT: Yale University Press, 2000), 25. To give some sense of the scope of the communication challenge, during an average offensive, a single British field army often needed to send ten thousand telegrams, twenty thousand phone calls, and five thousand written messages *per day*. Creveld, *Command in War*, 158. See also Brian N. Hall, "The British Army, Information Management, and the First World War Revolution in Military Affairs," *Journal of Strategic Studies* 41, no. 7 (2018): 1012.

27. British gunners fired over 1.5 million artillery shells before to the Somme offensive in 1916; more than three million shells in the lead up to the Battle of Messines in June 1917; and approximately six million shells prior to the Third Battle of Ypres in July 1917. G. C. Wynne, *If Germany Attacks: The Battle in Depth in the West* (London: Faber and Faber, 1940; reprint, Westport, CT: Greenwood, 1976), 106, 268, 299. To support a single army group in 1917, the German Army needed seven trains per day just to carry artillery shells and another twenty-six thousand horses to move the shells from the trains to the front lines per day. Herwig, "The Dynamics of Necessity," 94.

28. Writing immediately after the war, Lucas Pascal suggested that the German Army lost more men in two months of defending along the Somme River than it did in six months of attacking at Verdun. Pascal, *The Evolution of Tactical Ideas in France and Germany during the War of 1914–1918*, 83–84. See also Wynne, *If Germany Attacks*, 131.

29. The 1906 edition of the German exercise regulations for infantry dedicated 5 pages to the subject, which was twice the number of the 1888 edition. Samuels, *Command or Control?* 160–61. The British Army's 1912 *Field Service Regulations* devoted 13 of its 229 substantive pages to defensive operations. Despite its reputed preference for attacking, the French Army does seem to have at least given more thought to defensive tactics than history subsequently gave it credit for. Lucas, *The Evolution of Tactical Ideas in France and Germany during the War of 1914–1918*, 4–8.

30. Wynne, *If Germany Attacks*, 269.

31. Erich Ludendorff, *Ludendorff's Own Story, August 1914–November 1918: The Great War from the Siege of Liège to the Signing of the Armistice as Viewed from the Grand Headquarters of the German Army*, 2 vols. (New York: Harper, 1919), 1:289–90.

32. Suppression involves firing weapons in the general direction of an adversary to prevent him or her from taking well-aimed shots at you.

33. Joseph Jacques Césaire Joffre, *The Personal Memoirs of Joffre: Field Marshal of the French Army*, 2 vols., trans. Timothy Bentley Mott (London: Harper & Brothers, 1932), 1:185; Douglas Porch, "The French Army in the First World War," in *Military Effectiveness*, Vol. 1 (Boston: Allen & Unwin, 1988), 215; Ian Sumner, "French Poilu," *War on the Western Front*, 57.

34. House, *Combined Arms Warfare in the Twentieth Century*, 39; Bradley John Meyer, "Operational Art and the German Command System in World War I" (PhD diss., Ohio State University, 1988), 279–89.

35. Shelford Bidwell and Dominick Graham, *Fire-Power: British Army Weapons and Theories of War, 1904–1945* (London: George Allen & Unwin, 1982), 73; Samuels, *Command or Control?* 105–9; Wynne, *If Germany Attacks*, 25, 42; Haig, *The Private Papers of Douglas Haig, 1914–1919*, 87.

36. A quick technical discussion is useful for understanding why registration rounds were necessary prior to the introduction of predicted fire. Rifle and machine-gun bullets have a relatively flat trajectory, which allow gunners to see what and where their bullets are striking. Howitzers, on the other hand, fire at a higher angle and over such long distances that gunners cannot see where their shells land. Because of the distances involved, other variables also affect where a shell lands. Some factors, such as wind, humidity, temperature, and Earth's rotation, affect all guns in the same way. Other factors, such as minor variations in construction and wear and tear, are idiosyncratic to each gun. Before predicted firing, gunners had to fire practice rounds to make sure they their shells were landing where they thought they would. Guns had to fire one at a time to ensure that forward observers (the only ones who could see where the shells were landing) could match each impact to the respective gun that fired it.

37. For a detailed discussion of the myriad innovations and technical achievements that made predicted fire possible, see Meyer, "Operational Art and the German Command System in World War I," 318–33; Bidwell and Graham, *Fire-Power*, 101–10; David T. Zabecki, *The German 1918 Offensives: A Case Study in the Operational Level of War* (New York: Routledge, 2006), 1547–69, Kindle.

38. Meyer, "Operational Art and the German Command System in World War I," 349–50; Biddle, *Military Power*, 46–48; House, *Combined Arms Warfare in the Twentieth Century*, 40–43.

39. Biddle, *Military Power*, 28.

40. See Robert Michael Citino, *The Path to Blitzkrieg: Doctrine and Training in the German Army, 1920–1939* (Boulder, CO: Lynne Rienner, 1999); Robert Michael Citino, *Blitzkrieg to Desert Storm: The Evolution of Operational Warfare* (Lawrence: University Press of Kansas, 2004).

3. The German Army on the Western Front

1. *Report of a Conference of General Staff Officers at the Staff College 18th to 21st January, 1909* (1909), 60–61, Joint Services Command and Staff College Archives, Shrivenham.

2. Timothy T. Lupfer, *The Dynamics of Doctrine: The Changes in German Tactical Doctrine during the First World War* (Fort Leavenworth, KS: Combat Studies Institute, 1981), 57.

3. German units captured and acted upon both copies of Laffargue's memorandum and Note 5779, which the French high command had circulated to disseminate the lessons it learned during the initial stages of the Second Battle of Artois. Jonathan Krause, *Early Trench Tactics in the French Army: The Second Battle of Artois, May–June 1915* (New York: Routledge, 2016), 4–5.

4. Holger H. Herwig, "The Dynamics of Necessity: German Military Policy during the First World War," in *Military Effectiveness*, Vol. 1, ed. Allan R. Millet and Williamson Murray (Boston: Allen & Unwin, 1988), 86–92.

5. Jonathan Boff, *Haig's Enemy: Crown Prince Rupprecht and Germany's War on the Western Front* (Oxford: Oxford University Press, 2018), 182.

6. Herwig, "The Dynamics of Necessity," 86. For a discussion of how this fear gave rise to an obsession with decisive military action in the decades leading up to the First World War, see Gunther E. Rothenberg, "Moltke, Schlieffen, and the Doctrine of Strategic Envelopment," in *Makers of Modern Strategy: From Machiavelli to the Nuclear Age*, ed. Peter Paret, 296–325 (Princeton, NJ: Princeton University Press, 1986); Strachan, *The First World War*, 166–80.

7. Kaiser Wilhelm II's weltpolitik (place in the sun) policies fueled German bellicosity. Hew Strachan, *The First World War*, Vol. 1, *To Arms* (Oxford: Oxford University Press, 2003), 4–35.

8. Russia and France signed a political agreement in 1891. The military components of this alliance were agreed upon in later years. Robert A. Doughty, "French Strategy in 1914: Joffre's Own," *Journal of Military History* 67, no. 2 (2003): 433.

9. According to Hew Strachan, although in 1905 General Schlieffen put on paper the basic concepts behind how the German Army might fight a two-front war, his ideas represented neither a war plan nor an operation order. Strachan, *The First World War*, 163–66. See also Terence Zuber, *Inventing the Schlieffen Plan: German War Planning, 1871–1914* (Oxford: Oxford University Press, 2002).

10. Boff, *Haig's Enemy*, 83–84.

11. Erich von Falkenhayn, *The German General Staff and Its Decisions, 1914–1916* (New York: Dodd, Mead and Company, 1920), 256–257, 268–273, 325–326. Some historians question this narrative, suggesting that Falkenhayn's plan was muddled and failed to distinguish between attrition and maneuver. See Boff, *Haig's Enemy*, 92–93.

12. The Germans suffered 465,000 casualties at the Somme. One hundred thirty-eight German divisions rotated through the battle, although some divisions rotated through the battle multiple times. Pascal Lucas, *The Evolution of Tactical Ideas in France and Germany during the War of 1914–1918*, trans. P.V. Kieffer (Paris: Berger-Leorault, 1925), 83–84, LCCN 5102270, Library of Congress, Washington, DC.

13. General Staff, *SS 356: Handbook of the German Army in War, November 1918*, 15, Z478, Joint Services Command and Staff College Archives, Shrivenham. See also John Charteris, "Fluctuations in German Strength during 1916" (General Staff, October 23, 1916), Joint Services Command and Staff College Archives, Shrivenham.

14. Erich Ludendorff, *Ludendorff's Own Story, August 1914–November 1918: The Great War from the Siege of Liège to the Signing of the Armistice as Viewed from the Grand Headquarters of the German Army*, 2 vols. (New York: Harper and Brothers, 1919), 1:361. As of January 1917, Germany had 154 divisions on the Western Front. The Entente had 190.

15. Alexander Lanoszka and Michael Hunzeker, "Rage of Honor: Entente Indignation and the Lost Chance for Peace," *Security Studies* 24, no. 4 (2015): 662–95.

16. Stephen Bull, "The Somme and Beyond," in *War on the Western Front*, ed. Gary D. Sheffield (Oxford, UK: Osprey, 2007), 251–52; Ludendorff, *Ludendorff's Own Story*, 2:158–67.

17. The Allies suffered more than 490,000 casualties between March 21 and June 5, 1918. The German Army lost approximately 430,000 soldiers over the same period. David T. Zabecki, *The German 1918 Offensives: A Case Study in the Operational Level of War* (New York: Routledge, 2006), tables 6.9, 7.7, 8.7, Kindle.

18. Timothy Travers, *How the War Was Won: Command and Technology in the British Army on the Western Front, 1917–1918* (New York: Routledge, 1992), 154.

19. Bruce I. Gudmundsson, *Stormtroop Tactics: Innovation in the German Army, 1914–18* (Westport, CT: Praeger, 1995), 1.

20. Ibid., 20–21.

21. Details on the 1906 and 1908 documents are taken from English translations made by the British Army. War Office, *Field Service Regulations (Felddienst Ordnung, 1908) of the German Army, 1908*, trans. General Staff, War Office (London: Harrison and Sons, 1908), Joint Services Command and Staff College Archives, Shrivenham; General Staff, *Handbook of the German Army (Home and Colonial), 1912*, (London: Harrison and Sons, 1912), Joint Services Command and Staff College Archives, Shrivenham. Details on the contents of the 1888 and 1906 ExRfdIs manuals are taken from Lucas, *The Evolution of Tactical Ideas in France and Germany during the War of 1914–1918*, 18–20; Martin Samuels, *Command or Control? Command, Training and Tactics in the British and German Armies, 1888–1918* (London: Frank Cass, 1995), chap. 3; Theodore Schwan, *The Organization of the German Army* (Washington, DC: US Government Printing Office, 1902); Gudmundsson, *Stormtroop Tactics*, 17–25.

22. Historians often refer to this as assault power. To keep "assault power" distinct from "assault tactics," I instead use the term "shock power" instead. This and what follows are from Samuels, *Command or Control?*, 71–73; and Gudmundsson, *Stormtroop Tactics*, 7–9.

23. For a particularly egregious example, see Gudmundsson, *Stormtroop Tactics*, 9–13.

24. For examples of translated German after-action reports on the Boer War, see Colmar Von Der Goltz, "What Can We Learn from the Boer War?," *Journal of the Royal United Service Institution* 46, no. 298 (December 1902): 1534–39; Lindenau, "What Has the Boer War to Teach Us, as Regards to Infantry Attack?," *Journal of the Royal United Service Institution* 47, no. 302 (January 1903): 443–49.

25. Samuels, *Command or Control?*, 77.

26. Stephen Bull, "The Early Years of the War," in *War on the Western Front*, ed. Gary D. Sheffield (Oxford, UK: Osprey, 2007), 176–77; Gudmundsson, *Stormtroop Tactics*, 22.

27. General Staff, *Handbook of the German Army, 1912*, 234–35.

28. Note that this differed from the 1888 and 1906 doctrines, in which all attackers except those in the front line advanced in close-order formations.

29. The 1908 FSR warned that even when in skirmisher formations, units that try to cross open terrain "will suffer severely from the fire of unshaken [i.e., unsuppressed] infantry at medium and even at long ranges. Their losses will increase with the density of the skirmishing lines. Long and uninterrupted advances of dense skirmishing lines are therefore impossible under effective hostile fire." *Field Service Regulations of the German Army, 1908*, 177–78.

30. Ian Drury, "German Stormtrooper," in *War on the Western Front*, ed. Gary D. Sheffield (Oxford, UK: Osprey, 2007), 46.

31. Bull, "The Early Years of the War," 203.

32. Wilhelm Balck, *Development of Tactics: World War I*, trans. Harry Bell (Fort Leavenworth, KS: General Service Schools Press, 1922; reprint, West Chester, OH: The Nafziger Collection, 2011), 19–21.

33. Bull, "The Early Years of the War," 205; Gudmundsson, *Stormtroop Tactics*, 32–35. By mid-1915, many frontline regiments had created some kind of shock-troop detachment to lead larger assaults. By 1916, some thirty Western Front divisions had a self-made storm troop unit. Drury, "German Stormtrooper," 15–16.

34. Samuels, *Command or Control?*, 232.

35. Drury, "German Stormtrooper," 14; Gudmundsson, *Stormtroop Tactics*, 46–47.

36. Samuels, *Command or Control?*, 89; Gudmundsson, *Stormtroop Tactics*, 46–47.

37. Gudmundsson, *Stormtroop Tactics*, 47–49.

38. Drury, "German Stormtrooper," 14.

39. Samuels, *Command or Control?*, 90–93; Gudmundsson, *Stormtroop Tactics*, 49.

40. Samuels, *Command or Control?*, 239; Drury, "German Stormtrooper," 14.

41. Balck, *Development of Tactics*, 40–41.

42. Gudmundsson, *Stormtroop Tactics*, 85.

43. Drury, "German Stormtrooper," 15.

44. Gudmundsson suggests that the German Army's artillery techniques, which I discuss below, played a more prominent role than assault tactics at Riga. For an in-depth analysis of both Riga and Caporetto, see Gudmundsson, *Stormtroop Tactics*, 107–37.

45. Balck, *Development of Tactics*, 61–62; Lupfer, *The Dynamics of Doctrine*, 16–21; Erich Ludendorff, "Experiences in Flanders and at Lens" in *Translation of a German Document*, August 22, 1917, Joint Services Command and Staff College Archives, Shrivenham.

46. Ludendorff, *Ludendorff's Own Story*, 2:112; Gudmundsson, *Stormtroop Tactics*, 145.

47. Gudmundsson, *Stormtroop Tactics*, 141–45.

48. Douglas Haig, *The Private Papers of Douglas Haig, 1914–1919: Selections from the Private Diary and Correspondence of Field-Marshal the Earl Haig of Bemersyde*, ed. Robert Blake (London: Eyre and Spottiswoode, 1952), 270–73.

49. Erich Ludendorff, "Notes on the Offensive Battle" in *Translation of German Documents*, January 25, 1918, Joint Services Command and Staff College Archives, Shrivenham.

50. Drury, "German Stormtrooper," 30–31, 37.

51. Gudmundsson, *Stormtroop Tactics*, 148.

52. Samuels, *Command or Control?*, 245–46; Lupfer, *The Dynamics of Doctrine*, 48–49.

53. Zabecki, *The German 1918 Offensives*, location 3896, Kindle. Lupfer points out that "In the Somme battles of 1916 the British and French had labored for 140 days at the cost of more than one-half million casualties to capture a total of ninety-eight square miles of ground. In twenty-four hours in March 1918 the Germans secured about 140 square miles at a cost in casualties of less than one-tenth the Allied expenditure at the Somme." Lupfer, *The Dynamics of Doctrine*, 50.

54. Travers, *How the War Was Won*, 88–89; Paddy Griffith, *Battle Tactics of the Western Front: The British Army's Art of Attack, 1916–18* (New Haven, CT: Yale University Press, 2000), 92–93.

55. Lucas, *The Evolution of Tactical Ideas in France and Germany during the War of 1914–1918*, 19.

56. General Staff, *Handbook of the German Army, 1912*, 235.

57. Zabecki, *The German 1918 Offensives*, location 1374, Kindle.

58. The German Army divided its artillery into two branches: Field Artillery, which used lightweight mobile guns, such as the German 77mm, to support infantry maneuver, and Foot Artillery, which operated larger guns designed to defend and/or destroy fixed positions. The German Army started the war with 5,086 77mm field guns and 2,280 heavier pieces. The French Army had 3,480 75mm field guns and 308 heavy guns. The British Army had a higher ratio of heavy to light guns but, given its small size in 1914, had fewer of both types: 1,608 light guns and 1,248 heavy guns. Zabecki, *The German 1918 Offensives*, locations 1435–50, Kindle.

59. Lupfer, *The Dynamics of Doctrine*, 1–2.

60. Zabecki, *The German 1918 Offensives*, location 1380, Kindle.

61. Samuels, *Command or Control?*, 84–86.

62. Holger Herwig, "You Are Here to Learn How to Die: German Subaltern Officer Education on the Eve of the Great War," in *Forging the Sword: Selecting, Educating, and Training Cadets and Junior Officers in the Modern World*, ed. Elliott V. Converse (Chicago: Imprint Publications, 1998), 40.

63. G. C. Wynne, *If Germany Attacks: The Battle in Depth in the West* (London: Faber and Faber, 1940; reprint, Westport, CT: Greenwood, 1976), 64; Herwig, "The Dynamics of Necessity," 95–96.

64. Lucas, *The Evolution of Tactical Ideas in France and Germany during the War of 1914–1918*, 50.

65. Divisions previously controlled their own artillery.

66. Bradley John Meyer, "Operational Art and the German Command System in World War I" (PhD diss., Ohio State University, 1988), 300–4, 308–15.

67. Bruchmüller was a fierce proponent of predicted fire techniques, but Captain Erich Pulkowski deserves credit for developing them. Zabecki, *The German 1918 Offensives*, locations 1553–58, Kindle.

68. For example, attackers rarely used the same boundaries as defenders. To knock out a command post controlling the defenses against an assault unit therefore might require firing artillery into a sector that another division was slated to attack. Centralized control eliminated the need for time-consuming cross-unit coordination.

69. Balck, *Development of Tactics*, 61–62.

NOTES TO PAGES 77–82

70. For examples of German artillery plans in support of Operations Michael, Georgette, Blücher-Yorck, and Marneschutz-Reims, see Zabecki, *The German 1918 Offensives*, tables 6.8, 7.6, 8.6, 10.6, Kindle.

71. Lupfer, *The Dynamics of Doctrine*, 1.

72. The 1888 ExRfdI devoted two pages to defensive tactics, and the 1906 ExRfdI allotted only five. Samuels, *Command or Control?*, 160–61; Balck, *Development of Tactics*, 10; Lucas, *The Evolution of Tactical Ideas in France and Germany during the War of 1914–1918*, 20.

73. Balck, *Development of Tactics*, 29–30.

74. Samuels, *Command or Control?*, 161–65.

75. Wynne, *If Germany Attacks*, 15–17; Balck, *Development of Tactics*, 30–32.

76. Drury, "German Stormtrooper," 49.

77. Units typically put about half their soldiers in the forward-most trenches, which usually meant one soldier every three meters. Samuels, *Command or Control?*, 162–63.

78. Balck, *Development of Tactics*, 40; Samuels, *Command or Control?*, 162–69.

79. Krause, *Early Trench Tactics in the French Army*, 2–4.

80. Wynne, *If Germany Attacks*, 30–31; John Strawson, *Gentlemen in Khaki and Camouflage: The British Army, 1890–2008* (Barnsley, UK: Pen and Sword Military, 2009), 113.

81. Lucas, *The Evolution of Tactical Ideas in France and Germany during the War of 1914–1918*, 48.

82. Balck, *Development of Tactics*, 30.

83. Wynne, *If Germany Attacks*, 44.

84. Lucas, *The Evolution of Tactical Ideas in France and Germany during the War of 1914–1918*, 48; Samuels, *Command or Control?*, 165.

85. Samuels, *Command or Control?*, 169; Wynne, *If Germany Attacks*, 90–96.

86. Wynne, *If Germany Attacks*, 100–101.

87. Ibid.,103.

88. In the seven-day bombardment preceding the Somme offensive, 1,537 British guns fired 1,627,824 shells. Zabecki, *The German 1918 Offensives*, location 1473, Kindle. Following the battle, the German 55th Reserve Infantry Regiment reported that "all the trenches bombarded on the 1st July were completely flattened out. Only shell holes remained." General Staff, *SS 536: Report on the Defence of Gommecourt on the 1st July, 1916 (Translation of a German Document)*, July 1916, 8, Joint Services Command and Staff College Archives, Shrivenham.

89. Wynne, *If Germany Attacks*, 113, 122; Balck, *Development of Tactics*, 45; Robert T. Foley, "A Case Study in Horizontal Military Innovation: The German Army, 1916–1918," *Journal of Strategic Studies* 35, no. 6 (2012): 808–9.

90. Shelford Bidwell and Dominick Graham, *Fire-Power: British Army Weapons and Theories of War, 1904–1945* (London: Allen and Unwin, 1982), 114.

91. Samuels, *Command or Control?*, 175–77.

92. Bidwell and Graham, *Fire-Power*, 114.

93. Samuels, *Command or Control?*, 178; Foley, "A Case Study in Horizontal Military Innovation," 810–11.

94. Ludendorff, *Ludendorff's Own Story*, 1:321.

95. Ibid., 1:459.

96. Chief of the General Staff of the Field Army, *SS 561: Manual of Position Warfare for All Arms, Part 8, The Principles of Command in the Defensive Battle in Position Warfare (Translation of a German Document)*, March 1, 1917, Joint Services Command and Staff College Archives, Shrivenham.

97. Boff, *Haig's Enemy*, 146.

98. More commonly referred to as the Hindenburg Line in English language scholarship. Hew Strachan, *The First World War* (New York: Penguin Books, 2005), 195.

99. What follows is from General Staff, "Notes on the Construction of Positions on the Ypres Battle Front for the Coming Winter (Captured Order)," October 2, 1917, Joint Services Command and Staff College Archives, Shrivenham; Wynne, *If Germany Attacks*, 152–57; Balck, *Development of Tactics*, 90–93; Samuels, *Command or Control?*, 180–82.

100. Chief of the General Staff of the Field Army, *SS 561*, 8.

101. Ibid., 4, 7–9.

102. Robert Foley argues that the distinction emerged during the Battle of the Somme as frontline units began to defy the directive to immediately retake any lost ground regardless of the cost. Foley, "A Case Study in Horizontal Military Innovation," 809–10.

103. To be sure, the British had limited aims in attacking there. Their primary objective was to draw German units away from the site of the French Army's offensive along the Aisne River—something they achieved. Strachan, *The First World War*, 244–45.

104. Ibid., 242–48; Lupfer, *The Dynamics of Doctrine*, 33–34.

105. The German Army technically consisted of four distinct national armies: Prussian (which included soldiers from all of the smaller states), Bavarian, Saxon, and Wurttembergian. Each army had its own War Ministry and General Staff. The Bavarian Army was the most independent of the three. The Prussian Army was roughly six times larger than the Bavarian Army, ten times larger than the Saxon Army, and twenty times larger than the Wuttermburgian contingent. General Staff, *Handbook of the German Army, 1912*, 71, 97.

106. Meyer, "Operational Art and the German Command System in World War I," 46. See also, Jörg Muth, *Command Culture: Officer Education in the U.S. Army and the German Armed Forces, 1901–1940, and the Consequences for World War II* (Denton: University of North Texas Press, 2011), 168.

107. Ibid., 102.

108. Martin Van Creveld, *Command in War* (Cambridge, MA: Harvard University Press, 1985), 169; Dennis Showalter, "Goltz and Bernhardi: The Institutionalization of Originality in the Imperial German Army," *Defense Analysis* 3, no. 4 (December 1987): 313–14; Samuels, *Command or Control?*, 11.

109. Meyer points out that the German Army did not formally adopt the term *Auftragstaktik* until the interwar period. See Meyer, "Operational Art and the German Command System in World War I," 391–92. I nevertheless use the term instead of its predecessor concept, *Weisungsfuerhrung*, because it captures the same command philosophy, and because it is already familiar to English-language readers. That said, Muth argues that the English translation for the term "mission-type order" and the British translation for "directive control" are misleading. As Muth frames it, "Often *Aufgtragstaktitk* is misunderstood as a technique to issue orders, while in fact it is a command philosophy. The basic concept . . . means that there is direction by the superior, but no tight control." Muth, *Command Culture*, 173.

110. *Field Service Regulations of the German Army, 1908*, 12–31.

111. Ibid., 12–13, para. 49 and 50 (emphasis in the original).

112. Samuels, *Command or Control?*, 10–15, 22.

113. Meyer, "Operational Art and the German Command System in World War I," 131–32.

114. Ibid., 131–32.

115. Ibid., 117.

116. Boff, *Haig's Enemy*, 115–18.

117. Ibid., 115.

118. Bull, "The Early Years of the War," 203. Up to this point, the German Army had not mounted an attack by a force any smaller than a battalion. The prewar doctrines were also written in terms of battalion-size elements. The Garde Schutzen Division was the first to try a company-level attack.

119. Boff, *Haig's Enemy*, 115–18.

120. Summarizing the German Army's defensive practices at the end of 1916, Ludendorff stated that "the group (of a non-commissioned officer and eight men), the importance of which had been strongly emphasized by many intelligent commanders before the war, now became officially the unit of the infantry in fighting disposition. The position of the non-commissioned officer as group leader thus gained in importance. Tactics became more and more individualized." Ludendorff, *Ludendorff's Own Story*, 1: 459. As another example of this shift, during the Somme offensive, units began delegating near total autonomy to battalion-level commanders "so that they hardly had to consult division headquarters at all." Meyer, "Operational Art and the German Command System in World War I," 373. See also, Samuels, *Command or Control?*, 174–75.

121. Nor did German commanders hesitate to fire subordinates who failed to make sound decisions. This started at the top of the organization. Weeks after the new defensive doctrine was published, Ludendorff fired two generals who kept too many men in the front lines while defending against a French counterattack at Verdun. Wynne, *If Germany Attacks*, 168.

122. Lupfer, *The Dynamics of Doctrine*, 20–21.

123. Ludendorff, *Ludendorff's Own Story*, 1: 468.

124. Lupfer, *The Dynamics of Doctrine*, 20.

125. For a detailed analysis of the General Staff system and its origins, see Trevor N. Dupuy, *A Genius for War: The German Army and General Staff, 1807–1945* (Englewood Cliffs, NJ: Prentice Hall, 1977).

126. The German Army was administratively divided into twenty-four districts (plus an additional one for the Prussian Guards). Each district recruited, trained, and equipped approximately one corps. In time of war and during large-scale maneuvers, these corps fell under the operational command of one of seven field armies. General Staff, *Handbook of the German Army, 1912*, 41, 71, 73.

127. Ibid., 79–81.

128. This and what follows are from ibid., 47–50.

129. Robert T. Foley, "Dumb Donkeys or Cunning Foxes? Learning in the British and German Armies during the Great War," *International Affairs* 90, no. 2 (2014): 286.

130. Like Meyer, I use the term "German General Staff" to describe the Prussian General Staff. Meyer, "Operational Art and the German Command System in World War I," 16.

131. Foley, "A Case Study in Horizontal Military Innovation," 818.

132. "The General Staff, while unquestionably a corps d'elite, is in no sense a closed corporation; that it is made up of officers at once scientific and thoroughly practical, and that its members, having come from and kept up their intimate connection with the troops, enjoy the respect and confidence of the latter in a high degree. This respect and confidence they possess all the more since they owe their distinction not to the advantage of birth, wealth, or influence, but solely to their own efforts and merit." Schwan, *The Organization of the German Army*, 99.

133. And this was in a prewar army that was notoriously slow to promote company-grade officers to field grade (i.e., captain to major). Samuels, *Command or Control?*, 27.

134. Boff, *Haig's Enemy*, 52.

135. Samuels, *Command or Control?*, 15. It is, however, important to note that the army had what Robert Foley refers to as a "deep reservoir" of officers with staff expertise, given that the War Academy had been graduating approximately one hundred staff officers a year between 1876 and 1914. Foley, "Dumb Donkeys or Cunning Foxes?," 286.

136. Lupfer, *The Dynamics of Doctrine*, 10, 12, 28; Gudmundsson, *Stormtroop Tactics*, 46–47.

137. Lupfer, *The Dynamics of Doctrine*, 10–12; Samuels, *Command or Control?*, 93.

138. Lupfer, *The Dynamics of Doctrine*, 11; Herwig, "The Dynamics of Necessity," 95–96.

139. Lupfer, *The Dynamics of Doctrine*, 38–39.

140. Ibid., 22; Samuels, *Command or Control?*, 186.

141. Lupfer, *The Dynamics of Doctrine*, 9, 12–13. See, for example, General Staff, *SS 462: German Raid on the British Trenches Near La Boisselle, 11th April, 1916 (Translation of a German Document)*, August 1916, 13–19, Joint Services Command and Staff College Archives, Shrivenham.

142. Foley, "Dumb Donkeys or Cunning Foxes?," 287. These reports were written on an ad hoc basis prior to mid-1916, but were required after every engagement thereafter. The OHL initially tried to prevent units from sharing these reports with one another. However, given the officer corps' well-established culture of deviating from orders when they believed that the situation required, units readily distributed their reports both up the chain of command and to one another. Foley, "A Case Study in Horizontal Military Innovation," 814–15.

143. Foley, "A Case Study in Horizontal Military Innovation," 817.

144. Ludendorff, *Ludendorff's Own Story*, 2:102–3.

145. Samuels, *Command or Control?*, 187.

146. Meyer, "Operational Art and the German Command System in World War I," 361.

147. Wynne, *If Germany Attacks*, 161.

148. Ibid., 302.

149. General Staff, *Education and Training of the German Infantry* (July 1909), 9, Z160 Joint Services Command and Staff College Archives, Shrivenham.

150. What follows is taken from General Staff, *Education and Training of the German Infantry*, 10–19.

151. Steven Errol Clemente, "'Mit Gott! Für König und Kaiser!': A Critical Analysis of the Making of the Prussian Army Officer, 1860–1914" (PhD diss., University of Oklahoma, 1989), 112.

152. Schwan, *The Organization of the German Army*, 87.

153. Ibid., 42–51.

154. General Staff, *Education and Training of the German Infantry*, 18–19.

155. General Staff, *Handbook of the German Army, 1912*, 94.

156. For a detailed discussion of the officer selection process, see Clemente, "Mit Gott!," 112, 115–39.

157. Ibid., 260.

158. Gudmundsson, *Stormtroop Tactics*, 3–6.

159. Conscripts were still called up according to the year in which they turned twenty. However, as manpower shortages became acute, the German Army started calling them up earlier and earlier. General Staff, *SS 356: Handbook of the German Army in War*, 13–15.

160. Lupfer, *The Dynamics of Doctrine*, 23.

161. Drury, "German Stormtrooper," 14.

162. For a dissenting view, see Foley, "A Case Study in Horizontal Military Innovation," 818–20. Foley argues that training grew *more* decentralized from 1916 to 1918, because although the OHL directed the creation of these new schools, it gave them wide latitude to determine their own curriculum. I maintain that the doctrine developed by the General Staff and endorsed by Ludendorff formed the backbone for training and that the army would not have demonstrated as much consistency in applying assault tactics, combined-arms, and elastic defense-in-depth concepts as it did in late 1917 and early 1918 were it not for relatively uniform training. Indeed, it seems implausible that schools across the army would spontaneously converge on a remarkably consistent set of war-fighting concepts absent top-level doctrine. Unfortunately, testing these competing explanations, which would require a detailed assessment of what individual schools taught, is beyond the scope of this project.

163. Gudmundsson, *Stormtroop Tactics*, 77.

164. Samuels, *Command or Control?*, 240–41.

165. Herman Cron, *Imperial German Army, 1914–18: Organisation, Structure, Orders of Battle*, trans. C. F. Colton (Berlin, 1937: reprint, West Midlands, UK: Helion, 2006), 30.

166. Herwig, "The Dynamics of Necessity," 101–2; Meyer, "Operational Art and the German Command System in World War I," 351–52.

167. Cron, *Imperial German Army, 1914–18*, 30.

168. Wynne, *If Germany Attacks*, 162.

169. Lupfer, *The Dynamics of Doctrine*, 24; Samuels, *Command or Control?*, 184. These schools were initially established at Solesmes and Sedan. The first cohort of students arrived on February 1, 1917.

170. For example, units at Arras in 1917 almost allowed British forces to break through after German commanders did a poor job of implementing the army's new defensive doctrine. Lupfer, *The Dynamics of Doctrine*, 29–30; Wynne, *If Germany Attacks*, 184–85.

171. Cron, *Imperial German Army, 1914–18*, 31.

172. Lupfer, *The Dynamics of Doctrine*, 46–47.

173. Ibid., 46; Williamson Murray, *Military Adaptation in War: With Fear of Change* (New York: Cambridge University Press, 2011), 111.

174. Ludendorff, *Ludendorff's Own Story*, 2:209.

4. The British Army on the Western Front

1. I use the term "BEF" to refer specifically to the part of the British Army that fought in Western Europe from August 1914 until November 1918.

2. For a discussion on the origins of this narrative, see Gary Sheffield, *Forgotten Victory: The First World War: Myths and Realities* (London: Headline Book Publishing 2001; reprint, London: Sharpe Books, 2018), 14–44, Kindle.

3. See Alan Clark, *The Donkeys* (London: Hutchinson, 1961); A. J. P. Taylor, *The First World War: An Illustrated History* (London: Hamish Hamilton, 1963); Richard Boden and J. Lloyd, *Blackadder Goes Forth*, BBC, 1990; Norman F. Dixon, *On the Psychology of Military Incompetence* (New York: Basic Books, 2016), 74–80.

4. Shelford Bidwell and Dominick Graham, *Fire-Power: British Army Weapons and Theories of War, 1904–1945* (London: George Allen & Unwin, 1982); Paddy Griffith, *Battle Tactics of the Western Front: The British Army's Art of Attack, 1916–18* (New Haven, CT: Yale University Press, 2000); M. A. Ramsay, *Command and Cohesion: The Citizen Soldier and Minor Tactics in the British Army, 1870–1918* (Westport, CT: Praeger, 2002); Andy Simpson, *Directing Operations: British Corps Command on the Western Front, 1914–18* (Stroud, UK: Spellmount, 2006); Jonathan Boff, *Winning and Losing on the Western Front: The British Third Army and the Defeat of Germany in 1918* (Cambridge: Cambridge University Press, 2012); Robert T. Foley, "Dumb Donkeys or Cunning Foxes? Learning in the British and German Armies during the Great War," *International Affairs* 90, no. 2 (2014): 279–98; Aimée Fox, *Learning to Fight: Military Innovation and Change in the British Army, 1914–1918* (Cambridge: Cambridge University Press, 2018); Jonathan Boff, *Haig's Enemy: Crown Prince Rupprecht and Germany's War on the Western Front* (Oxford: Oxford University Press, 2018); Sheffield, *Forgotten Victory*.

5. Correlli Barnett, *Britain and Her Army: A Military, Political and Social History of the British Army, 1509–1970* (London: Cassell, 2000): 299–370; Michael Carver, *Britain's Army in the Twentieth Century* (London: Macmillan, 1998); David French and Brian Holden Reid, eds., *The British General Staff: Reform and Innovation* (London: Frank Cass, 2002); Timothy Bowman and Mark Connelly, *The Edwardian Army: Manning, Training, and Deploying the British Army, 1902–1914* (Oxford: Oxford University Press, 2012), 1–6.

6. Harold R. Winton, *To Change an Army: General Sir John Burnett-Stuart and British Armored Doctrine, 1928–1938* (Lawrence, KS: University of Kansas Press, 1988), 8.

7. Hew Strachan, *Wellington's Legacy: The Reform of the British Army, 1830–54* (Manchester, UK: Manchester University Press, 1984), 268.

8. Barnett, *Britain and Her Army*, 373.

9. Ibid., 337–49.

10. John Strawson, *Gentlemen in Khaki and Camouflage: The British Army, 1890–2008* (Barnsley, UK: Pen & Sword Military, 2009), 83–89; Hew Strachan, "The British Army, Its General Staff and the Continental Commitment, 1904–14," in *British General Staff: Reform and Innovation*, ed. David French and Brian Holden Reid (London: Frank Cass, 2002), 63–79.

11. Or, in Field Marshal Sir Henry Hugh Wilson's words, the BEF's six divisions were "fifty too few." Hew Strachan, *The First World War, Vol. 1, To Arms* (Oxford: Oxford University Press, 2003), 200.

12. Barnett, *Britain and Her Army*, 371–72.

13. The BEF was initially divided into two corps of two infantry divisions each. The remaining two divisions arrived in France prior to the Battle of the Marne.

14. Holger H. Herwig, *The Marne, 1914: The Opening of World War I and the Battle That Changed the World* (New York: Random House, 2011).

15. Sheffield, *Forgotten Victory*, 110–12.

16. Ibid., 109.

17. The British Army had 733,514 soldiers on its rolls in 1914. Of these, 247,432 were regulars. Foley, "Dumb Donkeys or Cunning Foxes?," 283. Nearly two and half million men voluntarily enlisted by the end of 1915. By November 1918, 5.7 million men served in the British Army. Strachan, *The First World War*, 160.

18. Ilana R. Bet-El, *Conscripts: Lost Legions of the Great War* (Gloucestershire, UK: Sutton, 1999), 48.

19. G. C. Peden, *Arms, Economics and British Strategy: From Dreadnaughts to Hydrogen Bombs* (Cambridge: Cambridge University Press, 2009), 60; Paul Kennedy points out that the British munitions industry was told to produce 7 million bullets per week before the war, only to find that the first wartime order was for 176 million. Paul Kennedy, "Britain in the First World War," in *Military Effectiveness*, Vol. 1, ed. Allan R. Millett and Williamson Murray (Boston: Allen & Unwin, 1988), 34. The shortage of artillery shells was even more acute. Prewar establishments planned for each cannon to deploy with one thousand rounds of ammunition. War Office, *War*

Establishments: Part I, Expeditionary Force, 1914 (London: HMSO, 1914), 6, Z216, Joint Services Command and Staff College Archives, Shrivenham. Units found that a gun could fire its entire allotment of ammunition in France in a matter of seventy-five minutes. Jonathan B. A. Bailey, *Field Artillery and Fire Power* (Abingdon, UK: Routledge, 2004), 118.

20. Paddy Griffith, *The Great War on the Western Front: A Short History* (Barnsley, UK: Pen & Sword Military, 2008), 19–20. Gary Sheffield suggests that it is more accurate to think of the debate as one between those who thought of the war as total and those who thought it could be kept limited. Sheffield, *Forgotten Victory*, 117–18.

21. Peter Hart, *Gallipoli* (Oxford: Oxford University Press, 2011).

22. Barnett, *Britain and Her Army*, 382. By late August 1915, even Kitchener admitted that his original plan to wait until 1917 to launch the war winning effort was infeasible. Sheffield, *Forgotten Victory*, 116.

23. Joseph Jacques Césaire Joffre, *The Personal Memoirs of Joffre: Field Marshal of the French Army*, 2 vols., transl. Timothy Bentley Mott (London: Harper & Brothers, 1932), 2:327.

24. Sheffield, *Forgotten Victory*, 164.

25. Bidwell and Graham, *Fire-Power*, 70.

26. Barnett, *Britain and Her Army*, 393.

27. Joffre, *The Personal Memoirs of Joffre*, 2:410–17; Martin Samuels, *Command or Control? Command, Training and Tactics in the British and German Armies, 1888–1918* (London: Frank Cass, 1995), 124–26.

28. Peter Hart, *The Somme: The Darkest Hour on the Western Front* (New York: Pegasus, 2010).

29. Sheffield, *Forgotten Victory*, 131–33.

30. Ibid., 207.

31. Ibid., 217.

32. Ibid., 222.

33. Barnett, *Britain and Her Army*, 400.

34. Nick Lloyd, *Passchendaele: The Lost Victory of World War I* (New York: Basic, 2017).

35. Sheffield, *Forgotten Victory*, 239.

36. Ibid., 239.

37. Ibid., 253–54.

38. Douglas Haig, *The Private Papers of Douglas Haig, 1914–1919: Selections from the Private Diary and Correspondence of Field-Marshal the Earl Haig of Bemersyde*, ed. Robert Blake (London: Eyre and Spottiswoode, 1952), 281; Timothy Travers, *How the War Was Won: Command and Technology in the British Army on the Western Front, 1917–1918* (New York: Routledge, 1992), 34–37; Samuels, *Command or Control?*, 199.

39. Haig, *The Private Papers of Douglas Haig, 1914–1919*, 271.

40. Travers, *How the War Was Won*, 35.

41. Haig, *The Private Papers of Douglas Haig, 1914–1919*, 297–301; Ferdinand Foch, *The Memoirs of Marshal Foch*, trans. Timothy Bentley Mott (Garden City, NY: Doubleday, Doran, 1931), 264, 276–77.

42. Halik Kochanski, "Planning for War in the Final Years of Pax Britannica, 1889–1903," in *The British General Staff: Reform and Innovation c. 1890–1939*, ed. David French and Brian Holden Reid (London: F. Cass, 2002), 15–19; Strawson, *Gentlemen in Khaki and Camouflage*, 62, 71.

43. Ramsay, *Command and Cohesion*, 25–32.

44. Ibid.; T. H. E. Travers, "The Offensive and the Problem of Innovation in British Military Thought, 1870–1915," *Journal of Contemporary History* 13, no. 3 (July 1978): 537–39; Bidwell and Graham, *Fire-Power*, 50–58; Samuels, *Command or Control?*, 102.

45. For an example of the firepower perspective, see Cecil Battine, "The Offensive versus the Defensive in the Tactics of To-Day," *Journal of the Royal United Service Institution* 47, no. 304 (June 1903): 655–72.

46. F. N. Maude, "Continental versus South African Tactics: A Comparison and Reply to Some Critics," *Journal of the Royal United Services Institution* 46, no. 289 (March 1902): 318–54.

47. We should not overstate the degree to which British officers recognized these manuals as official doctrine. The army had long resisted promulgating a formal doctrine for fear that it might undermine intellectual flexibility and commonsense problem solving. Amieé Fox

suggests that even after the army published the FSR, "the prerogative of the individual com-mander overruled any desire for uniformity, particularly where training and tactics were concerned." Fox, *Learning to Fight*, 37. She also aptly reminds us that the FSR technically re-mained in force throughout the war. The introduction to a manual for division commanders published in January 1918 reminded readers that "the general principles laid down in Field Service Regulations, Part I, Chapter VII, as to attack and defence in battle hold good to-day." Yet the manual then goes on to point out that it is still necessary to modify the way that such principles are applied in practice. General Staff, *SS 135: The Training and Employment of Divi-sions, 1918* (January, 1918), 5, Z435, Joint Services Command and Staff College Archives, Shrivenham. Given this book's emphasis on learning as it pertains to tactical systems, appli-cation is arguably more important than principle. For this reason, I treat the various regula-tions, manuals, and associated documents published by the GHQ over the course of the war doctrine.

48. Ramsay, *Command and Cohesion*, 96.

49. Bowman and Connelly, *The Edwardian Army*, 66.

50. What follows is a summary of War Office, *Infantry Training (Provisional)* (London: HMSO, 1902), 190–202, Z111, Joint Services Command and Staff College Archives, Shrivenham.

51. Ibid., 200.

52. Ibid., 207–8.

53. Ibid., 207.

54. Ibid., 201.

55. War Office, *Field Service Regulations, Part I* (London: HMSO, 1912), 135. See also Travers, "The Offensive and the Problem of Innovation in British Military Thought, 1870–1915," 538.

56. War Office, *Infantry Training (Provisional)*, 209.

57. Travers, "The Offensive and the Problem of Innovation in British Military Thought, 1870–1915," 538.

58. War Office, "Report of a Conference of General Staff Officers at the Staff College 18th to 21st January, 1909," 10, Joint Services Command and Staff College Archives, Shrivenham; Griffith, *Battle Tactics of the Western Front*, 49.

59. War Office, *Field Service Regulations, Part I*, 138–39.

60. Ibid., 133.

61. War Office, "Report of a Conference of General Staff Officers at the Staff College 18th to 21st January, 1909," 11.

62. What follows is from War Office, *Field Service Regulations, Part I*, 130–39.

63. Griffith, *Battle Tactics of the Western Front*, 50. See also Bidwell and Graham, *Fire-Power*, 18–19; Ramsay, *Command and Cohesion*, 93.

64. Sheffield, *Forgotten Victory*, 145–46.

65. General Staff, *Notes from the Front: Part I, 1914* (London: HMSO, 1914), 2–5, Z204, Joint Services Command and Staff College Archives, Shrivenham; General Staff, *Notes from the Front: Part II, 1914* (London: HMSO, 1914), 13, Z204, Joint Services Command and Staff College Ar-chives, Shrivenham.

66. Barnett, *Britain and Her Army*, 372.

67. Ramsay, *Command and Cohesion*, 176.

68. Ibid., 176–77.

69. Sheffield, *Forgotten Victory*, 161.

70. Samuels, *Command or Control?*, 109.

71. Wynne, *If Germany Attacks*, 19–35.; Samuels, *Command or Control?*, 104–5.

72. Wynne, *If Germany Attacks*, 30–31.

73. Ibid., 42. For an example of the army's efforts to integrate engineers and lightweight ar-tillery into infantry operations at the time, see General Staff, *Trench Warfare, Notes on Attack and Defence*, February 1915, 3–7, Z227, Joint Services Command and Staff College Archives, Shriven-ham. Units were already wrestling with the challenges of maintaining positive communication between the assault waves and their supporting. General Staff, "Tactical Notes," 1915, 1, WO 33/721, National Archives, London.

74. The Germans lost approximately nine hundred. Wynne, *If Germany Attacks*, 51.

75. Samuels, *Command or Control?*, 105–9.

76. Ibid., 103.

77. Wynne, *If Germany Attacks*, 72; Bidwell and Graham, *Fire-Power*, 77.

78. Wynne, *If Germany Attacks*, 78.

79. Ibid., 114–15; Griffith, *Battle Tactics of the Western Front*, 54.

80. Fifth Army was also referred to as Reserve Army. "Memorandum on Trench to Trench Attack by a Battalion Commander in the Fifth Army," October 31, 1916, WO 158/344, National Archives, London.

81. General Staff, *SS 135: Instructions for the Training of Divisions for Offensive Action*, December 1916, 9, Joint Services Command and Staff College Archives, Z280, Shrivenham.

82. Ibid., 15–16, 47.

83. Griffith, *Battle Tactics of the Western Front*, 57.

84. Simon Robbins, *British Generalship on the Western Front 1914–18: Defeat into Victory* (London: Frank Cass, 2005), 99–101.

85. Ibid., 94; Bidwell and Graham, *Fire-Power*, 126–27.

86. These included integrating combat engineers with advance guards during an assault to breach obstacles, letting platoons and even sections maneuver independently, attaching as many Lewis guns as possible to assault platoons, and exploring diamond, "blob," and "dribbling" formations. General Staff, *SS 158: Notes on Recent Operations on the Front of First, Third, Fourth and Fifth Armies*, May 1917, 2–3, Z357, Joint Services Command and Staff College Archives, Shrivenham; Griffith, *Battle Tactics of the Western Front*, 97–98.

87. General Staff, *SS 143: Instructions for the Training of Platoons in Offensive Action*, February 1917, 3, Z854, Joint Services Command and Staff College Archives, Shrivenham. As laid out in a subsequent manual, each infantry battalion would thereafter consist of a headquarters element and four line companies, each infantry company was divided into a headquarters element and four platoons, and each line platoon was organized into four sections. General Staff, *SS 600: The Organization of an Infantry Battalion and the Normal Formation for the Attack*, April 1917, 2, Z390, Joint Services Command and Staff College Archives, Shrivenham.

88. James Beach, "Issued by the General Staff: Doctrine Writing at British GHQ, 1917–1918," *War in History* 19, no. 4 (2012): 470; Sheffield, *Forgotten Victory*, 226–27.

89. General Staff, *SS 143: Instructions for the Training of Platoons in Offensive Action*, 8–9; General Staff, *SS 144: The Normal Formation for the Attack*, February 1917, OB/1919/T, Imperial War Museum Archive, London. *SS 600*, which was explicitly written to be read in conjunction with *SS 143* and *SS 144*, further specified that platoons should "constitute a unit for fighting and training, and should consist of a homogenous combination of all the weapons with which the infantry is now armed." General Staff, *SS 600*, 3.

90. General Staff, *SS 143: Instructions for the Training of Platoons in Offensive Action*, 6.

91. For a comprehensive list of relevant infantry-specific manuals published in 1917, see Beach, "Issued by the General Staff," 469, 472 and 476.

92. Sheffield, *Forgotten Victory*, 253–54.

93. General Staff, *SS 600*, 4–6, 8–12.

94. General Staff, *SS 143: Instructions for the Training of Platoons in Offensive Action*, 9.

95. General Staff, *SS 135: The Division in Attack*, November 1918, 23, Z441, Joint Services Command and Staff College Archives, Shrivenham.

96. Ibid., 5–6.

97. Ibid., 20, 24.

98. Ibid., 19.

99. General Staff, *SS 143: The Training and Employment of Platoons, 1918*, February 1918, 4, Z854, Joint Services Command and Staff College Archives, Shrivenham.

100. Griffith, *Battle Tactics of the Western Front*, 95.

101. Beach, "Issued by the General Staff," 477.

102. Ibid., 481.

103. General Staff, *SS 135: The Division in Attack*, 9. This also meant bypassing strongpoints and bunkers, leaving tanks and follow-on forces to reduce and destroy them and using reserves to reinforce success, not failure. Ibid., 8–9.

104. Ivor Maxse, *Hints on Training (Issued by XVIII Corps)*, August 1918, 10, Z854/2, Joint Services Command and Staff College Archives, Shrivenham.

105. Sheffield, *Forgotten Victory*, 226–27.

106. Bidwell and Graham, *Fire-Power*, 139.

107. For examples, see Boff, *Winning and Losing on the Western Front*, 127–30.

108. Robbins, *British Generalship on the Western Front*, 30.

109. For an analysis of the sources and causes of tactical diversity within the BEF at this point in the war, see Boff, *Winning and Losing on the Western Front*, 153–59.

110. See the corresponding discussions of German and French prewar artillery doctrine in chapters 3 and 5, respectively.

111. "Each arm of the service possesses a power peculiar to itself; yet is dependent, to a greater or less degree, upon the aid and co-operation of the other arms." War Office, *(Provisional)* (London: HMSO, 1902), 13, Z112, Joint Services Command and Staff College Archives, Shrivenham. See also Bowman and Connelly, *The Edwardian Army*, 84–85.

112. War Office, "Report of a Conference of General Staff Officers at the Staff College 7th to 10th January, 1908" (1908), 44–45, Joint Services Command and Staff College Archives, Shrivenham. See also War Office, "Report of a Conference of General Staff Officers at the Staff College 18th to 21st January, 1909," 6; War Office, "Report of a Conference of General Staff Officers at the Staff College 17th to 19th January, 1910," 69, Joint Services Command and Staff College Archives, Shrivenham; War Office, "Report of a Conference of General Staff Officers at the Staff College 9th to 12th January, 1911," 53–74, 81–82, Joint Services Command and Staff College Archives, Shrivenham.

113. War Office, *Field Service Regulations, Part I*, 138–39.

114. "Artillery fire will be continued until it is impossible for the artillery to distinguish between its own and the enemy's infantry. The danger from shells bursting short is more than compensated for by the support afforded." War Office, *Field Service Regulations, Part I*, 138.

115. Spencer Jones, "Applying Colonial Lessons to European War: The British Expeditionary Force 1902–1914," in *The Greater War: Other Combatants and Other Fronts, 1914–1918*, ed. Jonathan Krause (New York: Palgrave Macmillan, 2014), 91.

116. Sanders Marble, *The Infantry Cannot Do with a Gun Less: The Place of the Artillery in the British Expeditionary Force, 1914–1918* (New York: Columbia University Press, 2002), location 39, American Council of Learned Societies E-Book, 2008 edition.

117. This and what follows are from ibid., locations 63–71.

118. According to Marble, there was "too much talk of a 'spirit of close support.'" By highlighting the artillery's direct-fire role, prewar regulations robbed it of its primary advantage: range. Ibid., location 58.

119. Bidwell and Graham, *Fire-Power*, 19.

120. Samuels, *Command or Control?*, 101–3.

121. Peden, *Arms, Economics and British Strategy*, 63.

122. Marble, *The Infantry Cannot Do with a Gun Less*, locations 64, 81.

123. Ibid., locations 73, 88.

124. Ibid., location 47.

125. Ammunition and artillery shortages persisted until 1917. Bidwell and Graham, *Fire-Power*, 61.

126. Ibid., 73, 102.

127. Shell shortages were an important reason for the short bombardment.

128. Bidwell and Graham, *Fire-Power*, 73; Sheffield, *Forgotten Victory*, 164.

129. Marble, *The Infantry Cannot Do with a Gun Less*, location 94.

130. Bidwell and Graham, *Fire-Power*, 75.

131. Wynne, *If Germany Attacks*, 51–52. See also Sheffield, *Forgotten Victory*, 164.

132. Wynne, *If Germany Attacks*, 60; Samuels, *Command or Control?*, 109.

133. Bidwell and Graham, *Fire-Power*, 77.

134. Sequencing fire and maneuver meant that infantry tactics needed to conform to artillery plans. But this imperative did not make timetable tactics inevitable. Although rigid formations and inflexible time lines certainly represented an easier way to synchronize infantry maneuver with the artillery's firepower, there was no reason the two had to go hand in hand.

Infantry units could have continued to explore flexible formations or adding more organic fire-power, even as BEF operations emphasized "shoot then move" and attacking for limited objectives, as they did later in the war. As Sanders Marble aptly points out, "the ultimate solution was flexible infantry tactics so that the infantry could fight their way forward if the barrage did not do all the work for them." Marble, *The Infantry Cannot Do with a Gun Less*, location 248.

135. Sheffield, *Forgotten Victory*, 165; Marble, *The Infantry Cannot Do with a Gun Less*, locations 245–46.

136. Ernest D. Swinton suggested the idea behind the tank to Colonel Maurice Hankey in October 1914. However, at least within the army, the concept only existed on paper until Swinton wrote a memo to Sir John French in June 1915, which led to the creation of the joint Admiralty–War Office Landship Committee. Of course, Sir Winston Churchill famously created an armored car unit within the Royal Naval Air Service in late 1914, which served as another source of inspiration behind the tank. But this initiative did not generate a similar effort within the army in 1914. See Foley, "Dumb Donkeys or Cunning Foxes?," 292–92. For these reasons, I do not consider the BEF to have seriously experimented with the tank concept until after the Battle of Neuve Chapelle.

137. As Sanders Marble points out, "the BEF never quite believed that artillery conquered and infantry occupied, but a corps could write 'if the artillery plan is complete and the gunners are given full time to carry through . . . the battle is three-quarters won before our infantry appear on the scene at all.'" Marble, *The Infantry Cannot Do with a Gun Less*, location 273. For other references to British artillery doctrine adhering to the spirit of this approach in 1916 and 1917, see Stephen Bull, "The Somme and Beyond," in *War on the Western Front*, ed. G. D. Sheffield (Oxford, UK: Osprey, 2007), 223–24; Sheffield, *Forgotten Victory*, 207.

138. Wynne, *If Germany Attacks*, 106.

139. Sheffield, *Forgotten Victory*, 208.

140. Marble, *The Infantry Cannot Do with a Gun Less*, location 127.

141. "Memorandum on Trench to Trench Attack by a Battalion Commander in the Fifth Army."

142. Bidwell and Graham, *Fire-Power*, 102.

143. Ibid., 85.

144. General Staff, *SS 135 Instructions for the Training of Divisions for Offensive Action*, 9.

145. Wynne, *If Germany Attacks*, 113–14.

146. Foley, "Dumb Donkeys or Cunning Foxes?," 291–93.

147. Elizabeth Greenhalgh, "Technology Development in Coalition: The Case of the First World War Tank," *International History Review* 22, no. 4 (2000): 812.

148. Boff, *Winning and Losing on the Western Front*, 140–45.

149. General Staff, *SS 135 Instructions for the Training of Divisions for Offensive Action*, 9.

150. Sheffield, *Forgotten Victory*, 245.

151. British gunners fired three million shells a week at the bombardment's peak. Wynne, *If Germany Attacks*, 299; Bidwell and Graham, *Fire-Power*, 88–90.

152. The GHQ ultimately overruled him. The Third Army therefore began its bombardment on March 20. Its infantry went over the top on April 9. Marble, *The Infantry Cannot Do with a Gun Less*, location 144.

153. Ibid., locations 135–44. "Not until November 1917 would destruction be abandoned as a primary goal of artillery attack." Ibid., location 103.

154. Griffith, *Battle Tactics of the Western Front*, 151. See also Marble, *The Infantry Cannot Do with a Gun Less*, location 366.

155. Bidwell and Graham, *Fire-Power*, 99–100.

156. The GHQ briefly flirted with this approach in late 1915, only to reverse course almost immediately. The senior artillery officer in each corps therefore remained in an advisory capacity until December 1916. Marble, *The Infantry Cannot Do with a Gun Less*, location 369.

157. Griffith, *Battle Tactics of the Western Front*, 152.

158. Bidwell and Graham, *Fire-Power*, 101–11.

159. This and what follows are from William Van der Kloot, "Lawrence Bragg's Role in the Development of Sound-Ranging in World War I," *Notes and Records of the Royal Society* 59, no. 3 (2005): 273–84.

160. Ibid., 277.

161. Bidwell and Graham, *Fire-Power*, 110.

162. Marble, *The Infantry Cannot Do with a Gun Less*, location 162.

163. That said, the Mark IV tank could only achieve a maximum speed of four miles per hour and could operate for only eight hours before exhausting the crew. General Staff, *SS 164: Notes on the Use of Tanks and on the General Principles on Their Employment as an Adjunct to the Infantry Attack*, May 1917, 1, Z365, Joint Services Command and Staff College Archives, Shrivenham.

164. Third Army, "Training Note: Tank and Infantry Operations without Methodical Preparation," October 30, 1917, WO 158/347, National Archives, London.

165. Marble, *The Infantry Cannot Do with a Gun Less*, location 137.

166. What follows is taken from Wilhelm Balck, *Development of Tactics: World War I*, trans. Harry Bell (Fort Leavenworth, KS: General Service Schools Press, 1922; reprint, West Chester, OH: The Nafziger Collection, 2011), 60; Griffith, *The Great War on the Western Front*, 164–69; Marble, *The Infantry Cannot Do with a Gun Less*, location 160–62.

167. The Mark V (Heavy) was a faster, more reliable attack tank than the Mark IV. The Mark (One Star) was even larger and carried supplies. The Whippet, the army's first light tank, only had machine guns and was designed to support semiopen and mobile warfare. Each of these three new variants saw action in 1918. General Staff, *SS 214: Tanks and Their Employment in Co-Operation with Other Arms*, August 1918, 4–5, Z438, Joint Services Command and Staff College Archives, Shrivenham.

168. Sheffield, *Forgotten Victory*, 284.

169. Marble, *The Infantry Cannot Do with a Gun Less*, locations 167, 283.

170. Ibid., location 177.

171. Ibid., location 172.

172. Sheffield, *Forgotten Victory*, 298.

173. Bidwell and Graham, *Fire-Power*, 131–46; Boff, *Winning and Losing on the Western Front*, 123–59; Robbins, *British Generalship on the Western Front 1914–18*, 106–13.

174. Ernest Dunlop Swinton, *The Defence of Duffer's Drift*, reprint (Washington, DC: Journal of the United States Infantry Association, 1904).

175. The 1902 *Combined Training (Provisional)* manual states: "The tactical outcome of the effects of modern fire and of smokeless powder is that a small force, judiciously posted, with its flanks secure, can easily hold its own against superior numbers. To a certain extent this favors the force that stands on the defensive." War Office, *Combined Training (Provisional)*, 16.

176. What follows is taken from War Office, *Field Service Regulations, Part I*, 140–50; War Office, "Report of a Conference of General Staff Officers at the Staff College 17th to 19th January, 1910."

177. At the 1910 General Staff Conference, officers discussed using engineering officers to build defensive trenches in light of the increasingly powerful artillery available to attackers. War Office, "Report of a Conference of General Staff Officers at the Staff College 17th to 19th January, 1910," 15–20. Officers at the 1912 conference called on troops to make entrenching a regular part of peacetime maneuver but lamented the fact that troops could not dig holes on public lands in Britain.

178. General Staff, *Notes from the Front: Part I*, 8.

179. General Staff, *Notes from the Front: Part II*, 17.

180. What follows is from Samuels, *Command or Control?*, 200.

181. General Staff, *Notes on Trench Warfare for Infantry Officers* (London: HMSO, 1916), Z310, Joint Services Command and Staff College Archives, Shrivenham.

182. General Staff, *Notes from the Front: Part III and Further Notes on Field Defences*, February 1915, Joint Services Command and Staff College Archives, Shrivenham; General Staff, *Trench Warfare*.

183. Balck argues that second and third lines were no more than twenty-five yards behind the front line. Balck, *Development of Tactics*, 32.

184. Samuels, *Command or Control?*, 200–202.

185. What follows is taken from General Staff, *Notes for Infantry Officers on Trench Warfare* (London: HMSO, 1917), 10–33, Z251, Joint Services Command and Staff College Archives, Shrivenham.

186. Ibid., 11.

187. General Staff, *SS 143: Instructions for the Training of Platoons in Offensive Action*, 10.

188. Samuels, *Command or Control?*, 202.

189. British units captured a copy of the new German defensive manual in April 1917. Wynne, *If Germany Attacks*, 249.

190. What follows is taken from Samuels, *Command or Control?*, 202–9.

191. L. E. Kiggell, "Defensive Organisation of British Front, Special Instructions as to Manner of Dealing with FLESQUIERES and PASSCHENDAELE and Salient," December 13, 1917, WO 158/209, National Archives, London.

192. "Defensive Scheme, Army Battle Zone, VIII Corps Divisional Sector," January 1918, WO 158/411, National Archives, London.

193. Samuels, *Command or Control?*, 208–9; Travers, *How the War Was Won*, 58–60.

194. Griffith, *The Great War on the Western Front*, 90–91.

195. Travers, *How the War Was Won*, 56–65; Samuels, *Command or Control?*, 214–21.

196. On December 20, 1917, Haig wrote in his diary that his chief of intelligence, Charteris, anticipated a major German offensive in March 1918. Haig received additional intelligence and situation reports confirming this prediction on February 16, February 28, March 3, and March 19. Haig, *The Private Papers of Douglas Haig, 1914–1919*, 274, 285, 291, 292.

197. Samuels, *Command or Control?*, 222.

198. General Staff, *SS 210: The Division in Defence*, May 1918, 4, Z436, Joint Services Command and Staff College Archives, Shrivenham.

199. For their part, ordinary soldiers were still told that "so far as they are concerned, there is only one degree of resistance, and that is to the last round and to the last man." General Staff, *SS 210*, 5.

200. Ibid., *SS 210*, 8.

201. Ramsay, *Command and Cohesion*, 153; Jones, "Applying Colonial Lessons to European War," 82.

202. Gary Sheffield, *Leadership in the Trenches: Officer-Man Relations, Morale and Discipline in the British Army in the Era of the First World War* (New York: St. Martin's, 2000), 21; Ramsay, *Command and Cohesion*, 61–62, 153.

203. Sheffield, *Leadership in the Trenches*, 5–6. As Sheffield points out, there was a give-and-take aspect to this relationship. In exchange for their obedience, officers were expected to take care of their men's needs. This itself was progress, since officer-enlisted relations were even more asymmetric in pre-Edwardian Britain.

204. Samuels, *Command or Control?*, 58. Tim Travers ascribes this tendency toward the public school education shared by almost all officers. Tim Travers, "The Hidden Army: Structural Problems in the British Officer Corps, 1900–1918," *Journal of Contemporary History* 17, no. 3 (July 1, 1982): 524. See also Ramsay, *Command and Cohesion*, 56–60; Sheffield, *Leadership in the Trenches*, 2–3; Robbins, *British Generalship on the Western Front 1914–18*, 11.

205. For a discussion of junior officer training in the prewar period, see Tim Travers, "Learning the Art of War: Junior Officer Training in the British Army from the Eighteenth Century to 1914," in *Forging the Sword: Selecting, Educating, and Training Cadets and Junior Officers in the Modern World*, ed. Elliott V. Converse, 13–25 (Chicago: Imprint, 1998).

206. Fox, *Learning to Fight*, 43–44. Martin Samuels takes a more critical view, suggesting that the army was too deferential to its senior commanders. He argues that senior British officers had a tendency to "umpire," which meant they avoided "'interfering' out of an excessive respect for the feelings and reputation of the subordinate," thereby allowing decentralization to become "an end in itself." Samuels, *Command or Control?*, 51–53.

207. For a brief discussion of the history behind the regimental system, see Winton, *To Change an Army*, 8–9; Strachan, *Wellington's Legacy*, 211–19.

208. Ramsay, *Command and Cohesion*, 60.

209. Sheffield, *Leadership in the Trenches*, 3; Strawson, *Gentlemen in Khaki and Camouflage*, 34–35; Robbins, *British Generalship on the Western Front 1914–18*, 12.

210. Battine, "The Offensive versus the Defensive in the Tactics of To-Day," 672; Alsager Pollock, "The Training of the Army," *Journal of the Royal United Service Institution* 47, no. 300 (February 1903):176.

211. War Office, *Infantry Training (Provisional)*, 191.

212. War Office, *Combined Training (Provisional)*, 3.

213. Samuels, *Command or Control?*, 96–97.

214. Sheffield, *Leadership in the Trenches*, 24.

215. It is certainty easy to understand why an officer—who spent a career climbing to a point where he finally had the opportunity to exercise considerable discretion, prerogative, and latitude—might then prove reluctant to cede some of that hard-earned authority back down the chain of command to leaders who had not yet paid their dues. Promotions were, after all, notoriously slow in the prewar officer corps. For example, it generally took artillery lieutenants thirteen years to make captain and another ten years to make major. Marble, *The Infantry Cannot Do with a Gun Less*, location 26.

216. Herwig, *The Marne*, 153–54, 182–83. The BEF had roughly 150,000 soldiers in France in August 1914. The German Army's First Army alone had 320,000 men. Barnett, *Britain and Her Army*, 374. The "Old Contemptibles'" performance was even more astonishing given that nearly 60 percent were reservists. F. W. Perry, *The Commonwealth Armies: Manpower and Organisation in Two World Wars* (New York: St. Martin's, 1988), 8.

217. Jones, "Applying Colonial Lessons to European War," 92–93.

218. Ibid., 93.

219. Herwig, *The Marne*, 177.

220. Jones, "Applying Colonial Lessons to European War," 93.

221. According to one lessons learned document circulated by the army in early 1915, "it is essential that the most minute details should be thought out and prepared, in order that the detachments detailed for the assault may all leave their trenches at the same moment and reach the objective at one rush without firing a shot." General Staff, *Trench Warfare*, 3. See also, Ramsay, *Command and Cohesion*, 168.

222. Robbins, *British Generalship on the Western Front 1914–18*, 61.

223. Ramsay, *Command and Cohesion*, 169.

224. As quoted in Robbins, *British Generalship on the Western Front 1914–18*, 62.

225. Kennedy, "Britain in the First World War," 52–54.

226. As quoted in Robbins, *British Generalship on the Western Front 1914–18*, 61.

227. Ramsay, *Command and Cohesion*, 169.

228. Griffith, *The Great War on the Western Front*, 35.

229. As quoted in Samuels, *Command or Control?*, 141.

230. Sheffield, *Leadership in the Trenches*, chap. 5.

231. Martin Van Creveld, *Command in War* (Cambridge, MA: Harvard University Press, 1985), 166.

232. Murray, *Military Adaptation in War*, 22.

233. Samuels, *Command or Control?*, 151.

234. Marble, *The Infantry Cannot Do with a Gun Less*, location 254.

235. Sheffield, *Forgotten Victory*, 223.

236. Ibid., 223–24.

237. Robbins, *British Generalship on the Western Front 1914–18*, 99–100; Sheffield, *Forgotten Victory*, 225–26.

238. General Staff, *SS 159: Notes on Tactical Schemes Compiled by Fourth Army*, May 1917, 1 Joint Services Command and Staff College Archives, Shrivenham.

239. General Staff, *SS 135: The Division in Attack*, 5.

240. Bowman and Connelly, *The Edwardian Army*, 64–65.

241. Strachan, *Wellington's Legacy*, 146–48.

242. Kochanski, "Planning for War in the Final Years of Pax Britannica, 1889–1903," 10; Fox, *Learning to Fight*, 30.

243. The Imperial General Staff was established in 1905. It received a chief in 1906. The billet was originally named the First Military Member, but was redesignated as the Chief of the Imperial General Staff in 1909. Bidwell and Graham, *Fire-Power*, 44–46.

244. Ibid., 128. During a meeting in 1910, the staff discovered that it did not even possess a complete record of the army's nineteenth-century campaigns. War Office, "Report of a Confer-

ence of General Staff Officers at the Staff College 17th to 19th January, 1910," 77–78. Officers assigned to the General Staff were divided into two main groupings: those who served in the War Office (including the Directorate of Military Operations, the Directorate of Staff Duties, and the Directorate of Military Training) and those who served in the regional commands. Samuels, *Command or Control?*, 39–40. See also, Barnett, *Britain and Her Army*, 360.

245. This point was part of a larger call by the chief of the General Staff to develop a mechanism for collecting opinions and ideas from units for analysis and decision by the General Staff during the 1908 General Staff Conference. War Office, "Report of a Conference of General Staff Officers at the Staff College 7th to 10th January, 1908," 47.

246. Fox, *Learning to Fight*, 30.

247. Bidwell and Graham, *Fire-Power*, 44.

248. Samuels, *Command or Control?*, 40.

249. Ibid., 38–39.

250. Ibid., 40.

251. Ibid., 46–48.

252. Strachan, *Wellington's Legacy*, 146–48.

253. Aimée Fox challenges this stereotype, suggesting that anti-intellectualism did not mean the officer corps was unthinking. Fox, *Learning to Fight*, 45. While acknowledging this important insight, ACT theory suggests that certain types of thinking—in particular rigorous doctrinal analysis—require formal training and preparation.

254. War Office, "Report of a Conference of General Staff Officers at the Staff College 13th to 16th January, 1913," 47, Joint Services Command and Staff College Archives, Shrivenham.

255. Bowman and Connelly, *The Edwardian Army*, 75.

256. Long overseas postings made it hard even for those who wanted to apply to the Staff College or to serve as staff officers. The army tried to reduce the fear that attending school would hurt an officer's standing in the regiment was by alternating post–Staff College assignments between the staff corps and the officer's regiment. Anthony Clayton, *The British Officer: Leading the Army from 1660 to the Present* (New York: Pearson Longman, 2006), 109–11.

257. Samuels, *Command or Control?*, 100–102.

258. Ibid., 103; Sheffield, *Forgotten Victory*, 162.

259. Robbins, *British Generalship on the Western Front 1914–18*, 34.

260. Foley, "Dumb Donkeys or Cunning Foxes?," 286. Ostensibly, not all of these trained staff officers were actually serving on the general staff at the start of the war.

261. Robbins, *British Generalship on the Western Front 1914–18*, 35–36.

262. Bidwell and Graham, *Fire-Power*, 42–43.

263. Ramsay, *Command and Cohesion*, 164.

264. Ibid., 167.

265. Stephen Bull, "The Early Years of the War," in *War on the Western Front*, ed. G. D. Sheffield (Oxford, UK: Osprey, 2007), 203.

266. Ramsay, *Command and Cohesion*, 167.

267. Marble, *The Infantry Cannot Do with a Gun Less*, location 113. These updates received the Stationary Service (SS) moniker in November. Fox, *Learning to Fight*, 78–79.

268. Travers, "Learning and Decision-Making on the Western Front, 1915–1916: The British Example," *Canadian Journal of History* 18, no. 1 (1983): 95.

269. Tim Travers, "A Particular Style of Command: Haig and GHQ, 1916–18," *Journal of Strategic Studies* 10, no. 3 (1987): 366. To be fair, attrition rates among officers who attended the staff college before the war were horrific. Forty-seven percent did not live to see November 1918. Robbins, *British Generalship on the Western Front 1914–18*, 37.

270. Robbins, *British Generalship on the Western Front 1914–18*, 8–9; Paddy Griffith aptly summarizes the situation in the first half of the war as one in which "the high command too often willfully closed its ears to voices of reason from below, too often responded too hastily to imperatives from above and, in Haig's case especially, too often made destabilising last-minute alterations in the perfectly sound plans of subordinates." Griffith, *Battle Tactics of the Western Front*, 6–7.

271. Robbins, *British Generalship on the Western Front 1914–18*, 20–25.

272. Beach, "Issued by the General Staff," 469.

273. Griffith, *Battle Tactics on the Western Front*, 183.

274. Strachan, "Review: The First World War," *The Historical Journal* 43, no. 3 (2000): 902.

275. Ramsay, *Command and Cohesion*, 183.

276. Murray, *Military Adaptation in War*, 20; Travers, "A Particular Style of Command," 374.

277. Samuels, *Command or Control?*, 140–41.

278. Fox, *Learning to Fight*; Foley, "Dumb Donkeys or Cunning Foxes?"

279. Robbins, *British Generalship on the Western Front*, 94–95.

280. Beach, "Issued by the General Staff," 490–91.

281. Ibid., 471.

282. Beach suggests that by 1918 Training Branch made significant strides toward harmonizing and codifying doctrine within the BEF. See ibid., 464–91.

283. For a complete list, see ibid., 472, 476.

284. Bowman and Connelly, *The Edwardian Army*, 69–70.

285. Clayton, *The British Officer*, 103–4.

286. War Office, "Report of a Conference of General Staff Officers at the Staff College 18th to 21st January, 1909," 17.

287. Bidwell and Graham, *Fire-Power*, 43.

288. Clayton, *The British Officer*, 74–75.

289. War Office, "Report of a Conference of General Staff Officers at the Staff College 7th to 10th January, 1908," 6.

290. War Office, "Report of a Conference of General Staff Officers at the Staff College 18th to 21st January, 1909," 44–48; War Office, "Report of a Conference of General Staff Officers at the Staff College 17th to 19th January, 1910," 33–38.

291. Perry, *The Commonwealth Armies*, 11; Martin Pegler, "British Tommy, 1914–1918," in *War on the Western Front*, ed. G. D. Sheffield (Oxford, UK: Osprey, 2007), 96–97.

292. Pegler, "British Tommy," 95–96.

293. Robbins, *British Generalship on the Western Front 1914–18*, 91.

294. Ibid.

295. What follows is taken from Bet-El, *Conscripts*, 42–57; and Perry, *The Commonwealth Armies*, 19–21.

296. Perry, *The Commonwealth Armies*, 19–21.

297. Bidwell and Graham, *Fire-Power*, 125–26.

298. General Staff, *SS 152: Instructions for the Training of the British Armies in France (Provisional)*, June 1917, 4–11, OB/1146, Imperial War Museum Archive, London.

299. Ibid., *SS 152*, 8.

300. Ibid., *SS 152*, 66.

301. General Staff, *Training at Home* (London: HMSO, 1917), Joint Services Command and Staff College Archives, Shrivenham.

302. Ramsay, *Command and Cohesion*, 195.

303. Robbins, *British Generalship on the Western Front 1914–18*, 96.

304. Ibid.

305. Ibid.

5. The French Army on the Western Front

1. The Third Bureau managed the army's operations and doctrine.

2. Kristen A. Harkness and Michael Hunzeker, "Military Maladaptation: Counterinsurgency and the Politics of Failure," *Journal of Strategic Studies* 38, no. 6 (2015): 777–800.

3. Eliot A. Cohen, *Supreme Command: Soldiers, Statesmen, and Leadership in Wartime* (New York: Free Press, 2002), 52–94.

4. Jonathan Krause, *Early Trench Tactics in the French Army: The Second Battle of Artois, May–June 1915* (New York: Routledge, 2016), 6, Kindle.

5. Elizabeth Greenhalgh, "Writing about France's Great War," *Journal of Contemporary History* 40, no. 3 (July 2005): 605–6. Greenhalgh also discusses the official war history's inaccessibility, quoting Cyril Falls in calling it "one of the most inhuman documents that one can imagine." Finally, she points to the relative absence of empirical work on the French army and its battlefield activities and performance (609–11). A relatively recent wave of English-language scholarship is starting to reverse this trend. See Krause, *Early Trench Tactics in the French Army*; Michel Goya, *Flesh and Steel during the Great War: The Transformation of the French Army and the Invention of Modern Warfare*, Andrew Uffindell trans. (Barnsley, UK: Pen and Sword, 2018); Elizabeth Greenhalgh, "The French Army on the Western Front," *War and Society* 38, no. 4 (2019): 250–67.

6. It is composed of 11 tomes and 102 volumes.

7. Ronald Harvey Cole, "'Forward with the Bayonet!': The French Army Prepares for Offensive Warfare, 1911–1914" (PhD diss., University of Maryland College Park, 1975), 8–9; Anthony Clayton, *Paths of Glory: The French Army, 1914–18* (London: Cassell, 2005), 27–31; Ian Sumner, "French Poilu," in *War on the Western Front*, ed. Gary D. Sheffield (Oxford, UK: Osprey, 2007), 54.

8. Clayton, *Paths of Glory*, 28.

9. By 1914 Frenchmen were technically liable for twenty-eight years of service: three years on active duty, eleven in the reserves, seven in the territorial army, and seven in the territorial reserves. General Staff, *Handbook of the French Army*, August 1914, 15, Joint Services Command and Staff College Archives, Shrivenham.

10. Shelford Bidwell and Dominick Graham, *Fire-Power: British Army Weapons and Theories of War, 1904–1945* (London: George Allen & Unwin, 1982), 16; Walter Shepherd Barge Sr., "The Generals of the Republic: The Corporate Personality of High Military Rank in France, 1889–1914" (PhD diss., University of North Carolina at Chapel Hill, 1982), 153–54.

11. France saw Russia as the more important and reliable partner. French leaders had serious doubts that Britain would actually send its expeditionary force in the event of war. They were, in fact, so skeptical that the French army had plans to preemptively violate Belgian neutrality. And even if the British Expeditionary Force did arrive, French leaders knew it would be too small to divisively tip the scales. Robert A. Doughty, "French Strategy in 1914: Joffre's Own," *Journal of Military History* 67, no. 2 (2003): 435–40.

12. Hew Strachan, *The First World War, Vol. 1, To Arms* (Oxford, UK: Oxford University Press, 2003), 191; Doughty, "French Strategy in 1914." For a dissenting view, which suggests that alliance dynamics had less influence over French planning than is commonly assumed, see Douglas Porch, "The Marne and After: A Reappraisal of French Strategy in the First World War," *Journal of Military History* 53, no. 4 (1989): 372–73.

13. Doughty, "French Strategy in 1914"; Strachan, *The First World War, Vol. 1, To Arms*, 180–86, 191–98.

14. What follows is taken from Joseph Jacques Césaire Joffre, *The Personal Memoirs of Joffre: Field Marshal of the French Army*, 2 vols., transl. Timothy Bentley Mott (New York: Harper & Brothers, 1932), 1:26. It is worth pointing out that Joffre's memoirs were almost certainly ghostwritten. Goya, *Flesh and Steel during the Great War*, 25.

15. Strachan, *The First World War, Vol. 1, To Arms*, 184.

16. Porch, "The Marne and After," 378.

17. Robert A. Doughty, *Pyrrhic Victory: French Strategy and Operations in the Great War* (Cambridge, MA: Harvard University Press, 2008), 37–38.

18. Ian Sumner, *They Shall Not Pass: The French Army on the Western Front, 1914–1918* (Barnsley, UK: Pen & Sword Military, 2012), 51.

19. Greenhalgh, "The French Army on the Western Front," 252.

20. The so-called *L'union sacree*.

21. Douglas Porch, "The French Army in the First World War," in *Military Effectiveness*, Vol. 1 (Boston: Allen & Unwin, 1988), 193; Doughty, *Pyrrhic Victory*, 83.

22. Jonathan Krause suggests that Joffre was able to quickly shift French forces because of Plan XVII's inherent flexibility. Krause, *Early Trench Tactics in the French Army*, 17–18.

23. Goya, *Flesh and Steel during the Great War*, 151. At the start of 1915, the French army held approximately 88 percent of the Western Front, the British army 8 percent, and the Belgian army 4 percent. These percentages are based on figures provided by Doughty, *Pyrrhic Victory*, 108.

24. Porch, "The French Army in the First World War," 203–4.

25. Pascal Lucas, *The Evolution of Tactical Ideas in France and Germany during the War of 1914–1918*, trans. P.V. Kieffer (Paris: Berger-Leorault, 1925), 34, LCCN 5102270, Library of Congress, Washington, DC.

26. "Herein lay the reason for operations, however fruitless they may now seem, such as those we had already undertaken, and for continuing along the same line with others. If we were not yet in a position to achieve victory, we could at least force the enemy to retain on the western front all the forces which he [the German Army] had accumulated there and thus prevent him from moving them to the eastern theater." Ferdinand Foch, *The Memoirs of Marshal Foch*, trans. Timothy Bentley Mott (Garden City, NY: Doubleday, Doran, 1931), 191–92.

27. Joseph Joffre, "Memorandum Laid before the Second Allied Military Conference at Chantilly, 6th December, 1915," FirstWorldWar.com, https://www.firstworldwar.com/source/chantillymemo.htm. Joffre initially planned to contribute forty-two divisions. Only six participated in the assault on July 1.

28. Joffre, *The Personal Memoirs of Joffre*, 2:472.

29. Martin Horn, *Britain, France, and the Financing of the First World War* (Montreal: McGill-Queen's University Press, 2002), 80.

30. Pierre-Cyrille Hautcoeur, "Was the Great War a Watershed? The Economics of World War I in France," in *The Economics of World War I*, ed. Stephen Broadberry and Mark Harrison (Cambridge: Cambridge University Press, 2005), 183, 185.

31. Hautcoeur, "Was the Great War a Watershed?," 185.

32. Goya suggests that Nivelle engaged in a "skillful 'messaging'" campaign aimed at senior politicians. Goya, *Flesh and Steel during the Great War*, 160.

33. Sumner, *They Shall Not Pass*, 156.

34. Ibid., 159–69.

35. Petain called these the *batailles de redressement*.

36. Goya, *Flesh and Steel during the Great War*, 18.

37. The French army promulgated new field service regulations (operational doctrines) in 1883, 1895, and 1913 and issued new, updated, or amended *Infantry Training Regulations* manuals (as well as associated and instructions) in 1875, 1884, 1887, 1888, 1889,1894, 1901, 1902, 1904 and 1914. Goya, *Flesh and Steel during the Great War*, 33, 36–37, 40–41, 43, 48, 50.

38. The 1895 *Service of Armies on Campaign* conveyed operational-level doctrine. The 1901, 1902, and 1904 *Infantry Training Regulations* described the associated tactical concepts for infantry units. As I discuss below, a new set of regulations replaced these manuals in 1913 and 1914. However, the 1895 doctrine shaped French operations for fifteen years and so also invariably impacted the army's operations at the start of the war. Moreover, because the army published the 1913/1914 manuals in October 1913, December 1913, and April 1914, it is unlikely that units had sufficient time to absorb—let alone embrace—the most significant changes before the war broke out.

39. What follows is taken from General Staff, *Handbook of the French Army* (London: Harrison and Sons, 1906), 15, Z140, Joint Services Command and Staff College Archives, Shrivenham, 166–69; and Goya, *Flesh and Steel during the Great War*, 44–45.

40. "The final assault is to be made by masses which have been accumulated at a convenient distance from the defense. Very great importance is attached to artillery fire, both preparatory to the attack and in supporting it." General Staff, *Handbook of the French Army, 1906*, 168.

41. Goya, *Flesh and Steel during the Great War*, 45–48.

42. Ibid., 46.

43. Ibid., 47.

44. Ibid.

45. Ibid., 48–52.

46. Ibid., 51.

47. Lucas, *The Evolution of Tactical Ideas in France and Germany during the War of 1914–1918*, 4. *The Conduct of Large Units* provided operational-level doctrine for larger formations. *The Decree on the Service of Armies in the Field* established tactical-level doctrine for regiments and divisions.

Greenhalgh, "The French Army on the Western Front," 252. The *Regulations for Infantry Maneuver* focused on infantry-specific tactics, techniques, and procedures.

48. Joffre, *The Personal Memoirs of Joffre*, 1:34.

49. As quoted in Lucas, *The Evolution of Tactical Ideas in France and Germany during the War of 1914–1918*, 4.

50. Cole, "Forward with the Bayonet!," 67.

51. As quoted in Lucas, *The Evolution of Tactical Ideas in France and Germany during the War of 1914–1918*, 9 (emphasis in the original).

52. Article 119, *The Conduct of Large Units*, as quoted in Lucas, *The Evolution of Tactical Ideas in France and Germany during the War of 1914–1918*, 9.

53. Cole, "Forward with the Bayonet!," 229–31, 285–86.

54. Lucas, *The Evolution of Tactical Ideas in France and Germany during the War of 1914–1918*, 9.

55. Ibid., 13.

56. Cole, "Forward with the Bayonet!," 287–88.

57. Goya, *Flesh and Steel during the Great War*, 27.

58. Ibid., 31.

59. Lucas, *The Evolution of Tactical Ideas in France and Germany during the War of 1914–1918*, 13; Sumner, "French Poilu," 82–83; Goya, *Flesh and Steel during the Great War*, 100–103.

60. Goya, *Flesh and Steel during the Great War*, 104–5.

61. Ibid.

62. Ibid., 119.

63. Ibid., 106.

64. Ibid., 151–52.

65. Ibid., 150.

66. This and what follows are from Lucas, *The Evolution of Tactical Ideas in France and Germany during the War of 1914–1918*, 35–36.

67. Joffre, *The Personal Memoirs of Joffre*, 2:355.

68. Doughty, *Pyrrhic Victory*, 170.

69. Goya, *Flesh and Steel during the Great War*, 153.

70. This and what follows are from Lucas, *The Evolution of Tactical Ideas in France and Germany during the War of 1914–1918*, 36–40; Wilhelm Balck, *Development of Tactics: World War I*, trans. Harry Bell (Fort Leavenworth, KS: General Service Schools Press, 1922; reprint, West Chester, OH: The Nafziger Collection, 2011), 36–37.

71. Lucas, *The Evolution of Tactical Ideas in France and Germany during the War of 1914–1918*, 38.

72. Krause, *Early Trench Tactics in the French Army*, 21.

73. Goya, *Flesh and Steel during the Great War*, 154.

74. Ibid., 156.

75. Doughty, *Pyrrhic Victory*, 189; Lucas, *The Evolution of Tactical Ideas in France and Germany during the War of 1914–1918*, 50–51.

76. Krause, *Early Trench Tactics in the French Army*, 26–27.

77. André Laffargue, *Impressions and Reflections of a French Company Commander regarding the Attack* (London: Harrison and Sons, 1916), 4, 9, 12, 24, Joint Services Command and Staff College Archives, Shrivenham.

78. Ibid., 17.

79. Ibid., 12–14.

80. Williamson Murray, *Military Adaptation in War: With Fear of Change* (New York: Cambridge University Press, 2011), 92.

81. Ibid.

82. Goya, *Flesh and Steel during the Great War*, 158.

83. Ibid., 157–158.

84. Greenhalgh, "The French Army on the Western Front," 256.

85. Krause, *Early Trench Tactics in the French Army*, 19.

86. Jonathan Boff, *Haig's Enemy: Crown Prince Rupprecht and Germany's War on the Western Front* (Oxford: Oxford University Press, 2018), 78–82, 89–90.

87. This and what follows are from Lucas, *The Evolution of Tactical Ideas in France and Germany during the War of 1914–1918*, 55–56.

88. Goya, *Flesh and Steel during the Great War*, 159.

89. The GQG issued an *Interim Note Appended to the Instruction of 8 January 1916 on the Offensive Combat of Small Units* in late September. A final update to methodical battle came in December, when the GQG sought to identify ways to reduce the delay between successive attacks for limited objectives. Goya, *Flesh and Steel during the Great War*, 161–62.

90. Lucas, *The Evolution of Tactical Ideas in France and Germany during the War of 1914–1918*, 93.

91. Goya, *Flesh and Steel during the Great War*, 237.

92. Ibid., 144.

93. Ibid., 159–160.

94. Joffre, *The Personal Memoirs of Joffre*, 2:564–65.

95. Goya, *Flesh and Steel during the Great War*, 160.

96. This and what follows are from Lupfer, *The Dynamics of Doctrine*, 33–34; Balck, *Development of Tactics*, 47–49; Lucas, *The Evolution of Tactical Ideas in France and Germany during the War of 1914–1918*, 99–102.

97. Each assault division designated a single regiment to lead the attack. This regiment would advance with all three battalions forward. The battalions would have two companies in the first wave and two more companies in a second wave, about eighty meters in trace. Thus, in a division sector, six companies would advance in line in the first wave, with six more behind. The division's other two regiments would form reserve waves that would follow several hundred meters behind the assault force.

98. Lupfer, *The Dynamics of Doctrine*, 33–34.

99. Nivelle knew about the new German defenses but did not think they could stop his *bataille de rupture*. Balck, *Development of Tactics*, 57.

100. Ibid., 55.

101. These included *Instruction of 4 June 1917, Directive Number 3, Amendment of 27 July 1917 to the Instruction of 16 December 1916,* and *Note on the Reorganization of the Infantry Company* (September). Goya, *Flesh and Steel during the Great War*, 230 and 237–38.

102. Ibid., 150, 230.

103. This and what follows are from Balck, *Development of Tactics*, 22, 59; Sumner, "French Poilu," 76; Goya, *Flesh and Steel during the Great War*, 236–39.

104. Goya, *Flesh and Steel during the Great War*, 245.

105. Ibid., 232.

106. Ibid.

107. This and what follows are from ibid., 230–32.

108. Each assault division was supported by five artillery *groupements*.

109. Goya, *Flesh and Steel during the Great War*, 170.

110. Ibid., 248.

111. Ibid., 245.

112. Ibid., 247.

113. Ibid.

114. Ibid., 248.

115. Sumner, *They Shall Not Pass*, 196.

116. Cole, "Forward with the Bayonet!," 279.

117. Goya, *Flesh and Steel during the Great War*, 50–51.

118. Ibid., 85–86. Goya also argues that the army lacked the training space to conduct realistic live-fire training.

119. Sixty-one of the army's seventy-seven artillery regiments were equipped with French 75s in 1914. Ibid., 84.

120. Ibid., 175.

121. Ibid., 90.

122. Bradley John Meyer, "Operational Art and the German Command System in World War I" (PhD diss., Ohio State University, 1988), 272–73; Krause, *Early Trench Tactics in the French Army*, 22.

123. Bidwell and Graham, *Fire-Power*, 14–15.

124. Lucas, *The Evolution of Tactical Ideas in France and Germany during the War of 1914–1918*, 10.

125. Goya, *Flesh and Steel during the Great War*, 51.

126. Cole, "Forward with the Bayonet!," 108. "As Charles De Gaulle wrote in 1938, 'When the war came, the German army was prepared to fire, at a greater distance, with greater ease, twice the amount of lead of its opponent.'" Ibid., 119.

127. Goya, *Flesh and Steel during the Great War*, 109–11 and 177.

128. A decision for which Joffre was heavily criticized when the German Army attacked at Verdun in 1916. Sumner, *They Shall Not Pass*, 97.

129. Before the war, the army planned on needing 13,600 75mm shells per day. To keep up with demand, French industry produced 210,000 shells *per day* by August 1916. Doughty, *Pyrrhic Victory*, 116–17.

130. Cole, "Forward with the Bayonet!," 119.

131. For a discussion of these initial efforts, see Krause, *Early Trench Tactics in the French Army*, 32.

132. Greenhalgh, "The French Army on the Western Front," 256.

133. Goya, *Flesh and Steel during the Great War*, 177–78.

134. Krause, *Early Trench Tactics in the French Army*, 23.

135. Ibid.

136. Goya, *Flesh and Steel during the Great War*, 154.

137. Lucas, *The Evolution of Tactical Ideas in France and Germany during the War of 1914–1918*, 51.

138. As quoted in Goya, *Flesh and Steel during the Great War*, 205.

139. Greenhalgh, "Technology Development in Coalition," 807–8.

140. Goya, *Flesh and Steel during the Great War*, 206.

141. Ibid., 112.

142. Lucas, *The Evolution of Tactical Ideas in France and Germany during the War of 1914–1918*, 64.

143. Ibid., 66.

144. Ibid., 87.

145. Goya, *Flesh and Steel during the Great War*, 211.

146. Ibid., 211. French tanks were smaller and lighter. French prototypes weighed seven tons. British prototypes weighed thirty. Greenhalgh, "Technology Development in Coalition," 815–16.

147. Goya, *Flesh and Steel during the Great War*, 206.

148. Greenhalgh, "Technology Development in Coalition," 816.

149. The British army began sharing lessons learned with French Assault Artillery liaison officers in late 1916. Goya, *Flesh and Steel during the Great War*, 211.

150. Ibid., 176.

151. William Van der Kloot, "Lawrence Bragg's Role in the Development of Sound-Ranging in World War I," *Notes and Records of the Royal Society* 59, no. 3 (2005): 274.

152. Greenhalgh suggests that 128 French tanks participated in the operation. Greenhalgh, "Technology Development in Coalition," 821. Sumner and Goya put the number at 132. Goya, *Flesh and Steel during the Great War*, 212; Sumner, *They Shall Not Pass*, 151.

153. Sumner, *They Shall Not Pass*, 151.

154. Goya, *Flesh and Steel during the Great War*, 212.

155. Ibid., 212–13.

156. Ibid., 216.

157. Ibid., 214.

158. Greenhalgh, "Technology Development in Coalition," 823.

159. Goya, *Flesh and Steel during the Great War*, 215.

160. Ibid., 214.

161. René Louis Jules Radiguet, *The Making of a Modern Army and Its Operations in the Field: A Study Based on the Experience of Three Years on the Western Front (1914–1917)*, trans. Henry P. du Bellet (New York: Putnam, 1918; reprint, Ann Arbor, MI: University of Michigan Library, n.d.), 84–86.

162. Goya, *Flesh and Steel during the Great War*, 242.

163. Ibid. Some French officers questioned British success with the hurricane barrage at Cambrai, believing it might not work against German defenses elsewhere. Radiguet, *The Making of a Modern Army and Its Operations in the Field*, 141.

164. Goya, *Flesh and Steel during the Great War*, 242.

165. Clayton, *Paths of Glory*, 149.

166. Goya, *Flesh and Steel during the Great War*, 241.

167. Goya, *Flesh and Steel during the Great War*, 241.

168. Ibid., 178.

169. Ibid., 219.

170. Clayton, *Paths of Glory*, 186–87; Goya, *Flesh and Steel during the Great War*, 220. In the phrasing of one manual for junior French officers, "troops must never be launched to the attack, when such attack is not *prepared and supported by an effective artillery action. It is impossible to fight with men against material.*" French General Staff, *French Trench Warfare, 1917–1918*, A Reference Manual (Originally published as "Manual of the Chief of Platoon of Infantry," 1918; reprint, Nashville: Battery Press, 2002), 149 (emphasis in the original).

171. On the 37mm field gun and its role in supporting infantry operations, see French General Staff, *French Trench Warfare*, 171–72.

172. Goya, *Flesh and Steel during the Great War*, 248.

173. This and what follows in the next paragraph are from Lucas, *The Evolution of Tactical Ideas in France and Germany during the War of 1914–1918*, 4–13.

174. As quoted in Lucas, *The Evolution of Tactical Ideas in France and Germany during the War of 1914–1918*, 8 (emphasis in the original). The *Regulations for Infantry* went on to stipulate "an infantry unit whose mission it is to hold a point of terrain must never abandon it without an order. It will resist to the end."

175. Goya, *Flesh and Steel during the Great War*, 108.

176. Lucas, *The Evolution of Tactical Ideas in France and Germany during the War of 1914–1918*, 33.

177. Balck, *Development of Tactics*, 32; Lucas, *The Evolution of Tactical Ideas in France and Germany during the War of 1914–1918*, 40–41.

178. Greenhalgh, "The French Army on the Western Front," 256.

179. Lucas, *The Evolution of Tactical Ideas in France and Germany during the War of 1914–1918*, 46.

180. Goya, *Flesh and Steel during the Great War*, 146.

181. This and what follows are from Clayton, *Paths of Glory*, 71–72.

182. Boff, *Haig's Enemy*, 90.

183. Goya, *Flesh and Steel during the Great War*, 132–33. Goya attributes the reluctance to develop elastic defense-in-depth concepts to French soldiers' "unwilling[ness] to make the effort to learn something new." Ibid., 133. However, this explanation seems implausible given the degree to which French soldiers and officers were willing to aggressively experiment with new offensive warfare techniques.

184. Clayton, *Paths of Glory*, 122.

185. Ibid., 152.

186. This and what follows are from Radiguet, *The Making of a Modern Army and Its Operations in the Field*, 58–69.

187. This and what follows are from Doughty, *Pyrrhic Victory*, 424–26; Clayton, *Paths of Glory*, 153.

188. Doughty, *Pyrrhic Victory*, 426.

189. Sumner, "French Poilu," 84; Porch, "The French Army in the First World War," 219–20.

190. French General Staff, *French Trench Warfare*, 178.

191. Ibid., 287 (emphasis in the original).

192. Goya, *Flesh and Steel during the Great War*, 244.

193. General Staff, *Handbook of the French Army, 1906*, 166.

194. Goya, *Flesh and Steel during the Great War*, 47.

195. Lucas, *The Evolution of Tactical Ideas in France and Germany during the War of 1914–1918*, 15–16.

196. Ironically, the army's commissioning of so many of its noncommissioned officers caused many officers to doubt the intellectual abilities of those noncommissioned officers who either chose to remain in the ranks or could not earn a commission. Sumner, "French Poilu," 77.

197. Steven Errol Clemente, "'Mit Gott! Für König und Kaiser!': A Critical Analysis of the Making of the Prussian Army Officer, 1860–1914" (PhD diss., University of Oklahoma, 1989), 107.

198. Gary D. Sheffield, *Leadership in the Trenches: Officer-Man Relations, Morale and Discipline in the British Army in the Era of the First World War* (New York: St. Martin's, 2000), 165. Nevertheless, the army's commitment to meritocracy did not extend to promotion to the higher ranks. In 1905, prior-service noncommissioned officers made up 45 percent of the army's new officers but only 5 percent of its colonels. Furthermore, nearly 30 percent of the army's prewar general officers had an aristocratic background. Goya, *Flesh and Steel during the Great War*, 11.

199. Clemente, "'Mit Gott! Fuer Koenig Und Kaiser!'," 106–7.

200. For details on the number of men called to service, exempted, postponed, or otherwise allowed to avoid being conscripted prior to the war, see General Staff, *Handbook of the French Army, 1914*, 63–64.

201. Joffre, *The Personal Memoirs of Joffre*, 1:185.

202. Sumner, *They Shall Not Pass*, 27; Doughty, *Pyrrhic Victory*, 59; Goya, *Flesh and Steel during the Great War*, 103.

203. Cole, "Forward with the Bayonet!," 232–34.

204. Clayton, *Paths of Glory*, 56. At least some French reserve officers agreed with the assessment that they were not ready for the rigors of combat. Ian Sumner relates the tragic story of one reserve officer who "took the desperate step of committing suicide on the outbreak of war, 'fearful of the responsibility of commanding, at a time of mobilization, a regiment which in his opinion was inadequately prepared.'" Sumner, *They Shall Not Pass*, 15.

205. Goya, *Flesh and Steel during the Great War*, 119.

206. Krause, *Early Trench Tactics in the French Army*, 16.

207. As related in Doughty, *Pyrrhic Victory*, 167. See also, ibid., 123–24.

208. Ibid., 186.

209. Goya, *Flesh and Steel during the Great War*, 121.

210. Lucas, *The Evolution of Tactical Ideas in France and Germany during the War of 1914–1918*, 68.

211. Goya, *Flesh and Steel during the Great War*, 144.

212. Ibid., 237.

213. Lucas, *The Evolution of Tactical Ideas in France and Germany during the War of 1914–1918*, 96.

214. At least one French officer thought Pétain was too lenient and wanted him to set an example by executing two thousand soldiers. Sumner, *They Shall Not Pass*, 183.

215. Porch, "The French Army in the First World War," 221.

216. Goya, *Flesh and Steel during the Great War*, 119, 238.

217. This staff's actual title was *état major de l'armée*, or army staff. The head of this staff was called the *chef d'état-major général de l'armée*, which translates to "Chief of the General Staff." See General Staff, *Handbook of the French Army, 1914*, 134–35. In the interest of terminological consistency, I use the term "General Staff" in lieu of "army staff" throughout.

218. For a description of the curriculum and the selection process, see ibid., 161–66.

219. The CHEM was a top-gun school for French staff officers and was akin to the US Marine Corps' School of Advanced Warfighting or the US Army's School of Advanced Military Studies programs. Each year, the war minister selected twenty to twenty-five majors and lieutenant colonels to attend the CHEM. The original plan was to select from among the top graduates of the Ecole Supérieure de Guerre, but the army quickly abandoned this idea for fear that it might create a rift within the staff corps. The CHEM curriculum included courses taught by War College professors, lectures given by bureau heads from the army staff, and staff rides led by members of the Conseil Supérieur de la Guerre (Superior War Council). General Staff, *Handbook of the French Army, 1914*, 163.

220. Cole, "Forward with the Bayonet!," 67.

221. Ibid. Foch was the commandant of the War College while the 1913 regulations were being written.

222. General Staff, *Handbook of the French Army, 1914*, 134.

223. Strachan, *The First World War*, Vol. 1, *To Arms*, 189.

224. Goya, *Flesh and Steel during the Great War*, 2.

225. Strachan, *The First World War*, Vol. 1, *To Arms*, 189.

226. General Staff, *Handbook of the French Army, 1914*, 128–30.

227. Goya, *Flesh and Steel during the Great War*, 34.

228. Porch, "The French Army in the First World War," 211.

229. Goya, *Flesh and Steel during the Great War*, 2

230. Joffre, *The Personal Memoirs of Joffre*, 1:137.

231. Goya, *Flesh and Steel during the Great War*, 34.

232. Ibid., 105.

233. Ibid., 138–39.

234. Greenhalgh, "The French Army on the Western Front," 255.

235. General Staff, *Handbook of the French Army, 1914*, 135.

236. Goya, *Flesh and Steel during the Great War*, 139–40.

237. G. C. Wynne, *If Germany Attacks: The Battle in Depth in the West* (1940; reprint, Westport, CT: Greenwood, 1976), 58.

238. Goya, *Flesh and Steel during the Great War*, 141–42.

239. Ibid., 140.

240. This and what follows are from ibid., 142–43.

241. Ibid., 237–38.

242. France had forty-one active divisions in 1914. Each division had two brigades. Each brigade had two regiments. General Staff, *Handbook of the French Army, 1914*, 108; Sumner, "French Poilu," 57; Sumner, *They Shall Not Pass*, 15.

243. Sumner, "French Poilu," 57–58.

244. General Staff, *Handbook of the French Army, 1914*, 135.

245. Porch, "The French Army in the First World War," 215.

246. By comparison, he estimates that German units needed to learn approximately nine hundred pages. Goya, *Flesh and Steel during the Great War*, 62.

247. Ibid., 63.

248. Sumner, *They Shall Not Pass*, 53–54.

249. Goya, *Flesh and Steel during the Great War*, 144–45.

250. Ibid., 146.

251. Ibid., 145.

252. This and what follows are from Sumner, "French Poilu," 60–61, 75.

253. Goya, *Flesh and Steel during the Great War*, 146.

254. Ibid., 147.

255. Murray, *Military Adaptation in War*, 103–5.

256. Goya, *Flesh and Steel during the Great War*, 147.

257. Ibid., 178. In January 1918 the Directorate General of Artillery Training, with more power and authority, replaced the inspectorate-general of artillery post.

258. Clayton, *Paths of Glory*, 152.

259. Porch, "The French Army in the First World War," 224.

260. Goya, *Flesh and Steel during the Great War*, 149.

261. Ibid., 148.

262. Ibid.

263. Ibid., 259.

264. Porch, "The French Army in the First World War," 224.

265. Goya, *Flesh and Steel during the Great War*, 178.

266. The fact that the army designated tanks as assault artillery and organized them as a branch of the artillery arm suggests that the GQG also treated tank training as highly specialized and technical.

Conclusion

1. With regard to assault tactics, the BEF moved from exploration to selection in the winter of 1917 and from selection to action in the winter of 1918. The dates for combined arms are the winter of 1917 and the fall of 1917. Both occurred in the late spring/early summer of 1918 for elastic defenses in depth.

2. Just a few months before, the Wilson administration had suspended war loans to the Entente and tried to broker peace.

3. Hein Goemans argues that because military defeat would have threatened their domestic survival, Germany's autocratic leaders decided to "gamble for resurrection" instead of negotiating in 1917. Alexander Lanoszka and I counter that Goeman's account cannot explain why Germany launched Operation Michael in early 1918 instead of using the Treaty of Brest-Litovsk to bargain from a position of strength and undercut domestic opposition. We suggest that the British decision to reject the various 1916 peace offers convinced the German high command that the Entente was an implacable adversary committed to Germany's destruction. This perception caused Germany to bypass multiple bargaining opportunities and fight on until it was exhausted. See Hein Goemans, *War and Punishment: The Causes of War Termination and the End of the First World War* (Princeton, NJ: Princeton University Press, 2000); Alexander Lanoszka and Michael A. Hunzeker, "Rage of Honor: Entente Indignation and the Lost Chance for Peace in the First World War," *Security Studies* 24, no. 4 (2015), 662–95.

4. Paddy Griffith, *Battle Tactics of the Western Front: The British Army's Art of Attack, 1916–18* (New Haven, CT: Yale University Press, 1994), 87–89; Paddy Griffith, *The Great War on the Western Front: A Short History* (Barnsley, UK: Pen & Sword Military, 2008), 73–74.

5. See Rupert Smith, *The Utility of Force: The Art of War in the Modern World* (New York: Knopf, 2007); Emile Simpson, *War from the Ground Up: Twenty-First Century Combat as Politics* (Oxford: Oxford University Press, 2018).

6. The US commitment to the ground war technically ended by 1972. Michael G. Kort, *The Vietnam War Reexamined* (Cambridge: Cambridge University Press, 2018), 166, Kindle.

7. Although the transition to the All Volunteer Force may have changed the army's organizational culture after Vietnam, American strategic culture, as the term is usually employed, is unlikely to have shifted in such a short period of time. On the origins and definition of the term, see Jack L. Snyder, *The Soviet Strategic Culture: Implications for Limited Nuclear Operations* (Santa Monica, CA: Rand Corporation, 1977); Colin S. Gray, "National Style in Strategy: The American Example," *International Security* 6, no. 2 (Fall, 1981): 21–47; Alastair Iain Johnston, *Cultural Realism: Strategic Culture and Grand Strategy in Chinese History* (Princeton, NJ: Princeton University Press, 1998). On how the All Volunteer Force affected the US Army's organizational culture, see Austin Long, *The Soul of Armies: Counterinsurgency Doctrine and Military Culture in the US and UK* (Ithaca, NY: Cornell University Press, 2016), 171–72.

8. As I use the term, a population-centric COIN doctrine focuses on shielding civilians from insurgent violence; generating intelligence by developing enduring networks within the local population; using precise and proportional firepower; emphasizing nonmilitary goals, such as economic development, alongside military objectives; developing a close working relationship with both host and partner civilian government agencies; and demonstrating a lasting commitment to operate among the people by both mastering the local culture, language, and traditions and forgoing traditional military force protection measures.

9. Some scholars argue that US ground forces did learn how to conduct COIN operations toward the end of the war. See, for example, Lewis Sorley, *A Better War: The Unexamined Victories and Final Tragedy of America's Last Years in Vietnam* (New York: Harcourt, 1999); Jonathan Askonas, "A Muse of Fire: Why the U.S. Military Forgets What It Learns in War" (D.Phil. diss., Oxford University, 2019).

10. John Gerring, "Case Selection for Case-Study Analysis: Qualitative and Quantitative Techniques," in *The Oxford Handbook of Political Methodology*, ed. Janet M. Box-Steffensmeier, Henry E. Brady, and David Collier (Oxford: Oxford University Press, 2008), 655–56.

11. Kort, *The Vietnam War Reexamined*, 14–21.

12. South Vietnam cycled through seven different governments in 1964 alone. Kort, *The Vietnam War Reexamined*, 118. US Army advisers played a key role by attempting to transform the ARVN into an effective fighting force. See Caitlin Talmadge, *The Dictator's Army: Battlefield Effectiveness in Authoritarian Regimes* (Ithaca, NY: Cornell University Press, 2015), 50–62; Jerad Harper, "A Tug of War for Effectiveness: U.S. Efforts to Build the Republic of Vietnam Armed Forces (1955–1973)" (PhD diss., George Mason University, 2020).

13. This and what follows are from Kort, *The Vietnam War Reexamined*, 26–35.

14. Walter E. Kretchik, *U.S. Army Doctrine: From the American Revolution to the War on Terror* (Lawrence: University Press of Kansas, 2011), 188–89.

15. Andrew J. Birtle, *US Army Counterinsurgency and Counterinsurgency Doctrine, 1942–1976* (Washington, DC: US Army Center of Military History, 2006), 361. By 1966, approximately fifty-eight thousand PAVN soldiers were operating in South Vietnam. That number more than tripled by 1968. Michael L. Lanning and Dan Cragg, *Inside the VC and the NVA the Real Story of North Vietnam's Armed Forces* (College Station: Texas A&M University Press, 2008), 38.

16. To be fair, not everyone agreed with this setup. Ambassador Maxwell Taylor wanted to send ARVN forces to fight the PAVN while leaving American ground troops to protect airbases and major population centers. Andrew F. Krepinevich, *The Army and Vietnam* (Baltimore: Johns Hopkins University Press, 1988), 140–41; Birtle, *US Army Counterinsurgency and Counterinsurgency Doctrine, 1942–1976*, 363–64.

17. Thomas W. Scoville, *Reorganizing for Pacification Support* (Washington, DC: US Army Center of Military History, 1999), 16–17; Robert W. Komer, *Bureaucracy Does Its Thing: Institutional Constraints on U.S.-GVN Performance in Vietnam* (Santa Monica, CA: The Rand Corporation, 1972), 47.

18. Kort, *The Vietnam War Reexamined*, 152–54.

19. Ibid., 161–66.

20. Ibid., 166.

21. John Nagl claims that "the United States Army entered the Vietnam War with a doctrine well suited to fighting conventional war in Europe, but worse than useless for the counterinsurgency it was about to combat." John Nagl, *Learning to Eat Soup with a Knife: Counterinsurgency Lessons from Malaya and Vietnam* (Chicago: University of Chicago Press, 2005), 115. This critique is almost certainly overstated in light of the number of relatively prescient COIN manuals that the US Army produced between the Second World War and Vietnam, which I briefly introduce below.

22. According to Gregory Daddis, "contrary to arguments that almost all officers wedded themselves to a concept of conventional battle on the European plains, the army made serious and thoughtful attempts to develop unconventional warfare doctrine." Gregory A. Daddis, *No Sure Victory: Measuring U.S. Army Effectiveness and Progress in the Vietnam War* (Oxford UK: Oxford University Press, 2011), 41–42; See also Long, *The Soul of Armies*, 107–9. Although the Kennedy administration is often credited with pushing the US Army and Marine Corps to pay more attention to COIN, much of this work preceded his presidency. See, for example, *Field Manual 100-5: Operations* (1954), *Field Manual 33-5: Psychological Warfare Operations* (1954), *Field Manual 31-20: Operations against Guerilla Forces* (1951), and *Field Manual 31-15: Operations against Airborne Attack, Guerrilla Action and Infiltration* (1953).

23. Birtle, *US Army Counterinsurgency and Counterinsurgency Doctrine, 1942–1976*, 146–47; Austin Long, *Doctrine of Eternal Recurrence: The US Military and Counterinsurgency Doctrine, 1960–1970 and 2003–2006* (Santa Monica, CA: Rand Corporation, 2008), 5–9.

24. Kretchik, *U.S. Army Doctrine*, 189–90.

25. Long, *Doctrine of Eternal Recurrence*, 15.

26. Ibid., 15–17.

27. Kort, *The Vietnam War Reexamined*, 145.

28. Long, *The Soul of Armies*, 116–17. The US Army's long-standing institutional aversion to COIN almost certainly played a role in this outcome as well. Long, *The Soul of Armies*, 127–28.

29. Birtle, *US Army Counterinsurgency and Counterinsurgency Doctrine, 1942–1976*, 367.

30. Sorley, *A Better War*, 64–74; Nagl, *Learning to Eat Soup with a Knife*, 165–69.

31. Austin Long suggests that a "closer inspection of what actually took place after Tet reveals that change was more apparent than real." Long, *The Soul of Armies*, 131.

32. Even at its peak, the highly effective CORDS program involved less than 3 percent of the half million US soldiers and civilians in Vietnam. Komer, *Bureaucracy Does Its Thing*, 126.

33. Sorley, *A Better War*, 30 and 102–3.

34. Birtle, *US Army Counterinsurgency and Counterinsurgency Doctrine, 1942–1976*, 371; Robert A. Doughty, "The Evolution of US Army Tactical Doctrine, 1946–1976," *Leavenworth Papers* (1979): 31.

35. Sorley, *A Better War*, 102–3.

36. Komer, *Bureaucracy Does Its Thing*, 70; Nina A. Kollars "War's Horizon: Soldier-Led Adaptation in Iraq and Vietnam," *Journal of Strategic Studies* 38, no. 4 (2015): 542–43; Askonas, "A Muse of Fire," 178–89.

37. Birtle, *US Army Counterinsurgency and Counterinsurgency Doctrine, 1942–1976*, 385.

38. Krepinevich, *The Army and Vietnam*, 171–72.

39. According to Dennis Vetock, the US Army's doctrine development process came of age after it organized the CDC in 1962. Dennis J. Vetock, *Lessons Learned: A History of US Army Lesson Learning* (Carlisle, PA: US Army Military History Institute, 1988), 94.

40. Askonas, "A Muse of Fire," 64. For a deeper discussion of the body count method, see ibid., 116–21.

41. Vetock, *Lessons Learned*, 97, 100.

42. Ibid., 105.

43. Charles R. Shrader, *History of Operations Research in the United States Army, Volume 2: 1961–1973* (Washington, DC: US Army Center of Military History, 1999), 81.

44. Vetock, *Lessons Learned*, 91. See also Julian J. Ewell and Ira Augustus Hunt, *Sharpening the Combat Edge: The Use of Analysis to Reinforce Military Judgment* (Washington, DC: Department of the Army, 1974).

45. Shrader, *History of Operations Research in the United States Army*, 295.

46. Ibid., 156.

47. This and what follows are from ibid., 124–46.

48. Ibid., 146.

49. Information overload created its own problems. The Hamlet Evaluation System alone generated ninety thousand pages of data a month. "Resolve (January 1966–June 1976)," Episode 4, *The Vietnam War: A Film by Ken Burns and Lynn Novick* (Arlington, VA: Public Broadcast Service, 2017), http://www.pbs.org/kenburns/the-vietnam-war/episodes/episode-4/.

50. This and what follows are from Shrader, *History of Operations Research in the United States Army*, 304–9.

51. For its part, MACV sponsored studies on the rural pacification program and the remote sensor program and for limiting the use of harassment and interdiction fires. Shrader, *History of Operations Research in the United States Army*, 311.

52. Benjamin King, *Victory Starts Here: A 35-year History of the US Army Training and Doctrine Command* (Fort Leavenworth, KS: Combat Studies Institute Press, 2008), 1; Krepinevich, *The Army and Vietnam*, 28. Before the CDC's creation in 1962, CONARC retained control over both doctrine and training. The two functions were separated from 1962 to the creation of TRADOC in 1973.

53. Birtle, *US Army Counterinsurgency and Counterinsurgency Doctrine, 1942–1976*, 231–32.

54. Ibid., 266.

55. Daddis, *No Sure Victory*, 55.

56. Krepinevich notes that COIN training took up less than 12 percent of these units' overall schedule. Krepinevich, *The Army and Vietnam*, 111–12. The problem with this critique is the fact that these units were also tasked with preparing for global contingencies, to include conventional operations against the Soviet Union.

57. Kort, *The Vietnam War Reexamined*, 14–21.

58. Askonas, "A Muse of Fire," 66. It is telling that at the peak of the war in 1968, only 9 of the army's 19.5 divisions were in Vietnam. Suzanne C. Nielsen, *An Army Transformed: The U.S. Army's Post-Vietnam Recovery and the Dynamics of Change in Military Organizations* (Carlisle, PA: Strategic Studies Institute, 2010), 35–37.

59. Long argues that the army's organizational culture, not MACV's overarching strategy, prevented it from mastering COIN. Long, *The Soul of Armies*, 127–28 and 136–38. I maintain that the absence of an overarching COIN-centric military strategy made it possible for commanders at every level to revert to their preferred war-fighting methods. As other scholars have argued (see the next footnote), is it not self-evident that MACV should have adopted such a strategy.

60. The standard narrative, forcefully argued by Krepinevich, is that the US Army's failure to adopt a COIN-centric strategy led to its defeat. Other former officers, such as Harry Summers Jr., make the opposite case, suggesting that the United States might have prevailed had it prioritized its conventional operations against the PAVN. Dale Andrade offers a third perspective:

that the combination of PAVN-led conventional operations and National Liberation Frong guerrilla operations put American ground forces on the horns of another dilemma and that the only way to win was to effectively integrate conventional and COIN operations. Krepinevich, *The Army and Vietnam*; Harry G. Summers Jr., *On Strategy: A Critical Analysis of the Vietnam War* (New York: Random House, 1995); Dale Andrade, "Westmoreland Was Right: Learning the Wrong Lessons from the Vietnam War," *Small Wars and Insurgencies* 19, no. 2 (2008): 145–281. For a detailed summary of this debate, see Kort, *The Vietnam War Reexamined*, 139–45.

61. Large-scale ground combat operations began with the invasion in March 2003 and ended when the last US Army combat brigade departed Iraq in August 2010.

62. James A. Russell, "Innovation in War: Counterinsurgency Operations in Anbar and Ninewa Provinces, Iraq, 2005–2007," *Journal of Strategic Studies* 33, no. 4 (2010): 595–624; Askonas, "A Muse of Fire," 227–28.

63. Richard W. Stewart, ed., *American Military History: The United States Army in a Global Era, 1917–2008*, Vol. 2 (Washington, DC: US Army Center of Military History, 2010), 480–81. For a status-based explanation, see Ahsan I. Butt, "Why Did the United States Invade Iraq in 2003?," *Security Studies* 28, no. 2 (2019): 250–85.

64. Michael R. Gordon and Bernard E. Trainor, *Cobra II: The Inside Story of the Invasion and Occupation of Iraq* (New York: Random House, 2007), 162–68.

65. Stewart, *American Military History*, 494.

66. Kretchik, *U.S. Army Doctrine*, 261.

67. Stewart, *American Military History*, 495.

68. As quoted in Kretchik, *U.S. Army Doctrine*, 262.

69. Nigel Aylwin-Foster, "Changing the Army for Counterinsurgency Operations," *Military Review* (November–December 2005): 5.

70. Ahmed Hashim, *Insurgency and Counter-insurgency in Iraq* (Ithaca, NY: Cornell University Press, 2005), 325.

71. As quoted in Aylwin-Foster, "Changing the Army for Counterinsurgency Operations," 3.

72. Stephen Biddle, Jeffrey A. Friedman, and Jacob N. Shapiro, "Testing the Surge: Why Did Violence Decline in Iraq in 2007?," *International Security* 37, no. 1 (2012): 15.

73. Stewart, *American Military History*, 503.

74. Biddle, Friedman, and Shapiro, "Testing the Surge," 7–8.

75. Recent scholarship suggests that although the surge was not singularly responsible for Iraq's dramatic turnaround, the other factors that abetted this outcome (e.g., the Sunni Awakening) would not have been possible were it not for surge forces and their sound application of COIN tactics. See Biddle, Friedman, and Shapiro, "Testing the Surge."

76. The US Army redesignated its FM 100-5 series FM 3-0 in 2001.

77. This and what follows are from Kretchik, *U.S. Army Doctrine*, 262–63.

78. Long, *The Soul of Armies*, 179.

79. As an interim step, the army published *Field Manual-Interim 3-07.22: Counterinsurgency Operations* in late 2004. Long, *The Soul of Armies*, 179.

80. Stewart, *American Military History*, 505–6.

81. John Nagl, "Constructing the Legacy of Field Manual 3-24," *Joint Forces Quarterly*, no. 58 (July 2010): 118–20.

82. David H. Petraeus and James F. Amos, *The U.S. Army, U.S. Marine Corps Counterinsurgency Field Manual* (Chicago: University of Chicago Press, 200), 174–78.

83. Ibid., 247–48. FM 3-24 also dedicates an entire chapter to leadership and ethics in a COIN campaign.

84. Ibid., chap. 2.

85. James A. Russell, *Innovation, Transformation, and War: Counterinsurgency Operations in Anbar and Ninewa Provinces, Iraq, 2005–2007* (Palo Alto, CA: Stanford University Press, 2011). At the same time, these were far from mainstream practices among most US Army combat units, where a focus on firepower, raids, and mass detainments was the norm. Long, *The Soul of Armies*, 180–84, 192–93.

86. This and what follows are from Stewart, *American Military History*; Biddle, Friedman, and Shapiro, "Testing the Surge."

87. Long suggests that "whatever success Petraeus achieved in ensuring Army compliance with written doctrine in Baghdad was limited outside the capital." Long, *The Soul of Armies*, 195.

88. To ensure that these assignments attracted qualified officers, the army told promotion boards to treat advisory tours as equivalent to traditional command tours.

89. For examples of relevant doctrine in force at the time, see Department of the Army, *Field Manual 7–22: The Army Non-Commissioned Officer Guide* (Washington, DC: Department of the Army, 2002), 3–1 to 3–18; Department of the Army, *Field Manual 6–22: Army Leadership; Competent, Confident, and Agile* (Washington, DC: Department of the Army, 2006).

90. Russell, "Innovation in War," 74.

91. Company- and battalion-level movements were simply too unwieldy to be effective.

92. Long, *Doctrine of Eternal Recurrence*, 22.

93. Kollars, "War's Horizon," 545–48; Askonas, "A Muse of Fire," 226–43.

94. Russell, "Innovation in War," 5, 86, 89, 90, 113, 120, 130, 148, 156, 162.

95. Examples include General James N. Mattis, Colonel H. R. McMaster, and Lieutenant Colonel John Nagl.

96. Nielsen, *An Army Transformed*, 41–45.

97. Ibid., 40; Conrad C. Crane, *Avoiding Vietnam: The US Army's Response to Defeat in Southeast Asia* (Carlisle, PA: Strategic Studies Institute, 2002), 6.

98. Vetock, *Lessons Learned*, 119; Robert T. Foley, Stuart Griffin, and Helen McCartney, "'Transformation in Contact': Learning the Lessons of Modern War," *International Affairs* 87, no. 2 (2011): 256–58.

99. TRADOC implemented this change in 2006. Brigade commands and above had to report after major operations. Individual soldiers and small-unit commanders could submit reports whenever they wanted via the Internet.

100. US Army, *Commander's Guide to Operational Records and Data Collection: Tactics, Techniques, and Procedures* (Fort Leavenworth, KS: Combined Arms Center, 2009), 18.

101. CALL's analysts did not hesitate to criticize the army for its performance, issuing a "scathing" report on the army's poor job of collecting, analyzing, and distributing intelligence during the Iraq War's earliest phases. Hashim, *Insurgency and Counter-Insurgency in Iraq*, 322.

102. US Army, *Commander's Guide to Operational Records and Data Collection*, 18.

103. Nielsen, *An Army Transformed*, 43.

104. General Paul F. Gorman, as quoted in Anne W. Chapman, *The Army's Training Revolution, 1973–1990: An Overview* (Fort Monroe, VA: US Army Training and Doctrine Command, 1994), vii.

105. Kretchik, *U.S. Army Doctrine*, 202–3.

106. King, *Victory Starts Here*, 8.

107. Kretchik, *U.S. Army Doctrine*, 201.

108. Chapman, *The Army's Training Revolution, 1973–1990*, 5–6, 9; King, *Victory Starts Here*, 10, 43–44; Kretchik, *U.S. Army Doctrine*; John L. Romjue, Susan Canedy, and Anne W. Chapman, *Prepare the Army for War: A Historical Overview of the Army Training and Doctrine Command, 1973–1993* (Fort Monroe, VA: US Army Training and Doctrine Command, 1993).

109. Chapman, *The Army's Training Revolution, 1973–1990*, 7.

110. David Fitzgerald, "Vietnam, Iraq and the Rebirth of Counter-Insurgency," *Irish Studies in International Affairs* 21, no. 1 (2010): 149–59; Foley, Griffin, and McCartney, "'Transformation in Contact'"; Kretchik, *U.S. Army Doctrine*, 263–68.

111. Foley, Griffin, and McCartney, "'Transformation in Contact,'" 257.

112. King, *Victory Starts Here*, 16, 25, 35; Kretchik, *U.S. Army Doctrine*, 270.

Index